CCNP Self-Study
CCNP BCRAN Exam Certification Guide
Second Edition

Brian Morgan, CCIE No. 4865
Craig Dennis

Cisco Press

Cisco Press
800 East 96th Street
Indianapolis, IN 46240 USA

CCNP BCRAN Exam Certification Guide
Second Edition

Brian Morgan

Craig Dennis

Copyright© 2004 Cisco Systems, Inc.

Published by:
Cisco Press
800 East 96th Street
Indianapolis, Indiana 46240 USA

Printed in the United States of America 3 4 5 6 7 8 9 0

Third Printing February 2004

Library of Congress Cataloging-in-Publication Number: 2002116291

ISBN: 1-58720-084-8

Warning and Disclaimer

This book is designed to provide information about selected topics for the Building Cisco Remote Access Networks (BCRAN) exam for the CCNP certification. Every effort has been made to make this book as complete and as accurate as possible, but no warranty or fitness is implied.

The information is provided on an "as is" basis. The authors, Cisco Press, and Cisco Systems, Inc., shall have neither liability nor responsibility to any person or entity with respect to any loss or damages arising from the information contained in this book or from the use of the discs or programs that may accompany it.

The opinions expressed in this book belong to the author and are not necessarily those of Cisco Systems, Inc.

Feedback Information

At Cisco Press, our goal is to create in-depth technical books of the highest quality and value. Each book is crafted with care and precision, undergoing rigorous development that involves the unique expertise of members from the professional technical community.

Readers' feedback is a natural continuation of this process. If you have any comments regarding how we could improve the quality of this book or otherwise alter it to better suit your needs, you can contact us through e-mail at feedback@ciscopress.com. Please make sure to include the book title and ISBN in your message.

We greatly appreciate your assistance.

Corporate and Government Sales

Cisco Press offers excellent discounts on this book when ordered in quantity for bulk purchases or special sales. For more information, please contact: **U.S. Corporate and Government Sales**   1-800-382-3419   corpsales@pearsontechgroup.com

For sales outside of the U.S. please contact: **International Sales**   1-317-581-3793   international@pearsontechgroup.com

Trademark Acknowledgments

Publisher: John Wait

Editor-In-Chief: John Kane

Executive Editor: Brett Bartow

Acquisitions Editor: Michelle Grandin

Development Editor: Jill Batistick

Production Manager: Patrick Kanouse

Production Team: Argosy Publishing

Book and Cover Designer: Louisa Adair

Cisco Press Program Manager: Sonia Torres Chavez

Cisco Representative: Anthony Wolfenden

Cisco Marketing Communications Manager: Scott Miller

Cisco Marketing Program Manager: Edie Quiroz

Technical Editor(s): Henry Benjamin, Howard Hecht, Charles Mann

Team Coordinator: Tammi Barnett

Copy Editor: Bill McManus

CISCO SYSTEMS

Corporate Headquarters
Cisco Systems, Inc.
170 West Tasman Drive
San Jose, CA 95134-1706
USA
www.cisco.com
Tel: 408 526-4000
    800 553-NETS (6387)
Fax: 408 526-4100

European Headquarters
Cisco Systems International BV
Haarlerbergpark
Haarlerbergweg 13-19
1101 CH Amsterdam
The Netherlands
www-europe.cisco.com
Tel: 31 0 20 357 1000
Fax: 31 0 20 357 1100

Americas Headquarters
Cisco Systems, Inc.
170 West Tasman Drive
San Jose, CA 95134-1706
USA
www.cisco.com
Tel: 408 526-7660
Fax: 408 527-0883

Asia Pacific Headquarters
Cisco Systems, Inc.
Capital Tower
168 Robinson Road
#22-01 to #29-01
Singapore 068912
www.cisco.com
Tel: +65 6317 7777
Fax: +65 6317 7799

Cisco Systems has more than 200 offices in the following countries and regions. Addresses, phone numbers, and fax numbers are listed on the
Cisco.com Web site at www.cisco.com/go/offices.

Argentina • Australia • Austria • Belgium • Brazil • Bulgaria • Canada • Chile • China PRC • Colombia • Costa Rica • Croatia • Czech Republic
Denmark • Dubai, UAE • Finland • France • Germany • Greece • Hong Kong SAR • Hungary • India • Indonesia • Ireland • Israel • Italy
Japan • Korea • Luxembourg • Malaysia • Mexico • The Netherlands • New Zealand • Norway • Peru • Philippines • Poland • Portugal
Puerto Rico • Romania • Russia • Saudi Arabia • Scotland • Singapore • Slovakia • Slovenia • South Africa • Spain • Sweden
Switzerland • Taiwan • Thailand • Turkey • Ukraine • United Kingdom • United States • Venezuela • Vietnam • Zimbabwe

About the Authors

Brian Morgan, CCIE No. 4865, is a certified Cisco Systems instructor teaching ICND, BSCI, CVOICE, BCRAN, CBCR, CIT, and CATM courses. Brian has been instructing for more than five years. He is currently serving as a director for Paranet Solutions, a nationwide consulting firm.

During his 12 years in the networking industry, Brian has developed and taught Cisco Dial Access Solutions boot camp classes for Cisco Systems internally (Tiger Team) as well as for various Training Partner sponsored courses.

Prior to teaching, Brian spent a number of years with IBM in Network Services where he attained MCNE and MCSE certifications. He was involved with a number of larger LAN/WAN installations for many of IBM's Fortune 500 clients.

Brian is the proud father of fraternal twin girls (Emma and Amanda) and husband to Beth. His hobbies include spending time with family and friends, scuba diving, and writing the occasional book.

Craig Dennis is a CCDA currently working as an independent consultant for LANS UnLimited specializing in small business solutions, primarily SDSL and ADSL installations, in the Northern Virginia area. Craig is a certified Cisco Systems instructor. During the past six years he has taught classes for PSC, GeoTrain, Global Knowledge, and Mentor Technologies. He is certified to teach ICND, BSCI, BCRAN, CID, and BCMSN.

About the Contributing Authors

Neil Lovering, CCIE No. 1772, is CEO of Neil Lovering Enterprises, Inc., a network consulting and training company. He has been a network consultant for more than eight years and has worked on various routing, switching, dialup, and security projects for many customers all over North America. Neil continues to teach advanced networking classes across the United States.

When not at the keyboard or at a customer site, Neil enjoys spending time with his wife and two children in North Carolina.

Shawn Boyd is a senior network consultant for ARP Technologies, Inc. Shawn is active in course development and is a certified Cisco Systems instructor with Global Knowledge, responsible for teaching most of the CCNP, CCDP, and Security courses. His background is in network security and design at a service provider level. He has worked for Canada's largest telco providers performing network designs and implementations and was lead contact on many large government contracts.

About the Technical Reviewers

Henry Benjamin, CCIE No. 4695, is a triple CCIE, having certified Routing and Switching in May 1999, ISP Dial in June 2001, and Communications and Services in May 2002. He has more than 10 years of experience in Cisco networks, including planning, designing, and implementing large IP networks running IGRP, EIGRP, BGP, and OSPF. Recently Henry has worked for a large IT organization based in Sydney, Australia, as a key network designer, designing and implementing networks all over Australia and Asia. Henry is a formal CCIE lab proctor.

Howard Hecht is a consultant for the Cisco Networking Academy® Program. He holds both the CCNA and CCNP certifications with a masters degree in media management. He has been an author, reviewer, and subject matter expert for several different networking titles.

Charles Mann is a consultant with Chesapeake NetCraftsmen, LLC, based in the Washington, D.C. metro area (http://www.netcraftsmen.NET). He is a certified Cisco Systems instructor and holds the CCNP certification. Charles has over 10 years of experience in networking and telecommunications. Currently, Charles assists large government organizations with enterprise network design, implementation, and troubleshooting.

Dedications

Brian Morgan: This book is dedicated to my three giggling girls Beth, Amanda, and Emma. Thank you for making me complete, not to mention putting up with me while I got this book to production.

Oh, pay no attention to our friends behind "The Curtain."

Craig Dennis: This book is dedicated to the memory of my parents, Pearl and Rally, who died last year leaving many friends and family. They will be sorely missed by all.

Neil Lovering: This book is dedicated to my family: my wife Jody, my son Kevin, and my daughter Michelle. Thank you for understanding when dad is busy and glued to his computer.

Shawn Boyd: This book is dedicated to my family and friends.

Acknowledgments

Brian Morgan: I'd like to thank my wife, Beth, and kids, Emma and Amanda, for putting up with me during the time this book was being produced. It has taken me away from them more than I'd like to admit. Their patience in temporarily setting some things aside so I could get the book done has been incredible, even when my patience wore a bit thin in trying to meet timelines.

I'd like to give special recognition to Bill Wagner just for being Bill. I couldn't wish for a better friend.

A big "thank you" goes out to the production team for this book. John Kane, Michelle Grandin, and the crew have been incredibly professional and a pleasure to work with.

Craig, thoughts are with you and your family.

Thank you to Neil Lovering, Shawn Boyd, Howard Hecht, and Charles Mann for their part in this production. Their assistance and contributions have proved invaluable.

Hi Mom and Dad!

Craig Dennis: There are so many people who have helped me in one way or another during the rewrite of this book—I hope I can remember them all.

First, I want to thank the entire Cisco Press team for gently guiding me through this and for their sympathy in the loss of my parents. Thank you, Chris Cleveland, Jill Batistick, Michelle Grandin, and all the others who worked behind the scenes to make this project another reality.

Thanks to Brian and his usual Herculean efforts on his parts.

A special thanks goes to my wife, Sharon, who always held the family together while we were going in ten different directions over the last year. Thanks also to Sandra, Jacob, Joseph, and David, my children, for just being there.

Neil Lovering, Shawn Boyd, Henry Benjamin, Charles Mann, and Howard Hecht had to read the rough stuff, and their comments and suggestions were always succinct and furthered the project. Thanks.

Neil Lovering: I'd like to start by thanking both Michelle Grandin and Chris Cleveland at Cisco Press. Without their patience, guidance, and understanding, this project could have never happened. I also must thank my wife, Jody, for tending to the house and kids while I studied and worked on this book. And of course I must thank my kids, Kevin and Michelle, for understanding that even when home, Daddy must work at times.

Shawn Boyd: I would like to thank my friends and family for always supporting me in any endeavor I have tried, especially my parents, Pat and Dwaine. Without your unwavering love and support I could not have come this far. I am especially grateful for all the trust and guidance you have given me over the years.

To Tammy Brown, thank you for giving me your love and support. You mean the world to me.

A special thanks to the production team. Your professionalism and great organizational skills kept us on track.

Contents at a Glance

Table of Contents

Icons Used in This Book

Router

Bridge

Hub

DSU/CSU

Catalyst Switch

Multilayer Switch

ATM Switch

ISDN/Frame Relay Switch

Communication Server

Gateway

Access Server

PC

PC with Software

Sun Workstation

Macintosh

Terminal

File Server

Web Server

Cisco Works Workstation

Modem

Printer

Laptop

IBM Mainframe

Front End Processor

Cluster Controller

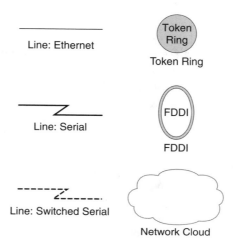

Line: Ethernet

Token Ring

Line: Serial

FDDI

Line: Switched Serial

Network Cloud

Command Syntax Conventions

The conventions used to present command syntax in this book are the same conventions used in the *Cisco IOS Command Reference*, as follows:

- **Boldface** indicates commands and keywords that are entered literally as shown. In actual configuration examples and output (not general command syntax), boldface indicates commands that are manually input by the user (such as a **show** command).

- *Italics* indicate arguments for which you supply actual values.

- Square brackets ([ ]) indicate optional elements.

- Braces ({ }) indicate a required choice.

- Vertical bars (|) separate alternative, mutually exclusive elements.

- Braces within square brackets ([{ }]) indicate a required choice within an optional element.

Foreword

CCNP BCRAN Exam Certification Guide, Second Edition, is a complete study tool for the CCNP BCRAN exam, allowing you to assess your knowledge, identify areas in which to concentrate your study, and master key concepts to help you succeed on the exam and in your daily job. The book is filled with features that help you master the skills to configure, operate, and troubleshoot WAN and other remote access networks while maximizing bandwidth utilization over remote links. This book was developed in cooperation with the Cisco Internet Learning Solutions Group. Cisco Press books are the only self-study books authorized by Cisco Systems for CCNP exam preparation.

Cisco Systems and Cisco Press present this material in text-based format to provide another learning vehicle for our customers and the broader user community in general. Although a publication does not duplicate the instructor-led or e-learning environment, we acknowledge that not everyone responds in the same way to the same delivery mechanism. It is our intent that presenting this material via a Cisco Press publication will enhance the transfer of knowledge to a broad audience of networking professionals.

Cisco Press will present study guides on existing and future exams through these Exam Certification Guides to help achieve Cisco Internet Learning Solutions Group's principal objectives: to educate the Cisco community of networking professionals and to enable that community to build and maintain reliable, scalable networks. The Cisco Career Certifications and classes that support these certifications are directed at meeting these objectives through a disciplined approach to progressive learning.

In order to succeed on the Cisco Career Certifications exams and in your daily job as a Cisco certified professional, we recommend a blended learning solution that combines instructor-led, e-learning, and self-study training with hands-on experience. Cisco Systems has created an authorized Cisco Learning Partner program to provide you with the most highly qualified instruction and invaluable hands-on experience in lab and simulation environments. To learn more about Cisco Learning Partner programs available in your area, please go to www.cisco.com/go/authorizedtraining.

The books Cisco Press creates in partnership with Cisco Systems will meet the same standards for content quality demanded of our courses and certifications. It is our intent that you will find this and subsequent Cisco Press certification and training publications of value as you build your networking knowledge base.

Thomas M. Kelly
Vice-President, Internet Learning Solutions Group
Cisco Systems, Inc.
August 2003

Introduction

Professional certifications have been an important part of the computing industry for many years and will continue to become more important. Many reasons exist for obtaining these certifications, but the most popularly cited reason is that of credibility. Although the Remote Access exam is just one of the foundation topics in the CCNP certification, if you pass the exam, you can consider yourself a truly skilled routing/switching engineer or specialist. All other considerations being equal, a certified employee/consultant/job candidate is considered more valuable than one who is not certified.

Goals and Methods

As the title of this book indicates, the most important goal of this book is to help you pass the BCRAN exam (642-821). However, the methods used in this book to help you pass the CCNP BCRAN exam are designed to also make you much more knowledgeable about how to do your job. In other words, this book helps you to truly learn and understand the topics, not just memorize them long enough to pass the exam. To that end, the book uses the following methods to help you pass the Remote Access exam:

- Presents questions that help you to discover which test topics you have not mastered and need to review in more depth

- Provides explanations and information to fill in your knowledge gaps

- Supplies exercises and scenarios that enhance your ability to recall and deduce the answers to test questions

- Provides practice exercises on the topics and the testing process via test questions on the CD-ROM, enabling you to prove to yourself that you have mastered the topics

Who Should Read This Book?

This book is intended for network administrators who want to significantly increase their chances of passing the CCNP BCRAN exam. (It is also a good general reference for networking topics, although that is not its intended purpose.) Passing the CCNP BCRAN exam is one of the milestones toward getting the CCNP certification. The reasons for getting CCNP certification vary. It could mean a raise, a promotion, professional recognition, or an important enhancement to your resume. Perhaps you want to demonstrate that you are serious about continuing the learning process. Or, perhaps you want to please your reseller-employer, who needs more certified employees to obtain a higher discount from Cisco. Regardless of the reason, you first need to pass the CCNP BCRAN exam, and this book will help you to do so.

Strategies for Exam Preparation

The strategy you use to prepare for CCNP BCRAN exam might be slightly different than strategies used by other readers, mainly based on the skills, knowledge, and experience you already have obtained. For instance, if you have attended the BCRAN course, then you might take a different approach than someone who learned remote access via on-the-job training. Later in this introduction, the section "All About the Cisco Certified Network Professional and Design Professional Certification" includes different strategies for various backgrounds so that you can choose a strategy that closely matches your own background.

Regardless of the strategy you use or the background you have, the book is designed to help you get to the point where you can pass the exam with the least amount of time required. For instance, there is no need for you to practice or read about IP addressing and subnetting if you fully understand it already. However, many people like to make sure that they truly know a topic, and thus read over material that they already know. Several book features will help you to determine confidently which material you already know and which material you need to study more.

How This Book Is Organized

Although this book could be read cover to cover, it is designed to be flexible and allow you to easily move between chapters and sections of chapters to cover just the material that you need more work with. Chapter 1 provides an overview of the CCNP and CCDP certifications, and offers some strategies for how to prepare for the exams. Each chapter in this book covers a section of the critical objectives that you need to know for the BCRAN exam. If you intend to read all chapters, the order of the book is an excellent sequence to use.

The chapters cover the following topics:

- Chapter 1, "Remote Access Solutions," provides an overview of the remote-access product line from Cisco Systems and coverage of WAN technologies.

- Chapter 2, "Identifying Site Requirements," addresses appropriate selection criteria for the placement of equipment, WAN access methods for remote access, and site requirements.

- Chapter 3, "Network Overview," steps you through the issues involved in choosing WAN equipment and assembling and cabling the equipment.

- Chapter 4, "Configuring Asynchronous Connections with Modems," gives a solid background in modem signaling, configuration using reverse Telnet, router line numbering, and basic asynchronous configuration.

- Chapter 5, "Configuring PPP and Controlling Network Access," discusses the background and basics of the PPP and its use in today's remote-access networks.

- Chapter 6, "PPP Link Control Protocol Options," discusses features of PPP to enhance the operation and security of implementing it. Options such as authentication, callback, and multilink are discussed in some detail.

- Chapter 7, "Using ISDN and DDR Technologies," covers the basics and background of ISDN as a technology. ISDN remains a staple of remote-access networking throughout the industry. This chapter explores the ins and outs of the technology.

- Chapter 8, "Advanced DDR Options," discusses dial-on-demand routing issues such as dialer profiles and rotary groups. These two implementations further augment the functionality of ISDN services in a remote-access network.

- Chapter 9, "Using ISDN Primary Rate Interface," provides an introduction to T1 and E1 PRI implementations. These connections are useful in providing central site connectivity and ISP-type dialup capabilities for a remote-access network.

- Chapter 10, "Broadband Options to Access a Central Site," discusses various options for high-speed Internet connectivity available in today's marketplace. Satellite, cable, and wireless networking will have a profound effect on the access market in the years to come.

- Chapter 11, "Using DSL to Access a Central Site," discusses the basics and background of DSL technologies. DSL is emerging as the forerunner in the SOHO Internet connectivity market. This chapter builds on the information covered in Chapter 10.

- Chapter 12, "Establishing a Frame Relay Connection," discusses the basics and background of Frame Relay as a technology. Frame Relay has proven itself to be a robust and reliable technology for interoffice connectivity.

- Chapter 13, "Frame Relay Traffic Shaping," discusses the manipulation of traffic traversing Frame Relay circuits. This is a key function in Frame Relay hub-and-spoke environments where there typically exists a speed mismatch between the ends of a particular circuit.

- Chapter 14, "Enabling a Backup to the Permanent Connection," discusses various methods that are used to provide redundancy in connectivity if a circuit or interface fails. Issues such as dial backup and snapshot routing are covered.

- Chapter 15, "Managing Network Performance with Queuing and Compression," provides an overview of queuing, with coverage Class-Based Weighted Fair Queuing, Low-Latency Queuing, and compression techniques.

- Chapter 16, "Scaling IP Addresses with NAT," examines Network Address Translation, with discussion of its characteristics, overloading, overlapping networks, and TCP load distribution. This chapter also covers port address translation (PAT).

- Chapter 17, "Using AAA to Scale Access Control in an Expanding Network," covers authentication, authorization, and accounting. Security protocols are discussed, and a complete overview of TACACS and RADIUS is provided.

- Chapter 18, "Securing Remote Access Network Connections," helps you to understand the process Cisco Systems uses to create VPN networks with its line of products and IPSec and other encryption algorithms. As a CCNP candidate, you must come up with solutions for remote access that are secure, reliable, and cost effective, and this chapter describes how to do so.

Each of these chapters uses several features to help you make the best use of your time in that chapter:

- **"Do I Know This Already?" quiz**—Each chapter begins with a quiz that helps you determine the amount of time you need to spend studying that chapter. The quiz is broken into subdivisions, each of which corresponds to a section of the chapter. Based on your score on the quiz, you will be directed to study all or particular parts of the chapter.

- **Foundation Topics**—This is the core section of each chapter that explains the protocols, concepts, and configuration for the topics in the chapter.

- **Foundation Summary**—This section is designed to help you review the key concepts in the chapter, and it is an excellent tool for last-minute review.

- **Q&A**—These end-of-the-chapter questions focus on recall, covering topics in the "Foundation Topics" section by using several types of questions. It is a tool for final review when your exam date is approaching.

- **CD-ROM-based practice exam**—The companion CD-ROM contains a large number of questions that are not included in the text of the book. You can answer these questions by using the simulated exam feature, or by using the topical review feature. This is the best tool for helping you prepare for the test-taking process.

Approach

Retention and recall are the two features of human memory most closely related to performance on tests. This exam preparation guide focuses on increasing both retention and recall of the topics on the exam. The other human characteristic involved in successfully passing the exam is intelligence; this book does not address that issue!

Adult retention is typically less than that of children. For example, it is common for four-year-old children to pick up basic language skills in a new country faster than their parents. Children retain facts as an end unto itself; adults typically either need a stronger reason to remember a fact or must have a reason to think about that fact several times to retain it in memory. For these reasons, a student who attends a typical Cisco course and retains 50 percent of the material is actually quite an amazing student.

Memory recall is based on connectors to the information that needs to be recalled—the greater the number of connectors to a piece of information, the better chance and better speed of recall.

Recall and retention work together. If you do not retain the knowledge, it will be difficult to recall it. This book is designed with features to help you increase retention and recall. It does this in the following ways:

- By providing succinct and complete methods of helping you decide what you recall easily and what you do not recall at all.

- By giving references to the exact passages in the book that review those concepts you did not recall so that you can quickly be reminded about a fact or concept. Repeating information that connects to another concept helps retention, and describing the same concept in several ways throughout a chapter increases the number of connectors to the same pieces of information.

- By including exercise questions that supply fewer connectors than multiple-choice questions. This helps you exercise recall and avoids giving you a false sense of confidence, as an exercise with only multiple-choice questions might do. For example, fill-in-the-blank questions require you to have better recall than multiple-choice questions.

Finally, accompanying this book is a CD-ROM that has exam-like, multiple-choice questions as well as simulation-based questions. These are useful for you to practice taking the exam and to get accustomed to the time restrictions imposed during the exam.

All About the Cisco Certified Network Professional Certification

The Cisco Certified Network Professional (CCNP) certification proves that an individual has completed rigorous testing in the network arena. In addition, the CCNP certification is becoming more important than ever because Cisco is providing greater and greater incentives to its partners that have employees with CCNP-level expertise.

The CCNP track requires the candidate to be comfortable with advanced routing techniques, switching techniques, and dialup or Remote Access Server (RAS) technology. On top of those areas, the CCNP must be able to, without consulting a book or other resource, configure and troubleshoot a routed and switched network.

The CCNP is a hands-on certification that requires a candidate to pass the Cisco Internetwork Troubleshooting exam. The emphasis in the exam is on troubleshooting the router if the configuration for it has failed. CCNP is currently one of the most sought-after certifications, short of the Cisco Certified Internetworking Expert (CCIE).

The CCNP track is daunting at first glance because it requires a candidate to pass a number of tests. To become a CCNP, a candidate must first be a Cisco Certified Network Associate (CCNA). The CCNP certification requires study and proficiency in the three areas of advanced routing, in switching and RAS, and in either design or troubleshooting.

Some of the information in this book overlaps with information in the routing field, and you may have seen some of this book's information while studying for the BCMSN exam. In addition, there are other certification books that specifically focus on advanced routing and switching. You might find some overlap in those manuals also. This is to be expected—all the information taken as a whole is what produces a CCNP.

The exam is a computer-based exam that has multiple choice, fill-in-the-blank, and list-in-order style questions. The fill-in-the-blank questions are filled in using the complete syntax for the command, including dashes and the like. For the fill-in-the-blank questions, a tile button is given to list commands in alphabetical order. This is a real lifesaver if you can't remember whether there is a dash or an *s* at the end of a command. Knowing the syntax is key, however, because the list contains some bogus commands in addition to the real ones.

The exam can be taken at any Pearson VUE testing center (http://www.PearsonVue.com/cisco/) or Thomson Prometric testing center (866-PROMETRIC or www.prometric.com). As with most Cisco exams, you cannot mark a question and return to it. In other words, you must answer a question before moving on, even if this means guessing. Remember that a blank answer is scored as incorrect.

Most of the exam is straightforward; however, the first answer that leaps off the page may be incorrect. You must read each question and each answer completely before making a selection. If you find yourself on a question that is incomprehensible, try restating the question a different way to see if you can understand what is being asked. Very few candidates score 100 percent in all categories—the key is to pass. The exam has so few questions that giving up just one question because of lack of diligence can mean the difference between passing and failing. Four questions one way or the other can mean a change of 10 to 20 percent!

Many people do not pass on the first try, but success is attainable with study. This book includes questions and scenarios that are designed to be more difficult and more in depth than most questions on the test. This was not done to show how much smarter we are, but to allow you a certain level of comfort when you have mastered the material in this book.

The CCNP certification is difficult to achieve, but the rewards are there, and will continue to be there, if the bar is kept where it is.

How This Book Can Help You Pass the CCNP BCRAN Exam

The primary focus of this book is not to teach material in the detail that is covered by an instructor in a five-day class with hands-on labs. Instead, we tried to capture the essence of each topic and to present questions and scenarios that push the envelope on each topic that is covered for the BCRAN exam.

The audience for this book includes candidates that have successfully completed the Building Cisco Remote Access Networks (BCRAN) class and those that have a breadth of experience in this area. The **show** and **debug** commands from that class are fair game for questions within the Remote Access exam, and hands-on work is the best way to commit those to memory.

If you have not taken the BCRAN course, the quizzes and scenarios in this book should give you a good idea of how prepared you are to skip the class and test out based on your experience. On the flip side, however, you should know that although having the knowledge from just a classroom setting can be enough to pass the test, some questions assume a CCNA level of internetworking knowledge.

Overview of Cisco Certifications

Cisco fulfills only a small portion of its orders through direct sales; most times, a Cisco reseller is involved. Cisco's main motivation for developing the current certification program was to measure the skills of people working for Cisco Resellers and Certified Partners.

Cisco has not attempted to become the only source for consulting and implementation services for network deployments using Cisco products. In 1996 and 1997, Cisco embarked on a channel program in which business partners would work with smaller and midsize businesses with whom Cisco could not form a peer relationship. In effect, Cisco partners of all sizes carried the Cisco flag into these smaller companies. With so many partners involved, Cisco needed to certify the skill levels of the employees of the partner companies.

The CCIE program was Cisco's first cut at certifications. Introduced in 1994, the CCIE was designed to be one of the most respected, difficult-to-achieve certifications. To certify, a written test (also at Thomson Prometric) had to be passed, and then a two-day hands-on lab test was administered by Cisco. The certifications were a huge commitment for the smaller resellers that dealt in the commodity-based products for small business and home use.

Cisco would certify resellers and services partners by using the number of employed CCIEs as the gauge. This criterion worked well originally, partly because Cisco had only a few large partners. In fact, the partners in 1995–1997 were generally large integrators that targeted the midsize corporations with whom Cisco did not have the engineering resources to maintain a personal relationship. This was a win-win situation for both Cisco and the partners. The partners had a staff that consisted of CCIEs that could present the product and configuration with the same adroitness as the Cisco engineering staff and were close to the customer.

As stated, Cisco used the number of CCIEs on staff as a criterion in determining the partner status of another company. That status in turn dictated the discount received by the reseller when buying from Cisco. The number of resellers began to grow, however, and with Cisco's commitment to the lower-tier market and smaller-sized businesses, it needed to have smaller integrators that could handle that piece of the market.

The CCIE certification didn't help the smaller integrators who were satisfying the small business and home market; because of their size, the smaller integrators were not able to attain any degree of discount. Cisco, however, needed their skills to continue to capture the small-business market, which was—and is—one of the largest markets in the internetworking arena.

What was needed by Cisco was a level of certification that was less rigorous than CCIE but that would allow Cisco more granularity in judging the skills on staff at a partner company. So Cisco created several additional certifications, CCNP and CCDP included.

Two categories of certifications were developed—one to certify implementation skills and the other to certify design skills. Service companies need more implementation skills, and resellers working in a pre-sales environment need more design skills. So, the CCNA and CCNP are implementation-oriented certifications, whereas the Cisco Certified Design Associate (CCDA) and CCDP are design-oriented certifications.

Rather than just one level of certification besides CCIE, Cisco created two additional levels: Associate and Professional. CCNA is more basic, and CCNP is the intermediate level between CCNA and CCIE. Likewise, CCDA is more basic than CCDP.

Several certifications require other certifications as a prerequisite. For instance, CCNP certification requires CCNA first. Also, CCDP requires both CCDA and CCNA certification. CCIE, however, does not require any other certification prior to the written and lab tests—mainly for historical reasons.

Cisco certifications have become a much needed commodity in the internetworking world as companies scramble to position themselves with the latest e-commerce, e-business, and e-life that is out there. Because Novell, Windows NT, Linux, or any other routed protocols generally need to be routed somewhere, the integrators want a piece of that business as well. Because Cisco cannot form a relationship with every new startup business, it looks for certified partners to take on that responsibility. The CCNP and CCDP certifications are truly another win-win situation for resellers, integrators, you, and Cisco.

The BCRAN Exam and the CCNP Certification

Passing the BCRAN exam proves mastery of the features used in larger corporate dial-in facilities and ISP operations. Skills required for CCNP and CCDP certifications include the ability to install, configure, operate, and troubleshoot remote-access devices in a complex WAN environment. Specifically, the remote-access skills required demonstrate that the CCNP or CCDP candidate can ensure minimal WAN costs to the customer or client using the Cisco IOS features.

The Cisco features that are critical to this endeavor include dial-on-demand, bandwidth-on-demand, dial backup, snapshot routing, dialer maps, and dialer profiles. In addition, successful candidates should be comfortable with Frame Relay, ISDN, queuing, and broadband services.

The target audience for CCNP certification includes the following:

- Gold- or Silver-certified partners
- CCNAs who want increased earning power, professional recognition, job promotions, and so on
- Level 1 network support individuals who want to progress to level 2
- ISP professionals who want to gain a larger understanding of the Internet picture and its intricacies

A CCNP's training and experience enables them to accomplish the following:

■ Install and configure a network to minimize WAN costs and to ensure connectivity from remote sites

■ Maximize performance over a WAN link

■ Improve network security

■ Provide access to remote customers or clients

■ Configure queuing for congested links to alleviate occasional congestion

■ Provide dialup connectivity over analog and digital networks

■ Implement DDR backup services to protect against down time

Exams Required for Certification

As described earlier, you are required to pass a group of exams to achieve CCNP certification. The exams generally match the same topics that are covered in one of the official Cisco courses. Table I-1 outlines the exams and the courses with which they are most closely matched.

Table I-1 *Exam-to-Course Mappings for CCNP Certification*

Certification	Exam Number	Name	Course Most Closely Matching the Exam's Requirements
CCNA	640-801	CCNA	Interconnecting Cisco Network Devices (ICND)
CCNP	642-801	BSCI	Building Scalable Cisco Internetworks (BSCI)*
	642-811	BCMSN	Building Cisco Multilayer Switched Networks (BCMSN)
	642-821	BCRAN	Building Cisco Remote Access Networks (BCRAN)
	642-831	CIT	Cisco Internetwork Troubleshooting (CIT)

* Passing the Foundation exam 640-841, which is also a recertification exam for CCNP, meets the same requirements as passing exams 642-801 and 642-811.

What Is on the BCRAN Exam?

The BCRAN exam evaluates the knowledge of network administrators and specialists who must configure and maintain a RAS and the associated peripheral components that accompany it. Candidates attempting to pass the BCRAN exam must perform the following tasks:

■ Describe how different WAN technologies can be used to provide remote access to a network, including asynchronous dial-in, Frame Relay, ISDN, cable modem, and DSL

■ Describe traffic-control methods used to manage traffic flow on WAN links

■ Explain the operation of remote network access control methods

- Identify PPP components, and explain the use of PPP as an access and encapsulation method
- Describe the structure and operation of VPN technologies
- Describe the process of Network Address Translation
- Configure asynchronous modems and router interfaces to provide network access
- Configure an ISDN solution for remote access
- Configure Frame Relay operation and traffic control on WAN links
- Configure access control to manage and limit remote access
- Configure DSL operation using Cisco IOS
- Configure VPN operation using Cisco IOS
- Configure Network Address Translation
- Design a Cisco remote-access solution using asynchronous dialup technology
- Plan a Cisco ISDN solution for remote access or primary link backup
- Design a Cisco Frame Relay infrastructure to provide access between remote network components
- Design a solution of access control to meet required specifications
- Plan traffic shaping to meet required quality of service on access links
- Troubleshoot nonfunctional remote-access systems
- Troubleshoot a VPN system
- Troubleshoot traffic-control problems on a WAN link

Recommended Training Path for CCNP

The recommended training path for the Cisco professional-level certifications is, of course, the instructor-led courses:

- **Building Scalable Cisco Internetworks (BSCI)**—Covers the advanced routing protocols and the scaling issues involved with a large, routed network with multiple protocols.
- **Building Cisco Multilayer Switched Networks (BCMSN)**—Covers the switch infrastructure and the configuration in a large network environment.
- **Building Cisco Remote Access Networks (BCRAN)**—Covers the dialup and RAS issues involved in large-scale remote-access designs and implementations.

After these courses, the CCNP requires Cisco Internetwork Troubleshooting as the final course.

The previously listed courses are the recommended training events for passing the exams for the CCNP track. However, as Cisco evolves the testing, the tests might not necessarily correlate to the given class. In other words, the tests can cover material that is germane to the material in the class but that might not have been covered per se. In essence, Cisco is looking for each test to be less a fact-stuffing event and more a gauge of how well you know the technology.

How to Use This Book to Pass the Exam

There are four sections in each chapter: a short pre-assessment quiz, the main topics of the chapter, a summary of the key points of the chapter, and a test to ensure that you have mastered the topics in the chapter.

Each chapter begins with a "Do I Know This Already?" quiz, which maps to the major topic headings in the chapter. If you get a high score on these quizlets, you might want to review the "Foundation Summary" section at the end of the chapter and then take the chapter test. If you score high on the test, you should review the summary to see if anything else should be added to your crib notes for a final run-through before taking the live test.

The "Foundation Summary" section in each chapter provides a set of "crib notes" that can be reviewed prior to the exam. These notes are not designed to teach, but merely to remind the reader what was in the chapter.

If you score well on one group of questions in the quiz, but low on another, you are directed to the section of the chapter that corresponds to the questions on which you scored low. You'll notice that the questions in the quizlet are not multiple choice in most cases. This testing format requires you to think through your answer to see if the information is already where you need it—in your brain! If you score poorly on the overall quiz, it is recommended that you read the whole chapter, because some of the topics build on others.

All "Do I Know This Already?" and Q&A questions, with answers, are in Appendix A, "Answers to the 'Do I Know This Already?' Quizzes and Q&A Sections." These conveniently located questions can be read and reviewed quickly prior to taking the live test. The CD-ROM has testing software and many additional questions that are similar to the format of the Remote Access exam. These questions should be a valuable resource when you are making final preparations for the exam.

Anyone preparing for the BCRAN exam can use the guidelines at the beginning of each chapter to guide their study. However, if you would like some additional guidance, the final parts of this introduction give additional strategies for study, based on how you have prepared before buying this book. So, find the section that most closely matches your background in the next few pages, and then read some additional ideas to help you prepare. There is a section for the reader who has passed other CCNP exams and is ready for the BCRAN exam, one for the reader who has passed the CCNA and is starting the CCNP track, and one for the reader who has no Cisco certifications and is starting the CCNP track.

One Final Word of Advice

The "Foundation Summary" section and your notes are your "crib note" knowledge of remote access. These pieces of paper are valuable when you are studying for the CCIE or Cisco recertification exam. You should take the time to organize them so that they become part of your paper "long-term memory."

Reviewing information that you actually wrote in your own handwriting is the easiest data to put back into your brain's RAM. Gaining a certification but losing the knowledge is of no value. For most people, maintaining the knowledge is as simple as writing it down.

You Have Passed Other CCNP Exams and Are Preparing for the BCRAN Exam

Consider the following scenarios as you plan your study time.

Scenario 1: You Have Taken the BCRAN Course

Because you have taken other Cisco exams and have taken the BCRAN course, you know what you are up against in the test experience. The BCRAN exam is like all the others. The questions are "Sylvanish" and the answers are sometimes confusing if you read too much into them.

The best approach with this book is to take each chapter's "Do I Know This Already?" quiz and then focus your study on the parts of the chapter that cover the questions you answered incorrectly. It is best not to jump to the final exam until you have given yourself a chance to review the entire book. Save the final exam to test your knowledge after you have mentally checked each section to ensure that you have an idea of what the whole test could cover. Remember that the CD-ROM testing engine spools out a sampling of questions and might not give you a good picture the first time you use it; the test engine could spool a test that is easy for you, or it could spool one that is very difficult.

Before the test, make your own notes using the "Foundation Summary" sections and your own handwritten notes. Once you have your bank of notes, study them, and then take the final exam three or four times. Each time you take the test, force yourself to read each question and each answer, even if you have seen them before. Again, repetition is a super memory aid.

Scenario 2: You Have Not Taken the BCRAN Course

Because you have taken other Cisco exams, you know what you are up against in the test experience. The BCRAN exam is like all the others. The questions are "Sylvanish" and the answers are sometimes confusing if you read too much into them.

The best approach with this book, because you have not taken the class, is to take each chapter's "Do I Know This Already?" quiz to determine what to look for as you read the chapter. Once you have completed a chapter, take the end-of-chapter test to see how well you have assimilated the material. If there are sections that do not seem to gel, you might want to consider buying a copy of the Cisco

Press book *Building Cisco Remote Access Networks,* which is a hard copy of the material found in the BCRAN course.

After you have completed each chapter, you should go back through the book and do the scenarios, where available, to verify that you can apply the material you have learned. At that point, you should then use the CD-ROM testing engine to find out how well you know the material.

Before the test, make notes using the "Foundation Summary" sections and your own additions. Writing something down, even if you are copying it, makes it easier to remember. Once you have your bank of notes, study them, and then take the final practice exam on the CD-ROM testing engine three or four times. Each time you take the test, force yourself to read each question and each answer, even if you have seen them before. Again, repetition is a super memory aid.

You Have Passed the CCNA and Are Preparing for the BCRAN Exam

Consider the following scenarios as you plan your study path.

Scenario 1: You Have Taken the BCRAN Course

Because you have taken other Cisco exams and have taken the BCRAN course, you know what you are up against in the test experience. The BCRAN exam is like all the others. The questions are "Sylvanish" and the answers are sometimes confusing if you read too much into them.

The best approach with this book is to take each chapter's "Do I Know This Already?" quiz and focus on the parts that draw a blank. It is best not to jump to the final exam until you have given yourself a chance to review the entire book. Save the final exam to test your knowledge after you have mentally checked each section to ensure that you have an idea of what the whole test could cover. The CD-ROM testing engine spools out a sampling of questions and might not give you a good picture the first time you use it; the test engine could spool a test that is easy for you, or it could spool one that is very difficult.

Before the test, make your own notes using the "Foundation Summary" sections and your own additions. Writing something down, even if you are copying it, makes it easier to remember. Once you have your bank of notes, study them, and then take the final practice exam on the CD-ROM testing engine three or four times. Each time you take the test, force yourself to read each question and each answer, even if you have seen them before. Again, repetition is a super memory aid.

Scenario 2: You Have Not Taken the BCRAN Course

Because you have taken other Cisco exams, you know what you are up against in the test experience. The BCRAN exam is like the others. The questions are "Sylvanish" and the answers are sometimes confusing if you read too much into them.

The best approach with this book, because you have not taken the course, is to take each chapter's "Do I Know This Already?" quiz to determine what to look for as you read the chapter. Once you have completed a chapter, take the end-of-chapter test to see how well you have assimilated the material. If there are sections that do not seem to gel, you might consider buying a copy of the Cisco Press book *Building Remote Access Networks*, which is a hard copy of the material found in the course.

After you have completed each chapter, you should go back through the book and do the chapter scenarios to ensure that you can apply the material you have learned. At that point, you should then use the CD-ROM testing engine to find out how well you know the material.

Before the test, make your own notes using the "Foundation Summary" sections and your own additions. Writing something down, even if you are copying it, makes it easier to remember. Once you have your bank of notes, study them, and then take the final practice exam on the CD-ROM testing engine three or four times. Each time you take the test, force yourself to read each question and each answer, even if you have seen them before. Again, repetition is a super memory aid.

You Have Experience and Want to Skip the Classroom Experience and Take the BCRAN Exam

Consider carefully the following scenarios.

Scenario 1: You Have CCNA Certification

Because you have taken other Cisco exams, you know what you are up against in the test experience. The BCRAN exam is like the others. The questions are "Sylvanish" and the answers are sometimes confusing if you read too much into them.

The best approach with this book, because you have not taken the course, is to take each chapter's "Do I Know This Already?" quiz to determine what to look for as you read the chapter. Once you have completed a chapter, take the end-of-chapter test to see how well you have assimilated the material. If there are sections that do not seem to gel, you might want to buy a copy of the Cisco Press book *Building Remote Access Networks*, which is a hard copy of the material found in the course.

After you have completed each chapter, you should go back through the book and do the chapter scenarios to see if you can apply the material you have learned. At that point, you should use the CD-ROM testing engine to find out how well you know the material.

Before the test, make your own notes using the "Foundation Summary" sections and your own additions. Writing something down, even if you are copying it, makes it easier to remember. Once you have your bank of notes, study them, and then take the final practice exam on the CD-ROM testing engine three or four times. Each time you take the test, force yourself to read each question and each answer, even if you have seen them before. Again, repetition is a super memory aid.

Scenario 2: You Do Not Have CCNA Certification

Why don't you have the certification? The prerequisite for the CCNP certification is to be certified as a CCNA, so you really should pursue your CCNA certification before tackling the CCNP certification. Beginning with the BCRAN exam gives you a skewed view of what is needed for the Cisco Professional certification track.

That being said, if you *must* pursue the certifications out of order, follow the spirit of the book. Read each chapter and then do the quiz at the front of the chapter to see if you caught the major points. After you have done that, try the test on the CD-ROM and pay particular attention to the VUE/Sylvan-way of testing so that you are prepared for the live test.

Good luck to all!

PART I: Identifying Remote Access Needs

Chapter 1 **Remote Access Solutions**

Chapter 2 **Identifying Site Requirements**

Chapter 3 **Network Overview**

This part of the book covers the following BCRAN exam topics:

- Describe how different WAN technologies can be used to provide remote access to a network, including asynchronous dial-in, Frame Relay, ISDN, cable modem, and DSL

- Explain the operation of remote network access control methods

This chapter covers the following subjects:

- Questions for Evaluating Remote Access Products

- Discussion of Remote Access Products

- WAN Connections

- Determining the Site Requirements

- Introduction to QoS

CHAPTER 1

Remote Access Solutions

Most corporations now recognize that to remain competitive, their employees must be able to access the corporate network remotely at all times and from a variety of locations. Whether this access is by a home user, a "road warrior" (an employee who connects to the office from numerous different remote locations), or a remote office, as a network administrator, you must consider the many different scenarios in which employees might need to access the network remotely and provide support for that access.

Depending on where the users may be located, you have to consider many types of access technologies. Because there are so many access technologies available, the choice of infrastructure equipment that will support the appropriate technology is critical. You need to support current access technologies and also be able to support future technologies. You also have to take into account such factors as security, availability, reliability, and cost.

One important consideration in today's networks is the ability to guarantee quality of service (QoS) for certain types of traffic, such as voice and video. You also need to consider the fundamentals of QoS, so that when a remote user is running an application that needs priority or guaranteed bandwidth, you can try to accommodate that need. Accomodating this need is usually accomplished between remote offices or home offices with high-speed connections, because the amount of bandwidth available to a dialup user is just too small to send toll-quality voice and video in addition to regular data across.

"Do I Know This Already?" Quiz

The purpose of the "Do I Know This Already?" quiz is to help you decide whether you really need to read the entire chapter. If you already intend to read the entire chapter, you do not necessarily need to answer these questions now.

The 15-question quiz, derived from the major sections in the "Foundation Topics" portion of the chapter, helps you to determine how to spend your limited study time.

Table 1-1 outlines the major topics discussed in this chapter and the "Do I Know This Already?" quiz questions that correspond to those topics.

Table 1-1 *"Do I Know This Already?" Foundation Topics Section-to-Question Mapping*

Foundation Topics Section	Questions Covered in This Section
Questions for Evaluating Remote Access Products	1–3
Discussion of Remote Access Products	4–6
WAN Connections	7–9
Determining the Site Requirements	10–12
Introduction to QoS	11–15

CAUTION   The goal of self-assessment is to gauge your mastery of the topics in this chapter. If you do not know the answer to a question or are only partially sure of the answer, you should mark this question wrong for purposes of the self-assessment. Giving yourself credit for an answer you correctly guess skews your self-assessment results and might provide you with a false sense of security.

1.   Who is usually considered to be using remote access?

   a.   Anyone who is not logged on locally to the resource

   b.   Anyone in a branch office

   c.   A user on a different subnet

   d.   Anyone who has to use some form of WAN connection

2.   What are some common considerations for remote access usage?

   a.   Security

   b.   Reliability

   c.   Cost

   d.   Availability

   e.   All of the above

3.   What are the two main categories for Cisco's product lineup?

   a.   Modular

   b.   Layer 3

   c.   Fixed

   d.   Layer 2

4. Where does the Cisco 800 Series router fit into the product lineup?

   a. Small office

   b. Remote office

   c. Branch office

   d. Head office

5. Where does the Cisco 2600 Series router fit into the product lineup?

   a. Small office

   b. Remote office

   c. Branch office

   d. Head office

6. Where does the PIX 501 Firewall fit into the product lineup?

   a. Small office

   b. Remote office

   c. Branch office

   d. Home office

7. What is the most common dedicated WAN connection?

   a. xDSL

   b. Wireless

   c. X.25

   d. Leased line

   e. Frame Relay

8. What is the typical maximum speed of an asynchronous dialup connection?

   a. 1 Mbps

   b. 1.544 Mbps

   c. 128 kbps

   d. 53 kbps

9. What are three emerging WAN technologies?

   a. Frame Relay

   b. Wireless

   c. xDSL

   d. Cable

10. What are typical network growth estimates at a head office site?

   a. 0%

   b. 5%

   c. 10%

   d. 15%

   e. 20%

11. To save costs, fixed-configuration devices are used at the branch-office level.

   a. True

   b. False

12. At home office or small office sites, what is the predominant deciding factor when choosing the connection type?

   a. Reliability

   b. Speed

   c. Cost

   d. Bandwidth

13. What is the default interface queuing option on serial interfaces?

   a. FIFO

   b. WFQ

   c. Round robin

   d. No queuing turned on

14. What is a common problem with Priority Queuing?

   a. Cannot be used with most types of traffic

   b. No way of differentiating packets

   c. Only two classes of traffic, high and normal

   d. Lower-priority queues could be starved for bandwidth

15. How many user-definable queues are available with Custom Queuing?

   a. 1

   b. 2

   c. 4

   d. 16

The answers to the "Do I Know This Already?" quiz are found in Appendix A, "Answers to the 'Do I Know This Already?' Quizzes and Q&A Sections." The suggested choices for your next step are as follows:

■ **8 or fewer overall score**—Read the entire chapter. This includes the "Foundation Topics," "Foundation Summary," and "Q&A" sections.

■ **9, 10, or 11 overall score**—Begin with the "Foundation Summary" section and then go to the "Q&A" section.

■ **12 or more overall score**—If you want more review on these topics, skip to the "Foundation Summary" section and then go to the "Q&A" section. Otherwise, move to the next chapter.

Foundation Topics

As you progress through this chapter, you will discover the need for remote access to your data. You will see that when designing remote access solutions, you need to consider many things, such as the bandwidth required for the applications being used, whether the application needs guaranteed bandwidth, and which Cisco devices offer the features and interfaces that you may need. As you decide on what options fulfill your current needs, you also have to consider future growth and new technologies that may need to be added, such as VPN support or different access technologies such as DSL, wireless, or cable. Considering all of your options will help you narrow down the choices of equipment and access technologies.

Cisco has a complete lineup of devices that meets the demanding criteria for today's data infrastructures. The challenge is to narrow down the list to what fits into your network and supports your network's goals for remote access.

The first objective is to become familiar with the technologies offered by Cisco. There are two types of platforms:

- **Modular**—Provides the capability to support different configurations of ports and modules by placing the appropriate interface modules into the modular chassis of the device to support your current network solution, while leaving the flexibility to add new options later.

- **Fixed**—Provides the capability to support a fixed type/number of interfaces or modules. You cannot change the configuration of the specific types of interfaces/modules that are in the device. If new options arise, you must buy a new device that supports that type of interface.

Cisco has built most of its current product line on a modular chassis format.

The next consideration is how many remote users you need to support and where they are located. If the majority of your users are located at a remote office, then you need to support some type of connection that is permanently available. If the majority of remote access users are connecting from home or on the road, you need to support some type of connection that is an on-demand circuit. Usually, support for a combination of both access methods needs to be provided.

These are just some considerations to keep in mind as you familiarize yourself with Cisco's product line. This chapter focuses on the routers and remote access devices in the Cisco product line. For a complete lineup of Cisco's products, go to http://www.cisco.com and search for "Cisco Products."

Discussion of Remote Access Products

This section provides a brief overview of some of the more popular remote access equipment in the Cisco product lineup. Please see the white papers about the specific product on the Cisco website if you need more details.

Cisco 700 Series

The Cisco 700 Series router supports IP and IPX routing over ISDN. Routers from this family have no scalability for adding ports and were designed for remote offices (ROs) and small offices, home offices (SOHOs).

The 700 Series router is an inexpensive ISDN access device. Figure 1-1 shows a Cisco 700 Series router.

Figure 1-1 *Cisco 700 Series Router*

Cisco 800 Series

The Cisco 800 Series router is the lowest-priced entry-level router that runs the Cisco IOS software. Because the base operating system for the 800 Series router is the same as for the higher-end router platforms, this platform enables the corporate staff to use the same language to configure the remote device. The Cisco 800 Series router is ideal for the RO or SOHO.

The WAN options for the 800 Series are the same as for the 700 Series. Figure 1-2 shows a Cisco 800 Series router.

Figure 1-2 *Cisco 800 Series Router*

Cisco 1600 Series

The Cisco 1600 Series router offers a modular construction that enables the WAN interfaces to be changed by the customer as needed.

The WAN cards in a 1600 Series router can be shared with routers from the 2600 and 3600 router Series. This enables the maintenance of only a small set of hot-spare boards.

The 1600 uses the trademark Cisco IOS software and is generally positioned at a branch-office site and not at a RO or SOHO.

Figure 1-3 shows a Cisco 1600 Series router.

Figure 1-3 *Cisco 1600 Series Router*

Cisco 1700 Series

The Cisco 1700 Series router is a replacement for the 1600 Series. It is designed to support small to medium-sized branch-office networks. It has near wire speed capability for VPN and IPSec networks, including support for stateful firewall and intrusion detection. It also supports converged networking by offering Voice over IP capabilities and QoS services.

Cisco 2500 Series

The Cisco 2500 Series router is the oldest router platform mentioned so far. A router from this series is a fixed-configuration router that offers a wide range of options for the branch or central office.

This router series is not modular. If a different port configuration is needed, a new 2500 is required.

Figure 1-4 shows a Cisco 2500 Series router.

Figure 1-4   *Cisco 2500 Series Router*

Cisco 2600 Series

The Cisco 2600XM Series router is replacing the current 2600 Series router because of its flexibility with the WAN card design and added CPU processing power and RAM. The 2600XM Series router can support many different hardware configurations in a single chassis. In fact, the customer can mix and match both LAN and WAN resources by simply changing boards on the chassis. The 2600XM Series router is generally positioned in a branch-office site or small, central facility.

Figure 1-5 shows a Cisco 2600XM Series router.

Figure 1-5   *Cisco 2600XM Series Router*

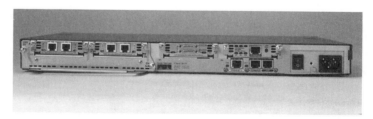

Cisco 3600 Series

The Cisco 3600 Series router provides two, four, or six module slots, depending on the model. The 2600 Series router provides only two module slots. A 3600 Series router is considered a central-office piece of equipment because its flexibility and port density are so high.

Figure 1-6 illustrates a Cisco 3600 Series router.

Figure 1-6 *Cisco 3600 Series Router*

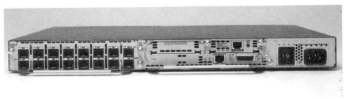

Cisco 3700 Series

The Cisco 3700 Series router is replacing the 3600 Series. It is the cornerstone to Cisco's Architecture for Voice, Video and Integrated Data (AVVID). It offers many of the advanced features of today's top-end equipment. Some of the features include in-line power for IP phones, high-density port population, and support for multiple Advanced Integration Modules (AIMs).

Cisco AS5000 Series

The Cisco AS5000 Series router (specifically, the 5200 and 5300 routers) provides a high port density and is typically found at an Internet service provider's (ISP) point of presence (POP).

The AS5000 chassis incorporates the functions of modems, switches, routers, and channel banks into a single platform. In addition, the AS5000 Series can support serial, digital, ISDN, and asynchronous access through a single physical interface. This support of mixed media makes this router very useful for a central office environment in which many different branch offices and remote offices must be supported.

Figure 1-7 illustrates a Cisco AS5300 Series router.

Figure 1-7 *Cisco AS5300 Series Router*

Cisco 7200 Series

The Cisco 7200 Series router is used in a remote access services (RAS) environment. The 7200 Series can provide a central site with many high-speed interfaces in which many branch offices can be aggregated.

Figure 1-8 shows several Cisco 7200 Series routers.

Figure 1-8 *Cisco 7200 Series Router*

PIX Firewall Series

The Cisco PIX Firewall Series is an excellent choice for firewalls. There are many different models to choose from, but the focus here is what fits in a small branch office or home office. There are two models to choose from. The PIX 501 offers basic site-to-site VPN configuration and connectivity for asymmetric digital subscriber line (ADSL) with Point-to-Point Protocol over Ethernet (PPPoE) connections and offers a built-in four-port 10/100 switch. The PIX 506E offers a little more horsepower than the PIX 501, for more VPN site-to-site traffic, and offers the same robust firewall features. Cisco has recently released a PIX Firewall Services Module for the 7200 Series router or the Catalyst 6500 Series switch. It offers many of the same advantages as the PIX Firewall, but with a much higher throughput.

VPN 3000 Concentrator Series

Cisco offers many flexible solutions for small to large VPN networks. For a SOHO scenario, you could consider installing a VPN 3002 hardware client that does the VPN tunneling for many PCs and devices connected to it, instead of having each PC run its own client software and connect back to the main site.

The preceding device descriptions represent much of the Cisco product line. To properly install this equipment, you should consult Cisco's website (http://www.cisco.com) to get the most up-to-date information.

Although it is possible to review the entire suite of Cisco products before you make a product decision for an installation, to do so would be extremely time consuming. To help you with the selection task, you should use the Cisco Product Selection Tool, which is available on CD-ROM and at Cisco's website (http://www.cisco.com/warp/public/779/smbiz/service/advisor).

This tool enables you to quickly narrow a selection to a small number of router platforms by paring down the Cisco product line so that only the router platforms that match the search criteria are displayed.

In addition to using the Product Selection Tool, you can simply provide the requirements to a Cisco-certified value-add reseller (VAR) or to a Cisco sales engineer and ask which products satisfy the requirements. This advice might sound a bit trite, but Cisco is truly focused on ensuring that the right solution is provided in every instance in which its products are used. The emphasis that Cisco has placed on the certification process for its VARs is just one piece of evidence that supports this statement.

WAN Connections

Now that you have looked at what Cisco's product lineup can support, you need to review what WAN connections are available and decide which one will meet your needs.

There are many different types of WAN connections, such as the ones described in the sections that follow.

Traditional WAN Technologies

These are the traditional WAN technologies:

- **Asynchronous dialup**—This is a standard dialup connection across a service provider's network (PSTN) that provides an on-demand dedicated circuit, usually running at speeds up to 53 kbps. Dialup is the least expensive access method if the calls are local and for short periods of time. This may be the only wire-based access technology available in some areas. If more bandwidth is required, you can use Multilink PPP connections that bond two asynchronous dialup connections together, but then you have twice the cost for long-distance toll charges, and so on. This could give you speeds up to approximately 100 kbps if you bond two lines together.

- **Integrated Services Digital Network (ISDN)**—ISDN offers more bandwidth than standard PSTN connections because it offers a digital circuit-switched connection from end to end. It can achieve speeds of 128 kbps with the bonding of two B channels, which is common with a BRI interface. As with Asynchronous connections, if you need more bandwidth, multiple B channels can be bonded together. ISDN can also come in a PRI style interface. It is 23B channels and 1 signaling channel. Typical speeds are 1.544 Mbps.

- **Leased line**—If the company needs to control all aspects of the connection, such as protocol encapsulation and bandwidth division, you should consider a leased-line solution. This is one of the higher-cost solutions, but it offers many advantages such as complete control of the bandwidth including channelizing voice and data across the same leased line, very high data rates available, and access to the full bandwidth 100 percent of the time. It is not shared with anyone else. Typical speeds are between 1.544 Mbps and 45 Mbps.

- **Frame Relay**—Frame Relay circuits are still the most popular WAN connection method for dedicated access. Frame Relay offers many of the advantages of a dedicated leased line while retaining the cost savings of shared bandwidth. Frame Relay specifies a committed information rate (CIR), which is the minimum amount of throughput a customer needs. From there, the customer can burst to the port speed for periods at a time as long as the network is not too busy. The service provider decides on what information above the CIR is allowed through. Even though Frame Relay is shared bandwidth, you still have some security because each customer gets its own permanent virtual circuit (PVC) through the service provider's cloud. In the United States, you must specify the port speed, minimum CIR, and the number of PVCs or data-link connection identifiers (DLCIs) you need per location. In Canada, in which the service provider network is overprovisioned, you only have to specify the port speed and the number of PVCs or DLCIs that you need per location. You do not need to purchase CIR in Canada unless you have a mission-critical application, in which case it is suggested that you buy enough CIR to allow your applications to function properly. Typical port speeds are from 56 kbps to 1.544 Mbps.

- **Asynchronous Transfer Mode (ATM)**—ATM is not normally used for WAN connections by end customers; it is usually a service provider backbone technology. However, it is possible to purchase ATM when remote sites need high bandwidth, guaranteed throughput, and low latency. It works by fragmenting packets into 53-byte cells and transporting them (usually) across a fiber-optic network. ATM is considered to be the grandfather of LAN extensions. Typical speeds are 5 Mbps to 622 Mbps.

Emerging WAN Technologies

The following are the emerging WAN technologies:

- **xDSL LAN Extension**—This is a newer technology that offers WAN connectivity to remote sites by simulating an Ethernet environment over xDSL technologies. It is used for higher-bandwidth solutions and, because of the common infrastructure that it uses, service providers can offer it at lower prices. Typical speeds are up to 1 Mbps synchronous or 640 kbps upload and up to 8 Mbps download if you get an asynchronous flavor of DSL.

- **Cable access**—In most places where a cable network is already in place, service providers can connect you to a coaxial cable infrastructure that allows data and television signals to traverse across the same network. This solution is usually low cost and provides a medium to high data rate. Typical speeds are up to 4 Mbps upload and up to 28 Mbps download.

■   **Wireless**—This is a general term used to describe any type of connectivity that is not based on a physical cable between sites. With the advancements of today's wireless technologies, very high-rate data transfers can be established over great distance. Some of the common deployments are site-to-site tertiary connections (when you have line of site for distances of up to a few kilometers) or connections using the cellular phone infrastructure for connecting back to the office through a dialup scenario or VPN access across the Internet. Typical speeds are from 19.2 kbps to 10 Gbps.

Determining the Site Requirements

In general, each company site can be placed into one of three categories: central office, branch office, or SOHO or RO (which are grouped into one category because of the small number of end users at these sites). Each type of site provides different opportunities for growth. The sections that follow provide insight into which platforms would be used at each site.

Central Site Installations

When the installation is in a central site or corporate headquarters, you should strongly consider the need for growth. Typical considerations are purchasing expansion capabilities for approximately 20 percent growth. Room for growth is important because remote or branch sites can be added or deleted over time and the hardware platform should be flexible so that a "forklift" upgrade is not needed every time a change in corporate strategy occurs.

The criteria for the central office should include evaluation of speeds and technologies available. The speeds should be sufficient to aggregate the information flows from the branch and remote sites. With speed, cost is a major consideration because the recurring WAN charges are the dominant cost factor. Hardware costs usually pale in comparison to the ongoing costs for WAN charges. Firewalls and access control (feeds) are also top considerations, because the central site must maintain and enable outside communication but protect against unauthorized access.

Branch-Office Installations

When the installation is for a branch office, there is usually less need for flexibility than with the central site, and cost becomes more of an issue. This does not mean that a fixed-configuration device is acceptable, however. It is still strongly suggested that a router contain enough ports for expansion, but possibly on a smaller scale (such as 10 percent growth). Branch-office support may include access to smaller, single-function remote offices or remote users.

Considerations at the branch office include dedicated WAN connections to the head office and possibly on-demand circuits for home users or small remote offices. The monthly costs are still a strong consideration. Additionally, the branch office must be able to authenticate itself to the central site.

The issue of availability is another critical factor in the branch office. You should take into account how much the company would lose if the network goes down. Estimating the potential for loss builds a strong case for considering some form of backup connection. The central office generally uses links that are always available or highly reliable, whereas the branch office might not want to pay for that reliability.

Remote Office or Home Office Installations

As you look to support end users or small remote offices/home offices, cost becomes the predominant factor. Usually, fixed-function devices are chosen, with cost as a main factor. Another important criteria is WAN connection availability in the area. Once you decide on which type of access method to use, it is unlikely to change in the near future.

The traffic or data that exits the RO or HO can usually be categorized very neatly. An example of this categorization would be a remote salesperson who must download corporate pricing and upload sales data and e-mail.

The overriding consideration at these offices is generally cost. In addition, the RO must maintain a method for authentication to the branch or central site and justify the connection time to a central or branch office. In general, these offices would use a dial-on-demand methodology to minimize WAN charges.

Introduction to QoS

As you add more and more services to your data networks, you need to consider the traffic types and service guarantees for the different types of traffic on the network. Today's networks carry different types of traffic, such as file transfers, interactive sessions, and voice and video, to name a few. Each of these types of traffic has different characteristics that the network must accommodate.

The problem with network equipment is that most of it is configured by default to work on a first-in, first-out (FIFO) basis. If you are using the Internet as a WAN technology (VPN networks), you have another problem, because there is no guaranteed class of service (CoS) across the Internet. If you use service providers for WAN connections, you can purchase different classes of service depending on your data needs. All of these factors must be considered.

Here are some guidelines when deciding to implement QoS services:

■   Prioritization of delay-sensitive traffic is important if you have interactive sessions and file transfers on the same WAN links. Large file transfers could make interactive sessions seem sporadic. Always give delay-sensitive traffic (interactive traffic) explicit priority over less time-sensitive traffic (file transfers).

■ If slower WAN links are at 100 percent usage all the time, QoS will not help. It is most effective on slower WAN connections that spike to 100 percent usage some of the time, causing temporary congestion.

■ QoS is usually only applied to lower-bandwidth links because of the added processing time.

■ If you do not experience congestion or sporadic interactive sessions, you probably don't need QoS.

There are many options within the QoS portfolio, as follows:

■ **Compression**—QoS does not provide more bandwidth on the link; rather, it just makes better use of the available bandwidth by using compression to reduce the size of the packets traversing the link to give the appearance of more bandwidth. You could introduce compression on the whole packet, on just the header, or on just the payload. Compression should only be done on links below T1/E1 speeds due to the added processing time and possible memory usage because of compressing each packet.

■ **Bandwidth Reservation Protocol**—If devices along the path support the reservation protocol, a connection from sender to receiver can be set up with a guaranteed CoS, providing time-sensitive or bandwidth-intensive traffic the necessary path through the network.

■ **QoS classification**—With the IP precedence bits, you can differentiate multiple classes of service for different traffic types. Therefore, you can provide different traffic-flow characteristics that the packets need to traverse the network properly.

■ **Congestion management**—As an abundance of packets enters a device, congestion management prioritizes the traffic as it places the packets on the outgoing link. The goal is to set a QoS class and prioritize the packets according to defined characteristics. Any delay-sensitive traffic, such as voice, should be given adequate bandwidth and always set into a priority queue. This is done at the expense of less critical data. Some of the Cisco IOS queuing methods that are currently supported are the following:

    — **Priority Queuing (PQ)**—PQ is based on four specific queues: high, medium, normal, and low. The high-priority queue is always serviced first. After the high-priority queue is empty, the process checks the medium-priority queue. If data is there, the device transmits a fixed amount and then goes back and checks the high-priority queue to see if any new traffic has arrived. This process is repeated, always checking the highest-priority queues first; if they are empty, the process services the next queue. This could lead to starvation in the normal- and low-priority queues if too much information is sent to the higher-priority queues.

    — **Custom Queuing (CQ)**—This method has up to 16 custom-defined queues. The administrator can decide on the number of bytes or packets serviced from each queue. This is one way of guaranteeing that no queue will be starved. This also provides a way to guarantee how much bandwidth each queue receives.

— **Weighted Fair Queuing (WFQ)**—This is the default method of queuing on links that are T1/E1 speeds or less. It offers fair access to the available bandwidth for each traffic flow. It can recognize IP precedence and apply a weight or priority to selected traffic to provide classification and determine how much bandwidth each conversation or flow is permitted.

- **Congestion avoidance**—Also known as *traffic policing*, this shapes traffic from different flows by limiting the bandwidth traffic can use, therefore causing the applications to reduce the amount of traffic they are sending. Traffic policing actually drops traffic above a certain rate, whereas traffic shaping simply limits the flow of traffic. Cisco supports Generic Traffic Shaping and three basic types of policing:

  — Committed Access Rate (CAR)

  — Random Early Detection (RED)

  — Weighted Random Early Detection (WRED)

Foundation Summary

The Foundation Summary section of each chapter lists the most important facts from the chapter. While this section does not list every fact from the chapter that will be on your Remote Access exam, a well-prepared CCNP candidate should at a minimum know all the details in each Foundation Summary before going to take the exam.

This chapter discussed what type of equipment is available to install at each of the different office types and what WAN technologies each office type could use. When designing a remote access solution, you need to look at many different components and then select the appropriate WAN technologies, device technologies, and option features such as QoS.

This chapter covered a few basic concepts of remote access. Some of the key points discussed regarding WAN connections were availability, reliability, and cost.

Q&A

The questions and scenarios in this book are more difficult than what you should experience on the actual exam. The questions do not attempt to cover more breadth or depth than the exam, but they are designed to make sure that you know the answer. Rather than enabling you to derive the answer from clues hidden inside the question, the questions challenge your understanding and recall of the subject. Hopefully, mastering these questions will help you limit the number of exam questions on which you narrow your choices to two options and then guess.

The answers to these questions can be found in Appendix A.

1. What are some of the considerations for remote access networks?

2. Why are modular chassis preferred over a fixed configuration?

3. What is the difference between traffic shaping and traffic policing?

4. How does Custom Queuing work?

5. Why is queuing only put on links that spike to 100 percent utilization and not on every single link?

6. What advantages does using wireless WAN links offer the designer?

This chapter covers the following topics that you will need to comprehend to master the BCRAN exam:

- **Determining Site Requirements**—The three sites described by Cisco Systems are the central office, remote office/branch office (ROBO), and small office/home office (SOHO). The successful CCNP candidate should be aware of these sites and their associated requirements.

- **Guidelines for Equipment Selection**—This section addresses the questions raised when planning a Cisco network: Is the device going to be used at a central office, a branch office, or in support of telecommuters? What are the cost factors and how volatile is the proposed location? What types of features are required to implement the network?

- **WAN Access Methods for Remote Access**—The WAN connection type directly affects the current and future needs of the customer and influences its level of satisfaction. This section addresses the selection process for the various WAN technologies available.

- **Technology Assessment**—You may need to address additional factors, such as encryption and security. Virtual private networks (VPNs) have become commonplace in today's networks. In some cases, a VPN might not be needed. But in others, data encryption is essential.

Identifying Site Requirements

This chapter covers the site preparation necessary to successfully deploy a remote-connection solution. First, you must understand the scope and requirements for different types of sites. Then, you can determine the appropriate connection technology to send data to that site. Today, a design engineer has a tremendous number of selections, including leased lines, packet switching (Frame Relay), ISDN, DSL, and even cable modems. Even analog modems are still used in locations where other services are not available, or just not needed.

After the site requirements are accepted, you can select the Cisco hardware to fulfill the design. The next chapter is dedicated to finding the correct Cisco product based on the site surveys and technology available at each of the sites in question.

"Do I Know This Already?" Quiz

The purpose of the "Do I Know This Already?" quiz is to help you decide whether you really need to read the entire chapter. If you already intend to read the entire chapter, you do not necessarily need to answer these questions now.

The eight-question quiz, derived from the major sections in the "Foundation Topics" portion of the chapter, helps you to determine how to spend your limited study time.

Table 2-1 outlines the major topics discussed in this chapter and the "Do I Know This Already?" quiz questions that correspond to those topics.

Table 2-1 *"Do I Know This Already?" Foundation Topics Section-to-Question Mapping*

Foundation Topics Section	Questions Covered in This Section
Determining Site Requirements	1–2
Guidelines for Equipment Selection	3–4
WAN Access Methods for Remote Access	5–6
Technology Assessment	7–8

> **CAUTION**   The goal of self-assessment is to gauge your mastery of the topics in this chapter. If you do not know the answer to a question or are only partially sure of the answer, you should mark this question wrong for purposes of the self-assessment. Giving yourself credit for an answer you correctly guess skews your self-assessment results and might provide you with a false sense of security.

1. Which of the following best describes some telecommunications parameters for a central office?

   a. Low-speed connections are an option

   b. Redundancy is required

   c. Cost is very important

   d. Fixed configuration routers are a must

2. Which of the following link connection speeds is considered appropriate for a remote office?

   a. 100 users with an ISDN BRI connection

   b. 10 users with a T1 connection

   c. 100 users with a cable-modem connection

   d. 100 users with a T1 connection

3. Which of the following terms describes whether a service provider is capable of providing a service in your area?

   a. Reliability

   b. Cost

   c. Availability

   d. Redundancy

4. How does QoS affect the flow of packets?

   a. QoS allows high-priority traffic to exit first

   b. QoS blocks certain traffic flows

   c. QoS puts smaller packets at the end of the line

   d. QoS has different behavior patterns based on the time of day

5. Which connection option guarantees consistent bandwidth availability all the time?

    a. Frame Relay

    b. Leased line

    c. ISDN

    d. DSL

6. What is the maximum speed of an ISDN BRI connection?

    a. 64 kbps

    b. 128 kbps

    c. 256 kbps

    d. 1544 kbps

7. Which of the following WAN connection methods establishes connections with an ISP instead of with another site?

    a. Frame Relay

    b. Leased line

    c. ISDN

    d. DSL

8. What type of VPN link creates a tunnel between a PC and a router?

    a. Site-to-site VPN

    b. VPN client

    c. Site-to-client VPN

    d. Host-to-host VPN

The answers to the "Do I Know This Already?" quiz are found in Appendix A, "Answers to the 'Do I Know This Already?' Quizzes and Q&A Sections." The suggested choices for your next step are as follows:

- **4 or fewer overall score**—Read the chapter. This includes the "Foundation Topics," "Foundation Summary," and "Q&A" sections, as well as the scenarios at the end of the chapter.

- **5 or more overall score**—If you want more review on these topics, skip to the "Foundation Summary" section, and then go to the "Q&A" section and the scenarios at the end of the chapter. Otherwise, move to the next chapter.

Foundation Topics

Determining Site Requirements

In general, each company site can be placed into one of three categories: central office, remote office/branch office (ROBO), or small office/home office (SOHO). Each type of site provides different opportunities for growth and has unique requirements for connectivity and equipment. The sections that follow provide insight into what constitutes each type of site.

Determine the Goals of the Network

You must lay out the goals of the overall network ahead of time. Regardless of the type of site that is chosen, you must first determine the goals of the network. Some of the questions you should consider include:

- What do you wish to gain from this specific deployment?
- How many users must it support?
- How much bandwidth is necessary to support the applications in use at and between each site?
- Has future growth been taken into account?
- Will the selected WAN components support an upgrade, or will a new component (forklift) be necessary?
- What type of corporate resources must be accessed from the SOHO location?

Figure 2-1 shows how various elements of a network may fit together. In the upper-left corner, two different types of SOHO sites are shown. One is permanently connected to the Internet via a cable or DSL modem, while the other uses a small Cisco router for temporary ISDN or analog dialup connectivity. On the bottom of the figure are two types of ROBOs. One uses Frame Relay as a primary connection back to the central office with ISDN as a backup. The second uses a leased line to the main office, and does not have any backup capabilities. And the central office has the ability to terminate connections from any of the small or remote offices.

Figure 2-1 *Typical Site Installations*

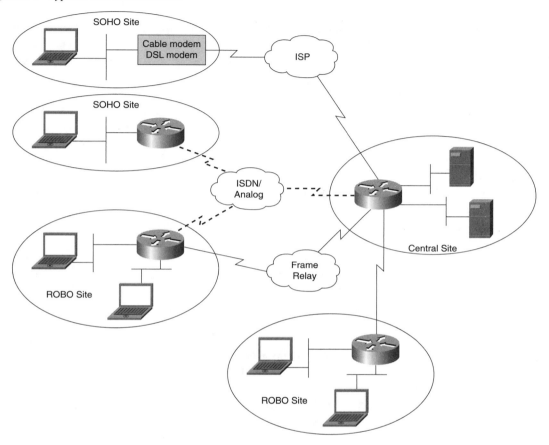

Central-Site Installations

The central site tends to be the administrative nucleus of a company (the headquarters). In most cases, this also is the largest site, whether it is a building or an entire campus. There is normally a requirement that all sites have communication to the central site, but they might not need to communicate with each other. This requires a diverse set of WAN connection methods.

In networks similar to that shown in Figure 2-1, the Frame Relay connection into the central site is typically much larger than any Frame Relay connection to a remote or branch office. In this case, the larger pipe is needed to be able to terminate multiple remote sites simultaneously. At the same time, it is rare to find a central-site Frame Relay connection that is simply the sum of all the bandwidth used at all the remote locations. Chances are, not all remote sites will be sending data to the central site at the same time.

If the installation is taking place in a central or corporate headquarters site, room for growth should be a strong consideration. Room for growth is important because remote or branch sites can be added or deleted over time, and the hardware platform should be flexible so that a "forklift" upgrade (an upgrade that requires physically changing equipment because the older equipment is too small/slow/inadequate) is not needed every time a change in corporate strategy occurs.

Decisions for the central office should include evaluation of speeds and feeds. The speeds should be sufficient to aggregate the information flows from the branch and remote sites. With speeds, cost is a major consideration, because the recurring WAN charges (for the size of pipe and distance traveled) are the dominant cost factor. In fact, hardware costs pale in comparison to the ongoing costs for WAN charges. But such costs are less critical at the central office.

Firewalls and access control (feeds) are also top considerations, because the central site must maintain and enable outside communication, but protect against unauthorized access. A network may have a requirement that all traffic passes through the central site before going to other locations.

Redundancy is also an important consideration at the central site. Normally, a network outage that would prevent any remote sites or customers from accessing the network is not acceptable. Such redundancy comes at a price (additional hardware and WAN circuits), but this cost is normally offset by the price of a network failure.

Remote Office/Branch Office Installations

A branch office is normally smaller than a central site, and it gives a corporate presence in a specific region. If the installation is to be done in a branch office, there is less need for flexibility than with the central site. This does not mean that a fixed configuration device is acceptable, however. It still might be more palatable for the router to contain enough ports for expansion. Branch-office support generally includes access to smaller, single-function remote offices or remote users.

Most modern Cisco devices that could be employed at a branch or central site are modular. This means that the devices can be changed by adding or removing cards, ports, and functionality. Only the smallest SOHO routers are still fixed, meaning no additional ports or capabilities can be added to the chassis.

Considerations at the branch office include the WAN connection method and the monthly costs. Additionally, the branch office must be able to authenticate itself to the central site. This authentication prevents unwanted devices from connecting to the resources at the main site. Authentication is especially important for temporary connections, like dialup ISDN or analog, used for backup circuits from a branch office.

The issue of availability is another critical factor in the branch office. You must know how often and how long the primary connection will be needed and whether a backup is necessary. Typical questions would be "Can the remote site tolerate an outage?"; if yes, "How long of an outage can the remote site tolerate?" and "Does the remote site need 24-hour access?" Normally, outages are not acceptable at the central site.

The central office generally uses links that are always available or highly reliable (leased lines), whereas the branch office might not want to pay for that reliability (Frame Relay). At the same time, a branch office may need a permanent connection (Frame Relay or leased line), but can temporarily do without a backup connection (no ISDN or analog backup).

Consider a small branch office of three users with low bandwidth needs. ISDN BRI might be a good fit for the installation. However, what if the office grows to 20 users in a short time? At that point, the 128 kbps may be inadequate to support them, yet ISDN BRI has no additional bandwidth to offer.

If the bandwidth becomes inadequate, a technology or router change becomes necessary. However, the time and costs involved may not be feasible. Would adequate planning and an alternate choice of technology have prevented the issue? Yes, they may have prevented the issue, if there were any indication that this particular office was going to grow as it did. Overall, it is a guessing game sometimes.

Small Office/Home Office Installations

An installation at either of these locations is likely to have a fixed function (but not fixed configuration) device that was chosen with cost as a main factor. Once the election of the access method is made, it is unlikely to change in the near term. Note that a single salesperson with a laptop and a modem constitutes a SOHO.

The traffic or data that exits the SOHO can usually be categorized very neatly. An example of this categorization is a remote salesperson who must download corporate pricing and upload sales data and e-mail. Normally, a SOHO location has so few subnets that a combination of static and default routes are employed. The SOHO site sends all traffic back to the central site (default route), while the central site has a specific static route pointing down to the SOHO. Although this method requires a bit more configuration, it alleviates the overhead (bandwidth consumption, CPU utilization, memory usage) associated with any dynamic routing protocol.

The overriding consideration at these offices is generally cost. In addition, the SOHO must maintain a method for authentication to the branch or central site and justify the connection time to a central or branch office. It is possible that these offices would use a dial-on-demand methodology to minimize WAN charges.

However, many SOHOs have DSL or cable modem connectivity to their ISP today. With such a connection, the only issue is now how to secure the corporate traffic as it travels from the SOHO to the branch or central office.

The utilization of today's networks often sees sales and design engineers working out of their house, and spending little if any time in the actual office. As such, they normally need complete access to both corporate data and phone resources. Thus, their SOHO is actually an encrypted extension of the main office that they rarely visit. And even if the office is a frequent destination, this type of SOHO VPN access allows for office work to be performed during times of bad weather, bad traffic, or just the lack of desire to commute (if allowed).

Guidelines for Equipment Selection

The selection of a hardware product for remote-access usage is an art form to some extent, and the biggest, most-scalable router possible is not always the best router. Information that you gather about the site is critical in the process of selecting the hardware and connection type. In addition, you must consider the connection speed (the size of the pipe) to ensure that various types of traffic can successfully be sent to and from each site.

Figure 2-2 shows the same network described earlier. However, this time, various considerations for network design are added to the diagram. In some cases, connectivity between two sites is simply a matter of passing traffic. However, in others, various factors are considered to ensure the proper movement of data. Figure 2-2 shows these options, which are also described in the subsequent list.

- **Bandwidth**—What speed is required for the applications that will use the link? This is normally measured in bits per second (bps). Bandwidth is generally thought of in increments of 64 thousand bits per second (kbps). A T1 (typically seen in North America) equates to 1544 kbps, or 1.544 Mbps (million bits per second). An E1 (seen in most places except North America) runs at 2.048 Mbps.

    It is important that the bandwidth handle the client's requirements at any particular site. In general, clients who are extremely cost-conscious might look for solutions that are doomed to failure. There is often truth in the statement "you get what you pay for." Proper network surveys can help determine bandwidth requirements up front.

    Also be aware that some solutions today offer asymmetrical speeds. This means that the transfer speed in one direction is different than the speed in the other. With some technologies, and some price packages, a site might have terrific download capabilities but lousy upload capabilities.

Figure 2-2 *Selection Criteria*

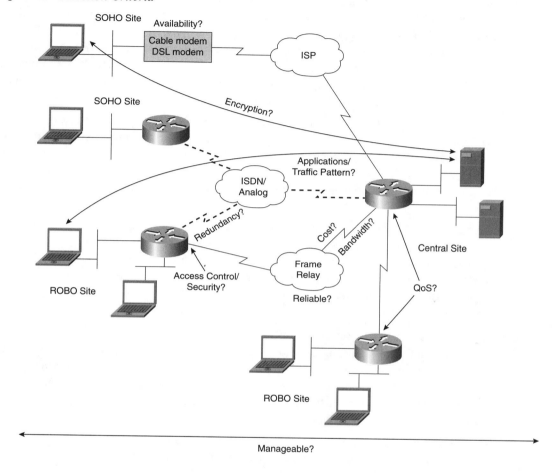

- **Availability**—The key question here is, "Is there ISDN or DSL in my area, and can I get it?" This book discusses remote access, yet it is not a given that the desired service is available. Sometimes a television commercial announcing availability of DSL or cable modem cannot be fulfilled to every location by the provider. Generally, dedicated lines (leased T1 or fractional T1 service) or packet-switching networks (Frame Relay) are universally available. But such services or expenses may not be required or desired.

  Often, metropolitan areas are rich in WAN options. However, branch offices in remote locations may suffer from service unavailability. It is often cost-ineffective for a carrier to offer certain services in remote locations until it can be shown that there will be enough customers to make the endeavor financially feasible. This catch-22 often leaves only high-cost WAN connection options or slow-speed dialup access in some locations.

- **Reliability**—For a brokerage house or an online banking institution, the aspect of reliability may override all other factors (including cost). However, for a local tire shop, which checks inventory at the warehouse, the reliability of the link may not be mission critical. The loss of this link during a bad storm or local power outage may be a minor concern to the tire shop. If there is no local power, then checking inventory and installing tires is probably not an option. But for sites that absolutely depend on WAN connectivity (banking systems), backup circuits, backup equipment, and backup power systems are common.

- **Cost**—This is one of the final selection criteria for an implementation. You must explore *all* the WAN options available, because costs can vary between regions. In general, cost is directly related to the bandwidth requirement and the distance between the sites. Many times, cost becomes the first criteria when selecting a WAN connection option. When doing this, often the selections become quite limited, which may cripple the site in question, or possibly the entire network.

  WAN expenses are typically the largest recurring cost incurred by any company, month after month after month. Dial-on-demand routing (DDR) connections only use a provider's network when there is a need to send traffic. This can greatly reduce cost; however, such connections are typically low-bandwidth and have limited options available. Bandwidth on demand (BoD) can also be used to add additional low-cost bandwidth to assist high-speed pipes at capacity.

- **Ease of management**—Given any installation at any site, the cost of moves, adds, and changes should be factored into the design. CiscoWorks is a good choice for management software, but it is not the only choice. Many Cisco products today have their own web-based management capabilities built into the product. Administrators have the ability to configure some Cisco devices with a web browser, instead of via the command-line utility. In larger networks, such GUI-based tools can simplify daily life.

  Management may go beyond the day-to-day operations of a network. Planning for scheduled outages, equipment upgrades, and circuit upgrades is a huge task. Ideally, the initial design eliminated this requirement. But reality sneaks in and makes this nearly impossible. Ideally, the amount of such change should be limited and invisible to the user community.

- **Applications and traffic patterns**—Working with applications and traffic patterns can be a difficult task; however, it is by far the most critical. Because of the difficulty involved, it is often the most neglected aspect in network design projects. For example, a remote law office repeatedly uploading and downloading thousand-page documents may require a different solution than a remote insurance agency that sends a few pages of client information and that accesses a SQL database. The traffic patterns and needs define the bandwidth requirement, which in turn drives the cost.

It often helps to be aware of what applications are used in a network, and to understand their traffic patterns. Some applications (such as routing protocols) are rather chatty themselves, without actually sending user data; some (such as file transfers) might be bursty in nature, with peaks and valleys in bandwidth requirements; while others (such as voice) have predetermined requirements for consistent bandwidth.

■ **Redundancy**—The need for backup, or redundant, links is potentially important. For instance, what is the cost (meaning loss) of downtime? If the loss is great, the high-speed Frame Relay or leased-line circuit should be backed up by a low-cost ISDN line. Another consideration is the cost of loss of service if a dialup link fails. If this happens, backup needs and costs should be weighed against the track record of the suppliers in the area for a given access technique. It is also important to consider that a backup link should not be too different from the primary link in throughput. For example, a T1 leased line should not be backed up by a 56K modem. Someone is bound to notice the difference when the backup is operational.

The feasibility of a backup connection is typically compared to the importance of data or personnel at any given site. If a single telecommuter is temporarily unavailable, the impact may not be felt. However, if an entire engineering plant is out of service for many hours, the cost of the outage may far outweigh the price of a backup circuit.

Redundancy can extend beyond the duplication of a circuit or connection method. It can mean additional network equipment, feature cards, power sources, servers, and client machines. The level of redundancy that any site may employ is truly based on the policy that defines this requirement. The ability to have complete redundancy under any circumstance drives the cost way up.

■ **Quality of service (QoS)**—Quality of service is often directly compared to the bandwidth to any given site. Most folks figure that a large pipe can handle any data or application requirement. However, when a mix of traffic shares a single connection, some applications may deserve a greater share of the available bandwidth than others. And certain applications may even be allowed to take bandwidth away from others in times of need. Such behavior can be implemented with various QoS options.

There are a variety of QoS methods that can be implemented by Cisco routers. Some allow small packets to sneak between large packets. This is typically done when attempting to transport voice packets across a data network. Other methods allow the administrator to prioritize certain data streams. And it is possible to ensure that certain traffic will have high priority under all conditions, and that the remainder of the traffic will be sorted based on administrator rules. All of this can be employed without increasing the WAN costs.

■ **Access control requirements and security**—In implementations for remote access, security is a major consideration. Because the users are not "local" to the location where the data and applications are, it is imperative to consider access control. This can be as simple as a local username/password database or as complex as using an authentication, authorization, and auditing (AAA) server such as Cisco Secure ACS.

The core issue is to know the amount of security needed and the sensitivity of the data being transferred between sites. For example, Joe and Bob's Tire Shop might require a simple password scheme for security, whereas Einstein's Genetic Research Corporation would want an environment that provides more control.

Simply letting someone "in" or denying access might not be enough. Different users may have different levels of access, and the need to limit access to resources and devices may be a requirement, not an option. Normally, the importance or need for privacy for data determines how much security may be needed at any given site. As with reliability, additional security increases the implementation cost.

It is important to remember that the additional security normally adds cost and decreases throughput on any given link between sites. Some people are caught off guard when they discover that, after a super-security plan is put in place, the difference in throughput is quite noticeable.

■ **Encryption**—Controlling access to network resources and locations and tracking what users access might not provide sufficient security. Hiding the actual data that travels the links between sites is often a requirement in modern networks. VPNs allow encryption of data sent between any combination of sites. A VPN tunnel can be permanently constructed for all traffic between a remote site and the central office. And even an individual PC can establish its own private VPN tunnel to a remote office location, or back to the main site.

For ROBO or SOHO sites that connect to other sites through a DSL or cable modem, VPN tunnels are a must.

Because such connection methods are with the provider, and not directly to any of your sites, great care must be taken when transferring data across these types of links.

You must be very careful when using a public transport system (such as the Internet) to connect business sites together—or, for that matter, to connect any two systems together. It is important to remember that the hackers and evil-doers are connected to the same Internet that your sites are. Any data that travels across this region can possibly be intercepted by folks who are not the intended recipients. Encryption (VPN tunnels) is a way to ensure that if the data falls into the wrong hands, it cannot be read, played back, or modified.

WAN Access Methods for Remote Access

After you define the customer needs, you must select carrier technology to support the applications that have been selected for the customer. This section identifies only the WAN connection options that are used in the remote-access arena. Super-high-speed (and high price) opportunities such as Asynchronous Transfer Mode (ATM), Synchronous Optical Network (SONET), Packet over SONET (POS), and Dynamic Packet Transfer (DPT) are not covered in this book.

Figure 2-3 shows the typical methods used to connect sites together. This is the same diagram used throughout the chapter, only this time the connection technologies are identified. There are many ways to employ such technologies, but a discussion of the alternatives is beyond the scope of this book.

Figure 2-3   *WAN Access Methods*

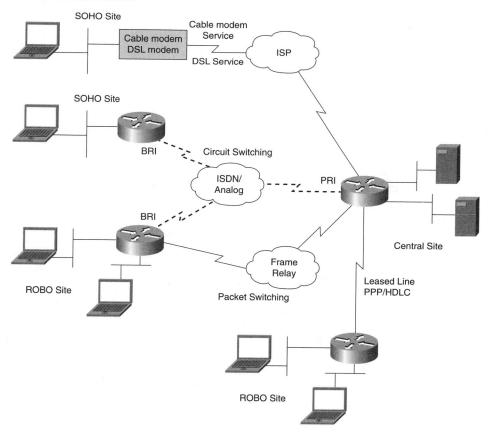

For remote access, the choices are as shown in Figure 2-3 and described in the subsequent list:

■ **Leased line**—A leased line gives the consumer complete control of the facility in terms of what data is to be put on it. The customer effectively owns the bandwidth of the link. This ownership offers high security and control to the customer; however, this is probably the highest-cost solution available. Although lease facilities with very high data rates (up to multiple megabit) can be obtained, the issue is how much bandwidth, and at what cost, the consumer is willing to purchase.

Leased lines typically come in increments of 64 kbps, or DS0s. There is a base price for a DS0 circuit, and the price goes up for each DS0 added. Normally, once a circuit from one site to another requires more than seven or eight DS0s, it becomes more cost-efficient to purchase an entire T1 (24 DS0s) or E1 (30 available DS0s).

A leased line is terminated on a serial port of a Cisco router. Any Cisco router can easily handle a T1 or E1 worth of bandwidth. There are no special interfaces needed for "leased lines." Each leased line uses one router interface to connect to one other site. Scalability becomes an issue with leased lines, because multiple router interfaces are needed to connect to multiple sites.

A leased line uses either the Point-to-Point Protocol (PPP) or the Cisco High-Level Data Link Control (HDLC) encapsulation protocol. Both ends of the circuit must use the same encapsulation type, or else the transfer of data across the circuit is impossible.

■ **Packet switching**—Packet switching technology, such as Frame Relay, carries a large number of business circuits in the United States. With Frame Relay, a single router serial interface is connected to the provider's network. However, it is possible to communicate with multiple remote locations through the use of virtual circuits (VCs). Normally, each remote site has its own VC, although it is possible to have multiple VCs between two sites.

Each VC has a theoretical guarantee of bandwidth called the committed information rate (CIR). This is the throughput rate that the provider strives to achieve for each VC through its network. Normally, the CIR of any circuit can be achieved. However, most Frame Relay clouds are purposefully oversubscribed. The provider knows that not every circuit will be used simultaneously. However, in times of heavy VC use, there might not be enough bandwidth available in the provider's cloud to honor all CIRs.

Frame Relay circuits tend to be more cost-effective than leased lines because each site needs only one connection to the provider (local loop) and one router interface to reach multiple destinations (via VCs). The incremental cost comes from the number of VCs and the distance each VC must travel. Each VC is labeled with a data-link connection identifier (DLCI) that is local only to the site assigned the DLCI.

- **ISDN**—ISDN offers more than twice the bandwidth of a simple dialup link; however, it is a circuit-switched connection and is subject to availability of the remote end. In other words, ISDN might not be available everywhere. The control of the circuit is given over to the provider. Speed for ISDN is limited to 128 kbps for a remote user using a Basic Rate Interface (BRI).

  An ISDN BRI connection consists of two 64 kbps bearer channels (B channels). Both can be used simultaneously to send data, or there can be two independent 64-kbps conversations. ISDN can also carry voice and video.

  An ISDN connection requires a special BRI interface in a Cisco router. Not all Cisco routers have ISDN BRI capabilities. Each ISDN call establishes a private circuit to the destination site.

  Normally, if remote sites are using ISDN BRI for connectivity back to the central site, the central site would employ a Primary Rate Interface (PRI) to terminate multiple BRI connections. A PRI, on a T1, has up to 23 B channels, whereas a PRI across an E1 has up to 30 B channels. Implementing a PRI requires only a single channelized T1/E1 interface on a Cisco router, compared to a 1:1 ratio of BRI ports for all the remote sites.

- **Digital subscriber line service**—DSL is one method of broadband access offered today by many telephone companies. DSL uses the same two-wire connection that normal phone service is delivered on. It uses frequencies above what people can hear to transmit high-speed data. A special modem is needed to split the high frequencies out of the phone line and convert them to an Ethernet frame. This modem can be integrated into some Cisco routers.

  Because the external DSL modem creates an Ethernet frame from the incoming telephone line signal, the DSL connection can terminate on any Ethernet port of any Cisco router. However, the DSL connection is from the site to the provider. There is no private circuit established between corporate sites. All security must be maintained through the use of VPNs.

  Some smaller sites use routers only as media converters. In other words, they need a serial interface to connect to the WAN (PPP or Frame Relay connection), and an Ethernet port to connect to the internal network. These sites might decide to use only a PIX Firewall at the location. The PIX has all Ethernet connections, and there is no need to convert any serial signals from a leased line or Frame Relay connection.

- **Cable-modem service**—Cable modems are quickly becoming another popular broadband method of Internet access. Like DSL, cable modems use a separate frequency across the normal cable-TV feed into a home office or small branch office. The cable modem simply splits out these frequencies and returns an Ethernet frame.

  Like DSL, the connection from a cable modem is between the site and the provider. Thus, there is no security between offices. VPNs are needed to provide secure connections.

Both DSL and cable-modem services offer a variety of connection speeds and prices. In some locations, these options are quite cost-effective, however offer little reliability. Such broadband offerings are typically used at sites where cost savings are important but reliability is not paramount.

It is also important to remember that both DSL and cable-modem services may be shared media. This means that multiple locations actually share bandwidth back to the carrier, such as multiple Ethernet frames going through a hub. Not all services adhere to this model, but some (typically residential) do. So, if you are using DSL or cable modems for business connectivity, it is important to quiz the provider about how the network is configured.

■ **Asynchronous dialup (analog modem)**—Simple analog-modem connectivity such as asynchronous dialup is sometimes all that is needed for communication. Speeds are limited to 53 kbps or slower, depending on the type of connection and the modem being used. Dialup is the most inexpensive of all communication methods and is available almost everywhere.

Note that V.90 defines the standard for 56-kbps modems. However, it is currently against United States federal law to have a modem communicate at the 56-kbps barrier. So when the term 56K modem is used, it really means that the modem can communicate at up to speeds of 53 kbps. Plus, in many cases, the copper used to physically connect across the last mile is below the quality needed to support 53-kbps traffic.

An asynchronous dialup connection needs an asynchronous port in a Cisco router. This can be accomplished with asynchronous ports or internal modem banks. Like ISDN, an asynchronous connection is a private connection between two sites.

Technology Assessment

Now that you have examined the different types of sites, the various parameters for selecting equipment, and the WAN connection types, you need to explore one final issue in this chapter: technology that supports additional security in today's networks.

Certain connection technologies may create a sense of data security between sites. Many people feel safe with point-to-point dedicated links (PPP or HDLC leased lines), or unique virtual circuits between sites across a Frame Relay cloud. And a call placed through an ISDN or asynchronous network goes directly from one modem to another.

However, all means of data transport are subject to some form of hacking. Data can be intercepted while in transit, and important information can be compromised. The only way to truly ensure that your data is safe during transfer from one site to another is to employ your own form of data encryption: virtual private networks (VPNs).

Figure 2-4 shows the different types of VPNs that can be constructed between sites. Again, the same site diagram is used to highlight the VPN connections. VPNs can be built to encrypt data between individual devices (server-to-server or host-to-host), between entire sites (site-to-site), or from one machine to a central site (VPN client). The following list describes each of these VPN methods:

Figure 2-4   *VPN Options*

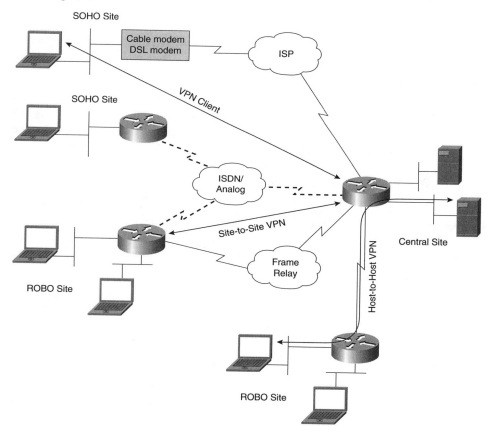

- **Server-to-server** — Sever-to-server VPNs (also known as host-to-host VPNs) encrypt traffic between selected devices when communicating between sites. There may be certain data streams between sites that are considered highly sensitive, whereas most other traffic does not need the overhead of encryption. VPNs can be established for individual conversations between selected devices. These VPNs are controlled by the routers or firewalls at the sites, and encrypt only the data streams in question.

  Traffic between sites that does not need encryption (or meet the criteria established for encryption) is not encrypted. And, traffic that is not specifically between the devices in question (such as Internet traffic) is sent out without being bothered.

- **Site-to-site**—On the surface, a site-to-site VPN has many similarities to its little cousin, the server-to-server VPN. In this case, the VPN between sites encrypts all data that flows between the sites. It is important to know that a VPN is a point-to-point tunnel. If there are many sites that require secure communications, many VPNs must be established.

  As with the server-to-server VPNs, Internet traffic is sent unencrypted. It would be impossible to encrypt all Internet traffic, because the number of destinations is impossible to count. And each destination requires its own VPN tunnel.

- **VPN client**—A client might also create a connection to a site. This is especially true when connections between sites do not use dedicated connections or circuits (leased lines, Frame Relay virtual circuits, ISDN, and asynchronous calls).

  When a site is connected to the Internet with a DSL or cable-modem connection, or is dialed into an Internet service provider (ISP) with an analog modem, a secure connection must be established from individual workstations to a branch or corporate office. VPN client software on a PC, such as Cisco VPN Client, can create an encrypted tunnel from the PC to the site where the necessary resources are located. Normally, such a VPN tunnel terminates on a router or a VPN concentrator.

It is important to remember that VPN tunnels add to the CPU overhead of the network device that is either originating or terminating the VPN tunnel. This additional CPU load could be crippling to smaller devices. Some Cisco routers have VPN accelerator cards that are used specifically for the establishment and maintenance of VPN tunnels. Most smaller routers do not have this capability.

Foundation Summary

This section is a collection of information that provides a convenient review of many key concepts in this chapter. For those of you already comfortable with the topics in this chapter, this summary could help you recall a few details. For those of you who just read this chapter, this review should help solidify some key facts. For any of you who are doing your final preparation before the exam, these tables and figures will hopefully be a convenient way to review the material the day before the exam.

In general, each company site can be placed into one of three categories: central office, ROBO, or SOHO. Table 2-2 outlines considerations for each type of site.

Table 2-2   *Site Considerations*

Site	Major Considerations
Central office	Cost of WAN services
	Bandwidth growth
	Flexibility
	Access control
ROBO	WAN availability
	Redundancy needs
	Ease of management
	Application traffic patterns
SOHO	Cost of equipment
	Ease of management

The selection of equipment should be based on the following criteria:

- Bandwidth
- Availability
- Reliability
- Cost
- Ease of management
- Applications and traffic patterns
- Redundancy

- QoS

- Access control requirements

- Encryption

Table 2-3 summarizes the WAN connection options for remote access. This table offers a quick comparison of all the connection methods available.

Table 2-3 *WAN Connection Options*

Method	Speeds	Notes
Leased lines	All speeds	High control; high bandwidth
	Up to T1 (1.544 Mbps)/T3 (45 Mbps)	High-cost, enterprise network usage
Frame Relay	Up to T1 (1.544 Mbps) speed	Medium-control, shared-bandwidth, branch office usage
ISDN	PRI-T1/E1 (2.048 Mbps); BRI-128 kbps	Low-control, low bandwidth that is faster than asynchronous dialup
DSL	128 kbps to 2.048 Mbps	Little control, good bandwidth, ROBO or SOHO, variety of pricing options
Cable modem	128 kbps to 4.0 Mbps	Little control, good bandwidth, ROBO or SOHO, variety of pricing options
Asynchronous	Up to 53 kbps	Low control, low bandwidth, variable cost that is effective for limited usage environments

Table 2-4 summarizes the VPN concepts that have been discussed in this chapter.

Table 2-4 *VPN Options*

Method	Sites	Notes
Host-to-host	SOHO to ROBO ROBO to ROBO	Specific control of encrypted streams
Site-to-site	SOHO to ROBO ROBO to central office ROBO to ROBO	All traffic between sites is encrypted, all off-site traffic is not
VPN client	SOHO to ROBO SOHO to central office	All traffic between the remote machine and site is encrypted

Q&A

The questions and scenarios in this book are more difficult than what you will experience on the actual exam. The questions do not attempt to cover more breadth or depth than the exam; however, they are designed to make sure that you know the answer. Rather than enabling you to derive the answer from clues hidden inside the question itself, the questions challenge your understanding and recall of the subject.

Hopefully, mastering these questions will help you to limit the number of exam questions on which you narrow your choices to two options and then guess.

The answers to these questions can be found in Appendix A.

1.   Which type of site has the most diverse forms of WAN connections?

2.   How is redundancy defined?

3.   What is the most important selection criteria at a SOHO?

4.   Which design selection criteria adds cost yet reduces throughput?

5.   How many leased-line circuits can terminate on one router serial port?

6.   The term "packet switching" describes which WAN access method?

7.   Which WAN access methods actually place phone calls from one location to another?

8.   Why is encryption important for a SOHO?

9.   What is a host-to-host VPN?

10.   What type of connection technologies are more likely to require VPNs?

Scenarios

The following case studies and questions are designed to draw together the content of the chapter and exercise your understanding of the concepts. There is not necessarily a right answer to each scenario. The thought process and practice in manipulating the related concepts is the goal of this section.

Scenario 2-1

You have decided to design a corporate headquarters that must have permanent connections to each of the ten branch offices. Also, a variety of engineers work from home and need access to corporate resources, which are located at the central site.

1. What type of WAN connection methods must be employed at the central office?

2. What type of WAN connection methods must be used at each of the remote offices?

3. What are the possible WAN connection methods for the SOHOs?

Scenario 2-2

You provide leased-line connectivity (T1s) from your central office to three branch offices that supply time-critical information for your customers. In addition, the central site maintains an ISP connection to the Internet for the branch-office users to do research. Each branch office has less than ten users who constantly upload small files to the corporate data warehouse. In addition, they use the leased line for e-mail and web surfing.

1. What options are available to ensure that the connection between each remote office and the central office is always available?

2. How would the available backup options compare to the speed of the leased lines between the offices?

Scenario Answers

The answers provided in this section are not necessarily the only possible correct answers. They merely represent one possibility for each scenario. The intention is to test your base knowledge and understanding of the concepts discussed in this chapter.

Should your answers be different (as they likely will be), consider the differences. Are your answers in line with the concepts of the answers provided and explained here? If not, go back and read the chapter again, focusing on the sections related to the problem scenario.

Scenario 2-1 Answers

1. Since a permanent connection is required between the central office and each of the ten remote offices, either leased lines or Frame Relay virtual circuits can be used. Leased lines give each connection its own private bandwidth, yet each connection needs a separate serial interface at the main site. Frame Relay needs only a single serial interface at the main site, but that interface could become congested if all ten remote offices were sending large amounts of data simultaneously.

    The main office also needs a modem bank to receive calls from all of the remote engineers in the field, or the ability to terminate many VPNs from all of the SOHO connections. A PRI could also be required if the SOHOs have BRI connections.

2. Each remote office needs a router with one serial interface, and one or more LAN ports. The serial interface can be used for either the leased-line connection back to the main site or the Frame Relay link back to the central office.

    No backup connections were called for, nor was the need to allow the SOHO users to connect to the ROBOs.

3. The SOHOs can use analog modems to dial the main office. If available, ISDN BRI could be used to call the main office and connect to the corporate resources. And, again depending upon availability, DSL or cable modems could be used to access the Internet; a VPN can then be used to the central office.

Scenario 2-2 Answers

1. The ROBOs could have a backup ISDN BRI connection that would be used if the primary leased line fails. Analog modems could also be used, but the available bandwidth (for backup purposes) is probably not comparable to the leased lines.

2. The ISDN BRI option allows either 64-kbps or 128-kbps connections back to the main office. Because each remote office has its own leased line, it is possible that only 64 kbps or 128 kbps is actually needed. For a site that has a leased line that is greater than 128 kbps, the ISDN BRI backup would offer less-than-normal access speeds.

    Note that a 56-kbps modem could offer speeds near that of a 64-kbps leased line. However, because the maximum speed of a modem is really 53 kbps, and this speed is not guaranteed, modem backup should be used only when other options are not available.

This chapter covers the following topics that you will need to comprehend to master the BCRAN exam:

- **Choosing WAN equipment**—This section discusses the basic guidelines behind the selection of routers for specific deployments.

- **Assembling and cabling the equipment**—This section goes over some of the possible types of physical connections that may be necessary for individual deployments.

- **Verifying the installation**—This section explains how to confirm the physical connectivity of the WAN devices.

CHAPTER 3

Network Overview

The CCNP Remote Access Exam requires you to have an in-depth understanding of various WAN technologies. The previous chapter helped you to understand the different types of sites (central office, ROBO, or SOHO) and how to interconnect the sites. This chapter first focuses on how to select the proper equipment for each site in the network. Then, it examines how to actually assemble the appropriate equipment for each site and how to verify the installation.

Cisco Systems has made cabling the WAN connections simple. Most Cisco routers have a common WAN port: the Cisco DB-60. The DB-60 connector takes up much less space than a typical WAN connector. And a 5-in-1 cable is used to convert the DB-60 end to any WAN interface (for example, EIA/TIA-232 or V.35). The biggest challenge is to determine whether any other equipment is necessary to complete the connection to the provider.

This chapter explores the basics behind selecting and cabling the remote-access devices discussed in this book. The discussion in this chapter focuses on routers.

"Do I Know This Already?" Quiz

The purpose of the "Do I Know This Already?" quiz is to help you decide whether you really need to read the entire chapter. If you already intend to read the entire chapter, you do not necessarily need to answer these questions.

The ten-question quiz, derived from the major sections in the "Foundation Topics" portion of the chapter, helps you to determine how to spend your limited study time.

Table 3-1 outlines the major topics discussed in this chapter and the "Do I Know This Already?" quiz questions that correspond to those topics.

Table 3-1 *"Do I Know This Already?" Foundation Topics Section-to-Question Mapping*

Foundation Topics Section	Questions Covered In This Section
Choosing WAN Equipment	1–4
Assembling and Cabling the Equipment	5–7
Verifying the Installation	8–10

> **CAUTION**   The goal of self-assessment is to gauge your mastery of the topics in this chapter. If you do not know the answer to a question or are only partially sure of the answer, you should mark this question wrong for purposes of the self-assessment. Giving yourself credit for an answer you correctly guess skews your self-assessment results and might provide you with a false sense of security.

1.   Which of the following routers is best used as a central-site router?

   a. 804

   b. 3620

   c. 1710

   d. 7206

2.   Which of the following routers best serves as a small office or home office (SOHO) router for telecommuters?

   a. 804

   b. 3620

   c. 1710

   d. 7206

3.   Which Cisco 800 Series router has a built-in DSL port?

   a. 801

   b. 804

   c. 805

   d. 827

4.   Which of the following Cisco SOHO/ROBO routers can use one or more WIC modules and has at least one network module (select 2)?

   a. 1751

   b. 3620

   c. 3660

   d. 827

   e. 2621

5. What type of port on a Cisco router is used to connect to a Frame Relay provider?

   a. Ethernet port

   b. Serial port

   c. Frame Relay port

   d. Asynchronous port

6. Which of the following WAN connection types use an Ethernet port to connect to the provider (select 2)?

   a. Frame Relay

   b. ISDN

   c. DSL

   d. Asynchronous modem

   e. Cable modem

7. Which of the following connection technologies use an RJ-45 port for connectivity (select 2)?

   a. Frame Relay

   b. ISDN BRI

   c. Analog (asynchronous) modem

   d. Ethernet

   e. PPP

8. What does the DTR indicator on a serial interface mean?

   a. Data transmit rejected

   b. Data terminal ready

   c. Data transmit ready

   d. Data terminal rejected

9. When looking at the **show interfaces** display for a serial interface, which of the following conditions would cause the interface to be up/down?

   a. Incorrect IP address

   b. Disconnected cable

   c. Mismatched encapsulation

   d. Administrator shut down

10. Which Cisco IOS command is used to verify the encapsulation type on any interface?

   a. show encapsulation

   b. show interfaces

   c. show interfaces encapsulation

   d. get interfaces encapsulation

The answers to the "Do I Know This Already?" quiz are found in Appendix A, "Answers to the 'Do I Know This Already?' Quizzes and Q&A." The suggested choices for your next step are as follows:

- **4 or fewer overall score**—Read the chapter. This includes the "Foundation Topics," "Foundation Summary," and "Q&A" sections, as well as the scenarios at the end of the chapter.

- **5 or more overall score**—If you want more review on these topics, skip to the "Foundation Summary" section, and then go to the "Q&A" section and the scenarios at the end of the chapter. Otherwise, move to the next chapter.

Foundation Topics

The discussions in this chapter revolve around a fictitious, albeit typical, network topology. Figure 3-1 depicts that topology.

Figure 3-1 *Network Topology for Chapter Discussion*

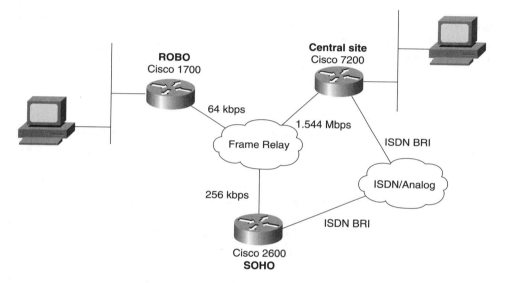

Figure 3-1 depicts a number of technologies in the network. These technologies (leased line, Frame Relay, ISDN, DSL, cable modem, and asynchronous modem) are discussed in this book at various times and are not discussed in this chapter.

You must understand the concepts and components involved in properly connecting WAN devices. A Layer 2 technology is an absolute necessity in your WAN deployment. Choosing the proper technology is a decision that is based on the goals of the network at each step. The previous chapter discussed the most popular means of connecting remote sites.

Now that you have a network design in mind, your next step is very important: to select the proper equipment to make that network a reality.

Choosing WAN Equipment

Once the goals of the network have been decided on, the hunt for proper equipment begins. Choosing the equipment that goes into each site is always an interesting endeavor. Vendors are contacted, and sales personnel visit and relentlessly tell you that their equipment is the best. Wisely, the decision is made to go with Cisco products (as if there were ever a doubt).

Obviously, the needs of each individual site in Figure 3-1 vary. The next few sections focus on each site and its unique technological requirements.

Cisco has an online tool called the Product Selection Tool that might help you procure the proper equipment for each site of the network. You can find this tool at http://www.cisco.com/pcgi-bin/front.x/corona/prodtool/select.pl. As with any tool, this one has its advantages and disadvantages. It does help to automate the product selection process. However, the tool does not consider all of the equipment that is actually "offered" by Cisco. This chapter uses some of the guidelines enforced by the Product Selection Tool, and provides an up-to-date list of Cisco equipment available to meet the needs of any site.

Central-Site Router Selection

The central site is usually the corporate office site and is also usually the largest of the sites. With this distinction comes the need for more diverse capabilities with regard to WAN connectivity. Whenever WAN connectivity is desired, a router is typically (although not always) used. Many times, multiple technologies must be supported at this site, and all facets of the network must be supported. Normally, each of the branch offices connects back to the central site, and remote and mobile users need to be able to connect to the network somehow. You can provide analog telephone and ISDN access to these users, and also provide a virtual private network (VPN) termination point for SOHO users who already have a DSL or cable-modem connection to the Internet.

All of these connection options must be supported from the central site. To do so, a number of technologies should be deployed and various issues should be considered. They include leased line (PPP or HDLC), Frame Relay, ISDN BRI/PRI (T1 or E1), DSL, cable modems, asynchronous modems, network authentication, bandwidth issues, and the list goes on. Many times, the solution involves a combination of the options listed here.

For serial connections (leased lines and Frame Relay) and T1/E1 PRI (using a channelized T1/E1 card), you should know that inside of North America, the customer (that is, your company) is responsible for providing a channel service unit/data service unit (CSU/DSU) for the installation of the network. The CSU/DSU is either an external device or built into the serial card in the Cisco router. For BRI connections, the customer typically provides the Network Termination 1 (NT1).

Outside of North America, however, these devices (the CSU/DSU and NT1) are generally telco-provided. Also be aware that most serial connections in the United States are based on the T1 connection, whereas most of the rest of the world uses the E1 standard. When connecting between the two (for example, between the United States and England), the E1 standard wins. T1 is a North American standard, whereas E1 is a global one.

Obviously, all the possibilities for a central-site router cannot be discussed at this time. There are too many variables (and the exam does not touch on all of them anyway). However, you should know that many mid- to high-range routers, including WAN access and access server routers, support multiple technologies and port densities for the central-site router.

The following sections discuss the Cisco 3600, AS5000, and 7200 Series routers for the central site. Keep in mind that there are high-end routers, such as the 7300 Series, 7400 Series, 7500 Series, 12000 Series, and so on. However, these high-powered routers are beyond the scope of the exam. Older models, such as the 4000 and 7100 Series that used to inhabit the central site, have been discontinued by Cisco. The 3600 Series is the evolution from the 4000, while the 7200 is the progression from the 7100.

Cisco 3600 Series Router

The 3600 Series is a versatile family of routers; for variations of supported technologies, it is hard to beat. It is a multifunctional platform that enables routing of data, voice, video, and dialup access capabilities in a single chassis. Figure 3-2 shows the 3600 family of routers.

Figure 3-2   *Cisco 3600 Series Routers*

The 3600 Series offers three chassis variants: 3620, 3640, and the new 3660. The 3620 has two network module slots, the 3640 has four slots, and the 3660 has six slots. Each module slot can contain MICA modems for dial-in access, voice network modules for telephone connectivity directly to the router, and data network modules for a variety of WAN and LAN access to the router.

As the number of network module slots increases, so does the CPU. The 3640 has a better CPU than the 3620, and the 3660 has a far better CPU than the 3640. It makes sense that as the number of modules increases, so does the CPU speed to drive the modules.

The beauty of this series is that all of these technologies can be implemented simultaneously in one chassis. All the interface components can be removed, serviced, and inserted without taking the chassis out of the rack. In addition, all the modules use spring screws that will not easily detach from the component, so there is no more looking for that dropped screw.

CAUTION   The modules for this router are not hot-swappable! You must turn off the power before inserting or removing any component. Always use the proper grounding techniques when swapping cards in routers.

The 3620 probably is not the best choice for a central installation. Although it is a highly versatile and capable router, it simply does not have the port density or CPU speed necessary for deploying a wide spectrum of technologies simultaneously. The 3620 does make a great ROBO router, however.

The 3640 and 3660 shine in their support of the varying technologies and speeds in the typical enterprise deployment. These two models combine mix-and-match capabilities with the horsepower necessary to support a wide array of variables. For instance, these two routers can provide dialup access (through MICA modem modules), ISDN, Frame Relay, and leased-line services in a single chassis. In any central-site deployment, this type of flexibility is imperative.

Both the 3620 and 3640 have no network interfaces by default. All interfaces come via the network modules that are added to the chassis. The 366X actually comes with one or two Fast Ethernet (FE) ports built in (the 3661 has one FE interface, while the 3662 has two). This allows the 3660 to concentrate on WAN or remote-access modules without having to sacrifice a slot for LAN connectivity. The CPU of the 3660 is also in a league of its own compared to its little brothers, the 3640 and 3620.

Cisco AS5000 Series Router

This family of routers is an Access Server line (hence the AS in the name). Today, these devices are called universal gateways, because they seamlessly integrate LAN, WAN, and dialup capabilities on a large scale. The available models in the line are the AS5350, the AS5400, and the AS5850. The series also includes a very high-end model known as AccessPath. It consists of a number of AS5300s operating together in a single integrated rack with a Catalyst switch collocated.

The AS5000 family of devices can provide carrier-class service scalability as well as multiprotocol routing services. These devices are usually deployed in an ISDN installation to provide to remote users dialup access to internetwork resources. The AS5350 is Voice-over-IP capable with the proper line cards installed. Figure 3-3 shows the Cisco 5350.

Figure 3-3 *Cisco 5350 Universal Server*

This family of routers is designed to perform best in dialup access environments. The routers offer high-density voice and data solutions. The AS5350 can terminate both digital and analog data calls. There are three slots in an AS5350. It also comes with two 10/100-Mbps Ethernet ports, and two serial interfaces for Frame Relay or leased-line connectivity. All of this fits in a single rack unit (RU).

The AS5350 supports four or eight T1/E1 ports in a single slot, with MICA modems or Voice over IP (VoIP) feature cards in the other two slots, which are typically PRI ports. With eight T1s, the incoming call volume can reach 192 calls (240 with E1s). With the other two slots populated with MICA modem blades, that capacity can easily be supported.

The AS5400 is a two-RU big brother to the 5350. It has seven slots, and can use all the same modules as the 5350. Due to the larger chassis size, the 5400 can support up to 648 concurrent calls. Figure 3-4 shows the Cisco 5400.

Figure 3-4 *Cisco 5400 Universal Server*

For extremely high call volume, the AS5800 model is available. It can handle six 12-port T1/E1 trunk cards (72 T1/E1 ports). This means that it can handle up to 1728 B channels at T1 or 2160 B channels at E1. This density enables hot sparing. Figure 3-5 shows the Cisco 5850.

Figure 3-5   *Cisco 5850 Universal Server*

The AS5800 model has the capability to handle 720 calls. The AS5800 has 14 line-card slots, and can combine both MICA modem cards and T1/E1 cards in the chassis at the same time.

Inbound calls to an AS5800 router can be digital from another ISDN device or analog from a dialup user. Therefore, this router is a good choice for central-site dialup facilities. In a mixed-technology environment with multiple WAN technologies, this router probably is not the best choice, but for dialup deployments, it is hard to beat.

Cisco 7200 Series Router

This family of routers has been around for a while and represents a wide install base. These devices provide high-power core LAN/WAN routing capabilities and voice integration capabilities. ATM, ISDN, and circuit emulation services are just a few of the available options supported.

If an AS5800 solution is being put in place, this router is absolutely necessary. It provides the router shelf function for the AS5800. The routing engine of the 7200 is the routing brain of the AS5800.

The 7200 comes in two flavors. The 7204 is a four-slot router that allows four different WAN connection options to be added to the chassis. The 7206 adds two more slots for additional WAN connections. Neither of the 7200 routers comes with any ports by default. Thus, a combination of WAN and LAN slots is normally implemented. Figure 3-6 shows the Cisco 7206.

Figure 3-6   *Cisco 7206 Router*

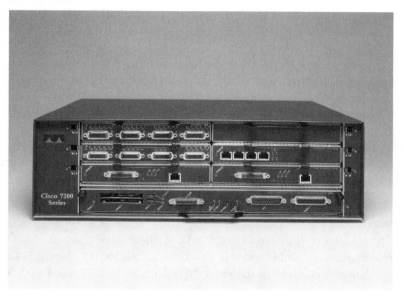

The port modules can be mixed and matched for varying degrees of connectivity and bandwidth. The newer VXR version of the 7200 includes a time-division multiplexing (TDM) bus, which provides better performance than its predecessors. This router is a great choice for the central site, based on its flexibility and overall power.

The 7200 Series can easily deal with remote-office connections. The port modules can support T1/E1 leased lines, Frame Relay connections, channelized T1/E1 (using different channels to connect with different remote sites instead of the entire interface dedicated to one remote location), ISDN PRI (for collecting multiple remote BRIs), and multiple Ethernet and Fast Ethernet ports (for connections to firewalls).

The 7200 Series can also deal with much higher-speed connections (for example, OC-3 – 155 Mbps, or Packet over SONET) if necessary. Thus, the 7200 can collect each of the remote sites via Frame Relay or BRI, and then have a high-speed connection to an ISP for corporate Internet access. In fact, the 7200 Series can terminate circuits ranging from a single DS0 (64 kbps) through OC-12 (622 Mbps).

Remote Office/Branch Office Router Selection

Branch-office sites are the source of many debates when the time comes to connect them to the central site through a WAN implementation. The amount of bandwidth necessary to adequately support the site is a crucial factor in the decision-making process. The technology implemented to provide the necessary bandwidth is also important. In addition, the router selection needed to terminate the current and potential future connections is equally important.

This section of the chapter focuses on some router families that meet the needs of the small- to medium-sized branch office. These are the Cisco 1700 and 2600 Series routers. Note that the 36X0 or 72X0 can also be a good choice for a large branch office, when flexibility is needed. However, these two routers were discussed in the previous section and need not be revisited.

There are other ROBO routers offered by Cisco. The 1600 Series has been replaced by the 1700, and most of the 2500 line has been replaced by the 2600 Series. A couple of 2500s that survived the chopping block are also discussed in this section.

Cisco 1700 Series Router

The 1700 Series router family is designed for the small- to medium-sized office. It can support one or two WAN connections and Ethernet or Fast Ethernet connectivity for the LAN. It tends to be a higher-horsepower device than its discontinued cousin, the 1600 Series. Figure 3-7 shows a Cisco 1760 router.

Figure 3-7   *Cisco 1760 Router*

The 1700 router can provide multiple WAN connections simultaneously and is a strong, stable router. It has a small footprint and is easy to work with. Most of the 1700s are not rack-mountable, although there is currently a version that is (the 1760). Thus, the 1700 Series normally needs its own shelf to sit on, or it sits on top of another piece of racked equipment. Figure 3-8 shows a Cisco 1710 router.

Figure 3-8 *Cisco 1710 Router*

The 1710 comes with two Ethernet interfaces, one 10 Mbps and the other 10/100 Mbps. All of the other 1700 Series routers come with only a single FE interface. The 1710 is the smallest of the Cisco routers that offer the ability to do VPNs, a firewall feature set, and advanced routing protocols. The 800 Series is somewhat limited in these areas of functionality.

The 1750 and 1760 offer voice capabilities built into the router. Thus, phones can be directly connected to the router, or phone lines can be run directly into the router. This flexibility and growth capacity make it an ideal choice for a small- to medium-sized branch office. As such, the 1750 and 1760 can offer alternate voice service to a site if the primary VoIP connection fails.

As mentioned earlier, the 1760 is actually rack-mountable. Thus, if there is a requirement to rack-mount the routers instead of shelf-mount them, the 1760 offers everything that the 1700 Series product line does in a 19-inch footprint.

Cisco 2500 Series Router

Most of the 2500 Series of routers have been discontinued. The 2600 routers are the stronger replacements for the older 2500s. However, two 2500 Series routers are still around today. The 2509 and 2511 are called access servers. They are very small cousins to the AS5000 family of routers.

The 2509 has eight asynchronous ports, while the 2511 has 16 such ports. These ports can be connected to modems and offer termination of asynchronous connections to the network.

The 2509/2511 routers are also popular for use as terminal servers to other racked devices. These routers allow a single console device (a PC using HyperTerminal, for example) to access multiple console ports in the same rack.

Cisco 2600 Series Router

The 2600 Series routers are replacements to the discontinued 2500 Series line. They offer greater throughput, and better interface options. Figure 3-9 illustrates the 2600 Series routers.

Figure 3-9 *Cisco 2600 Series Routers*

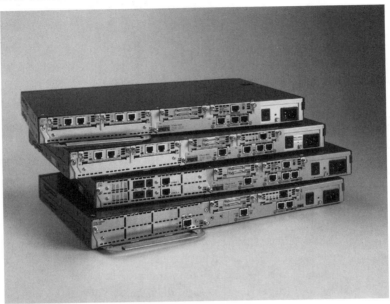

Whereas most of the 2500s were static routers (the ports could not be changed), all 2600s are modular. They have two wide-area interface card (WIC) slots and one network module (NM) slot.

The WIC slots use any of the WIC cards that can be used in the 3600 routers. And the NM slot also uses 3600 NMs. However, due to limited CPU, not every 3600 NM *should* go into the 2600 chassis. Normally, any NM that exceeds the normal T1/E1 speeds should not be added to the 2600 chassis. The 2650 and 2690 models do offer greater CPU capabilities, but are still below that of a 3600 Series router.

The 2600 Series can support multiservice offerings of voice, video, and data in a single chassis. Analog or digital telephony are options for this box. Traditional LAN/WAN routing options are, of course, available as well.

For branch offices with integrated voice and data, the 2600 Series router would be a good choice. However, in a data-only environment, it cannot offer the port density necessary for a medium-sized branch office.

Small Office/Home Office Router Selection

The SOHO market is an emerging market. The growing needs of the telecommuter are a very real aspect of today's internetwork deployments. Cisco offers a few options with regard to SOHO deployments. Depending on the company and the needs of the telecommuter, a 1700 or 2600 router could be utilized. However, Cisco 800 Series routers may be a more manageable and cost-effective solution.

Because both the 1700 and 2600 have been covered earlier, they will not be addressed again in this section.

Making Selections Among Available Series

Note that the selection between an 800 Series, 1700 Series, and 2600 Series router at a SOHO site is a matter of how large the site is, how much data will travel to/from that site, and any additional options needed at the site. The 1700 and 2600 have VoIP capabilities, whereas the 800 supports only phone connections into the router (across ISDN BRI connections).

At the central and branch offices, the demarcation is typically where the phone equipment entered the building. At a small site or home office, using DSL as a connection to the Internet, for example, the demarcation point is the phone box attached to the outside of the building. Normally, the phone company will not work on internal cabling without hefty fees. Thus, the connection from the DSL demarcation to the router would be a normal phone line into the building.

Cisco 800 Series Router

The 800 Series router connects small offices and corporate telecommuters to the Internet or to a corporate LAN through ISDN, serial connections (Frame Relay and leased lines), and DSL. It also enables customers to take advantage of value-added services, such as differentiated classes of service, integrated voice/data, business class security, and VPNs. Figure 3-10 illustrates the Cisco 806 router.

Figure 3-10   *Cisco 806 Router*

You should take care terminating VPN tunnels on an 800 Series router. The CPU cannot handle too much stress.

The 800 Series routers run the Cisco IOS Software and are a good choice if the needs of the SOHO include low port density with flexible WAN technology options. The 800s replaced the older 700 Series routers, which were not Cisco IOS based.

The 800 Series routers can be used for direct connectivity to DSL networks (827), at the end of an ISDN connection (801 and 803 have ISDN S/T connections, while the 802 and 804 have ISDN U connections), behind a cable modem (the 806 has two Ethernet ports), or connected to a Frame Relay or leased-line network (the 805 has a DB-60 serial interface). Because the CPU is limited, the 800 Series routers should be used only at home-based offices or very small remote offices. Thus, they certainly fit the SOHO mold.

Assembling and Cabling the Equipment

Numerous types of physical connectivity options are available based on the technologies being implemented. This section touches on the basics behind these connections. Much of what this section covers is review for most people with any significant time in the industry. For more in-depth information regarding physical connectivity, pinouts for individual cables, and other requirements, check out www.cisco.com.

The technologies discussed in this section are identified in Figure 3-11. Note that if all the labels are removed from the figure, the various connectivity possibilities become numerous.

A few of the connection options in Figure 3-11 come up on a regular basis:

- **Leased line**—A leased line is a full or fractional T1/E1 connection from one serial interface of a Cisco router to one other site. Remember that fractions come in increments of 64 kbps. Each serial interface can only support one leased-line circuit. And a leased line offers dedicated, full-time bandwidth between sites.

  All modern Cisco serial ports are either the well-known DB-60 format or a newer, smart serial connection. Two smart serial connectors occupy the footprint of one DB-60 connector. The leased-line connection is either a PPP or HDLC connection.

- **Frame Relay**—Frame Relay connections are serial connections between a site and a provider. This single connection to the provider allows multiple connections to multiple destinations via various virtual circuits (VCs). Because each Frame Relay connection terminates on a serial port of a Cisco router, the same cables are used for Frame Relay as are used for leased lines.

Figure 3-11 *Connection Types*

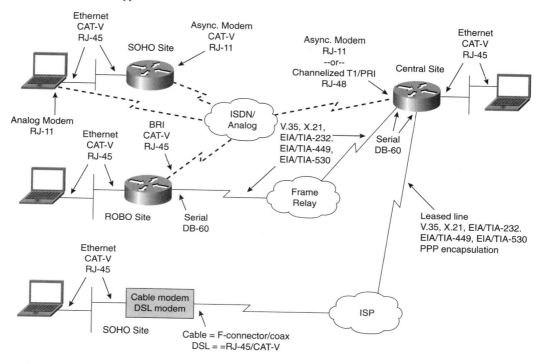

A Frame Relay interface at a central site shares the bandwidth on the single interface with multiple VCs to remote sites. Frame Relay is cost-effective, but offers less control of the data flow. A Frame Relay network offers no guarantee of service. If frames are dropped as they traverse the Frame Relay cloud, no error messages are generated to indicate the lost frame.

■ **ISDN BRI**—BRI connections are known as 1B+D or 2B+D connections. An ISDN BRI connection uses Category 5 cabling to connect to the phone company. It may be necessary to provide an external NT1 if one is not integrated into the router. A BRI interface with an integral NT1 is labeled as *BRI U*, and a BRI interface without an integral NT1 is labeled as *BRI S/T*. These connections use RJ-45 cables, which are typically Category 5 in quality.

It is important to note that for an ISDN U connection, only pins 4 and 5 are actually used. These are the same pins used for a normal phone connection. And for an ISDN S/T connection, pins 3 through 6 are used.

- **ISDN PRI**—This implementation varies, based on geographic location. PRI uses T1 or E1 characteristics. E1 PRI is generally used outside of North America. T1 PRI is prevalent within North America. The primary difference between the two is the number of bearer channels. T1 PRI uses 23B+D connectivity, and E1 PRI uses 30B+D connectivity. These connections use Category 5 RJ-45 cables.

  On a Cisco router, you need a channelized T1/E1 port to attach an ISDN PRI connection. A normal serial port cannot be used. As previously mentioned, the channelized T1/E1 port uses an RJ-45 connector.

- **DSL**—A Cisco router can be connected to DSL circuits in a variety of ways. The 827 router is specifically designed to terminate DSL connections from the provider. The 827 has an RJ-45 port to bring the DSL connection directly into the router. However, only pins 4 and 5 are actually used (the same pins used on a phone connection).

  A DSL modem can also be used to convert the frequencies on the phone line to Ethernet frames. If you use this method, then you can use any Cisco router with a spare Ethernet port to terminate the DSL connection. An 806, 1710, or 2600 works as a SOHO DSL router.

- **Cable modem**—Like DSL, a Cisco router can be connected to cable-modem circuits in a variety of ways. The best way is to use the Cisco 900UBR (universal broadband router). This router has a cable F connector in the router. However, this router is not covered in the BCRAN course.

  A cable modem can also be used to convert the frequencies on the cable line to Ethernet frames. With this method, you can use any Cisco router with a spare Ethernet port to terminate the cable-modem connection. An 806, 1710, or 2600 works as a SOHO cable-modem router.

- **Asynchronous**—These connections typically use RJ-11 cables (two, four, or six pins compared to RJ-45, which uses eight pins). They are dialup-connection interfaces designed to accept calls from remote users.

  External modems can be connected to the asynchronous ports of the 2509/2511 access routers. This normally takes a converter from the RJ-45 connector to the EIA/TIA-232 connector on the external modem. In any case, the modems typically have EIA/TIA-232 connectors. It is feasible to have all modems internal to the router as well, as with a 3600 or AS5300.

Verifying the Installation

The task of verifying physical connectivity is usually an easy one. If all is well, there is an LED on the front of the router (or on the back by the interface in question) that is green. If it is not green, it is time to figure out why.

LED Lights

During the boot process, the LEDs may flash green. This is completely normal. Other models of Cisco devices have an amber-colored light during the boot sequence. However, after the router has booted, all active and functioning LEDs should turn to solid green. The phrase "green is good" is heard over and over in many Cisco classes and environments.

For most routers, identifying the LEDs is the difficult part. For additional information, refer to the installation guide that came with your specific router and the specific module.

In most cases, a network administrator does not spend their entire life in the LAN room with all the routers and switches. So, in most cases, the lights on the chassis and modules have limited functionality. Learning how to determine the working status of any interface with the various IOS **show** commands becomes essential in the life of any network administrator.

Each router model has its own set of LEDs. They are usually located in the same places. Overall status LEDs, such as Enabled and Active LEDs, are usually on the front of the chassis. The interface-specific LEDs are on the back of the chassis, adjacent to the interface in question.

Router Interface Verification

As noted earlier, lights have value only if you are actually in the same room as the routers. Because most equipment is remotely managed, the appropriate **show** screen is the best tool to determine the status of any given interface.

The best thing about using the **show** screens is that the output is the same regardless of the type of router. An interface status on a SOHO 800 Series router looks the same as an interface status on a ROBO 3600 Series router. Once you learn how to read the screens, you can determine the status of any interface.

The following sections examine the two most popular types of interfaces used in routers: Ethernet and serial. An Ethernet port could be used to terminate a DSL or cable-modem connection. A serial interface is used to connect to leased-line (PPP or HDLC) or packet-switching (Frame Relay) environments.

show interfaces ethernet

Ethernet, or Fast Ethernet, interfaces are used at sites where a DSL modem or cable modem is used to create Ethernet frames. These Ethernet frames appear as if they were coming directly from the provider. As such, monitoring the status of the "outward-facing" Ethernet interface helps to determine the status of the WAN connection.

The display in Example 3-1 shows a Fast Ethernet interface on a Cisco 2600 router. Note that the information in this display is identical to any Ethernet interface on any Cisco router.

Example 3-1 *A* **show interfaces fastethernet** *Display*

```
Router#show interfaces fastethernet 0/0
FastEthernet0/0 is up, line protocol is up
  Hardware is AmdFE, address is 0002.160a.1cc0 (bia 0002.160a.1cc0)
  Description: Link to 2924 FA 0/24 (VLAN 1)
  Internet address is 192.168.1.1/24
  MTU 1500 bytes, BW 100000 Kbit, DLY 100 usec,
     reliability 255/255, txload 1/255, rxload 1/255
  Encapsulation ARPA, loopback not set
  Keepalive set (10 sec)
  Full-duplex, 100Mb/s, 100BaseTX/FX
  ARP type: ARPA, ARP Timeout 04:00:00
  Last input 00:00:00, output 00:00:00, output hang never
  Last clearing of "show interface" counters never
  Input queue: 0/75/0/0 (size/max/drops/flushes); Total output drops: 0
  Queueing strategy: fifo
  Output queue :0/40 (size/max)
  5 minute input rate 13000 bits/sec, 30 packets/sec
  5 minute output rate 504000 bits/sec, 60 packets/sec
     2996392 packets input, 1024956679 bytes
     Received 179135 broadcasts, 0 runts, 0 giants, 0 throttles
     0 input errors, 0 CRC, 0 frame, 0 overrun, 0 ignored
     0 watchdog
     0 input packets with dribble condition detected
     3384973 packets output, 2091655213 bytes, 0 underruns
     0 output errors, 0 collisions, 5 interface resets
     0 babbles, 0 late collision, 0 deferred
     0 lost carrier, 0 no carrier
     0 output buffer failures, 0 output buffers swapped out
Router#
```

The most critical portion of this display is the first line (after the **show** command itself). It shows that this interface is up/up. The first up refers to the physical connectivity of the interface. The second up refers to the line protocol, or the keepalive messages that travel in and out of the interface on a regular basis. The keepalive messages can travel only if the physical interface is operational.

There are four possible interface statuses, as shown in Table 3-2.

Table 3-2 *Ethernet Interface Status*

Physical	Line Protocol	Status
Up	Up	Operational
Up	Down	Incorrect pinouts
Down	Down	Physical problem, broken cable, bad pinout, cable not attached
Administratively down	Administratively down	Administrator disabled the interface

This interface status is the same on virtually any Cisco interface (Ethernet, Fast Ethernet, Serial, BRI, Async). The limited combination of ups and downs from the **show interfaces** screen helps you to determine the problem with the connectivity.

For an Ethernet interface, very few things could actually go wrong. If an Ethernet interface is down/down, then either the wrong type of cable has been used (straight vs. crossover) or the cable is not connected. Often, the lack of tabs on RJ-45 connectors causes Ethernet cables to slip loose from the router interfaces.

It actually takes work to get an Ethernet interface to be up/down. Normally, a router Ethernet port connects to a switch port. A probable cause of an up/down is a mispinned cable. Normally, Ethernet cables use pins 1, 2, 3, and 6. If a cable is mispinned, say, to pins 1, 2, 6, and 3, then one end would get a link and the other would not. The keepalives would eventually fail, and the status would go up/down. This can happen in places where cables are made (not very well) on site.

You can learn a few other important facts from any interface display. For Fast Ethernet interfaces, you can see the speed and duplex level. Table 3-3 represents the possible values.

Table 3-3 *Fast Ethernet Speed and Duplex*

Speed	Duplex
10 Mbps	Half
10 Mbps	Full
100 Mbps	Half
100 Mbps	Full

All Cisco 10/100-Mbps Ethernet interfaces have the ability to auto-sense both the speed and duplex. However, it is very important that these settings match for the two devices that are connected together. Because of inadequacies in the auto-sensing process, both speed and duplex should always be manually set to match the other end.

In Example 3-1, the interface has been manually set to 100 Mbps and full duplex. If auto-sensing were enabled, then the term (auto) would follow both the automatically determined speed and duplex value.

If the speed and duplex value do not match, then the most likely symptom is late collisions or input queue drops (shown at the bottom of Example 3-1) on the slower interface. Typically, the faster, full-duplex interface shows no problems. It is the slower interface that gets overwhelmed by the frame volume from its faster neighbor. Or, the half-duplex end receives what it believes to be late collisions because its neighbor is in full-duplex mode (receiving and transmitting simultaneously) yet it can only receive or transmit (half duplex).

It is important to note that not all network devices have this level of detailed examination. For example, if a Cisco router is attached to a cable modem at a remote site, the router has the display shown in Example 3-1, but the cable modem has no such troubleshooting display. Another example would be a Cisco router connected to an unmanaged switch. In each case, where both ends of a connection cannot be examined, it is even more important to manually configure the speed and duplex settings on the Cisco router.

show interfaces serial

Serial interfaces are used to connect a site to leased-line or Frame Relay services. As with Ethernet interfaces, the status of the interface helps to determine the cause of any problems. Example 3-2 shows a serial interface display.

Example 3-2   show interfaces serial *Display*

```
Router#show interfaces serial 0/2
Serial0/2 is up, line protocol is up
  Hardware is PowerQUICC Serial
  Internet address is 1.2.1.2/24
  MTU 1500 bytes, BW 1544 Kbit, DLY 20000 usec,
     reliability 255/255, txload 1/255, rxload 1/255
  Encapsulation HDLC, loopback not set
  Keepalive set (10 sec)
  Last input 00:00:05, output 00:00:05, output hang never
  Last clearing of "show interface" counters never
  Input queue: 0/75/0/0 (size/max/drops/flushes); Total output drops: 0
  Queueing strategy: weighted fair
  Output queue: 0/1000/64/0 (size/max total/threshold/drops)
     Conversations  0/1/256 (active/max active/max total)
     Reserved Conversations 0/0 (allocated/max allocated)
     Available Bandwidth 1158 kilobits/sec
```

Example 3-2   show interfaces serial *Display (Continued)*

```
    5 minute input rate 0 bits/sec, 0 packets/sec
    5 minute output rate 0 bits/sec, 0 packets/sec
       86 packets input, 6762 bytes, 0 no buffer
       Received 81 broadcasts, 0 runts, 0 giants, 0 throttles
       0 input errors, 0 CRC, 0 frame, 0 overrun, 0 ignored, 0 abort
       84 packets output, 5793 bytes, 0 underruns
       0 output errors, 0 collisions, 3 interface resets
       0 output buffer failures, 0 output buffers swapped out
       1 carrier transitions
       DCD=up  DSR=up  DTR=up  RTS=up  CTS=up
Router#
```

As with the Ethernet interface, the up/down status at the top of the display has only four possible states. Those states are listed in Table 3-4.

Table 3-4   *Serial Interface Status*

Physical	Line Protocol	Status
Up	Up	Operational
Up	Down	Keepalive mismatch, incorrect clock rate, clock rate not set, encapsulation mismatch
Down	Down	Physical problem, broken cable, cable not attached
Administratively down	Administratively down	Administrator disabled the interface

As Table 3-4 indicates, there are many more things that could go wrong with a serial interface. Aside from the physical problems that cause the interface to go down/down (the primary fault with Ethernet interfaces), there are many other problems that could cause the interface to be up/down.

Serial interfaces rely on a clock source. The DCE end of the cable, normally the carrier, provides the clock. If the clock rate is not configured or not detected, a serial interface will go up/down.

A serial cable can also be overwhelmed. For example, an EIA/TIA-232 cable should be used only for connections running 64 kbps or less. If the clock rate is set higher than this, the interface could fail and show an up/down status. Typically, most sites use V.35 cables to ensure that clock rates are not a problem. However, some networking equipment may use the EIA/TIA-232 connectors, and thus the speed of the router interface must be considered.

Also, because a serial interface can use various encapsulation types (for example, PPP, HDLC, and Frame Relay), a mismatch from end to end can be disastrous. The encapsulation is set on each end of the circuit: for the most part, the provider is not involved. If the two ends do not agree on the encapsulation, the line goes up/down.

The encapsulation on a Cisco serial interface (or any Cisco interface for that matter) is shown toward the top of the interface display. A serial interface can be in either point-to-point mode or packet-switching mode. The determination of which encapsulation is used is a matter of what type of service the provider is giving you. If your site has a single connection to another site, then a point-to-point circuit can be used (for example, a remote site connected back to the central site). However, if your site needs to communicate to multiple other sites via a single router interface, then something like Frame Relay is necessary (packet switching). This could apply to either a popular remote site or the central site itself. Normally, a SOHO would not have such a requirement.

If a point-to-point link is used, the two possible point-to-point encapsulations are HDLC (a Cisco proprietary standard, and the default) and PPP (the North American standard). There is no international point-to-point protocol standard. As long as the routers at either end of the circuit have the same encapsulation set (there is no auto-sensing for encapsulation), then the circuit should work. The carrier (provider) cannot impact your decision to select either PPP or HDLC.

If Frame Relay (packet switching) is employed, then the interface must connect to a provider offering such service. Frame Relay encapsulation cannot be configured across a point-to-point circuit offered from the provider. The router interface, when configured for Frame Relay, expects to talk to a Frame Relay switch. And if a Frame Relay switch is not found, the interface fails.

The final line of the **show interfaces serial** command also textually shows the status of the lights that are on the interface itself. Thus, if you do not have the ability to visit the router in the data center or LAN room, you can examine the light status with this screen. Table 3-5 describes the light statuses.

Table 3-5 *Serial Interface Light Display*

Light	Definition	Purpose
DCD	Data Carrier Detect	Provider switch detected
DSR	Data Set Ready	OK to send data
DTR	Data Terminal Ready	Notifies the far end that you can receive data
RTS	Request to Send	Asks the far end if it is OK to send data
CTS	Clear to Send	Tells the far end that it may send data

Foundation Summary

This section is a collection of information that provides a convenient review of many key concepts in this chapter. For those of you who are already comfortable with the topics in this chapter, this summary could help you recall a few details. For those of you who just read this chapter, this review should help solidify some key facts. For any of you doing your final preparation before the exam, this information is a convenient way to review the material the day before the exam.

Overall, this chapter dealt with:

■ Selecting the proper Cisco router at the appropriate site

■ Determining the physical connection requirements based on the type of service provided by the carrier

■ Examining the physical interfaces to determine whether it has been properly wired and configured

Table 3-6 documents the site types and the Cisco router options applicable to each location type. Although it may be possible to place larger-than-necessary routers at any given site, it may not be financially feasible to do so. However, it is never a good idea to have too small of a router at any site, because it limits the ability for that site to expand and add features in the future.

Table 3-6 *Cisco Routers Applicable to Central, Branch, and SOHO Locations*

Site	Applicable Routers
Central	3600 (3640 and 3660), AS5X00, 7200
ROBO	1700, 2600, 3600 (3620)
SOHO	800, 1700

There are a variety of services (connection options) that any Cisco router can be connected to. Table 3-7 summarizes the services that were covered in this chapter.

Table 3-7 *Services Covered in Chapter 3*

Connection Option	Encapsulation	Interface	Connector
Leased line	HDLC/PPP	Serial	DB-60 or smart serial
Frame Relay	Frame Relay	Serial	DB-60 or smart serial
ISDN (BRI)	HDLC/PPP	BRI	RJ-45

(continues)

Table 3-7   *Services Covered in Chapter 3 (Continued)*

Connection Option	Encapsulation	Interface	Connector
ISDN (PRI)	HDLC/PPP	Channelized serial	RJ-45
DSL	Ethernet (to modem)	Ethernet (to modem)	RJ-45
	— (to provider)	DSL (to provider)	
Cable modem	Ethernet (to modem)	Ethernet (to modem)	RJ-45
	— (to provider)	Cable (to provider)	F

Most cables are interface-specific in that they can be attached at only one place on the router. That is not always the case, however. For example, Category 5 UTP cable can be used with Ethernet, T1/E1 WIC, and ISDN interfaces. You should take the time to ensure that the correct cable is attached in the appropriate place. A straight-through Ethernet cable does not work in a T1/E1 WIC connection. The pinouts are dissimilar.

LEDs are an important part of the router. They provide a quick status of the router and its interfaces. A red or amber LED is worthy of investigation. Remember, green is good.

And the **show interfaces** display offers a view to the operational state of any particular interface of the Cisco router. An up/up status indicates that the interface is passing traffic. Anything else indicates a problem that needs to be investigated.

Q&A

The questions and scenarios in this book are more difficult than what you will experience on the actual exam. The questions do not attempt to cover more breadth or depth than the exam; however, they are designed to make sure that you know the answer. Rather than enabling you to derive the answer from clues hidden inside the question itself, the questions challenge your understanding and recall of the subject.

Hopefully, mastering these questions will help you to limit the number of exam questions on which you narrow your choices to two options and then guess.

The answers to these questions can be found in Appendix A.

1. At a central site where LAN and WAN access and hundreds of dialup ports are required, which type of router works best?

2. Which central-site router comes with two 10/100-Mbps auto-sensing Ethernet ports built into the chassis?

3. If a 3640 router is procured for use at a central site, but no modules are initially purchased, how can the router be used?

4. Which SOHO router can be rack-mounted?

5. How many serial ports are needed on a ROBO router that uses Frame Relay to connect to three other locations, including the central office?

6. How many serial ports are needed on a central-office router that uses Frame Relay to connect to three other locations?

7. The central office has decided to get PPP links between itself and each of the five remote sites. The remote sites are each connected to the central site. How many serial ports are needed at the central site?

8. How many ROBO and SOHO locations can a T1 PRI interface on a central router connect to simultaneously?

9. Which SOHO router can be used to directly terminate a DSL connection?

10. Which WAN connection methods use a serial port to connect to the provider?

11. Which condition would cause an Ethernet interface to be up/down?

12. Which conditions would cause a serial interface to be up/down?

13. What type of connector and what pins are used for an ISDN BRI connection?

Scenarios

The following scenario and questions are designed to draw together the content of the chapter and exercise your understanding of the concepts. There is not necessarily a right answer to each scenario. The thought process and practice in manipulating the related concepts is the goal of this section.

Scenario 3-1

Consider Figure 3-12 for the purposes of this scenario.

Figure 3-12 *Scenario 3-1 Topology*

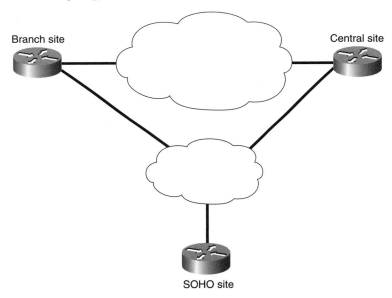

The goal in this case is to adequately deploy the proper technologies and line speeds to support the sites in the figure. Complete the scenario by meeting the needs of each step specified in the tasks that follow.

1. Make the decision as to which types of routers should be deployed at each site. For the central site, assume 100+ users and that the number is growing. For the branch site, assume ten users, and for the SOHO site, assume a single user.

2. Based on your router choices, deploy WAN topology appropriate to your choices.

Scenario Answers

The answers provided in this section are not necessarily the only possible correct answers. They merely represent one possibility for the scenario. The intention is to test your base knowledge and understanding of the concepts discussed in this chapter.

Should your answers be different (as they likely will be), consider the differences. Are your answers in line with the concepts of the answers provided and explained here? If not, go back and read the chapter again, focusing on the sections related to the problem scenario.

Scenario 3-1 Answers

1. For the growing central site, with 100+ users, it may be necessary to implement a 7200 router or higher. A 3640 could certainly handle the job. However, you must consider future growth. If the site has few or no plans for growth in the near future, the 3640 is a good choice. A 3660 has greater potential for growth. The branch office site with only ten users could function with a 1700, 2600, or even a 3620 (although this is probably overkill for now). The SOHO site with a single user will likely use ISDN for connectivity and an 800 Series router.

2. For the central site connecting to the branch site, a single dedicated circuit can be implemented. If future sites are to be added, Frame Relay may be appropriate to reduce the comparative cost of multiple dedicated circuits. Note that there is a secondary connection between the central and branch sites. Secondary connections are typically ISDN. The SOHO site shows connectivity to the same cloud as the secondary central-to-branch connection. Also, with the selection of an 800 Series router, the apparent connectivity choice is ISDN.

PART II: Enabling On-Demand Connections to the Central Site

Chapter 4   **Configuring Asynchronous Connections with Modems**

Chapter 5   **Configuring PPP and Controlling Network Access**

Chapter 6   **PPP Link Control Protocol Options**

This part of the book covers the following BCRAN exam topics:

- Describe traffic control methods used to manage traffic flow on WAN links
- Explain the operation of remote network access control methods
- Identify PPP components, and explain the use of PPP as an access and encapsulation method
- Configure asynchronous modems and router interfaces to provide network access
- Design a Cisco remote access solution using asynchronous dialup technology

This chapter covers the following subjects:

- Modem Signaling

- Modem Configuration Using Reverse Telnet

- Router Line Numbering

- Basic Asynchronous Configuration

- Configuration of the Attached Modem

- Chat Scripts to Control Modem Connections

CHAPTER 4

Configuring Asynchronous Connections with Modems

To configure a modem, the modem and its physical characteristics must be defined to the router. The router must be configured to see the modem at the right settings, and the router must be aware of the modem parameters.

The modem (modulator/demodulator) must be configured so that it understands the signaling on both the telephone-line side and the router-connection side. The modulation and demodulation function converts the data stream from digital (PC side) to analog (phone-line side). This information includes the line rate and the number of bits used for data and other physical settings for the modem. The particulars for the modem are discussed in the body of this chapter.

The second and third pieces of an asynchronous modem connection are configured on the router and provide both physical and logical aspects for a connection. The physical properties are configured on the line. These parameters include the line rate, the data link layer protocols supported on the line, and so on. These parameters are needed for the router line to communicate with the attached modem.

The last piece of an asynchronous modem connection is configuring the logical information on the router *interface*. The logical information includes the Layer 3 addresses, the network layer protocol, the authentication methods, and so forth.

This chapter covers the signaling of the modem and the configurations for a Remote Access Server (RAS) connection. The successful CCNP or CCDP candidate should be able to describe the signaling and pins used by the cabling and not just the syntax that is required for the connection. The signaling is just as important because it provides the basis for the physical layer troubleshooting that may be needed to establish a connection.

"Do I Know This Already?" Quiz

The purpose of the "Do I Know This Already?" quiz is to help you decide what parts of this chapter to use. If you already intend to read the entire chapter, you do not necessarily need to answer these questions now.

The 12-question quiz helps you determine how to spend your limited study time. Table 4-1 outlines the major topics discussed in this chapter and the "Do I Know This Already?" quiz questions that correspond to those topics.

Table 4-1 *"Do I Know This Already?" Foundation Topics Section-to-Question Mapping*

Foundation Topics Section	Questions Covered In This Section
Modem Signaling	1–2
Modem Configuration Using Reverse Telnet	3–4
Router Line Numbering	5–6
Basic Asynchronous Configuration	7–8
Configuration of the Attached Modem	9–10
Chat Scripts to Control Modem Connections	11–12

CAUTION The goal of self-assessment is to gauge your mastery of the topics in this chapter. If you do not know the answer to a question or are only partially sure of the answer, you should mark this question wrong for purposes of the self-assessment. Giving yourself credit for an answer you correctly guess skews your self-assessment results and might provide you with a false sense of security.

1. What pins are used for modem control?

    a. TD, RS, GRD

    b. RTS, CTS

    c. DSR, CD, DTR

    d. RTS, CTS, DSR

2. What is the standard for DCE/DTE signaling?

    a. EIA/TIA-232

    b. RS 232-C

    c. RS 232-Standard

    d. EIA/TIA-446

3. In character mode using reverse Telnet, what is the command to connect to the first async port on a 2509 router that has a loopback interface of 192.168.1.1?

    a. **telnet 192.168.1.1 port 1**

    b. **telnet 192.168.1.1 2001**

    c. **telnet 192.168.1.1 1**

    d. **telnet 192.168.1.1 async1**

4. What port range is reserved for accessing an individual port using binary mode?

    a. 4000–4xxx

    b. 5000–5xxx

    c. 6000–6xxx

    d. 7000–7xxx

5. If a four-port serial (A/S) module is in the second slot (slot 1) on a 3640 router, what are the line numbers for each port?

    a. 33–36

    b. 2/1–2/4

    c. 32–35

    d. a/s21–a/s24

6. What is the AUX port line number on a 3620 Series router?

    a. AUX1

    b. 65

    c. 21

    d. 63

7. On what interface would you apply the **physical-layer async** command?

    a. A/S interfaces

    b. Async interfaces

    c. Modem interfaces

    d. LAN interfaces

8. In what configuration mode must you be to configure the physical properties of an asynchronous interface?

    a. Global

    b. Line

    c. Physical

    d. Interface

9. When should **modem autoconfigure discovery** be used?

    a. Remotely, to possibly discover a modem type

    b. For convenience, so modems can be hot-swapped

    c. Never

    d. Always

10. Which of the following commands would you use to add an entry to a modemcap database called newmodem?

    a. **edit modemcap newmodem**

    b. **modemcap edit newmodem**

    c. **modemcap edit type newmodem**

    d. **modemcap add newmodem**

11. Which of the following is *not* a reason to use a chat script?

    a. **Line activation**—CD trigger (incoming traffic)

    b. **Line connection**—DTR trigger (outgoing traffic)

    c. **Line reset**—Asynchronous line reset

    d. **Disconnect of an active call**—Access server trigger

    e. **Dialer startup**—From a dial-on-demand trigger

12. Which of the following would, by default, trigger a chat script to start?

    a. Line reset

    b. DDR

    c. Line activation

    d. Manual reset

The answers to the "Do I Know This Already?" quiz are found in Appendix A, "Answers to the 'Do I Know This Already?' Quizzes and Q&A." The suggested choices for your next step are as follows:

- **6 or fewer overall score**—Read the entire chapter. This includes the "Foundation Topics," "Foundation Summary," and "Q&A" sections.

- **7, 8, or 9 overall score**—Begin with the "Foundation Summary" section and then go to the "Q&A" section.

- **10 or more overall score**—If you want more review on these topics, skip to the "Foundation Summary" section and then go to the "Q&A" section. Otherwise, move to the next chapter.

Foundation Topics

Modem Signaling

This chapter covers the signaling of the modem and the configurations for a RAS connection. The successful CCNP or CCDP candidate should be able to describe the signaling and pins used by the cabling and not just the syntax that is required for the connection. The signaling is just as important because it provides the basis for the physical layer troubleshooting that may be needed to establish a connection.

Asynchronous data communication occurs when an end device, such as a PC, calls another end device, such as a server, to exchange data. In asynchronous data communications, end devices are called data terminal equipment (DTE). These devices communicate through data circuit-terminating equipment (DCE). DCE devices clock the flow of information. In this case, the modem provides the DCE function to the PC and server.

The Electronic Industries Association/Telecommunications Industry Association (EIA/TIA) defines a standard for the interface between DCE and DTE devices. This standard is EIA/TIA-232 and was previously referred to as the RS-232-C standard (where the RS stood for "recommended standard").

A PC-to-server connection that uses asynchronous communications should not be thought of as a single circuit. The PC using a modem is one DTE-to-DCE path end. The far end DCE-to-DTE (modem to server) connection is another path. Each DTE-to-DCE or DCE-to-DTE connection must be made prior to data transfer.

With asynchronous communication, eight pins are used in a DB25 to transfer data and control the modem, as listed in Table 4-2. The table shows the pins and their definitions.

Table 4-2   *Standard EIA/TIA-232 Definitions and Codes*

Pin Number	Designation	Definition	Description Controlled by	Controlled by
2	TD	Transmits data	DTE-to-DCE data transfer	DTE
3	RD	Receives data	DCE-to-DTE data transfer	DCE
4	RTS	Request to send	DTE signal buffer available	DTE
5	CTS	Clear to send	DCE signal buffer available	DCE
6	DSR	Data set ready	DCE is ready	DCE

Table 4-2 *Standard EIA/TIA-232 Definitions and Codes (Continued)*

Pin Number	Designation	Definition	Description Controlled by	Controlled by
7	GRD	Signal ground	To ensure that both sides use the same ground potential	—
8	CD	Carrier detect	DCE senses carrier	—
20	DTR	Data terminal ready	DTE is ready	—

Pins 2, 3, and 7 enable data transfer, pins 4 and 5 enable flow control of data, and pins 6, 8, and 20 provide modem control.

Data Transfer

The pins used for data transfer are pins 2, 3, and 7. The DTE device raises the voltage on the RTS when it has buffer space available to receive from the DCE device. Once a call is established and the DTE device sees the DCE raise the voltage on the CTS, the DTE device transmits data on pin 2. Conversely, the DTE device raises the voltage on the RTS when it has buffer space available to receive from the DCE device. The GRD pin is needed to discern whether the voltage is positive or negative.

Data Flow Control

The RTS pin and the CTS pin control the flow of information. The DTE device controls the RTS pin (as shown in Table 4-2), which, when seen by the DCE, alerts the DCE that it can receive data. It might help you to think of the RTS as the ready-to-receive pin. The DCE device controls the CTS pin, which in turn signals the DTE that it has buffer available. These definitions are critical to a CCNP or CCDP candidate.

Modem Control

DSR and DTR are signal pins used to control how the modem operates. The DSR pin is raised when the modem is powered on. This raising lets the DTE device know that the modem is ready for use. The DTR pin is raised when the DTE device is powered and ready to receive information from the DCE.

In most cases, when the DTE device is powered on, the DTR pin is raised; however, there are cases in which the DTR pin is raised only if a software package begins to run. This might sound like a minor point, but when you are troubleshooting, it is important to know whether the DTE has signaled the modem that it is ready. In fact, just because the PC is on does not necessarily mean that DTR is asserted, and whether your DTE device raises the DTR when powering up or when you turn on your communication software, DTR is needed for a two-way conversation between the DCE and DTE device.

To be clear, just because a PC (the DTR) is turned on, that does *not* necessarily mean that the modem (the true DTR) is ready. On some laptop computers, the DTR is only raised when the communication software is invoked.

Note that the CD (sometimes referred to as DCD) pin is also a signal pin. When two DCE devices establish a connection, the CD pin is asserted to indicate that a carrier signal has been established between the DCE devices. Note also that because two devices constitute the DTE (PC) and DCE (modem) connection, either must be allowed to terminate the connection.

DTE Call Termination

When the DTE is ready to terminate the connection because the user has completed the call and signaled the PC to go back on-hook, the DTR is dropped. For this to happen, the modem must be configured to interpret the loss of the DTR as the end of a conversation. When the DTE drops the DTR, the modem is alerted that the carrier is no longer needed.

This configuration is done when the modem is first installed. This can be manually done for each call, or it can be scripted in a chat script that is sent to the modem each time a call is terminated. Each time a call is terminated, the router resets (rescripts) the modem. This low-level configuration is done on the modem to prepare the modem for reuse. In many cases, accepting the default configuration for a modem allows it to function properly.

Even accepting the default configuration provides a "configuration" to the modem. The details of each modem parameter are discussed in the section, "Configuration of the Attached Modem," later in this chapter.

DCE Call Termination

If a far-end modem drops the CD because the remote DTE has ended the transmission, the near-end modem must signal the near-end DTE that the transmission has been terminated. The modem must be programmed to understand and signal this termination. In other words, the modem must be told how to handle the loss of carrier detection. By default, most modems understand that this signal loss is an indication that the call is to be terminated. However, it is a configuration parameter that the modem must understand.

Modem Configuration Using Reverse Telnet

To configure a modem, a router must be set up to talk to it. Cisco refers to this as a *reverse Telnet connection*. A host that is connected to a router can Telnet to a Cisco reserved port address on the router and establish an 8-N-1 connection to a specific asynchronous port. An *8-N-1* connection declares the physical signaling characteristics for a line.

Table 4-3 shows reserved port addresses. The router must have a valid IP address on an interface and an asynchronous port. To establish a connection to the modem connected to the asynchronous port, you can Telnet to any valid IP address on the router and declare the Cisco reserved port number for the asynchronous interface. However, you can do this only from the router console or a remote device that has Telnet access to the router.

Table 4-3 *Reverse Telnet Cisco Reserved Port Numbers*

Connection Service	Reserved Port Range for Individual Ports	Reserved Port Range for Rotary Groups
Telnet (character mode)	2000–2xxx	3000–3xxx
TCP (line mode)	4000–4xxx	5000–5xxx
Telnet (binary mode)	6000–6xxx	7000–7xxx
Xremote	9000–9xxx	10000–10xxx

Most modem consoles operate using eight data bits, zero parity bits, and one stop bit. In addition, the use of reverse Telnet enables the administrator to configure locally attached devices. For example, suppose you want to set up an 8-N-1 connection to the first asynchronous interface on a router, which has the 123.123.123.123 address assigned to its E0 port. To connect in character mode using Telnet, you would issue the following command:

```
telnet 123.123.123.123 2001
```

where **123.123.123.123** is the router's E0 port and **2001** is the Cisco reserved port number for the first asynchronous port on the router. Table 4-3 shows the Cisco reserved port numbers for all port ranges.

The use of the rotary group reserved port number connects to the first available port that is in the designated rotary group. If a specific individual port is desired, the numbers from the second column of Table 4-3 are used.

You can establish a session with an attached modem using reverse Telnet and the standard AT command set (listed later in Table 4-4) to set the modem configuration. This, however, is the hard way because once a modem connection has been established using reverse Telnet, you must disconnect from the line for the modem to be usable again. In addition, to exit the connection, you would have to press Ctrl-Shift-6 and then x to suspend the session, and then issue the **disconnect** command from the router prompt. It is important to remember this simple sequence because the modem does not understand the **exit** command, as does a router.

Router Line Numbering

The line numbers on a router are obtained in a methodical manner. The console port is line 0. Each asynchronous (TTY) port is then numbered 1 through the number of TTY ports on the router. The auxiliary port is given the line number LAST TTY + 1, and the vty ports are numbered starting at LAST TTY + 2.

Example 4-1 has the **show line** output for a Cisco 2511 router, which has eight asynchronous ports available. Notice that the AUX port is labeled in line 17 and the vty ports are labeled in lines 18–22.

Example 4-1   **show line** *Output for Cisco 2511 Router*

```
2511Router>show line
  Tty Typ     Tx/Rx     A Modem  Roty AccO AccI   Uses   Noise   Overruns   Int
*   0 CTY                -    -    -    -    -       0      1      0/0        -
*   1 TTY    9600/9600   -    -    -    -    -       7     23      0/0        -
*   2 TTY    9600/9600   -    -    -    -    -       5      1      0/0        -
*   3 TTY    9600/9600   -    -    -    -    -      14     63      0/0        -
*   4 TTY    9600/9600   -    -    -    -    -       4      3      0/0        -
*   5 TTY    9600/9600   -    -    -    -    -      16      6      0/0        -
*   6 TTY    9600/9600   -    -    -    -    -      12      7      0/0        -
    7 TTY    9600/9600   -    -    -    -    -       3      1      0/0        -
    8 TTY    9600/9600   -    -    -    -    -       0      9      0/0        -
*   9 TTY    9600/9600   -    -    -    -    -      12      0      0/0        -
*  10 TTY    9600/9600   -    -    -    -    -      16      0      0/0        -
*  11 TTY    9600/9600   -    -    -    -    -      25      2      0/0        -
*  12 TTY    9600/9600   -    -    -    -    -       5      0      0/0        -
*  13 TTY    9600/9600   -    -    -    -    -       0      0      0/0        -
   14 TTY    9600/9600   -    -    -    -    -       0      2      0/0        -
   15 TTY    9600/9600   -    -    -    -    -       0      0      0/0        -
   16 TTY    9600/9600   -    -    -    -    -       3      0      0/0        -
   17 AUX    9600/9600   -    -    -    -    -       0      0      0/0        -
   18 VTY                -    -    -    -    -       0      0      0/0        -
   19 VTY                -    -    -    -    -       0      0      0/0        -
   20 VTY                -    -    -    -    -       0      0      0/0        -
   21 VTY                -    -    -    -    -       0      0      0/0        -
   22 VTY                -    -    -    -    -       0      0      0/0        -
```

The numbering scheme for interfaces was expanded for the 3600 Series routers. The console is still line 0 and the vty ports are similarly counted after the TTYs. However, Cisco chose to use reserved numbering for the available slots. Thus, slot 0 has reserved lines 1–32, slot 1 has reserved lines 33–64, slot 2 has reserved lines 65–97, and so on. Each slot is given a range of 32 line numbers, whether they are used or not.

Figure 4-1 shows the rear of the chassis for a 3620 and 3640 router and the line numbers associated with each slot.

Figure 4-1 *Line Numbers for 3620 and 3640 Routers*

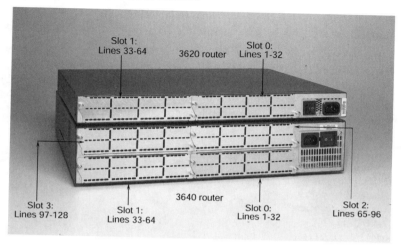

The line-numbering scheme is important when configuring a router. In the case of the 3600 and 2600 routers with the new modular interfaces, the line numbers are based on the slot that the feature card is in. For illustration, consider the output in Example 4-2, which is from a 3640 Series router with a modem card in slot 2. Notice that the line numbers for the internal modems are 65–70 because only one MICA card is installed in the slot.

Example 4-2 **show line** *Output from a 3640 Series Router with a Modem Card in Slot 2*

```
router#show line
  Tty Typ     Tx/Rx     A Modem  Roty AccO AccI   Uses  Noise  Overruns   Int
*   0 CTY                 -   -     -    -    -      0      0      0/0       -
I  65 TTY               - inout    -    -    -      0      0      0/0       -
I  66 TTY               - inout    -    -    -      0      0      0/0       -
I  67 TTY               - inout    -    -    -      0      0      0/0       -
I  68 TTY               - inout    -    -    -      0      0      0/0       -
I  69 TTY               - inout    -    -    -      0      0      0/0       -
I  70 TTY               - inout    -    -    -      0      0      0/0       -
I  97 TTY 115200/115200 - inout    -    -    -      0      0      0/0      Se3/0
*129 AUX   9600/9600     -   .     -    -    -      0      0      0/0       -
 130 VTY                 -   .     -    -    -      0      0      0/0       -
 131 VTY                 -   .     -    -    -      0      0      0/0       -
 132 VTY                 -   .     -    -    -      0      0      0/0       -
 133 VTY                 -   .     -    -    -      0      0      0/0       -
 134 VTY                 -   .     -    -    -      0      0      0/0       -
The following lines are not in asynchronous mode or are without hardware support: 164, 7196,
and 98128.
```

To properly configure a router, you must know the association between the line and interface numbers. The AUX port on the modular routers is the last line number, which would be the number of slots multiplied by 32, plus 1. In the case of the 3640 router output shown in Example 4-2, the AUX port number is 129, and the vty ports are 130–134 by default.

In Example 4-3, the configuration for a 3640 router has physical characteristics configured on line 97 for the asynchronous interface in slot 3/0. The remaining Cisco IOS commands are discussed in detail later in this chapter, but are presented here for completeness.

Example 4-3 *3640 Router Configuration*

```
interface Serial3/0
 physical-layer async
 ip unnumbered Ethernet0/0
 no ip directed-broadcast
 encapsulation ppp
 async mode interactive
 peer default ip address pool TESTPOOL
 no cdp enable
 ppp authentication chap
!
line 97
 password cisco
 autoselect during-login
 autoselect ppp
 login local
 modem InOut
 transport input all
 stopbits 1
 speed 115200
 flowcontrol hardware
line aux 0
line vty 0 4
 login local
!
```

Basic Asynchronous Configuration

To configure the modem (the DCE) from the router (the DTE), you must set up the logical and physical parameters for the connection. The logical parameters include the protocol addressing, the authentication method, and the encapsulation, all of which are configured on the asynchronous interface. The physical configuration is done on the line. The physical parameters include the flow control, the DTE-DCE speed, and the login request. It is important for the successful CCNP or CCDP candidate to be aware of the command mode needed for configuration.

The configuration in Example 4-4 demonstrates which commands are used on each line or interface. The highlighted lines are the most critical; however, as with most configurations, any one command can make or break a connection. As you can see under the line configuration, each command is highlighted. A CCNP or CCDP candidate should commit the line commands to memory, not just for the test, but for success in the field.

Example 4-4 *Configuration for a Serial Interface in Asynchronous Mode*

```
interface Serial3/0     !logical parameters go on the interface
    physical-layer async
    ip unnumbered Ethernet0/0
    no ip directed-broadcast
    encapsulation ppp %%%highlight this
    async mode interactive
    peer default ip address pool remaddpool
    no cdp enable
    ppp authentication chap
line 97    !physical parameters go on the line
    autoselect during-login
    autoselect ppp
    login
    modem InOut
    modem autoconfigure type usr_sportster
    transport input all
    stopbits 1
    rxspeed 115200
```

Example 4-4 shows the distinction between the physical and logical parameters and where they are defined in the router configuration file.

Three types of router interfaces can be configured for serial communication:

- Asynchronous interfaces
- Asynchronous/synchronous (A/S) interfaces
- Synchronous interfaces

Router interfaces that are synchronous only cannot be used for modem or asynchronous communication. On the router models with A/S ports (ports that can be used in the synchronous or asynchronous mode), the serial ports default to synchronous, and the interface must be declared for asynchronous usage using the **physical-layer async** command.

The configuration in Example 4-4 is for the first (port 0) synchronous/asynchronous interface on a four-port A/S card in the third slot of a 3600 router. The **physical-layer async** command is needed because this device has A/S ports. Hence, the **physical-layer async** command is entered at the

router(config-if)# prompt for Serial 3/0. On the other hand, in the case of those routers that have ports designated as asynchronous only, the **physical-layer async** command is not used.

Logical Configurations on the Router

Logical configurations can be done on the interface of the router. These include the network layer addressing, the encapsulation method, the authentication, and so on. The configuration in Example 4-5 is for a serial interface that is used to receive an inbound call.

Example 4-5   *Router Configuration for Serial Interface Receiving Inbound Calls*

```
interface Serial2
  physical-layer async
  ip unnumbered Ethernet0
  ip tcp header-compression passive
  encapsulation ppp
  bandwidth 38
  async mode interactive
  peer default ip address pool remaddpool
  no cdp enable
  ppp authentication chap
```

In Example 4-5, note the following:

■ The **physical-layer async** command places the serial 2 interface in asynchronous mode. Once this command is issued, the router treats the interface as an asynchronous port. This can be done on *only* those interfaces that are defined as A/S.

■ The **ip unnumbered Ethernet0** command declares that the interface assume the address of the E0 interface. This enables the saving of IP addresses but makes the physical asynch interface non-SNMP manageable. This command could be replaced with the desired IP address of the interface (refer to the discussion in this section that covers **ip address pool**).

Note that it is quite common for a large number of asynchronous interfaces to be unnumbered to a common physical interface and to use an address pool to assign the network layer addresses to the dialup users.

■ The **ip tcp header-compression passive** command states that if the other DCE device sends packets with header compression, the interface understands and sends in kind but does not initiate the compression.

■ The **encapsulation ppp** command declares the encapsulation method for the interface.

■ The **bandwidth 38** command tells the routing protocol and the router (for statistics) the speed of the line. This command has no effect on the actual negotiated speed of the modem or the speed at which the DTE talks to the modem.

- The **async mode interactive** command enables, once a connection is made, the dialup user to access the EXEC prompt.

- The **peer default ip address pool remaddpool** command specifies that the IP address assigned to the dialup user be from the address grouping or pool defined by the label **remaddpool**. The syntax for the pool definition, defined in global configuration mode, is as follows:

  `ip local pool remaddpool` *low-ip-pool-address high-ip-pool-address*

- A unique address from the pool of addresses is given to a dialup user for the duration of the session. The address is returned to the pool when the dialup user disconnects the session. In this fashion, it is not necessary to associate an IP address with each asynchronous interface. Each asynchronous interface uses an IP address that is part of the same subnet that the interface is "unnumbered" to. For more information and examples on the use of address pools and unnumbering, refer to Chapter 6, "PPP Link Control Protocol Options." The **no cdp enable** command turns off the Cisco Discovery Protocol for the interface. By default, this protocol is on, and because the interface is likely connected to a dialup user who does not understand CDP, the bandwidth it would use is saved.

- The **ppp authentication chap** command specifies that the Challenge Handshake Authentication Protocol (CHAP) be used on this link. Failure of the client to honor CHAP results in the link not being established.

Physical Considerations on the Router

Physical characteristics are configured in line mode. These include the speed, the direction of the call, modem setup, and so on. Example 4-6 shows a configuration used to connect to a USR Sportster modem on physical line 2.

Example 4-6 *Router Configuration Connecting USR Sportster Modem on Physical Line 2*

```
line 2
    autoselect during-login
    autoselect ppp
    login local
    modem InOut
    modem autoconfigure type usr_sportster
    transport input all
    stopbits 1
    rxspeed 115200
    txspeed 115200
    flowcontrol hardware
```

For Example 4-6, consider the following:

- The **login local** command is the same for this line as it is for the console and AUX ports.

- The **login local** command tells the physical line to request a username/password pair when a connection is made and to look locally on the router for a matching **username** *xxxx* **password** *yyyy* pair that has been configured in global mode (*xxxx* and *yyyy* represent a freely chosen username and password combination).

- The **autoselect during-login** and **autoselect ppp** commands automatically start the PPP protocol and issue a carriage return so that the user is prompted for the login. This feature became available in Cisco IOS Software Release 11.0. Prior to this "during-login" feature, the dialup user was required to issue an exec command or press the Enter key to start the session.

- The **modem InOut** command enables both incoming and outgoing calls. The alternative to this command is the default **no modem inout** command, which yields no control over the modem.

- The **modem autoconfigure type usr_sportster** command uses the **modemcap database usr_sportster** entry to initialize the modem. This initialization is discussed later in the chapter.

- The **transport input all** command enables the processing of any protocols on the line. This command defines which protocols to use to connect to a line. The default command prior to 11.1 was **all**; the default with 11.1 is **none**.

- In the router configuration, the number of **stopbits** must be the same for both communicating DCE devices. Remember that the physical layer parameters must match for the physical layer to be established. Failure to do so prevents the upper layers from beginning negotiation.

- In Example 4-6, **rxspeed** and **txspeed** are shown as separate commands. The **speed** command, however, sets both transmit and receive speeds and locks the speed between the modem and the DTE device. Failure to lock or control the DTE-to-DCE speed allows the speed of local communication to vary with the line speed negotiated between the DCE devices. This limits the capability of the DTE-to-DCE flow control.

- The **flowcontrol hardware** command specifies that the RTS and CTS be honored for flow control.

Example 4-6 provides the basic configuration for an asynchronous line. Once the DTE device has been configured, you must set the DCE device to communicate with the modem by using the AT commands.

Configuration of the Attached Modem

In the early modem days, the Hayes command set was the de facto standard; however, there was never a ratified industry command set. Today, rather than converging to a general standard, the modem industry has actually diverged. Nonetheless, the AT commands documented in Table 4-4 are considered "standard" and should work on most modems.

Table 4-4   *Standard AT Commands*

Command	Result
AT&F	Loads factory default settings
ATS0=n	Auto answers
AT&C1	CD reflects the line state
AT&D2	Hangs up on low DTR
ATE0	Turns off local echo
ATM0	Turns off the speaker

A CCNP or CCDP candidate should be familiar with these commands both to pass the CCNP test and to assist them in troubleshooting a live problem. There are other standard commands, but as was stated earlier, "standard" is a bit of a misnomer. For many modems on the market today, commands not in this table are used to configure the modem and fall into the category of not standard.

The correct initialization string must be sent to the modem for proper operation. You can do this by using a chat script or the **modem autoconfigure** (without the **type** argument) command. The former method is the most common.

Modem Autoconfiguration and the Modem Capabilities Database

Modem autoconfiguration is a Cisco IOS software feature that enables the router to issue the modem configuration commands, which frees the administrator from creating and maintaining scripts for each modem. The general syntax for modem autoconfiguration is as follows:

```
modem autoconfigure [discovery | type modemcap-entry-name]
```

The two command options for the **modem autoconfigure** command are as follows:

- **type**—This option configures modems without using modem commands, or so it is implied. The **type** argument declares the modem type that is defined in the modem capabilities database so that the administrator does not have to create the modem commands.

- **discovery**—Autodiscover modem also uses the modem capabilities database, but in the case of **discover**, it tries each modem type in the database as it looks for the proper response to its query.

As you can see, the **modem autoconfigure** command relies on the modem capabilities database, also known as the *modemcap* database. The modemcap database has a listing of modems and a generic initialization string for the modem type. The discovery of a modem using the **autoconfigure** feature uses the initialization strings from each modem in the modemcap database. If the modem is not in the database, it fails, and the administrator has to manually add the modem to the database.

Use of the Discovery Feature

The use of the discovery feature is not recommended because of the overhead on the router. Each time the line is reset, the modem is rediscovered. However, the discovery feature can be used to initially learn the modem type if you are not geographically near the router and cannot gather the information any other way. After discovery has taken place, you should use the **type** option to specify the entry in the modemcap database to use.

To discover a modem, the syntax would be as follows:

```
modem autoconfigure discovery
```

Again, once the modem type is determined, the final configuration for the router interface should be as follows:

```
modem autoconfigure type entry_name_from_modemcap
```

This configuration eliminates unnecessary overhead on the router.

Use the **show modemcap** command to see the entries in the modemcap database. Example 4-7 demonstrates the output from the **show modemcap** command.

Example 4-7   **show modemcap** *Command Output Reveals Modemcap Database Entries*

```
BCRANrouter#show modemcap

default
codex_3260
usr_courier
usr_sportster
hayes_optima
global_village
viva
telebit_t3000
microcom_hdms
microcom_server
nec_v34
nec_v110
nec_piafs
cisco_v110
mica
```

To view the detailed settings for a particular entry in the modemcap database, the entry name is added as an argument to the **show modemcap** command. The database has most models of modems. If your entry is not in the database, it can be added by editing the database.

Editing the database requires creating your own entry name and specifying the AT commands for the initialization string. This must be done for any modem that is not in the database. This might sound time-consuming or tedious, but it has to be done only once. The added information to the database is stored in NVRAM as part of the router configuration and can be copied to other routers that have the same modems.

Common practice dictates that multiple modem types not be used at a single RAS facility. Instead, you should use a single modem type and maintain spares of that particular type so that constant manipulation of the modemcap database is not necessary.

Consider an example of how a modem is added to the database. If an attached modem is a Viva plus modem that is not listed in the database, but another Viva modem is in the database, you could create a new entry and name it whatever you want. The AT commands that are unique to the Viva plus modem would be added to the local configuration in NVRAM, and the additional AT commands that are the same for all Viva modems would be obtained from the database.

To add the modem, you would use the following global commands:

```
modemcap edit viva_plus speed &B1
modemcap edit viva_plus autoanswer s0=2
modemcap edit viva_plus template viva
```

These commands use the initialization string from the entry **viva** and enable you to alter the newly created **viva_plus**. All changes and additions to the modemcap database are stored in the configuration file for the router. Because of this, Cisco can add to the modemcap database at any release, because the local NVRAM changes override the modemcap database.

To summarize, after you have bought some modems that you feel are the best for your application, those particular modems may, or may not, be defined in the modemcap database. If the modem is defined in the modemcap database, then you can simply use the **type** option to the **modem autoconfigure** command. If the modem is not defined in the database, then you must add it. After you add it, all future modem connections on this router can simply point to the added entry.

Chat Scripts to Control Modem Connections

Chat scripts enable you to talk to or through a modem to a remote system using whatever character strings or syntax is needed. A chat script takes the form

```
Expect-string - send-string - expect-string - send-string
```

where the *expect* strings are character strings sent from or through the modem to the DTE device, and the *send* strings are character strings sent from the DTE device to or through the modem.

Reasons for Using a Chat Script

As a CCNP or CCDP candidate, you should be aware that chat scripts are used for the following goals:

- **Initialization**—To initialize the modem
- **Dial string**—To provide the modem with a dial string
- **Logon**—To log in to a remote system
- **Command execution**—To execute a set of commands on a remote system

Reasons for a Chat Script Starting

Chat scripts can be manually started on a line using the **start-chap** command; they can also be configured to start for the following events:

- **Line activation**—CD trigger (incoming traffic)
- **Line connection**—DTR trigger (outgoing traffic)
- **Line reset**—Asynchronous line reset
- **Startup of an active call**—Access server trigger
- **Dialer startup**—From a dial-on-demand trigger

Using a Chat Script

The primary use of a chat script is to provide the dial number for the connection. The following line shows an example of this chat script:

```
Router(config)#chat-script REMDEVICE ABORT ERROR ABORT BUSY "" "ATZ" OK "ATDT \T"
TIMEOUT 30 CONNECT \c
```

You should take care with the character case that you use in this command. **ABORT ERROR** and **ABORT BUSY** cause the modem to abort if it sees **ERROR** or **BUSY**. Both arguments might be more easily understood if read as "abort if you see ERROR" and "abort if you see BUSY," respectively. If **error** or **abort** are entered in lowercase, the modem never sees these conditions because its search is case-sensitive. The **\T** inserts the called number from the **dial string** or **map** command into the chat script. A **\t** causes the script to look for a "table character"; hence, case is important here as well.

NOTE   Detailed information on the **dial string** and **map** commands is provided in Chapter 6.

The **REMDEVICE** chat script has been configured to drop the connection if the modem declares a busy or error condition. If no busy or error condition is declared, the router does not wait for anything except string = "". The router then issues the **ATZ**, or modem reset, command, using a send string. The router waits for the modem to respond OK, which is the normal modem response to **ATZ**. The router then sends the **ATDT** command and replaces the **\T** with the phone number to make the call. Last, the **TIMEOUT 30** declares that the call is considered "not answered" if no carrier is obtained in 30 seconds. Once the connection is made, the chat script sends a **c**, which is a carriage return.

Provided that the router, the modem, and the phone number are correct, the physical layer should now be established. Congratulations! You can now move on to the upper-layer protocols, such as PPP (see Chapter 5, "Configuring PPP and Controlling Network Access") and advanced uses (see Chapter 6).

Foundation Summary

The Foundation Summary is a collection of tables and figures that provides a convenient review of many key concepts in this chapter. If you are already comfortable with the topics in this chapter, this summary can help you recall a few details. If you just read this chapter, this review should help solidify some key facts. If you are doing your final preparation before the exam, these tables and figures are a convenient way to review the day before the exam.

Table 4-5 *Standard EIA/TIA-232 Definitions and Codes*

Pin Number	Designation	Definition	Description	Controlled by
2	TD	Transmits data	DTE-to-DCE data transfer	DTE
3	RD	Receives data	DCE-to-DTE data transfer	DCE
4	RTS	Request to send	DTE signal buffer available	DTE
5	CTS	Clear to send	DCE signal buffer available	DCE
6	DSR	Data set ready	DCE is ready	DCE
7	GRD	Signal ground	To ensure that both sides use the same ground potential	—
8	CD	Carrier detect	DCE senses carrier	—
20	DTR	Data terminal ready	DTE is ready	—

Table 4-6 *Cisco Reserved Port Numbers Used with Reverse Telnet*

Connection Service	Reserved Port Range for Individual Ports	Reserved Port Range for Rotary Groups
Telnet (character mode)	2000–2xxx	3000–3xxx
TCP (line mode)	4000–4xxx	5000–5xxx
Telnet (binary mode)	6000–6xxx	7000–7xxx
Xremote	9000–9xxx	10000–10xxx

Figure 4-2 *3600 Line Numbers*

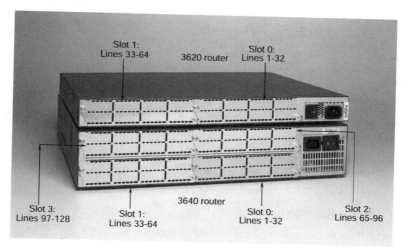

Table 4-7 **modem autoconfigure** *Commands*

Command	What It Does
modem autoconfigure discovery	Discovers the modem
modem autoconfigure type *entry_name_from_modemcap*	Creates the final configuration for the router interface, which eliminates unnecessary overhead on the router
show modemcap	Displays the entries in the modemcap database

Table 4-8 *Standard AT Commands*

Command	Result
AT&F	Loads factory default settings
ATS0=n	Auto answers
AT&C1	CD reflects the line state
AT&D2	Hangs up on low DTR
ATE0	Turns off local echo
ATM0	Turns off the speaker

The following are the reasons for using a chat script:

- **Initialization**—To initialize the modem
- **Dial string**—To provide the modem with a dial string
- **Logon**—To log in to a remote system
- **Command execution**—To execute a set of commands on a remote system

Chat scripts can be manually started on a line using the **start-chap** command; they can also be configured to start for the following events:

- **Line activation**—CD trigger (incoming traffic)
- **Line connection**—DTR trigger (outgoing traffic)
- **Line reset**—Asynchronous line reset
- **Startup of an active call**—Access server trigger
- **Dialer startup**—From a dial-on-demand trigger

Q&A

The questions and scenarios in this book are more difficult than what you should experience on the actual exam. The questions do not attempt to cover more breadth or depth than the exam, but they are designed to make sure that you know the answer. Rather than enabling you to derive the answer from clues hidden inside the question, the questions challenge your understanding and recall of the subject. Hopefully, mastering these questions will help you limit the number of exam questions on which you narrow your choices to two options and then guess.

The answers to these questions can be found in Appendix A.

1. If the user wants to terminate a call, what pin does the DTE device drop to signal the modem?

2. What must be done to terminate a reverse Telnet session with an attached modem?

3. Which interface is line 97 on a 3640 Series router?

4. When flow control is enabled, which pins are used?

5. What is the AT command to return a router to its factory default settings?

6. Which interface type provides clocking for a line?

7. What command lists the transmit and receive speeds for the asynchronous ports on the router?

8. On which pins does the DTE device send and receive?

9. What is the command to manually begin a chat script named remcon?

10. With asynchronous communication, how many pins are used in a DB25 to transfer data and control the modem?

11. On what does the DTE device raise the voltage when it has buffer space available to receive from the DCE device?

12. In most cases, when the DTE device is powered on, which pin is raised?

13. With what type of bits do most modem consoles operate?

14. To configure a modem (the DCE) from a router (the DTE), what parameters must you set up for the connection?

Scenarios

There are no scenarios for this particular chapter. The key issues and concepts here are syntax, syntax, and syntax. For further review, you should practice creating a configuration for a router and include all parts necessary for an asynchronous setup. The parts should include:

- Line configuration (physical)
- Interface configuration (logical)
- A new modemcap database entry (your choice)
- An alias to address the modem locally (reverse Telnet)
- A chat script for the connection (no phone number needed!)

This chapter covers the following subjects:

- PPP Background

- PPP Options

CHAPTER 5

Configuring PPP and Controlling Network Access

The CCNP Remote Access Exam requires you to have an-in depth understanding of various WAN technologies. In this chapter, the discussion focuses on Point-to-Point Protocol (PPP). The typical implementation of PPP has traditionally been in dialup and ISDN deployments.

The growing need of corporations to include dialup access to network resources for remote users has created a high demand for point-to-point technologies. Telecommuting personnel require access to network devices and information that looks and feels as it would at the office (albeit at slower access rates). PPP and its options enable this type of access to become a reality. The capabilities of PPP give it the versatility to remain flexible, yet viable, in many situations.

Most remote-access technology implementations center on PPP as the core access method. Dialup clients require a means of accessing the network. Windows 95, Windows 98, Windows 2000, and so forth include dialup networking client software as part of a standard installation. In addition, many companies have created proprietary dialup clients. PPP is the underlying architecture that makes it all work.

PPP creates a single connection over which multiple protocols can be multiplexed. IP, IPX, and AppleTalk, for example, can all traverse PPP links. The actual configuration of the dialup client is not discussed here. The discussions in this chapter center on the access server configuration. Whether the access server is a 3640 router or an AS5x00 router, the configuration is essentially the same.

Authentication plays a vital role in PPP connections. Having dialup lines with no user authentication is a dangerous game to play because of security concerns. Without authentication, anyone can dial in to the network at will. Password Authentication Protocol (PAP) and Challenge Handshake Authentication Protocol (CHAP) authentications provide varying degrees of security.

"Do I Know This Already?" Quiz

The purpose of the "Do I Know This Already?" quiz is to help you decide what parts of this chapter to use. If you already intend to read the entire chapter, you do not necessarily need to answer these questions now.

The eight-question quiz helps you determine how to spend your limited study time. Use the scoresheet in Table 5-1 to record your scores.

Table 5-1   *"Do I Know This Already?" Foundation Topics Section-to-Question Mapping*

Foundation Topics Section	Questions Covered in This Section
PPP Background	1–4
PPP Options	5–8

CAUTION   The goal of self-assessment is to gauge your mastery of the topics in this chapter. If you do not know the answer to a question or are only partially sure of the answer, you should mark this question wrong for purposes of the self-assessment. Giving yourself credit for an answer you correctly guess skews your self-assessment results and might provide you with a false sense of security.

1. Where is PPP typically deployed?

    a. ISDN implementations

    b. LAN segments

    c. Serial connections

    d. Dialup solutions

2. What is the difference between interactive and dedicated asynchronous implementations?

    a. Interactive mode keeps you from seeing a command prompt upon dial-in, whereas dedicated mode allows the command prompt.

    b. Dedicated mode keeps you from seeing a command prompt upon dial-in, whereas interactive mode allows the command prompt.

    c. Interactive mode and dedicated mode are different terms for the same function.

    d. None of the above

3. Which RFC deals with assigned numbers and protocol types?

    a. RFC 1630

    b. RFC 1700

    c. RFC 1483

    d. RFC 1918

4. Which command assigns a preassigned IP address to an async dialup user?

   a. **ip address** {*ip-address*}

   b. **peer default ip address** {*ip-address*}

   c. **set default ip address** {*ip-address*}

   d. **ip address default** {*ip-address*}

5. Which two are supported authentication types with PPP on Cisco routers?

   a. PPTP

   b. PAP

   c. CHAP

   d. SAP

6. Which PPP option is typically used to provide billing consolidation by entities with dialup users?

   a. Compression

   b. Callback

   c. Authentication

   d. Multilink

7. Which PPP option is typically used on low-speed WAN links in an effort to improve throughput?

   a. Compression

   b. Callback

   c. Authentication

   d. Multilink

8. What encryption algorithm is used in CHAP authentication?

   a. 3DES

   b. MD5

   c. IPSec

   d. None

The answers to the "Do I Know This Already?" quiz are found in Appendix A, "Answers to the 'Do I Know This Already?' Quizzes and Q&A Sections." The suggested choices for your next step are as follows:

- **4 or fewer overall score**—Read the entire chapter. This includes the "Foundation Topics," "Foundation Summary," and "Q&A" sections.

- **5–6 overall score**—Begin with the "Foundation Summary" section, and then go to the "Q&A" section.

- **7 or more overall score**—If you want more review of these topics, skip to the "Foundation Summary" section and then go to the "Q&A" section. Otherwise, move to the next chapter.

Foundation Topics

PPP Background

RFC 1661 defines PPP. PPP's basic function is to encapsulate network layer protocol information over point-to-point links. These point-to-point links can be utilized in establishing ISDN connections, dialup connections, and, of course, serial connections. The mechanics of PPP are as follows:

Step 1   To establish communications, each end of the PPP link must first send Link Control Protocol (LCP) packets to configure and test the data link.

Step 2   After the link has been established and optional facilities have been negotiated as needed, PPP must send Network Control Protocol (NCP) packets to choose and configure one or more network layer protocols.

Step 3   Once each of the chosen network layer protocols has been configured, traffic from each network layer protocol can be sent over the link.

Step 4   The link remains configured for communications until explicit LCP or NCP packets close the link down, or until some external event occurs (such as the expiration of an inactivity timer or the intervention of a network administrator). In other words, PPP is a pathway that is opened for multiple protocols simultaneously.

PPP was originally developed with IP in mind; however, it functions independently of the Layer 3 protocol that is traversing the link.

PPP Architecture

As mentioned, PPP encapsulates the network layer protocol(s) that are configured to traverse a PPP-configured link. PPP has a number of capabilities that make it flexible and versatile, including:

- Multiplexing of network layer protocols
- Link configuration
- Link quality testing
- Authentication
- Header compression
- Error detection
- Link parameter negotiation

PPP supports these functions by providing an extensible LCP and a family of NCPs to negotiate optional configuration parameters and facilities. The protocols to be transported, the optional capabilities, and the user authentication type are all communicated during the initial exchange of information when a link between two points is set up.

PPP Components

PPP can operate across any DTE/DCE interface. The only absolute requirement imposed by PPP is the provision of a duplex circuit, either dedicated or switched, that can operate in either an asynchronous or synchronous bit-serial mode, transparent to PPP link layer frames. Other than those imposed by the particular DTE/DCE interface in use, PPP does not impose any restrictions regarding transmission rates.

In just about every type of WAN technology in internetworking, a layered model is shown to provide a point of reference to the OSI model and to illustrate where each particular technology operates. PPP is not much different from other technologies. It too has its own layered model to define form and function. Figure 5-1 depicts the PPP layered model.

Figure 5-1   *PPP Layered Model*

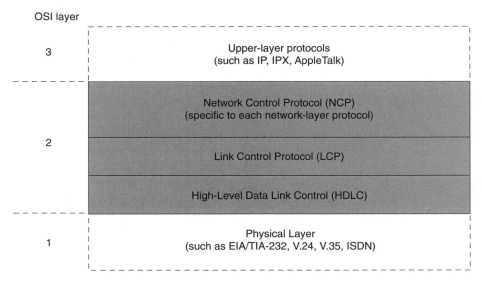

As with most technologies, PPP has its own framing structure. This structure enables the encapsulation of virtually any Layer 3 protocol. Because PPP is, by nature, point-to-point, no mapping of protocol addresses is necessary. Figure 5-2 shows the PPP frame format.

Figure 5-2 *PPP Frame Format*

1	1	1	2	Variable	2 or 4
Flag	Address	Control	Protocol	Data	FCS

The frame structure fields for PPP are as follows:

- **Flag**—A single byte that indicates the beginning or end of a frame. The Flag field consists of the binary sequence 01111110.

- **Address**—A single byte that contains the binary sequence 11111111, the standard broadcast address. PPP does not assign individual station addresses.

- **Control**—A single byte that contains the binary sequence 00000011, which calls for transmission of user data in an unsequenced frame.

- **Protocol**—Two bytes that identify the protocol encapsulated in the information field of the frame. The most up-to-date values of the Protocol field are specified in the most recent Assigned Numbers RFC. At press time, this was RFC 1700. For more information, see www.isi.edu/in-notes/rfc1700.txt.

- **Data**—Zero or more bytes that contain the datagram for the protocol specified in the Protocol field. The end of the Data field is found by locating the closing flag sequence and allowing 2 bytes for the FCS field. The default maximum length of the information field is 1500 bytes. By prior agreement, consenting PPP implementations can use other values for the maximum Data field length.

- **Frame Check Sequence (FCS)**—Normally 16 bits (2 bytes). By prior agreement, consenting PPP implementations can use a 32-bit (4-byte) FCS for improved error detection.

The LCP can negotiate modifications to the standard PPP frame structure. Modified frames, however, are always clearly distinguishable from standard frames. See Chapter 7 for additional information regarding the LCP options available to PPP implementations.

Dedicated and Interactive PPP Sessions

Asynchronous interfaces on an access server can be configured to accept inbound calls from remote users. There are two modes that can be used in this situation, interactive and dedicated. In interactive mode (the default), users who dial in to the network are able to access the user mode prompt. The user must enter the command **ppp connect** to initiate the connection. If access to the router prompt is unacceptable, dedicated mode should be used. Dedicated mode forces the connection into a PPP session once the call setup is complete. The command to implement interactive or dedicated mode for dialup connections is as follows:

```
RouterA(config-if)#async mode [dedicated | interactive]
```

IP addressing on serial interfaces can be done statically or dynamically. If assigned statically, the **ip address** command is used on the interface just as any other interface. To enable dynamic addressing, the **ip unnumbered** command is used:

```
RouterA(config-if)#ip unnumbered interface-type interface-number
```

Asynchronous interfaces can assign predefined IP addresses to dialup clients using the following command:

```
RouterA(config-if)#peer default ip address {ip-address | dhcp | pool poolname}
```

The **dhcp** and **pool** options require global configuration of a pool of addresses using the following command:

```
RouterA(config)#ip local pool poolname start-address end-address
```

The *poolname* must match the *poolname* in the **peer default ip address** command.

It is possible for the dialup clients to assign their own address. To do this, use the **async dynamic address** command at the interface level.

PPP Options

As mentioned, LCP negotiates a number of parameters. This section goes into more detail regarding those parameters.

LCP negotiation enables you to add features to your PPP configuration. Additional options are as follows (more details are in upcoming sections of this chapter):

■   **Authentication**—By using either PAP or CHAP (discussed later) to authenticate callers, this option provides additional security. Implementation of this option requires that individual dialup clients identify themselves and provide a valid username and password.

■   **Callback**—This option can be used to provide call and dialup billing consolidation. A user dials in to the network and disconnects; then, the access server dials the user back and a connection is established.

■   **Compression**—Compression is used to improve throughput on slower-speed links. Care should be taken when implementing compression.

- **Multilink PPP**—This option takes advantage of multiple ISDN B channels. Multilink is a standardized method of bundling B channels to aggregate their bandwidth. Data is transmitted across multiple links and reassembled at the remote end.

> **NOTE**   PPP options such as Callback, Compression, and Multilink PPP will be discussed in Chapter 7.

PPP Authentication

The topic of authentication has been touched on throughout this chapter. At this point, it is finally time to get down to specifics.

PPP authentication offers two options: PAP and CHAP. These two protocols offer differing degrees of protection. Both protocols require the definition of usernames and accompanying passwords. This can be done on the router itself or on a TACACS or RADIUS authentication server. The examples we deal with in this book are those in which the router itself is configured with all usernames and passwords.

Password Authentication Protocol

The Password Authentication Protocol is exactly what its name implies. It is a clear-text exchange of username and password information. When a user dials in, a username request is sent. Once that is entered, a password request is sent.

All communications flow across the wire in clear-text form. No encryption is used with PAP. There is nothing stopping someone with a protocol analyzer from gleaning passwords as they traverse the wire. At that point, simply playing back the packet allows authentication into the network. Although it may not provide the level of protection you may be seeking, it's better than nothing. It serves to keep honest people honest. Figure 5-3 depicts the PAP authentication procedure.

As is clearly shown, PAP is a one-way authentication between the user and the RAS. Example 5-1 shows a basic PPP PAP configuration.

Example 5-1   *PAP Configuration Example*

```
RouterA(config)#interface async 0
RouterA(config-if)#encapsulation ppp
RouterA(config-if)#ppp authentication pap
```

Figure 5-3 *PAP Authentication*

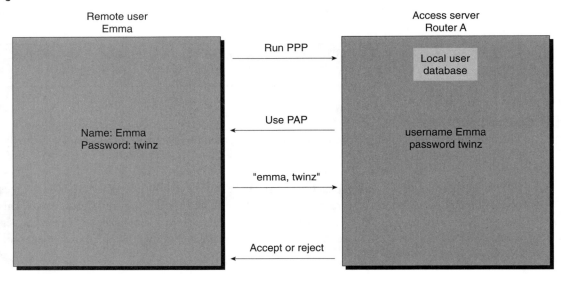

Challenge Handshake Authentication Protocol

CHAP is much more secure than PAP. It implements a two-way encrypted authentication process. Usernames and passwords still must exist on the remote router, but they do not cross the wire as they did with PAP.

When a user dials in, the access server issues a challenge message to the remote user after the PPP link is established. The remote end responds with a one-way hash function. This hash is generally an MD5 entity. If the value of the hash matches what the router expects to see, the authentication is acknowledged. If not, the connection terminates. Figure 5-4 depicts CHAP authentication.

The playback of packets captured by a protocol analyzer is not an issue with CHAP. The use of variable challenge values (that is, unique values) for each authentication attempt ensures that no two challenges are the same. CHAP also repeats a challenge every two minutes for the duration of the connection. If the authentication fails at any time, the connection is terminated. The access server controls the frequency of the challenges. Example 5-2 shows a basic CHAP configuration.

Example 5-2 *CHAP Configuration Example*

```
RouterA(config)#username amanda password twinz
RouterA(config)#interface async 0
RouterA(config-if)#encapsulation ppp
RouterA(config-if)#ppp authentication chap
```

Figure 5-4 *CHAP Authentication*

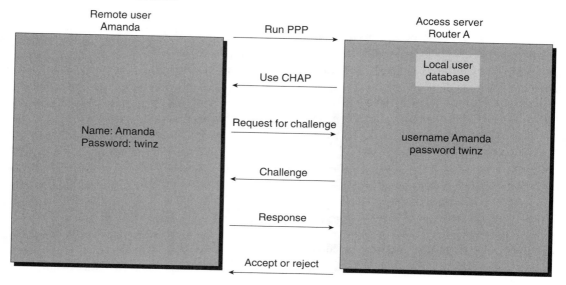

There are specific steps involved in a CHAP negotiation:

Step 1   Make a call. The inbound call arrives at the PPP configured interface. LCP opens the CHAP negotiation and the access server initiates a challenge.

Step 2   Convey the challenge. When the access server sends the challenge, a challenge packet is constructed. The packet consists of a challenge packet type identifier, a sequence number for the challenge, a random number (as random as an algorithm can be), and the authentication name of the *called* party.

The calling party must process the challenge packet as follows:

a. The ID value from the challenge packet is fed into the MD5 hash generator.

b. The random value is fed into the MD5 hash generator.

c. The authentication name of the called party is used to look up the password.

d. The password is fed into the MD5 hash generator.

The resulting value is the one-way MD5 CHAP challenge that is forwarded to the called party in response to the challenge. This value is always 128 bits in length.

Step 3   Answer the challenge. Once the reply is hashed and generated, it can be sent back. The response has a CHAP response packet type identifier, the ID from the challenge packet, the output from the hash, and the authentication name of the *calling* party.

The response packet is then sent to the called party.

Step 4   Verify. The called party processes the response packet as follows:

a. The ID is used to find the original challenge packet.

b. The ID is fed into the MD5 hash generator.

c. The original challenge random-number value is fed into the MD5 hash generator.

d. The authentication name of the calling party is compared to the username/password list in the router or in an authentication server.

e. The password is fed into the MD5 hash generator.

f. The hash value received in the response packet is compared to the result of the hash value just generated.

The authentication succeeds only if the hash value received from the calling party (from Step 2) matches the calculated hash value (from Step 4).

Step 5   Construct the result. If the values of the hash calculations match, the authentication is successful and a CHAP success packet is constructed. It contains a CHAP success message type and the ID from the response packet.

If the authentication fails, a CHAP failure packet is constructed. It contains a CHAP failure message type and the ID from the response packet.

Indication of success or failure is then sent to the calling party.

Foundation Summary

This section is a collection of information that provides a convenient review of many key concepts in this chapter. If you are already comfortable with the topics in this chapter, this summary can help you recall a few details. If you just read this chapter, this review should help solidify some key facts.

PPP was developed specifically for point-to-point connectivity, as its name implies. It has become one of the more versatile protocols in use today. ISDN implementations, serial connections, and other dialup connections now implement PPP.

Configuring PPP is not a difficult process; however, it does have some intricate differences when compared to other WAN technologies.

PPP authentication enables the use of PAP or CHAP. PAP uses clear-text passwords, which could enable packet playback if captured by a protocol analyzer. CHAP implements an MD5 hash challenge and response. Every challenge is unique, as is each response. At periodic intervals (two minutes) during the course of the connection, additional challenges are issued. In the event of a failed authentication, the call is immediately disconnected.

Any protocol can go across a PPP link. The only requirement is that the adjacent interfaces must be configured with the protocols that need to cross the link.

Q&A

The questions and scenarios in this book are more difficult than what you should experience on the actual exam. The questions do not attempt to cover more breadth or depth than the exam, but they are designed to make sure that you know the answer. Rather than enabling you to derive the answer from clues hidden inside the question, the questions challenge your understanding and recall of the subject.

Hopefully, mastering these questions will help you limit the number of exam questions on which you narrow your choices to two options and then guess.

The answers to these questions can be found in Appendix A.

1. List the two major components of the PPP architecture.

2. For what reason is it unnecessary to utilize any sort of protocol map commands on a PPP interface?

3. List the available PPP LCP options.

4. If the authentication methodologies on opposite sides of a single link are not configured, what will happen?

5. What command should be issued on a remote access router to keep dialup users from being able to access the user mode prompt?

6. What encryption algorithm is used in CHAP authentication?

7. What encryption algorithm is used in PAP authentication?

8. What is one potential security danger in using PAP authentication?

9. What happens in the event of a CHAP authentication failure?

10. What protocols can traverse a PPP link, and how are they differentiated?

This chapter covers the following topics that you will need to comprehend to master the BCRAN exam:

- PPP LCP

- PPP Options

- PPP Troubleshooting

CHAPTER 6

PPP Link Control Protocol Options

PPP Link Control Protocol (LCP) options provide granularity in control over network connections. By utilizing these options, the network administrator has the ability to maintain strict control while at the same time offering a wide breadth of functionality to customers and users.

These options were mentioned briefly in Chapter 5, "Configuring PPP and Controlling Network Access," in which PPP Authentication was discussed in detail. In this chapter, the remaining options will be discussed in more detail. Authentication remains an integral and vital component to these options; however, it will not be discussed again here.

PPP creates a single connection over which multiple protocols can be multiplexed. IP, IPX, and AppleTalk, for example, can all traverse PPP links. The actual configuration of the dialup client is not discussed here because the client configuration options are diverse and are not directly relevant to the actual exam.

"Do I Know This Already?" Quiz

The purpose of the "Do I Know This Already?" quiz is to help you decide which parts of this chapter to use. If you already intend to read the entire chapter, you do not necessarily need to answer these questions.

The eight-question quiz, derived from the major sections in the "Foundation Topics" portion of the chapter, helps you to determine how to spend your limited study time. Table 6-1 outlines the major topics discussed in this chapter and the "Do I Know This Already?" quiz questions that correspond to those topics.

Table 6-1   *"Do I Know This Already?" Foundation Topics Section-to-Question Mapping*

Foundation Topics Section	Questions Covered in This Section
PPP LCP	1
PPP Options	2–5
PPP Troubleshooting	6–8

> **CAUTION**   The goal of self-assessment is to gauge your mastery of the topics in this chapter. If you do not know the answer to a question or are only partially sure of the answer, you should mark this question wrong for purposes of the self-assessment. Giving yourself credit for an answer you correctly guess skews your self-assessment results and might provide you with a false sense of security.

1. What is the function of LCP (select 2)?

    a. Troubleshooting the connection

    b. Connection establishement

    c. Dialing the connection

    d. Configuring a connection

2. Which are PPP LCP negotiable options?

    a. Callback

    b. Authentication

    c. Multilink

    d. Compression

    e. All of the above

3. If there is a mismatch in the LCP negotiation, what will happen to the connection?

    a. The call will connect with diminished capabilities.

    b. The call will be disconnected.

    c. The call will be renegotiated with differing capabilities.

    d. The call will connect normally.

4. In PPP Callback implementations, which router is in charge of the authentication challenge and the disconnect of the initial call?

    a. Callback server

    b. Callback client

    c. Snapshot server

    d. Snapshot client

5. Which LCP option is used to add additional bandwidth to a link capacity as needed and available?

    a. Compression

    b. Callback

    c. Authentication

    d. Multilink

6. What command shows the status of individual B channels at any given time?

    a. **show isdn status**

    b. **show dialer**

    c. **show isdn q931**

    d. **debug isdn q921**

7. What command enables the real-time viewing of CHAP communications?

    a. **debug ppp callback**

    b. **debug isdn q931**

    c. **show isdn status**

    d. **debug ppp authentication**

8. What command enables the real-time viewing of dial events?

    a. **debug dialer**

    b. **show dialer**

    c. **show isdn status**

    d. **debug ppp callback**

The answers to the "Do I Know This Already?" quiz are found in Appendix A, "Answers to the 'Do I Know This Already?' Quizzes and Q&A Sections." The suggested choices for your next step are as follows:

- **4 or fewer overall score**—Read the chapter. This includes the "Foundation Topics," the "Foundation Summary," and the "Q&A" sections.

- **5 to six overall score**—Begin with the "Foundation Summary," then go to the "Q&A" section.

- **7 or more overall score**—If you want more review on these topics, skip to the "Foundation Summary," then go to the "Q&A" section. Otherwise, move to the next chapter.

Foundation Topics

PPP LCP

PPP LCP provides a method of establishing, configuring, maintaining, and terminating the point-to-point connection. LCP goes through four distinct phases:

1. A link establishment and configuration negotiation occurs. Before any network-layer datagrams (for example, IP) can be exchanged, LCP first must open the connection and negotiate configuration parameters. This phase is complete when a configuration-acknowledgment frame has been both sent and received.

2. A link-quality determination is made. LCP allows an optional link-quality determination phase following the link-establishment and configuration-negotiation phases. The link is tested to determine whether the quality is sufficient to initialize the network-layer protocols. Transmission of network-layer protocols can be held until this phase is complete.

3. The network-layer protocol configuration negotiation occurs. Network-layer protocols can be configured separately by the appropriate NCP and can be initialized and taken down at any time.

4. Link termination then occurs at the request of the user or a predefined inactivity timer, loss-of-carrier occurrence, or some other physical event.

Three classes of LCP frames are used to accomplish the work of each of the LCP phases:

- Link-establishment frames are used to establish and configure a link.
- Link-termination frames are used to terminate a link.
- Link-maintenance frames are used to manage and debug a link.

PPP Options

As mentioned in Chapter 5, LCP negotiates a number of options. LCP negotiation enables you to add features to your PPP configuration. If the LCP parameters on both sides of the link are mismatched, the call will not connect due to a negotiation failure. The additional options are as follows:

- **Authentication**—By using either PAP or CHAP to authenticate callers, this option provides additional security. Implementation of this option requires that individual dialup clients identify themselves and provide a valid username and password.

- **Callback**—This option can be used to provide call and dialup billing consolidation. A user dials into the network and disconnects; then, the access server dials the user back and a connection is established.
- **Compression**—Compression is used to improve throughput on slower-speed links. Use care when implementing compression.
- **Multilink PPP**—This option takes advantage of multiple ISDN B channels. Multilink is a standardized method of bundling B channels to aggregate their bandwidth. Data is transmitted across multiple links and reassembled at the remote end.

For brevity, only the last three of the preceding options are discussed in detail in this chapter.

PPP Callback

The PPP Callback option was developed to provide connectivity to remote users while controlling access and the cost of calls. Callback enables a router to place a call, and then request that the central router call back. Once the request is made, the call disconnects. The central router then dials the router back, which reverses the charges for the call. This callback feature adds another layer of protection because it only dials back authorized numbers. However, callback is not considered to be a security feature.

PPP Callback routers can play two roles, that of the callback client and that of the callback server. The client router passes authentication (PAP or CHAP) information to the server router, which in turn analyzes dial string and host name information to determine whether callback is authorized.

If authentication is successful, the server disconnects the call and then places the return call. The username of the client router is used as a call reference to associate it with the initial call. For the callback to be successful, the host name must exist in a **dialer-map** statement; otherwise, the router is unable to determine the proper dial string to use in calling back the client. If the return call fails, there are no retries. The client has to reissue the callback request.

For callback to function, both sides of a PPP link must be configured to support it. As mentioned, a server and a client must be specified. The client issues the initial call and the server places return calls. There is a catch, however. If a call is placed requesting callback, the server disconnects the call after authentication. It is possible that another call will come in on the same B channel during the idle time between disconnect and callback. If it is the last available B channel, callback will not occur. It is also possible that on DDR implementations, interesting traffic can force an outbound call on the last available B channel. Again, if this happens, callback does not occur. Example 6-1 shows a PPP Callback configuration for the client.

Example 6-1 *PPP Callback Client Configuration*

```
Client(config)#username Client password cisco
Client(config)#username Server password cisco
Client(config)#dialer-list 1 protocol ip permit
Client(config)#interface bri0
Client(config-if)#ip address 10.1.1.1 255.255.255.0
Client(config-if)#encapsulation ppp
Client(config-if)#dialer map ip 10.1.1.2 name Server 5551212
Client(config-if)#dialer-group 1
Client(config-if)#ppp callback request
Client(config-if)#ppp authentication chap
Client(config-if)#dialer hold-queue timeout 30
```

Example 6-2 shows the PPP Callback configuration for the server.

Example 6-2 *PPP Callback Server Configuration*

```
Server(config)#username Client password cisco
Server(config)#username Server password cisco
Server(config)#dialer-list 1 protocol ip permit
Server(config)#interface bri0
Server(config-if)#ip address 10.1.1.2 255.255.255.0
Server(config-if)#encapsulation ppp
Server(config-if)#dialer callback-secure
Server(config-if)#dialer map ip 10.1.1.1 name Client 6553434
Server(config-if)#dialer-group 1
Server(config-if)#ppp callback accept
Server(config-if)#ppp authentication chap
```

The callback client uses the **ppp callback request** command to request that the callback occur. The server router uses the **ppp callback accept** command as an indication that it should accept callback requests and place a call to the phone number configured for the requesting client (in this case, 5553434).

The **dialer callback-secure** command disconnects calls that are not properly configured for callback. It also forces a disconnect of any unconfigured dial-in users. This command ensures that the initial call is always disconnected at the receiving end and that the return call is made only if the username is configured for callback.

Figure 6-1 illustrates the PPP Callback procedure.

Figure 6-1 *PPP Callback Procedure*

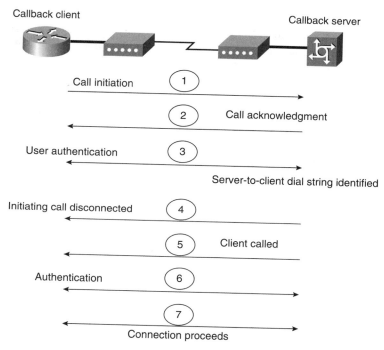

When the client router dials, its hold queue timer begins to count down. No additional calls to the same destination can be made until the time reaches zero. This value is configurable using the **dialer hold-queue** command detailed later in this chapter.

PPP Compression

Compression is covered in Chapter 15, "Managing Network Performance with Queuing and Compression," in more detail. This section is simply an overview of PPP's compression capabilities.

Compression is most useful on slower-speed links. In routing, there comes a point when it is faster to send information outright than it is to compress, send, and decompress it. Compression simply serves to decrease transit time across the WAN.

PPP or Layer 2 compression is determined during LCP negotiation. Therefore, if one side of the call doesn't support it or have it configured, it is not utilized for that call.

Cisco supports a number of compression algorithms. They include STAC, Predictor, MPPC, and TCP header compression. These are discussed in Chapter 15 and are therefore not covered here.

Multilink PPP

Multilink PPP is a specification that enables bandwidth aggregation of multiple B channels into one logical pipe. Its mission is comparable to that of Cisco bandwidth-on-demand (BOD). BOD is enabled when the **dialer load-threshold** command is utilized without the **ppp multilink** command. More specifically, the Multilink PPP feature provides load-balancing functionality over multiple WAN links, while providing multivendor interoperability, packet fragmentation and proper sequencing, and load calculation on both inbound and outbound traffic.

The Cisco implementation of Multilink PPP supports the fragmentation and packet sequencing specifications in RFC 1717. Multilink PPP enables packets to be fragmented and the fragments to be sent at the same time over multiple point-to-point links to the same remote address. See Chapter 7, "Using ISDN and DDR Technologies," for a more detailed discussion of Multilink PPP.

PPP Troubleshooting

Troubleshooting PPP is similar to troubleshooting many other WAN technologies. However, there is a key difference: the implementation of authentication adds another item to the list of things that can go wrong. This section details some of the commands useful in dealing with PPP issues.

The first step in troubleshooting PPP connections is to remove authentication of any kind from the configuration. If the service functions properly at that point, it is time to rethink your authentication configuration.

The **show dialer** command provides useful information about the current status of B channels. Example 6-3 shows sample output.

Example 6-3 show dialer *Command Output*

```
Example 6-3  show dialer Command Output Reveals B Channel Status
RouterA#show dialer
Dial String      Successes    Failures    Last called    Last status
4155551212           1            0        00:00:00       successful
4155551213           1            0        00:00:00       successful
0 incoming call(s) have been screened.
BRI0: B-Channel 1
Idle timer (300 secs), Fast idle timer (20 secs)
Wait for carrier (30 secs), Re-enable (15 secs)
BRI0: B-Channel 2
Idle timer (300 secs), Fast idle timer (20 secs)
Wait for carrier (30 secs), Re-enable (15 secs)
```

The **show dialer** command shows status and connection information regarding each B channel and the number to which the channel is connected. It also shows successful and failed calls. At the bottom of the output, the command breaks out the call settings for idle timeout, fast idle, wait for carrier, and re-enable.

The **debug ppp negotiation** and **debug ppp authentication** commands are useful in enabling the administrator to view the real-time communication between PPP-configured devices. They are mentioned together because they are often implemented simultaneously. Example 6-4 shows screen output from the commands.

Example 6-4 *Combined* **debug ppp negotiation** *and* **debug ppp authentication** *Command Output*

```
ppp: sending CONFREQ, type = 3 (CI_AUTHTYPE), value = C223/5
ppp: sending CONFREQ, type = 5 (CI_MAGICNUMBER), value = 28CEEF99
ppp: received config for type = 3 (AUTHTYPE) value = C223 value = 5 acked
ppp: received config for type = 5 (MAGICNUMBER) value = 1E23F5C acked
PPP BRI0: B-Channel 1: state = ACKSENT fsm_rconfack(C021): rcvd id E4
ppp: config ACK received, type. = 3 (CI_AUTHTYPE), value = C223
ppp: config ACK received, type = 5 (CI_MAGICNUMBER), value = 28CEEF99
BRI0: B-Channel 1: PPP AUTH CHAP input code = 1 id = 82 len = 16
BRI0: B-Channel 1: PPP AUTH CHAP input code = 2 id = 95 len = 28
BRI0: B-Channel 1: PPP AUTH CHAP input code = 4 id = 82 len = 21
BRI0: B-Channel 1: Failed CHAP authentication with remote.
Remote message is: MD compare failed
ppp: sending CONFREQ, type = 3 (CI_AUTHTYPE), value = C223/5
ppp: sending CONFREQ, type = 5 (CI_MAGICNUMBER), value = 28CEEFDB
%LINK-3-UPDOWN: Interface BRI0: B-Channel 1, changed state to down
%LINK-5-CHANGED: Interface BRI0: B-Channel 1, changed state to down
%LINK-3-UPDOWN: Interface BRI0: B-Channel 1, changed state to up
%LINK-5-CHANGED: Interface BRI0: B-Channel 1, changed state to up
ppp: sending CONFREQ, type = 3 (CI_AUTHTYPE), value = C223/5
ppp: sending CONFREQ, type = 5 (CI_MAGICNUMBER), value = 28CEF76C
ppp: received config for type = 3 (AUTHTYPE) value = C223 value = 5 acked
ppp: received conf.ig for type = 5 (MAGICNUMBER) value = 1E24718 acked
PPP BRI0: B-Channel 1: state = ACKSENT fsm_rconfack(C021): rcvd id E6
ppp: config ACK received, type = 3 (CI_AUTHTYPE), value = C223
ppp: config ACK received, type = 5 (CI_MAGICNUMBER), value = 28CEF76C
BRI0: B-Channel 1: PPP AUTH CHAP input code = 1 id = 83 len = 16
BRI0: B-Channel 1: PPP AUTH CHAP input code = 2 id = 96 len = 28
BRI0: B-Channel 1: PPP AUTH CHAP input code = 4 id = 83 len = 21
BRI0: B-Channel 1: Failed CHAP authentication with remote.
Remote message is: MD compare failed
```

As is noted in the output, this is an example of a failed CHAP authentication attempt. Authentication failures represent only one issue that can be encountered with PPP connections. Any mismatch in the features configured for PPP LCP options can cause calls to disconnect.

Foundation Summary

This section is a collection of information that provides a convenient review of many key concepts in this chapter. For those of you who are already comfortable with the topics in this chapter, this summary could help you recall a few details. For those of you who just read this chapter, this review should help solidify some key facts.

The options provided by PPP enable a level of control over network resources previously unknown. LCP negotiation of authentication, callback, compression, and PPP Multilink make this granularity possible.

PPP Callback enables the centralization of call-related costs. A central site provides callback services to remote clients. Client devices dial it and are authenticated. Upon successful authentication, the server disconnects the call and dials the client back.

PPP Compression enables a reduction in the delay associated with transmission of data over lower-speed links. You must exercise care when using compression because memory utilization on the router is greatly increased.

PPP Multilink enables the bundling of multiple bearer channels into one aggregate pipe. Traffic is broken up and sent across the redundant pathways to the remote side where it is reassembled.

Any protocol can go across a PPP link. The only requirement is that the adjacent interfaces must be configured with the protocols that need to cross the link.

Q&A

The questions and scenarios in this book are more difficult than what you will experience on the actual exam. The questions do not attempt to cover more breadth or depth than the exam; however, they are designed to make sure that you know the answer. Rather than enabling you to derive the answer from clues hidden inside the question itself, the questions challenge your understanding and recall of the subject.

Hopefully, mastering these questions will help you to limit the number of exam questions on which you narrow your choices to two options and then guess.

The answers to these questions can be found in Appendix A.

1. List at least three protocols that can traverse a PPP link.

2. What is the function of the PPP LCP?

3. List the three LCP frame types and their functions.

4. List the four PPP LCP options.

5. A PPP Callback router can perform one of two roles. List each and its function.

6. Where is compression most useful?

7. List the Cisco-supported compression algorithms.

8. If PPP Multilink is not enabled and the **dialer load-threshold** command is entered, will multiple channels be utilized if the threshold is reached? Why/Why not?

9. If an ISDN call completes successfully and then suddenly disconnects, what is a likely problem?

10. If IP and AppleTalk are successfully traversing a PPP link while at the same time IPX transmissions fail, what is a possible cause?

PART III: Using ISDN and DDR Technologies to Enhance Remote Connectivity

Chapter 7   Using ISDN and DDR Technologies

Chapter 8   Advanced DDR Options

Chapter 9   Using ISDN Primary Rate Interface (PRI)

This part of the book covers the following BCRAN exam topics:

- Configure an ISDN solution for remote access
- Troubleshoot non-functional remote access systems

This chapter covers the following subjects:

- Basic Rate Interface

- Implementing Basic DDR

- Additional Options Beyond Basic DDR Configuration

CHAPTER 7

Using ISDN and DDR Technologies

The CCNP Remote Access Exam requires you to have an in-depth understanding of various WAN technologies. In this chapter, the discussion focuses on Integrated Services Digital Network (ISDN). ISDN is not a new technology by any means. However, it is still widely implemented around the world. Even with the advent of newer (and faster) broadband technologies, ISDN continues to grow in the workplace, albeit at a slower rate than what has been seen in the recent past.

There are two specific implementation types of ISDN: Basic Rate Interface (BRI) and Primary Rate Interface (PRI). BRI is discussed in this chapter; PRI is discussed in Chapter 9. Although they are based on the same technologies and use the same protocols, their implementations are very different.

"Do I Know This Already?" Quiz

The purpose of the "Do I Know This Already?" quiz is to help you decide what parts of this chapter to use. If you already intend to read the entire chapter, you do not necessarily need to answer these questions now.

The eight-question quiz helps you determine how to spend your limited study time. Table 7-1 outlines the major topics discussed in this chapter and the "Do I Know This Already?" quiz questions that correspond to those topics.

Table 7-1   *"Do I Know This Already?" Foundation Topics Section-to-Question Mapping*

Foundation Topics Section	Questions Covered in This Section
Basic Rate Interface	1–5
Implementing Basic DDR	6–7
Additional Options Beyond Basic DDR Configuration	8

1. Which are the two most common implementations of ISDN?

    a. BRI

    b. PPP

    c. HDLC

    d. PRI

2. What type of information is carried over the D channel?

    a. Signaling

    b. Framing

    c. Data

    d. All the above

3. Which are the specifications that define Layer 2 and Layer 3 of ISDN?

    a. T.430

    b. Q.Sig

    c. Q.931

    d. Q.921

4. When is it necessary to use **dialer in-band** in an ISDN BRI configuration?

    a. When you have a BRI U interface

    b. When you have a BRI S/T interface

    c. When you have an NT1

    d. When you have a non-native ISDN interface

5. Which two state the difference between a router with a BRI S/T interface and one with a BRI U interface?

    a. BRI U interfaces have an integral NT1.

    b. BRI S/T interfaces have an integral NT1.

   c. BRI U interfaces require an external NT1.

   d. BRI S/T interfaces require an external NT1.

6. Which command defines only Telnet as interesting traffic for DDR?

   a. **Dialer-list 1 protocol ip permit**

     Interface BRI 0

     dialer-group 1

   b. **Access-list 100 permit tcp any any eq 23**

     Dialer list 1 protocol ip list 100

     Interface BRI 0

     Dialer-group 1

   c. **Access-list 100 permit tcp any any eq 20**

     Dialer list 1 protocol ip list 100

     Interface BRI 0

     Dialer-group 1

   d. **Access-list 100 permit tcp any any eq 21**

     Dialer list 1 protocol ip list 100

     Interface BRI 0

     Dialer-group 1

7. Which is the most common encapsulation in use on BRI interfaces?

   a. PPP

   b. HDLC

   c. ATM

   d. SDLC

8. An interface that has been configured not to send routing updates is known as what type of interface?

   a. ISDN

   b. BRI

   c. Active

   d. Passive

The answers to the "Do I Know This Already?" quiz are found in Appendix A, "Answers to the 'Do I Know This Already?' Quizzes and Q&A Sections." The suggested choices for your next step are as follows:

- **4 or fewer overall score**—Read the entire chapter. This includes the "Foundation Topics," "Foundation Summary," and "Q&A" sections.

- **5 or 6 overall score**—Begin with the "Foundation Summary" section, and then go to the "Q&A" section.

- **7 or more overall score**—If you want more review on these topics, skip to the "Foundation Summary" section and then go to the "Q&A" section. Otherwise, move to the next chapter.

Foundation Topics

ISDN refers to a set of digital services that has been available to end users for a number of years. It involves the digitizing of the telephone network so that carriers can provide end users with multiple services from a single end-user interface over existing telephone wiring.

ISDN is an effort to standardize subscriber services, user/network interfaces, and network and internetwork capabilities. The goal of standardizing subscriber services is to establish some level of international compatibility.

Compatibility between international carrier networks has long been at the forefront of more than a few heated debates in the global standards committees. Their pain, to a degree, has been good for the technology. This standardization, as it has evolved, has made reality of the myth of multivendor interoperability. By no means is it implied that multivendor interoperability is perfect. It is nowhere near perfect and will never be as long as there are global politics in the technology fields.

The ISDN community would like to ensure that ISDN networks communicate easily with one another. ISDN was developed with the idea that it would be used to transport voice calls, data traffic, and video traffic. The evolution of ISDN as a viable technology moves forward with the needs of those very different traffic types in mind. ISDN applications include high-speed image applications, additional telephone lines in homes to serve the telecommuting industry, high-speed file transfer, and video conferencing. ISDN is also becoming very common in small office/home office (SOHO) environments as many corporations extend their offices into the residential arena.

ISDN is the replacement of traditional analog plain old telephone service (POTS) equipment and wiring schemes with higher-speed digital equipment. The transition from POTS to ISDN changes the way connections at the local loop area are processed.

With POTS, a caller would have to dial up the operator and request a call setup. To accomplish this, the calling party would pick up the telephone and turn a crank to generate current on the line that would light up an LED on the operator console. The operator would answer the setup request and begin setting up the call, making a manual connection between the caller and the called party. The manual connection completed the analog local loop (that is, the connection between the telco switch and customer devices).

From the local loop, the call typically went through the central office (CO). Once digital technologies were born and implemented, the operator was replaced with digital facilities, leaving only the local loop as analog. The transition to ISDN completes the digital link by replacing the local loop with digital equipment.

Basic Rate Interface

ISDN interfaces can be either PRI or BRI. A PRI interface differs from a BRI interface mainly in the number of channels it offers. Again, PRI is discussed in Chapter 9.

ISDN channels are usually divided into two different types—B and D:

- **The bearer channel**—The B channel is the facility that carries the data. Each B channel has a maximum throughput of 64 kbps. B channels can carry encoded pulse code modulation (PCM) digital voice, video, or data. B channels are used mainly for circuit-switched data communications such as High-Level Data Link Control (HDLC) and Point-to-Point Protocol (PPP). However, they can also carry packet-switched data communications.

- **The D channel**—The D channel is used to convey signaling requests to an ISDN switch. In essence, it provides a local loop to the telephone company's central office. The router uses the D channel to dial destination phone numbers. It has a bandwidth of 16 kbps for BRI or 64 kbps for PRI. Although the D channel is used mainly for signaling, it too can also carry packet-switched data (X.25, Frame Relay, and so on).

BRI is the most typical ISDN connection and is a native ISDN interface on a router. The basic rate connection consists of two B channels and a single D channel (2B+D).

Each B channel provides 64,000 bps of bandwidth. The D channel is a 16,000-bps channel that provides signaling and framing for the B-channel payload. There also happens to be an additional 48,000 bps utilized for overhead that is not seen by the consumer. This constitutes the remainder of the channel not utilized by the D channel.

When both B channels are active, the aggregate bandwidth becomes 128,000 bps. However, total utilized bandwidth by an ISDN BRI implementation running 2B+D is 192,000 bps. You can purchase ISDN service with two, one, or zero B channels. Typical deployments use two B channels. Implementations of one B channel provide cost reduction, and zero B-channel implementations enable another technology (such as X.25) to be run across the D channel. In this book, we do not discuss zero B-channel deployments because such implementations are not typical in most internetworks. Figure 7-1 depicts the typical 2B+D model.

Figure 7-1   *BRI 2B+D*

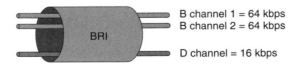

When you have ISDN BRI installed, the telephone company (or telco) places a Category 5 unshielded twisted-pair (UTP) cable at your site. The telco runs the cable to a location within your premises (usually a telephone room). Many times, the base installation charge covers only bringing the line into your premises. In that case, you must decide whether you want to extend the cable into your wiring closet or server room. Usually it is well worth the negligible additional charge to enable the telco installer to extend it to a point that is easy to reach from the router with another cable.

When you extend the cable, the extension begins at a 66 block on your premises. A 66 block is merely the location where all the lines coming into your premises are separated into individual pairs. After you decide where to put the cable and the cable is put in place, the installer attaches an eight-pin modular (RJ-45) jack to the cable and attaches the jack to the wall.

The installer should label the jack with the appropriate service profile identifiers (SPIDs) and a circuit identifier number. This information is necessary if a call for service is needed in the future. In North America, this jack is the *point of demarcation (demarc)*, where responsibility for the line changes hands. The equipment on your side of the point of demarc is known as customer premises equipment (CPE). The jack that the telco installs is a direct interface from the local CO switch to your CPE.

One important piece of equipment in any ISDN BRI installation is a Network Termination 1 (NT1). The NT1 is a device similar to a channel service unit/data service unit (CSU/DSU), which is used in serial connections. The NT1 terminates the local loop.

The NT1 has at least two interfaces: an S/T interface jack and a U interface. The S/T interface is attached to the router's BRI interface. The U interface is attached to the telco jack. Many of Cisco's BRI-capable routers are now available with an integrated NT1. These interfaces are labeled BRI U. If this feature is not available on the chassis, the interface is labeled BRI S/T and an external NT1 is necessary. This native ISDN interface is the router's Terminal Endpoint 1 (TE1) interface.

If you need to install ISDN but your router has no native BRI interface, it is still possible to use ISDN. However, in such cases, you must use a *terminal adapter (TA),* a hardware device that contains the BRI interface that your router is missing. In recent ISDN hype, telecommunications manufacturers marketed terminal adapters as ISDN modems. Terminal adapters are *not* modems. They do not modulate and demodulate signals. What they do is interface your router's universal I/O serial port. The terminal adapter interfaces the NT1 with a native BRI interface.

The non-native (that is, non-BRI) ISDN is known as the Terminal Endpoint 2 (TE2) interface. The interface between the TE2 and the TA is known as the R interface. It is important to note that a non-native ISDN interface (more specifically, a solution that lacks a D channel) requires you to use the **dialer in-band** command to issue signaling requests to the ISDN switch.

Using the **dialer in-band** configuration, each B channel, in effect, loses 8000 bps of available bandwidth for signaling. Therefore, the bandwidth available per B channel becomes 56,000 bps. In some cases, ISDN facilities are available only at 56,000 bps per B channel, regardless of whether the interface is native ISDN. Check with the telco provider for details for a particular installation. Figure 7-2 shows the ISDN reference points.

Figure 7-2 *ISDN Interface Detail*

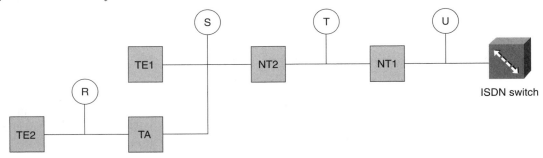

BRI Protocols

As is the standard for implementations in this industry, the ISDN implementation is divided into multiple layers. This division of labor for ISDN is not unlike the OSI model.

ISDN has three layers. Layer 1 deals with signal framing, Layer 2 deals with framing protocols, and Layer 3 deals with D-channel call setup and teardown protocols. Each of these protocols has a specific mission to accomplish. Figure 7-3 depicts the ISDN layer model.

Figure 7-3 *ISDN Protocol Layers*

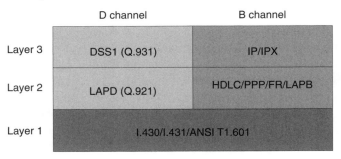

ISDN Layer 1

Layer 1 for ISDN is similar to that of the OSI model. It refers to physical connectivity. This connectivity is obviously an important piece of the picture. Without it, nothing happens.

In order for a router to communicate with an ISDN network, it must be configured for the type of switch to which it is connected. The carrier should provide the type of switch that is to be used. If it was not previously documented, you should call the carrier to obtain the information.

Manufacturers of ISDN CO switches (also known as local exchange equipment) divide the local exchange (LE) into two functions: local termination and exchange termination. The local-termination function deals with the transmission facility and termination of the local loop. The exchange-termination function deals with the switching portion of the local exchange.

The AT&T 5ESS and the Northern Telecom DMS-100 are the two principle ISDN switches used in North America. The recent release of National ISDN-1 software has corrected most incompatibility issues between the AT&T and Northern Telecom switches. Prior to the release of this software, for example, you could not use AT&T ISDN products with a Northern Telecom switch.

AT&T introduced the 5ESS switch in 1982. It can provide up to 100,000 local loops. Approximately 16,000 5ESS switches are in use worldwide, serving close to 40 million lines. In the United States, approximately 85 percent of the BRI lines in service connect to a 5ESS-equipped CO.

By comparison, the Northern Telecom DMS-100 switch family is intended to deliver a wide range of telecommunication services. The DMS-100, introduced in 1978, can terminate up to 100,000 lines. Although AT&T and Northern Telecom have deployed the most ISDN switches, there are other ISDN switch manufacturers.

Table 7-2 lists and describes the various switch types available for BRI implementations.

Table 7-2 *BRI Switch Types*

Switch Type	Description
Basic-1tr6	1TR6 switch type for Germany
Basic-5ess	AT&T 5ESS switch type for the U.S.
Basic-dms100	DMS-100 switch type
Basic-net3	NET3 switch type for the U.K. and Europe
Basic-ni1	National ISDN-1 switch type
Basic-nwnet3	NET3 switch type for Norway
Basic-nznet3	NET3 switch type for New Zealand
Basic-ts013	TS013 switch type for Australia
Ntt	NTT switch type for Japan

(continues)

Table 7-2 *BRI Switch Types (Continued)*

Switch Type	Description
vn2	VN2 switch type for France
vn3	VN3 and VN4 switch types for France
Basic-1tr6	1TR6 switch type for Germany

ISDN Layer 1 deals with not only physical connectivity but also how the bits traverse the wire. To accommodate transmission, a framing method must be established to enable communication between the NT and the TE and between the NT and the LE.

The framing between the NT and TE is defined in the ITU specification I.430. Figure 7-4 depicts the BRI frame.

Figure 7-4 *ISDN BRI Framing Between NT and TE*

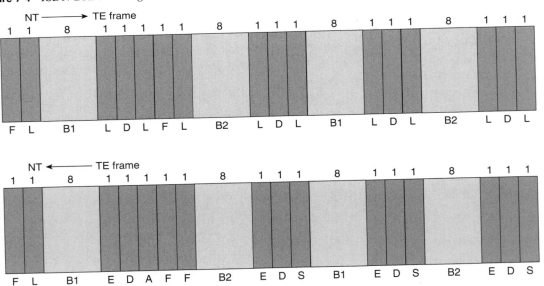

Notice in Figure 7-4 that 16 bits from each B (B1 and B2) channel and 4 bits from the D channel are being time-division multiplexed along with framing and alignment (A) bits. Frame transmission is constant regardless of whether data is actually being sent.

Between the NT and the LE, another framing convention is used, ANSI T1.601. The intricacies of ANSI T1.601 are not discussed at this time because they are not covered on the CCNP Remote Access Exam. For more information on this topic, check out http://www.ansi.org.

ISDN Layer 2

The Layer 2 processes of ISDN are defined in the ITU specifications Q.920 and Q.921. Q.921 defines the actual communication format. Obviously, Layer 2 communication does not take place unless Layer 1 is properly installed and functioning.

Q.921 institutes an addressing scheme similar to many other networking technologies. Just as in LAN implementations, ISDN Layer 2 addressing is meant to provide physical addressing on the network. Because multiple logical devices can exist in a single physical device, it is necessary to correctly identify the source and/or destination process or logical entity when transmitting or receiving data. In communication with the ISDN switch, an identifier must be issued by the switch. This is known as a Terminal Endpoint Identifier (TEI).

The telco has the option of creating a specific profile for your implementation. If it chooses to do so, it assigns an SPID for each of your B channels.

Terminal Endpoint Identifier

A terminal endpoint can be any ISDN-capable device attached to an ISDN network. The TEI is a number between 0 and 127, where 0–63 are used for static TEI assignment, 64–126 are used for dynamic assignment, and 127 is used for group assignments. (0 is used only for PRI.) The TEI provides the physical identifier, and the Service Access Point Identifier (SAPI) carries the logical identifier.

The process of assigning TEIs differs slightly between North America and Europe. In North America, Layer 1 and Layer 2 are activated at all times. In Europe, the activation does not occur until the call setup is sent (known as "first call"). This delay conserves switch resources. In Germany and Italy, and in other parts of the world, the procedure for TEI assignment can change according to local practices.

In other countries, another key piece of information to obtain is the bus type. Supported types are point-to-point or point-to-multipoint connection styles. In Europe, if you are not sure which is supported, specify a point-to-multipoint connection, which will enable dynamic TEI addressing. This is important if BRI connections are necessary, because Cisco does not support BRI using TEI 0, which is reserved for PRI TEI address 0. If you see a TEI of 0 on a BRI, it means that a dynamic assignment has not yet occurred, and the BRI may not be talking to the switch. In the United States, a BRI data line is implemented only in a point-to-point configuration.

Example 7-1 shows a typical ISDN Layer 2 negotiation.

Example 7-1 **debug isdn q921** *Output*

```
RouterA#debug isdn q921
BRI0: TX -> IDREQ   ri = 65279   ai = 127
BRI0: RX <- -UI sapi = 0   tei = 127 I = 0x0801FF0504038090A218018896250101
BRI0: TX -> IDREQ   ri = 61168   ai = 127
BRI0: RX <- -IDASSN   ri = 61168   ai =64
BRI0: TX -> SABMEp sapi = 0   tei = 64
BRI0: RX <- -UAf sapi = 0   tei = 64
BRI0: TX -> INFOc sapi = 0   tei = 64   ns = 0   nr = 0   i = x08017F5A080280D1
BRI0: RX <- -RRr sapi = 0   tei = 64   nr = 1
BRI0: RX <- -INFOc sapi = 0   tei = 64   ns = 0   nr = 1   i = x08007B963902EF01
BRI0: TX -> RRr sapi = 0   tei = 64   nr = 1
BRI0: RX <- -INFOc sapi = 0   tei = 64 ns = 1   nr = 1 i = 0x8007B962201013201013B0110
BRI0: TX -> RRr sapi = 0   tei = 64   nr = 2
BRI0: TX -> RRp sapi = 0   tei = 64 nr = 2
BRI0: RX <- -RRf sapi = 0   tei = 64   nr = 1
BRI0: TX -> RRp sapi = 0   tei = 64   nr = 2
BRI0: RX <- -RRf sapi = 0   tei = 64   nr = 1
```

The following paragraphs are a partial explanation of the output listed in Example 7-1. You should take the time to understand the rest of this section because the output gives a great deal of troubleshooting information. You may need more than one reading to get it all straight.

The **ri** is a reference indicator. It provides the router and the switch a way to keep straight all the calls they may be processing. Notice that in the **IDREQ** and the **IDASSN**, the **ri** value is the same. If the router sends an **IDREQ** and receives no response, it retries every two seconds. Each time the **ri** is different. The **ai** is an association indicator: **ai = 127** is the router's way of requesting a TEI from the switch; the switch reply is **ai = 64**. Therefore, 64 is the assigned TEI.

Notice that all remaining correspondence has **tei = 64** referenced. Once the router has a TEI, it sends a **SABME** (Set Asynchronous Balanced Mode Extended) message with **sapi = 0**. This means that this is a signaling connection (that is, this is all taking place over the D channel).

If no TEI is assigned, Layer 2 does activate and the output from the **debug isdn q921** command renders only **TX->IDREQ** lines. If all the Layer 2 processes are successful, you will see **MULTIPLE_FRAME_ESTABLISHED** under the **Layer 2 Status** section in the output of the

show isdn status command. See Example 7-3 in the upcoming "ISDN Call Setup" section for a demonstration of the **show isdn status** command output.

> **NOTE**   In some countries other than the United States, the TEI is negotiated as part of the call setup. Therefore, it will show only that Layer 1 is active. Layers 2 and 3 will negotiate their parameters once a call is attempted.

Service Profile Identifiers

Another key part of ISDN BRI Layer 2 is the SPID. SPIDs are used only in BRI implementations. PRI implementations do not require the use of SPIDs. The SPID specifies the services to which you are entitled from the switch and defines the feature set that you ordered when the ISDN service was provisioned.

The SPID is a series of characters manually entered into the router's configuration to identify the router to the switch. This is different from the TEI discussed earlier. The TEI address is dynamically assigned. The SPID is statically assigned to the router based on information provided by the service provider. If needed, two SPIDs are configured, one for each channel of the BRI. Usually, the SPID includes the ten-digit phone number of each B channel followed by four additional digits (sometimes 0101) assigned by the telco.

SPID requirements are dependent on both the software revision and the switch. Many switch manufacturers are moving away from SPIDs, as they have already done in Europe. SPIDs are required only in the U.S., and then are used only by certain switches. 5ESS, DMS-100, and NI-1 support the use of SPIDs; however, it is not necessary to configure them unless it is required by the LEC.

ISDN Layer 3

ISDN Layer 3 does not impose the use of any network layer protocol for the B channels. The use of the D channel is defined in Q.931 and specified in ITU I.451 and Q.931 and Q.932.

Q.931 is used between the TE and the local ISDN switch. Inside the ISDN network, the Signalling System 7 (SS7) Internal Signalling Utility Protocol (ISUP) is used. Link Access Procedure on the D channel (LAPD) is the ISDN data link layer protocol for the D channel. The data link layer protocol for the B channel, however, can be any of the available protocols, because the information can be passed transparently to the remote party. HDLC, PPP, or Frame Relay encapsulations can be used to pass data over the B channel.

LAPD

As mentioned, LAPD is the data link layer protocol for the D channel. It defines the framing characteristics for payload transmission, as illustrated in Figure 7-5.

Figure 7-5 *The LAPD Frame*

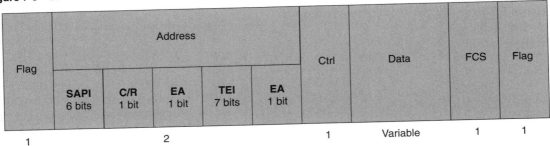

The following list defines the subfields of the Address portion of the LAPD frame:

- **SAPI**—Service access point identifier (6 bits)

- **C/R**—Command/response bit (1 bit)

- **EA**—Extended addressing bits (1 bit each)

- **TEI**—Terminal Endpoint Identifier (7 bits)

All fields of the LAPD frame are 1 byte except for the Address field, which is 2 bytes. The Data field is variable in length.

ISDN Call Setup

The setup procedure for ISDN calls is very similar to that of other circuit-switched technologies. It begins with a request, which is acknowledged. The acknowledging switch then forwards the setup request to the next switch in the line, and so on. Once the called party is reached, a connect message is sent, which also must be acknowledged. Figure 7-6 depicts the ISDN call setup procedure.

Prior to the actual Connect and Call Proceeding (CALL PROC) messages, there can be a number of different call progress messages. For instance, the calling party sends setup messages to the switch. The switch responds with the Setup Acknowledgement (SETUP ACK) and Call Proceeding messages. The remote switch then sends the setup message to the called party, which acknowledges with a CALL PROC message. Alerting messages can then be sent, although they are optional, depending on carrier implementation. Alerting messages are normally associated with voice traffic and are not usually implemented in data calls.

Figure 7-6 *ISDN Call Setup*

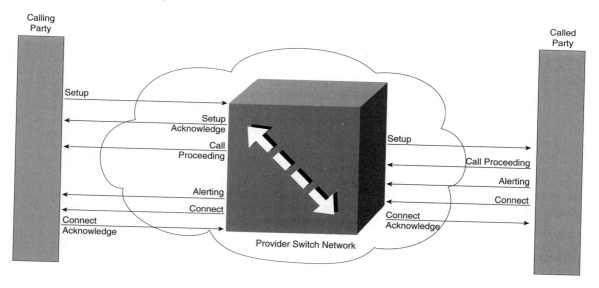

Connect messages flow from the called party to the calling party when the connection is established, and may be followed by a Connect Acknowledgement (CONNECT ACK) message, which is also optional. Once the calling party receives the CONNECT ACK, the call setup is complete.

Example 7-2 shows the beginning of a call setup. The output is from a **ping** to the remote side while the **debug isdn q931** command is active. Note the **ping** timeout (.), which is followed by a **ping** success (!) after the call setup.

Example 7-2 **debug isdn q931** *Command Output Reveals Call Setup Details*

```
RouterA#debug isdn q931
RouterA#ping 10.12.1.2
Type escape sequence to abort.
Sending 5, 100-byte ICMP Echos to 10.12.1.2, timeout is 2 seconds:
ISDN BR0: TX -> SETUP pd = 8  callref = 0x0E
    Bearer Capability i = 0x8890
    Channel ID i = 0x83
    Keypad Facility i = 0x3935353532303032
ISDN BR0: RX <- - SETUP_ACK pd = 8  callref = 0x8E
Channel ID i = 0x89
ISDN BR0: RX <- - CALL_PROC pd = 8  callref = 0x8E
ISDN BR0: RX <- - CONNECT pd = 8  callref = 0x8E
%LINK-3-UPDOWN:Interface BRI0:1, changed state to up
ISDN BR0: TX ->  CONNECT_ACK pd = 8  callref = 0x0E
%LINEPROTO-5-UPDOWN: Line protocol on Interface BRI0:1, changed state to up.!!!
Success rate is 60 percent (3/5), round-trip min/avg/max = 36/36/36 ms
%ISDN-6-CONNECT: Interface BRI0:1 is now connected to 2145553000 RouterB
```

The ICMP traffic falls within the parameters of what has been defined as interesting traffic. The call is placed and interface BRI 0, B channel 1, can be seen initializing and completing the call. Note that the first of the ICMP Echos failed. This is due to the amount of time necessary for the ISDN call setup to complete and negotiate LCP/NCP options. The last line of the output states that the call is connected to 2145553000, RouterB.

Once the call is up, you can monitor the call using the **show isdn status** command. This is a useful troubleshooting command because it shows the status of all three layers of ISDN that have been discussed in this chapter.

Example 7-3 shows the output from the **show isdn status** command. Note that both B channels are connected to the remote side. This is visible under the **Layer 2 Status** section.

Example 7-3 **show isdn status** *Command Output*

```
RouterA#show isdn status
The current ISDN Switchtype = basic-5ess
ISDN BRI0 interface
    Layer 1 Status:
            ACTIVE
    Layer 2 Status:
        TEI = 90, State = MULTIPLE_FRAME_ESTABLISHED
    Layer 3 Status:
            1 Active Layer 2 Call(s)
            Activated dsl 0 CCBs are 2, Allocated = 2
                callid=0, sapi=0, ces=2
                callid=8000, sapi=0, ces=1
```

ISDN Call Release

Any party in the network can release the call for whatever reason. Whether the release of the call is intentional or accidental (that is, due to some type of failure in the network), the call is torn down completely.

When either the calling or called party is ready to disconnect a call, that party issues a Disconnect (DISC) message. The disconnect is not negotiable. If necessary, the call can be reestablished, but once a disconnect is issued, the call comes down.

When a DISC is issued, it is acknowledged with a Released (RELEASED) message. The switch forwards the RELEASED message, which should be followed by a Release Complete (RELEASE COMPLETE) message. Figure 7-7 depicts the ISDN call-release process.

Figure 7-7 *ISDN Call Release*

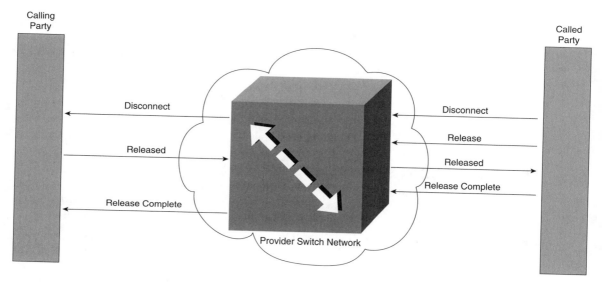

Implementing Basic DDR

Dial-on-demand routing (DDR) is a feature that is available on ISDN-capable Cisco routers. DDR was created to enable users to save money on usage-based ISDN, which assesses charges for every minute of ISDN circuit connect time.

Obviously, in a charge-by-the-minute scenario, the connection should be down during no or low-volume traffic times. DDR provides that capability and offers a wide array of commands and configuration variations. Many of those configuration options are covered in the remainder of this chapter.

The configuration tasks for implementing basic DDR are as follows:

Step 1   Set the ISDN switch type.

Step 2   Specify interesting traffic.

Step 3   Specify static routes.

Step 4   Define the interface encapsulation and ISDN addressing parameters.

Step 5   Configure the protocol addressing.

Step 6   Define any additional interface information.

Figure 7-8 depicts the network topology that is referenced throughout the rest of this chapter.

Figure 7-8 *Sample ISDN Topology*

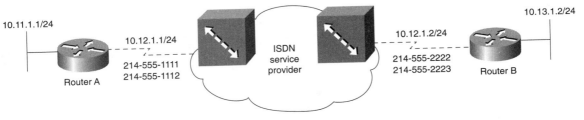

Step 1: Setting the ISDN Switch Type

The telephone company provides you the type of switch to which you are connecting. Manufacturers of ISDN central office switches (also known as *local exchange equipment*) divide the local exchange into two functions: local termination and exchange termination. The local termination function primarily deals with the transmission facility and termination of the local loop. The exchange termination function deals with the switching portion of the local exchange.

For your router to function, you must specify on the router the type of switch to which your router will connect. Use the **isdn switch-type** command to configure the router. Your telephone company should identify the type of switch that is located in the central office to which your router will connect. For a listing of supported switch types, refer to Table 7-2.

The **isdn switch-type** command has historically been issued from the global configuration prompt. However, as of Cisco IOS version 12.0, this command can be issued from the interface configuration prompt as well. (The use of this command is included in Example 7-4 in the next section.)

Note that once the switch type is set at the global configuration level, it is considered to be that type for all ISDN-capable interfaces. If it is changed at the global configuration level, the original switch type set will be dropped onto each individual interface. For example, assume that the switch type was initially set incorrectly to basic-dms100 when it should have been basic-5ess. The command **isdn switch-type basic-ni1** would have been entered at the global configuration prompt. Subsequently, the command **isdn switch-type basic-5ess** is entered at the global configuration prompt. Upon the issuance of a **show running-config** command, each ISDN-capable interface would show **isdn switch-type basic-ni1** and have to be manually altered to basic-5ess as well. The reasons for this anomaly are not known. This concept is merely stated here as a matter of assisting those who will call the support line for a telephone company and be told that the switch type should be "National ISDN 5ESS." As Table 7-2 indicates, National ISDN is a separate switch type from 5ESS.

To top off the discussion of switch types, note that once the switch type is changed, a router reload is in order.

Step 2: Specifying Interesting Traffic

The entire configuration of DDR depends on how the traffic types that cause a call setup to occur are triggered. This traffic is known as *interesting traffic.*

Cisco's implementation of DDR allows for as much or as little specificity of interesting traffic as you deem necessary; interesting traffic is defined by the creation of *dialer-lists* that can specify that an entire protocol suite, no matter the level of traffic, can trigger a call setup.

Dialer-lists can be associated with standard or extended access lists to be specific to various traffic types. Rather than associating an access list with an interface, it is associated with a dialer-list (discussed later in this section).

Example 7-4 shows a basic configuration in which all IP traffic has been specified as interesting. This is specified in the *dialer-list* line. The dialer-list is associated with the proper interface using a *dialer-group* line, as shown in the example. Because PPP is the most common encapsulation utilized in ISDN configurations, it is used on the interfaces for all examples.

Note that the list number and the group number are identical. This number ties the dialer-list and dialer-group together. This number cannot be reused by any other dialer-list or dialer-group in the same router.

Example 7-4 *Basic DDR Configuration on RouterA*

```
RouterA(config)#isdn switch type basic-5ess
!
RouterA(config)#interface BRI0
RouterA(config-if)#ip address 10.12.1.1 255.255.255.0
RouterA(config-if)#encapsulation ppp
RouterA(config-if)#dialer idle-timeout 180
RouterA(config-if)#dialer map ip 10.12.1.2 5552222
RouterA(config-if)#dialer-group 1
!
RouterA(config)#dialer-list 1 protocol ip permit
```

The remote router configuration should be similar. Example 7-5 details the basic configuration of the remote router.

Examples 7-4 and 7-5 deal with a blanket statement that enables entire protocol suites. This type of implementation is not always the best, or preferred, method of defining interesting traffic.

Example 7-5 *Basic DDR Configuration on RouterB*

```
RouterA(config)#isdn switch type basic-5ess
!
RouterA(config)#interface BRI0
RouterA(config-if)#ip address 10.12.1.2 255.255.255.0
RouterA(config-if)#encapsulation ppp
RouterA(config-if)#dialer idle-timeout 180
RouterA(config-if)#dialer map ip 10.12.1.1 5551111
RouterA(config-if)#dialer-group 1
!
RouterA(config)#dialer-list 1 protocol ip permit
```

To define specific traffic types as interesting traffic, you should use access lists. Any type of access list can be implemented to define interesting traffic. Rather than being associated with an interface, the access list is associated with the dialer-list.

This discussion assumes that you are already familiar with access lists to some degree and therefore focuses on IP access lists.

Example 7-6 shows a sample configuration using IP extended access lists to define interesting traffic. The explanation follows the output.

Example 7-6 *Extended Access Lists with Interesting Traffic*

```
RouterA#configure terminal
RouterA(config)#access-list 101 deny tcp any any eq ftp
RouterA(config)#access-list 101 deny tcp any any eq telnet
RouterA(config)#access-list 101 permit ip any any
!
RouterA(config)#interface bri 0
RouterA(config-if)#ip address 10.12.1.1 255.255.255.0
RouterA(config-if)#encapsulation ppp
<output omitted>
RouterA(config-if)#dialer-group 2
!
RouterA(config)#dialer-list 2 protocol ip list 101
```

Example 7-6 implements a more specific definition of interesting traffic. **access-list 101** is denying FTP and Telnet. That is, they are not allowed to trigger a call setup. Any other IP traffic that attempts to traverse the link triggers the call. Once the call is up, Telnet and FTP can go across freely.

Notice the dialer-list line in Example 7-6. Rather than enabling the entire IP protocol suite to trigger the call, this line specifies that all traffic attempting to exit through BRI 0 must be tested against **access-list 101**.

The interface configuration has not changed from our basic configuration model. Only the dialer-list has been altered to point to the access list. The dialer-list still must point to the dialer-group on the interface (that is, the dialer-list and dialer-group numbers must match). The access list number can be any valid standard or extended access list number (Example 7-6 demonstrates IP only). However, as stated earlier, interesting traffic for any protocol can be implemented using the appropriate access list command structure.

Step 3: Specifying Static Routes

In the classic DDR model, dynamic routing protocol updates do not move across the link, so it is important that static routes be used in place of dynamic updates. To provide bidirectional reachability between the two sites in the absence of routing protocol traffic, static routes should be configured at both the local and remote routers. As demonstrated in Example 7-6, any IP traffic that needs to cross the link has been defined as interesting and will trigger a call setup.

Do not confuse the definition of interesting traffic with the implementation of security measures. DDR defines only what types of traffic can initiate a call, not what can go across the link. Once a call has been established, any type of traffic that has been configured on the BRI interface can traverse the link freely. This includes routing updates. If the IP network on which the BRI interface exists is included in the routing protocol configuration (and the BRI interface isn't specified as passive), routing updates can flow across the link while it is active. Once static routes have been specified, it is important to make the BRI interface(s) passive. Passive interfaces are discussed later in this chapter (in the "Passive Interfaces" section).

Static routes are necessary in DDR because the ISDN link is not always active. In a dynamic routing environment, the fact that the link is down could be construed as a network-down condition and reachability could be lost. To combat this, the link shows that it's spoofing while it's down. Example 7-7 demonstrates this through the **show interface bri 0** command.

Example 7-7   show interface bri 0 *Command Output*

```
RouterA#show interface bri 0
BRI0 is up, line protocol is up (spoofing)
Hardware is BRI
MTU 1500 bytes, BW 64 Kbit, DLY 20000 usec, rely 255/255, load 1/255
Encapsulation PPP, loopback not set
Last input 0:00:06, output 0:00:06, output hang never
Last clearing of "show interface" counters never
Input queue: 0/75/0 (size/max/drops); Total output drops: 0
Output queue: 0/64/0 (size/threshold/drops)
   Conversations  0/1 (active/max active)
   Reserved Conversations 0/0 (allocated/max allocated)
5 minute input rate 0 bits/sec, 0 packets/sec
5 minute output rate 0 bits/sec, 0 packets/sec
```

continues

Example 7-7   **show interface bri 0** *Command Output (Continued)*

```
359 packets input, 5814 bytes, 1 no buffer
Received 0 broadcasts, 0 runts, 0 giants
0 input errors, 0 CRC, 0 frame, 0 overrun, 0 ignored, 0 abort
70 packets output, 307 bytes, 0 underruns
0 output errors, 0 collisions, 6 interface resets, 0 restarts
0 output buffer failures, 0 output buffers swapped out
5 carrier transitions
```

The first line in the output shows that the interface is up and the line protocol is down, but the line protocol is actually up because the router knows this is a DDR connection and keeps the line protocol state at **up (spoofing)**.

Obviously, while there is no connectivity, routing updates cannot flow. If all IP traffic is defined as interesting and the implementation in question is using a dynamic routing protocol, the routing updates keep the link up at all times. For example, IGRP uses a 90-second update cycle. Previous examples in this chapter placed a **dialer idle-timeout 180** command on the interface. This command states that the link should come down after 180 seconds of idle time. If IGRP updates are sent every 90 seconds, the idle timeout countdown is reset with each update. The very purpose of DDR has been defeated.

Step 4: Defining the Interface Encapsulation and ISDN Addressing Parameters

ISDN installations are capable of employing HDLC or PPP encapsulation (among others). PPP is most often used because of its rich feature set and flexibility. PPP offers the use of a single B channel or the combination of the two B channels in a single aggregate pipe. It enables you to decide when a connection should be dialed, when an additional channel should be brought up and used, when to disconnect the call, and other options that are discussed in the next couple of sections.

PPP encapsulates network layer protocol information over point-to-point links. Although the protocol can be configured on a variety of interfaces, our focus remains on the ISDN-capable interface. To establish communications over an ISDN link, each end of the PPP link must first send Link Control Protocol (LCP) packets to configure and test the data link. After the link has been established and optional facilities have been negotiated as needed, PPP must send Network Control Protocol (NCP) packets to choose and configure one or more network layer protocols.

After you have configured each of the network layer protocols that you have chosen, datagrams from each network layer protocol can be sent over the link. The link remains configured for communications until explicit LCP or NCP packets close the link down, or until some external event occurs (for example, a period of inactivity).

Functionally, PPP is simply a pathway opened for multiple protocols to share simultaneously. The call setup is initiated by interesting traffic as defined using access lists and terminated by an external event, such as manual clearing or idle timer expiration. Any interesting traffic that traverses the link resets the idle timer; noninteresting traffic does not.

Note that ISDN addressing uses phone numbers that are exactly like the phone numbers utilized by millions of people day in and day out. These numbers are telco-designated and locally significant. They usually include an area code, a local exchange, and additional digits.

To function, the router must understand what phone number to dial and when to dial it. How does it come to know this information? The same way it knows everything else it knows—the administrator tells it.

The administrator uses dialer maps to tell the router how and when to dial a particular destination. Dialer maps serve the same basic function as does ARP in a LAN: the mapping of network layer addresses to data link layer addresses. In this case, the data link layer address is the phone number. To get to a specific destination, the router must associate the proper destination phone number with the next logical hop protocol address.

Step 5: Configuring Protocol Addressing

After you have decided upon the type of encapsulation, you must apply a protocol addressing scheme. You can configure DDR with any routable protocol. Each protocol that must pass across the link must have a configured address.

For IP implementations, you must supply an IP address and subnet mask to the interface. You should choose the protocol addressing scheme well in advance of any deployment of any networking technology.

In Internetwork Packet Exchange (IPX) implementations, you must apply an IPX network number to the BRI interface. The host portion of the address is hard-coded in the global configuration or is taken from the Burned In Address (BIA) of the lowest-numbered LAN interface (that is, Ethernet 0). When IPX routing is enabled and IPX network numbers are configured on interfaces, the IPX Routing Information Protocol (RIP) and the Service Advertising Protocol (SAP) are automatically enabled for those interfaces.

IPX RIP and SAP are broadcast-based updates for routing table information and Novell NetWare service propagation, respectively. These broadcasts are on independent 60-second timers. You might or might not want this traffic to go across your ISDN link. To avoid this traffic, you can simply not include RIP and SAP in your interesting traffic definitions. This is accomplished by implementing IPX access lists to filter out RIP and SAP. The access lists are then associated with the dialer-list that defines interesting traffic. At this point, RIP and SAP go across the link only as long as the link is up.

You can also define IPX static routes and static SAP entries. In the example, the dialer map points to the next hop on the same logical IPX network, 80fa.0000.0000.0004, just as the dialer map for IP points to the next hop IP address on the same logical subnet. The host portion of the IPX address is either specified when the **IPX routing** command is issued or defaulted to the MAC address of the lowest-numbered LAN interface (ex. E0s MAC address). In the example, IPX was enabled with the command **ipx routing 0000.0000.0004**, which specifies that all IPX-enabled interfaces would use 0000.0000.0004 as the host portion of their address.

Example 7-8 shows the encapsulation and the application of an IPX network number and an IP address to the BRI interface.

Example 7-8 *Protocol Addressing*

```
RouterA(config)#interface BRI0
RouterA(config-if)#ip address 10.12.1.1 255.255.255.0
RouterA(config-if)#ipx network number 80fa
RouterA(config-if)#dialer map ip 10.12.1.2 broadcast 5551212
zzzz.   RouterA(config-if)#dialer map ipx 80fa.0000.0000.0004 broadcast
5551212RouterA(config-if)#encapsulation ppp
```

Step 6: Defining Additional Interface Information

The purpose of DDR is to bring down the ISDN link when the traffic volume is low or idle. However, at times, the traffic volume can simply be in a short lull. Indeed, LAN traffic is bursty—quiet times followed by an explosion of traffic.

If you want to avoid having the link come down too soon when traffic flow ceases, forcing you to redial, use the **dialer idle-timeout** command. Executing this command dictates that when traffic defined as interesting has ceased to flow across the link for the specified period of time (in seconds), go ahead and bring down the link. For instance, if the command **dialer idle-timeout 180** is used at the interface configuration mode, the link comes down three minutes after the last piece of interesting traffic has traversed the link. Note that only interesting traffic resets the timer. Any noninteresting traffic goes across, but does not contribute to keeping the link up.

SPIDs

Many BRI implementations use SPIDs. The SPID simply informs the switch of the purchased feature set for the particular installation. These SPIDs are not standardized in their format. The telco provider specifies the use of SPIDs and the appropriate values, if necessary.

To apply SPIDs to the interface, use the commands **isdn spid1** and **isdn spid2**. These commands have an optional parameter at the end known as *ldn*. This is the local dial number. Although this parameter is optional, in some implementations, the circuit does not perform optimally in the absence of the *ldn* parameter. It doesn't hurt to have the *ldn* parameter on the command line, but it can hurt sometimes not to have it, so it makes sense to add it.

As noted earlier, PRI does not use SPID information. The *ldn* parameter must be used if the switch is programmed to look for them (the telco will inform you of this). If they are expected and not specified, the circuit may not come up. This lack of coming up can be seen in the **show isdn status** command under the **Layer 2 status** section. It shows **invalid ldn** and **spid invalid**. Obviously, the circuit is not initialized in this state.

Caller ID Screening

Utilizing the features offered by caller ID, the router can be configured to accept calls only from specified callers. The **isdn answer** command is used for this purpose. The configuration is quite simple. Once this command has been issued, the router accepts calls only from numbers that have been specified. Use of this feature combats unauthorized use of the facilities.

Configuring Additional Interface Information

Example 7-9 illustrates the concepts of this section, including SPIDs, the **dialer idle-timeout** command, call screening, and dialer maps.

Example 7-9 *Optional Configuration Parameters*

```
RouterA(config)#interface BRI0
RouterA(config-if)#ip address 10.12.1.1 255.255.255.0
RouterA(config-if)#encapsulation ppp
RouterA(config-if)#dialer idle-timeout 180
RouterA(config-if)#isdn spid1 21455511110101 2145551111
RouterA(config-if)#isdn spid2 21455511120101 2145551112
RouterA(config-if)#isdn answer 2145552222
RouterA(config-if)#isdn answer 2145552223
RouterA(config-if)#dialer map ip 10.12.1.2 2145552222
RouterA(config-if)#dialer map ip 10.12.1.2 2145552223
RouterA(config-if)#dialer-group 1
!
RouterA(config)#dialer-list 1 protocol ip permit
!
RouterA(config)#ip route 10.13.1.0 255.255.255.0 10.12.1.2
```

Additional Options Beyond Basic DDR Configuration

Beyond basic DDR configuration, the following additional options can be used in various situations. Each option has a fairly specific use:

- Passive interfaces
- Static route redistribution

- Default routes
- Rate adaptation

Each of these options is explained in some detail in the following sections.

Passive Interfaces

Static routes used in place of dynamic routing functions also allow the link to be dropped. However, you must take care in your configuration.

To continue the discussion, an IGRP example is used; consider the basic IGRP/DDR configuration in Example 7-10.

Example 7-10 *Passive Interface Justification*

```
RouterA(config)#isdn switch type basic-5ess
!
RouterA(config)#interface ethernet 0
RouterA(config-if)#ip address 10.11.1.1 255.255.255.0
!
RouterA(config)#interface BRI0
RouterA(config-if)#ip address 10.12.1.1 255.255.255.0
RouterA(config-if)#encapsulation ppp
RouterA(config-if)#dialer idle-timeout 180
RouterA(config-if)#isdn spid1 21455511110101 2145551111
RouterA(config-if)#isdn spid2 21455511120101 2145551112
RouterA(config-if)#isdn answer 2145552222
RouterA(config-if)#isdn answer 2145552223
RouterA(config-if)#dialer map ip 10.12.1.2 2145552222
RouterA(config-if)#dialer map ip 10.12.1.2 2145552223
RouterA(config-if)#dialer-group 1
!
RouterA(config)#access-list 101 permit tcp any any eq telnet
RouterA(config)#access-list 101 permit tcp any any eq ftp
RouterA(config)#access-list 101 permit tcp any any eq ftp-data
!
RouterA(config)#dialer-list 1 protocol ip list 101
!
RouterA(config)#router igrp 100
RouterA(config-router)#network 10.0.0.0
!
RouterA(config)#ip route 10.13.1.0 255.255.255.0 10.12.1.2
```

There is a stub network on the remote side, network 10.13.1.0/24. This configuration has a problem: although the static route is properly defined, IGRP is still sending updates across the link. In addition, because interface BRI 0 is part of the classful network 10.0.0.0, it is included in routing updates. A simple alteration under the IGRP configuration remedies the problem, as demonstrated by Example 7-11.

Example 7-11 *Making the Configuration Work Properly*

```
RouterA(config)#router igrp 100
RouterA(config-router)#network 10.0.0.0
RouterA(config-router)#passive-interface bri 0
```

Making an interface passive lets the routing protocol know that it should not attempt to send updates out the specified interface.

The **passive-interface** command has a slightly different effect, depending on the type of routing protocol used. For RIP and IGRP, the operation is the same. These two protocols do not send updates out the passive interface, although they can receive updates through these interfaces.

OSPF and EIGRP also act the same. These protocols rely on the establishment of communications with neighboring routers. If the interface is passive, this cannot occur. Therefore, routing updates are neither sent nor received on the passive interface. If the neighbor relationship cannot be achieved, updates cannot flow.

Static Route Redistribution

An issue arises from time to time with static routes—static routes are just that, static. The dynamic routing protocol does not advertise the static route, so reachability can be affected. To remedy this, the static route can simply be redistributed into the dynamic routing protocol. It is important that a default metric be assigned in the configuration of the redistribution, or the routing protocol will not know how to treat the route. Redistribution is beyond our scope at this time and is not discussed further.

Default Routes

From time to time, a router is faced with a dilemma: what to do when it doesn't know what to do. As it stands now, in the absence of a suitable routing table entry to a given destination, a router has no choice but to return an ICMP "Destination Unreachable" message to the sender.

This dilemma, however, is easily remedied. By giving the router a default route, it can forward the traffic on to another router that may have a suitable entry in a routing table to keep the traffic flow alive. This is known as the *gateway of last resort.*

The default route can be entered in a number of different ways. Depending on the routing protocol and its configuration, the default route can even be injected into the routing table automatically.

If the default route must be entered manually (as with RIP), you can issue the **ip default-network** command. There is a catch here, however: the router must have a valid route (either static or dynamic) to the default network. If the routing table does not have an entry for the default network, one must be entered. Example 7-12 illustrates this concept.

Example 7-12 *Static Route with* **ip default-network**

```
RouterB(config)#ip route 10.11.1.0 255.255.255.0 10.12.1.1
RouterB(config)#ip default-network 10.11.1.0
```

As mentioned earlier, you may have the option of performing this function in another way: if the routing protocol supports it, a static default route to the network 0.0.0.0 0.0.0.0 is used. The entry is that of a static route. Example 7-13 illustrates the static default route.

Example 7-13 *Static Default Route*

```
RouterB(config)#ip route 0.0.0.0 0.0.0.0 10.12.1.1
```

Notice that a specific next hop is specified. This is significant in that a static route with a specific next hop is not redistributed automatically. If your overall goal is to have this route automatically redistributed, you can specify an outbound interface. This is true with all static routes, not just the static default route. Example 7-14 illustrates the same configuration, but with one that does have to be manually redistributed.

Example 7-14 *Automatically Redistributed Default Route*

```
RouterB(config)#ip route 0.0.0.0 0.0.0.0 Serial 0
```

In this case, any traffic for which the router does not have a suitable routing entry is forwarded out interface serial 0 to the device on the other side of the link.

Note that the example does not reference BRI 0 as the outbound interface. Although it is a valid command configuration to place BRI 0 at the end of the default route command (that is, the router allows it), this configuration will not function, because the routing table entry is the origin of the next hop address information that triggers the call to the other side of the network. In addition, the dialer map association ties a phone number to that next hop address. If there's no routing table entry, the device has no way of knowing the next hop address. Therefore, it does not know which dialer map to utilize for the call, and the call fails.

Rate Adaptation

Earlier in the chapter, a solution was discussed that involves placing non-native ISDN routers into service in an ISDN network. A short discussion described how this is possible using TA.

In this type of implementation, the **dialer in-band** command is a necessary part of the configuration, which effectively takes 8 kbps from each B channel for use by the signaling entity. In other words, the 16 kbps that would normally be out-of-band in the D channel now has to be taken from the B channels. Effectively, the throughput is now 56 kbps for each B channel.

Should a native solution dial into a non-native solution with out-of-band signaling, the native solution would need to step down its speed to 56 kbps. This is done with rate adaptation. The implementation of rate adaptation is simply an extension of the **dialer map** command. The **dialer map** command tells the router that to reach a specific next hop address, a specific phone number must be called. The **dialer map** command simply associates the destination protocol address with the appropriate phone number to dial to get there. Example 7-15 illustrates the configuration of the router dialing into the non-native 56-kbps installation.

Example 7-15 *Rate Adaptation*

```
RouterA(config)#interface BRI0
RouterA(config-if)#ip address 10.12.1.1 255.255.255.0
RouterA(config-if)#encapsulation ppp
RouterA(config-if)#dialer idle-timeout 180
RouterA(config-if)#dialer map ip 10.12.1.2 speed 56 2145552222
RouterA(config-if)#dialer map ip 10.12.1.2 speed 56 2145552223
RouterA(config-if)#dialer-group 1
!
RouterA(config)#dialer-list 1 protocol ip permit
!
RouterA(config)#ip route 10.13.1.0 255.255.255.0 10.12.1.2
```

Foundation Summary

This section provides a convenient review of many key concepts in this chapter. If you are already comfortable with the topics in this chapter, this summary can help you recall a few details. If you just read this chapter, this review should help solidify some key facts. If you are doing your final preparation before the exam, this information is a convenient way to review the day before the exam.

ISDN has been around for a number of years. Its primary purpose has evolved and changed with the times, as is necessary for any technology to survive in the marketplace. With that in mind, it can be considered a mature technology. It remains a tried and tested technology, albeit somewhat limited by today's standards.

With the newer offerings of broadband cable and DSL, the number of new ISDN deployments has significantly fallen. However, in many markets, ISDN may be the only non-dialup solution available.

ISDN is based on long-standing specifications that have been put to use in numerous other technologies. For example, Q.931 is utilized as a part of an H.323 (VoIP) call setup.

ISDN's purpose is essentially to provide a transport for the L2 protocol in use across the link, no matter whether it is configured to be PPP, HDLC, or Frame Relay. The rules don't change for the base ISDN call setup. When the router is configured for an ISDN call, a number of parameters must be in order. If, for whatever reason, the call setup fails, it is important to understand why and at what point the call failed. Was the issue caused by something in the Q.921, Q.931, or PPP LCP negotiation phase?

The configuration of ISDN can be somewhat complex. The specification of the switch type can cause a great deal of pain in and of itself. Once set, the switch type is relatively difficult to alter. If it is altered, the router requires a reload.

The configuration of DDR has a number of required pieces in order to make it function. Static or dynamic routing can be used to get traffic to the remote site. Once the router decides that traffic is to be pushed across an ISDN link, that traffic must be seen as interesting. Interesting traffic must be defined to force a call setup. It is possible, however, to allow any and all traffic to force a call setup. To support the call setup, a dialer map or dialer string must be provided to ensure connectivity to the next hop address specified in the routing table.

Once the circle of dependencies is satisfied and traffic flows, there comes the thought of bandwidth utilization and per-minute call charges. You can add additional links, if available to the connection, to increase available bandwidth.

Also of interest is the idea that once the link is no longer in use, it should be disconnected. This is configurable in by the **dialer idle-timeout** command.

Passive interfaces can be configured to keep routing updates from traversing the ISDN links, thereby keeping link traffic to a minimum and allowing the idle-timeout to disconnect the link. Oftentimes, administrators opt to provide default routes to remote sites to prevent the use of dynamic routing in any situation involving ISDN.

Table 7-3 summarizes the protocols used to define ISDN as a technology.

Table 7-3   *ISDN Protocols*

Layer	Protocol	Description
1	I.430/T1.601	This layer is the physical layer dealing with connectivity. I.430 specifies framing between TE1 and NT1. T1.601 specifies framing between TE and the LE.
2	Q.921	Q.921 institutes an addressing scheme for ISDN.
3	Q.931	Q.931 is used between the TE and the local ISDN switch. Call setup is handled by Q.931 as well.

Q&A

The questions and scenarios in this book are more difficult than what you should experience on the exam. The questions do not attempt to cover more breadth or depth than the exam, but they are designed to make sure that you know the answer. Rather than enabling you to derive the answer from clues hidden inside the question, the questions challenge your understanding and recall of the subject. Hopefully, these questions will help limit the number of exam questions on which you narrow your choices to two options and then guess.

The answers to these questions can be found in Appendix A.

1. How is ISDN different from traditional POTS lines?

2. A single bearer channel provides how much bandwidth?

3. A D channel provides how much bandwidth?

4. A typical 2B+D implementation utilizes how much total bandwidth overall?

5. If a router has an interface labeled "BRI U," is an external NT1 necessary to provide the proper connectivity?

6. The **dialer in-band** command is necessary in what circumstance?

7. If the **isdn switch-type** command is entered incorrectly, what steps are necessary to correct it?

8. What command is used to verify the status of the ISDN layers and what will the output show for Layer 1 and Layer 2 if properly configured and connected to the CO switch?

9. What message is issued by the router to the ISDN switch to initiate a call?

10. What message is issued by the router to the ISDN switch to terminate a call?

This chapter covers the following subjects:

- Basic DDR Review

- Enhancing DDR Functionality

- Advanced DDR Operations

CHAPTER 8

Advanced DDR Options

Dialer profiles and rotary groups are useful for extending the versatility of ISDN services. They allow ISDN BRI and PRI interfaces to function as a resource pool for connectivity's sake. The implementations can be somewhat complex when compared to other WAN technologies.

"Do I Know This Already?" Quiz

The purpose of the "Do I Know This Already?" quiz is to help you decide whether you really need to read the entire chapter. If you already intend to read the entire chapter, you do not necessarily need to answer these questions now.

The eight-question quiz, derived from the major sections in the "Foundation Topics" portion of the chapter, helps you to determine how to spend your limited study time. Table 8-1 outlines the major topics discussed in this chapter and the "Do I Know This Already?" quiz questions that correspond to those topics.

Table 8-1 *"Do I Know This Already?" Foundation Topics Section-to-Question Mapping*

Foundation Topics Section	Questions Covered in This Section
Enhancing DDR Functionality	1–3
Advanced DDR Operations	4–8

CAUTION The goal of self-assessment is to gauge your mastery of the topics in this chapter. If you do not know the answer to a question or are only partially sure of the answer, you should mark this question wrong for purposes of the self-assessment. Giving yourself credit for an answer you correctly guess skews your self-assessment results and might provide you with a false sense of security.

1. If the command **ppp multilink** is not entered, what methodology for link aggregation will be utilized?

   a. Bandwidth on Demand

   b. Multilink PPP

    c. Dial Backup

    d. Snapshot routing

2. If you want to use Multilink PPP or Bandwidth on Demand to force the initialization of additional B channels as the utilization of the link(s) already in use reaches approximately 60 percent, which command should you use?

    a. **dialer load-threshold 110**

    b. **dialer load-threshold 200**

    c. **dialer load-threshold 150**

    d. **dialer load-threshold 250**

3. Which of the following is a standard for link aggregation?

    a. Bandwidth on Demand

    b. Multilink PPP

    c. Dial Backup

    d. Snapshot

4. Which of the following could be specified under a dialer map-class configuration?

    a. Rate

    b. SPID

    c. Remote host name

    d. Load-threshold

5. When using the command **rotary-group 32**, what is the dialer interface that will be utilized?

    a. Virtual-template 32

    b. Interface dialer 23

    c. Interface virtual-template 32

    d. Interface dialer 32

6. What is the minimum snapshot quiet period?

    a. 10 minutes

    b. 15 minutes

    c. 5 minutes

    d. 1 minute

7. Which command will designate the use of a two-hour quiet period on a snapshot routing server?

    a. **snapshot server 120 5 dialer**

    b. **snapshot server 5 120 dialer**

    c. **snapshot server 2 720 dialer**

    d. **snapshot server 720 2 dialer**

8. Which command will force the quiet timer to zero and begin the routing update process in snapshot routing?

    a. **clear ip snapshot**

    b. **clear snapshot quiet-time**

    c. **clear snapshot**

    d. **clear quiet-time**

The answers to the "Do I Know This Already?" quiz are found in Appendix A, "Answers to the 'Do I Know This Already?' Quizzes and Q&A Sections." The suggested choices for your next step are as follows:

- **4 or fewer overall score**—Read the entire chapter. This includes the "Foundation Topics," "Foundation Summary," and "Q&A" sections.

- **5 or 6 overall score**—Begin with the "Foundation Summary" section and then go to the "Q&A" section.

- **7 or more overall score**—If you want more review on these topics, skip to the "Foundation Summary" section and then go to the "Q&A" section. Otherwise, move to the next chapter.

Foundation Topics

Basic DDR Review

ISDN as a technology has been introduced earlier in the book. Therefore, this section provides only a brief review of topics highly relevant to dialer profiles and rotary groups. The discussion of these topics assumes a starting point of a DDR environment that has already been implemented.

For review purposes, the configuration tasks for implementing basic DDR are repeated here. For an explanation of each step, refer to Chapter 7.

Step 1   Set the ISDN switch type.

Step 2   Specify interesting traffic.

Step 3   Specify static routes.

Step 4   Define the interface encapsulation and ISDN addressing parameters.

Step 5   Configure the protocol addressing.

Step 6   Define any additional interface information.

Figure 8-1 depicts the network topology that is referenced throughout this chapter.

Figure 8-1   *Sample ISDN Topology*

Enhancing DDR Functionality

DDR, as discussed in previous chapters, is a relatively versatile technology. This section discusses some methodologies of expanding the functionality of a DDR solution.

Bandwidth on Demand

Bandwidth on Demand (BoD) is a Cisco Systems proprietary implementation that allows the aggregation of multiple B channels into a single logical connection. This implementation is widely used in Cisco-centric networks.

The implementation of Cisco's BoD solution is accomplished through the **dialer load-threshold** command. The variable parameter in the command is *load*. When the interface is connected to the remote side, a measurement of *load* is kept and updated continually based on utilization of the link. The load is measured on a scale of 1–255, with 255 representing link saturation. This command is typically used in almost every DDR configuration to provide load sharing over both B channels. Example 8-1 demonstrates this concept.

Example 8-1 *Implementing Cisco's BoD Feature*

```
RouterA(config)#interface BRI0
RouterA(config-if)#ip address 10.12.1.1 255.255.255.0
RouterA(config-if)#encapsulation ppp
RouterA(config-if)#dialer idle-timeout 180
RouterA(config-if)#dialer load-threshold 110
RouterA(config-if)#dialer map ip 10.12.1.2 speed 56 2145552222
RouterA(config-if)#dialer map ip 10.12.1.2 speed 56 2145552223
RouterA(config-if)#dialer-group 1
!
RouterA(config)#dialer-list 1 protocol ip permit
!
RouterA(config)#ip route 10.13.1.0 255.255.255.0 10.12.1.2
```

The **dialer load-threshold 110** statement specifies that if the load of the first B channel reaches 110 (100(110/255) = approximately 43 percent utilization), the second B channel should be initialized and, once connected, the traffic should load-balance across both channels.

The router recalculates the load of the link every 5 minutes to maintain an accurate picture without unnecessarily using CPU cycles. In a multivendor environment, BoD may not be a viable choice due to its proprietary nature. For such cases, Multilink Point-to-Point Protocol is more appropriate.

Multilink PPP

Multilink PPP is a specification that enables the bandwidth aggregation of multiple links into one logical pipe. Its mission is comparable to that of Cisco's BoD. More specifically, the Multilink PPP feature provides load-balancing functionality over multiple WAN links, while providing multivendor interoperability, packet fragmentation and proper sequencing, and load calculation on both inbound and outbound traffic.

Cisco's implementation of Multilink PPP supports the fragmentation and packet sequencing specifications in RFC 1717. Multilink PPP enables packets to be fragmented and the fragments to be sent (at the same time) over multiple point-to-point links to the same remote address.

As with BoD, the multiple links come up in response to a **dialer load-threshold** command. The load can be calculated on inbound traffic or outbound traffic as needed for the traffic between the specific sites. Multilink PPP provides bandwidth on demand and reduces transmission latency across WAN links. Also, as in BoD, a router running Multilink PPP recalculates the load every 5 minutes.

At any time, you can use a **show interface** command to see the current load of the interface. Example 8-2 shows the configuration and the **show interface BRI 0** command output.

Example 8-2 *Multilink PPP*

```
RouterA(config)#interface BRI0
RouterA(config-if)#ip address 10.12.1.1 255.255.255.0
RouterA(config-if)#encapsulation ppp
RouterA(config-if)#ppp multilink
RouterA(config-if)#dialer idle-timeout 180
RouterA(config-if)#dialer load-threshold 110
RouterA(config-if)#dialer map ip 10.12.1.2 speed 56 2145552222
RouterA(config-if)#dialer map ip 10.12.1.2 speed 56 2145552223
RouterA(config-if)#dialer-group 1
!
RouterA(config)#dialer-list 1 protocol ip permit
!
RouterA(config)#ip route 10.13.1.0 255.255.255.0 10.12.1.2
RouterA(config)#end
!
RouterA#show interface bri 0 1
BRI0:1 is up, line protocol is up
 Hardware is BRI with integrated NT1
 MTU 1500 bytes, BW 64 Kbit, DLY 20000 usec, rely 255/255, load 1/255
 Encapsulation PPP, loopback not set, keepalive set (10 sec)
 LCP Open, multilink Open
 Open: IPCP
 Last input 00:00:01, output 00:00:01, output hang never
 Last clearing of "show interface" counters never
 Queueing strategy: fifo
 Output queue 0/40, 0 drops; input queue 0/75, 0 drops
 5 minute input rate 0 bits/sec, 0 packets/sec
 5 minute output rate 0 bits/sec, 0 packets/sec
 6148 packets input, 142342 bytes, 0 no buffer
 Received 6148 broadcasts, 0 runts, 0 giants, 0 throttles
 0 input errors, 0 CRC, 0 frame, 0 overrun, 0 ignored, 0 abort
 6198 packets output, 148808 bytes, 0 underruns
 0 output errors, 0 collisions, 0 interface resets
 0 output buffer failures, 0 output buffers swapped out
 9 carrier transitions
```

The preceding **show interface bri 0 1** command shows only the first B channel (hence the **bri 0 1**). If the second B channel were up, the command **show interface bri 0 2** could be entered to view its status. Notice that, as highlighted in Example 8-2, the load is currently 1/255. In other words, little or no traffic is flowing across the link.

Advanced DDR Operations

DDR installations are capable of utilizing dialer profiles (utilizing virtual dialer interfaces) and rotary groups. The installations also provide redundancy through dial backup and enable the use of dynamic routes across a DDR link while maintaining the routing table and keeping the link idle through snapshot routing.

Up to this point, the discussion has focused on the basics of DDR. Now that you have a more solid understanding of the technological base of ISDN and DDR implementations, it is appropriate to discuss some additional, more advanced features available with DDR.

Using Dialer Profiles

Dialer profiles allow the configuration of logical interfaces separate from the actual physical interfaces that receive or make calls. The separation of the physical and logical interfaces allows multiple physical interfaces to be shared by multiple dialer profile configurations. The logical definition of the differing interfaces can be bound dynamically to one or more physical interfaces on a per-call basis. This supports versatility in functionality because it allows physical interfaces to alter characteristics based on incoming or outgoing call requirements.

Dialer profiles first became a configuration option in Cisco IOS Release 11.2. The premise behind dialer profiles was to enable flexible design capabilities for deployment of custom profiles that meet users' dial access needs. This feature separates the logical function of DDR from the physical interface that places or receives the calls.

Prior to dialer profiles, B channels had no choice but to take on the configuration options applied to the physical interface. In this type of deployment, all users who dialed in to a particular access server received the same configuration, regardless of their access needs. With dialer profiles, each user's needs can be met by customized services and unique interfaces. In other words, each individual profile contains appropriately matched interface definitions and needs. The dialer profile solution need only be implemented at the hub site. No configuration changes are necessary at the spoke sites.

With this type of deployment, the logical and physical configurations are dynamically bound call by call. A dialer profile is made up of four components:

- **Dialer interfaces**—Logical entities that implement a dialer profile on a destination-by-destination basis. Destination-specific settings are applied to the dialer interface configurations. Multiple phone numbers (that is, dialer strings) can be specified for the same interface. Using a dialer map class, multiple configuration variations can be associated with a single phone number.

- **Dialer map class**—Defines specific characteristics for any call made to the specified dial string. Earlier configuration examples specified the *speed 56* parameter in the **dialer map** statement.

With dialer profiles, the map class can specify the speed based on the destination being dialed. At other times, again based on destination, the map class can specify *speed 64*. The speed can be altered on the fly based on the number being dialed. **dialer map** has an additional keyword, **broadcast**, that specifies that routing updates should be allowed to flow across the link. Without the **broadcast** keyword, routing updates would not reach across the cloud.

- **Dialer pool**—The dialer pool is a group of one or more physical interfaces associated with a logical interface. A physical interface can belong to multiple dialer pools. Contention for a specific physical interface is resolved with a configured priority.

- **Physical interfaces**—The actual interfaces to be utilized by dialer-profile-configured logical interfaces. Interfaces in a dialer pool are configured with individual parameters for encapsulation and dialer pool association. Dialer profiles support PPP and High-Level Data Link Control (HDLC) encapsulation.

When implementing dialer profiles with PPP, you must define specific parameters for the physical interface. The physical interface definition uses only the **encapsulation**, **authentication**, **ppp multilink**, and **dialer pool** configuration commands. All other settings are applied to the logical interface, and are applied only as needed for specific calls.

You can create a number of dialer interfaces on each router. Valid interface designations include numbers ranging from 1 through 255. Each logical dialer interface contains the complete configuration for a destination logical network and any networks reached through it. In other words, multiple physical interfaces can be forced to share a common set of characteristics. Example 8-3 shows a sample configuration for dialer profiles.

Example 8-3 *Dialer Profile Configuration*

```
RouterA(config)#isdn switch-type basic-5ess
!
RouterA(config)#interface ethernet 0
RouterA(config-if)#ip address 10.11.1.1 255.255.255.0
!
RouterA(config)#interface BRI0
RouterA(config-if)#encapsulation ppp
RouterA(config-if)#dialer pool-member 1
RouterA(config-if)#ppp authentication chap
RouterA(config-if)#ppp multilink
!
RouterA(config)#interface Dialer1
RouterA(config-if)#ip address 10.12.1.1 255.255.255.0
RouterA(config-if)#encapsulation ppp
RouterA(config-if)#dialer remote-name RouterB
RouterA(config-if)#dialer string 2145552222 class remote
RouterA(config-if)#dialer load threshold 50 either
RouterA(config-if)#dialer pool 1
RouterA(config-if)#dialer-group 1
```

Example 8-3 *Dialer Profile Configuration (Continued)*

```
RouterA(config-if)#ppp authentication chap
RouterA(config-if)#ppp multilink
!
RouterA(config)#map-class dialer remote
RouterA(config-map-class)#dialer isdn speed 56
!
RouterA(config)#ip route 10.12.1.2 255.255.255.255 Dialer1
RouterA(config)#ip route 10.13.1.0 255.255.255.0 10.12.1.2
RouterA(config)#dialer-list 1 protocol ip permit
```

In Example 8-3, there are a number of items of note. For instance, notice that there is no **dialer map** statement. The mapping is performed in separate statements. The **dialer string** statement defines the remote phone number and the map class (named *remote*) to use to dial that destination. This is why it is possible to use the outbound interface for the static route definition. This particular example also uses the rate adaptation capabilities. The **dialer pool** statements bind each interface (both logical and physical) together as a single operating entity.

Dialer profiles are a very useful addition to the configuration arsenal offered by Cisco IOS. However, they also represent a new set of issues and commands for troubleshooting. As with other implementations of ISDN, it is wise to simply utilize the **debug** commands discussed to this point.

To view the status of a dialer interface, the **show dialer interface bri 0** command can be of use, as demonstrated in Example 8-4.

Example 8-4 **show dialer interface bri 0** *Command Output*

```
RouterA#show dialer interface bri 0
BRI0 - dialer type = ISDN
Dial String Successes Failures Last called Last status
0 incoming call(s) have been screened.
BRI0: B-Channel 1
Idle timer (120 secs), Fast idle timer (20 secs)
Wait for carrier (30 secs), Re-enable (15 secs)
Dialer state is data link layer up
Dial reason: ip (s=10.12.1.1, d=10.12.1.2)
Interface bound to profile Dialer0
Time until disconnect 102 secs
Current call connected 00:00:19
Connected to 2145552222 (RouterB)
BRI0: B-Channel 2
Idle timer (120 secs), Fast idle timer (20 secs)
Wait for carrier (30 secs), Re-enable (15 secs)
Dialer state is idle
```

The **show dialer interface bri 0** command displays the status of each B channel and its configured settings. It specifies the reason for the call setup as well as the interface to which the physical interface is bound.

Rotary Groups

ISDN *rotary groups* are similar to dialer pools. One primary difference, however, is the lack of map class capabilities in rotary groups. The basic concept involves associating multiple physical interfaces with a single logical interface. When a call is placed, the member physical interfaces are scanned and the first available B channel is initialized. According to the needs of the traffic flow, and the capabilities of the remote side, additional B channels can be initialized, provided that there are available channels. The initialization of additional channels also assumes the presence of a Multilink PPP or Cisco BoD configuration.

Configuring rotary groups involves the creation of logical dialer interfaces (as is done in dialer pool configurations), the interface designation of which is an important detail.

Example 8-5 shows all the physical BRI interfaces associated with **dialer rotary-group 2**. The number 2 is used as a rotary group number, so it must also be used as the dialer interface number designator.

Example 8-5 *Rotary Group Configuration*

```
RouterA(config)#isdn switch-type basic-5ess
!
RouterA(config)#interface ethernet 0
RouterA(config-if)#ip address 10.11.1.1 255.255.255.0
!
RouterA(config)#interface BRI0
RouterA(config-if)#encapsulation ppp
RouterA(config-if)#dialer rotary-group 2
RouterA(config)#interface BRI1
RouterA(config-if)#encapsulation ppp
RouterA(config-if)#dialer rotary-group 2
RouterA(config)#interface BRI2
RouterA(config-if)#encapsulation ppp
RouterA(config-if)#dialer rotary-group 2
!
RouterA(config)#interface Dialer2
RouterA(config-if)#ip address 10.12.1.1 255.255.255.0
RouterA(config-if)#encapsulation ppp
RouterA(config-if)#dialer remote-name RouterB
RouterA(config-if)#dialer string 2145552222 class remote
RouterA(config-if)#dialer load threshold 50 either
RouterA(config-if)#dialer pool 1
RouterA(config-if)#dialer-group 1
```

Example 8-5 *Rotary Group Configuration (Continued)*

```
RouterA(config-if)#ppp authentication chap
RouterA(config-if)#ppp multilink
!
RouterA(config)#ip route 10.13.1.0 255.255.255.0 10.12.1.2
RouterA(config)#dialer-list 1 protocol ip permit
```

NOTE   The dialer interface designator (in this case, 2) must match the dialer rotary-group number. If these two numbers do not match, the configuration does not function properly.

Figure 8-2 depicts the concept of rotary groups.

Figure 8-2 *Rotary Group Configuration*

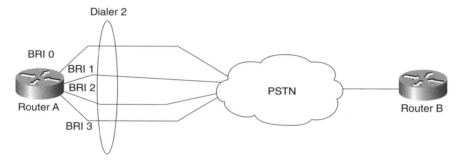

The only protocol or configuration attributes configured on the physical interface are the individual commands that make the BRI interface a part of the rotary group and the encapsulation. On dialer pool interfaces, you can set a priority to specify the order in which the interfaces are used. With rotary groups, that granularity is not possible. All protocol attributes are entered at the logical dialer interface configuration level.

The use of dialer profiles versus rotary groups comes down to one question: "How much control do I want to have over the link?" With dialer profiles, a map class can be created and applied on a per-destination basis. This allows a great degree of control over the characteristics of a particular call based on the destination being called. Rotary groups do not use the map class feature set. Therefore, they are limited to the characteristics applied to the dialer interface.

Snapshot Routing

Snapshot routing was developed to save bandwidth utilization across dialup interfaces. With snapshot routing, the routing table is placed in an update-restricted (that is, frozen) state. This implementation of DDR utilizes a *quiet* period and an *active* period. The routing table is not updated during the quiet period, which is the length of time that the routing table remains frozen. When the quiet period expires, a dialer interface initiates a call to a remote router. The active period is the length of time the call remains up in order for the two routers to exchange routing updates.

It is important to note that snapshot routing is designed for use only with distance vector routing protocols. In addition, you can configure the router to exchange routing updates each time the line protocol goes from "down" to "up" or from "dialer spoofing" to "fully up."

A router can fill one of two roles in a snapshot relationship: server or client. The *client* router is in charge of the quiet timer countdown. Once the counter reaches zero, the client router dials the *server* router. Snapshot routing enables dynamic distance vector routing protocols to run over DDR lines.

In many implementations, routing broadcasts (including routes and services) are filtered out on DDR interfaces and static definitions are configured instead. With snapshot routing implementations, normal updates are sent across the DDR interface for the short duration of the active period. After this, routers enter the quiet period, during which time the routing tables at both ends of the link remain unchanged. Snapshot routing is therefore a triggering mechanism that controls routing update exchange in DDR scenarios. Only during the active period are the neighboring routers exchanging routing protocol updates. During the quiet period, no updates traverse the link (even if the link is up to enable interesting traffic to cross) and the routing information previously collected is kept in an isolated state in the routing tables.

Snapshot routing is useful in two situations:

■ Configuring static routes for DDR interfaces

■ Reducing the overhead of periodic updates sent by routing protocols to remote branch offices over a dedicated serial line

In Examples 8-6 and 8-7, RouterA is defined as the server router and RouterB is defined as the client router. In this scenario, the quiet timer is slowly counting down to zero. Once the quiet period timer expires, the client router dials the server router. The defined quiet period is 12 hours (actually 720 minutes). Once the 12 hours have elapsed, the client and server routers "thaw" their routing tables and exchange updates for the duration of the active period, in this case, 5 minutes.

Example 8-6 *RouterA Snapshot Routing Configuration*

```
RouterA(config)#hostname RouterA
RouterA(config)#isdn switch-type basic-5ess
!
RouterA(config)#interface BRI0
RouterA(config-if)#snapshot server 5 dialer
RouterA(config-if)#dialer map snapshot 1 name RouterB 2145552222
```

Example 8-7 *RouterB Routing Configuration*

```
RouterB Snapshot Routing Configuration Example
RouterA(config)#hostname RouterB
RouterA(config)#isdn switch-type basic-5ess
!
RouterA(config)#interface BRI0
RouterA(config-if)#snapshot client 5 720 dialer
RouterA(config-if)#dialer map snapshot 1 name RouterA 2145551111
```

The active periods defined must match on both server and client routers. Five minutes is the minimum active period you can configure for any snapshot configuration.

Although the routing tables are frozen, routing updates are still sent at their regular intervals out of any LAN interfaces on the router. For example, if there is an Ethernet segment on the opposite side of a snapshot router, the routing updates still broadcast out of that interface at the normal update interval, while remaining dormant on the BRI interface. It is possible to force the quiet period to expire and start the active period manually using the **clear snapshot quiet-time** command. To monitor snapshot routing processes, use the **show snapshot** command.

Foundation Summary

This section is a collection of information that provides a convenient review of many key concepts in this chapter. If you are already comfortable with the topics in this chapter, this summary can help you recall a few details. If you just read this chapter, this review should help solidify some key facts.

DDR has long been one of the lesser understood technologies. The flexibility that DDR can provide has been underestimated due to its perceived complexity. Although it is true that ISDN configuration on the whole can be complex, it provides unsurpassed granularity and control. In previous chapters, the basic configuration and underlying technologies of ISDN and DDR have been discussed. This chapter took the discussion a few steps further into the realm of versatility.

DDR offers several valuable benefits. The implementation of map classes and dialer pools enables you to minimize configuration while maximizing technology capital. The ability to use multiple physical interfaces as one logical interface provides bandwidth scalability. Further, you can dynamically adjust utilized resources based on need.

The cost of ISDN connectivity has been an ever-present issue in any implementation. Because ISDN is a circuit-switched technology and uses the PSTN, charges related to long-distance telephony are indeed a large factor in the cost of ownership. To minimize the cost, DDR was implemented. To further aide in the quest to save capital, snapshot routing was created. Snapshot routing allows the use of a dynamic routing protocol across an ISDN/DDR link.

Traditionally, static routes have been the norm for DDR. With snapshot routing, they are no longer necessary. The routing table is frozen for a configured time and updates at the specified intervals. This relieves the pains typically associated with administering static routes.

All of these features combine to provide the most flexible and versatile technology available for a remote access solution. While other possibilities exist, none offer the same degree of customization as ISDN and DDR.

Q&A

The questions and scenarios in this book are more difficult than what you should experience on the actual exam. The questions do not attempt to cover more breadth or depth than the exam, but they are designed to make sure that you know the answer. Rather than enabling you to derive the answer from clues hidden inside the question itself, the questions challenge your understanding and recall of the subject. Hopefully, mastering these questions will help you limit the number of exam questions on which you narrow your choices to two options and then guess.

The answers to these questions can be found in Appendix A.

1. The load of a link is measured on what scale?

2. Multilink PPP serves what function?

3. What command can be issued to view the current load of interface Serial 0?

4. What is the principle benefit of dialer profiles?

5. In the absence of a dialer map statement, what can be used to define the phone number of the remote side of an ISDN link?

6. What commands would be entered to bind interfaces Bri 0, Bri 1, and Bri 2 to a common logical interface numbered 24? In the code that is your answer, also assign the IP address of 10.1.1.1/ 16 to the logical interface.

7. What is the purpose of a rotary group and how does it differ from a dialer pool configuration?

8. What are the two roles a router can fulfill in snapshot routing?

9. What are the periods in which a routing table can be placed when utilizing snapshot routing?

10. What is the minimum active period?

This chapter covers the following subjects:

- Primary Rate Interface

- Troubleshooting Multilink PPP and ISDN

CHAPTER 9

Using ISDN Primary Rate Interface

The CCNP Remote Access Exam requires you to have an in-depth understanding of various WAN technologies. In this chapter, the discussion focuses, once again, on ISDN. However, this chapter discusses Primary Rate Interface (PRI) rather than Basic Rate Interface (BRI), which was covered in Chapter 7.

Although they are based on the same technologies and use the same protocols, PRI implementations are very different than the BRI implementations previously discussed. This chapter touches on the background information necessary to give you a solid understanding of the PRI technology.

"Do I Know This Already?" Quiz

The purpose of the "Do I Know This Already?" quiz is to help you decide whether you really need to read the entire chapter. If you already intend to read the entire chapter, you do not necessarily need to answer these questions now.

The nine-question quiz, derived from the major sections in the "Foundation Topics" portion of the chapter, helps you to determine how to spend your limited study time.

Table 9-1 outlines the major topics discussed in this chapter and the "Do I Know This Already?" quiz questions that correspond to those topics.

Table 9-1 *"Do I Know This Already?" Foundation Topics Section-to-Question Mapping*

Foundation Topics Section	Questions Covered in This Section
Primary Rate Interface	1–5
Troubleshooting Multilink PPP and ISDN	6–9

CAUTION   The goal of self-assessment is to gauge your mastery of the topics in this chapter. If you do not know the answer to a question or are only partially sure of the answer, you should mark this question wrong for purposes of the self-assessment. Giving yourself credit for an answer that you correctly guess skews your self-assessment results and might provide you with a false sense of security.

1. What information is required of the telco to implement PRI implementations?

   a. Framing type

   b. Line coding

   c. Switch type

   d. All of the above

2. Which are options available for T1 framing and line code configuration?

   a. HDB3

   b. B8ZS

   c. MI

   d. SF

3. Which command configures the router to forward all incoming voice calls to internal MICA technology modems?

   a. **isdn incoming-voice voice**

   b. **isdn incoming-voice modem**

   c. **isdn incoming-voice data**

   d. **isdn incoming voice mica**

4. Which command is useful in viewing the state of Layers 1, 2, and 3 of ISDN simultaneously?

   a. **show dialer**

   b. **show isdn status**

   c. **show interface bri 0**

   d. **show isdn layer**

5. Which lists the number of bearer channels for BRI, T1 PRI, and E1 PRI?

   a. 30, 2, 23 respectively

   b. 2, 23, 30 respectively

   c. 23, 30, 2 respectively

   d. 30, 23, 2 respectively

6. Which command details the reason for the call as well as the B channels in use at a given time?

   a. show isdn protocol

   b. show isdn calls

   c. show dialer

   d. show calls

7. Which command allows the real-time viewing of the connection phase of a PPP session?

   a. debug isdn q921

   b. debug isdn q931

   c. debug dialer

   d. debug Multilink PPP

8. If a TEI is not properly negotiated, which command can be issued to view the message being exchanged between the router and switch at the appropriate layer?

   a. debug dialer

   b. debug ppp negotiation

   c. debug isdn q921

   d. debug isdn q931

9. If a call setup is not properly completing, which command can be issued to view the messages being exchanged between the router and switch at the appropriate layer?

   a. debug dialer

   b. debug ppp negotiation

   c. debug isdn q921

   d. debug isdn q931

The answers to the "Do I Know This Already?" quiz are found in Appendix A, "Answers to the 'Do I Know This Already?' Quizzes and Q&A Sections. The suggested choices for your next step are as follows:

- **4 or fewer overall score**—Read the entire chapter. This includes the "Foundation Topics," "Foundation Summary," and "Q&A" sections.

- **5 or 6 overall score**—Begin with the "Foundation Summary" section and then go to the "Q&A" section.

- **7 or more overall score**—If you want more review on these topics, skip to the "Foundation Summary" section and then go to the "Q&A" section. Otherwise, move to the next chapter.

Foundation Topics

Primary Rate Interface

PRI implementations are based on T1/E1 technologies. Although PRI is still ISDN, it is treated differently in regard to framing and signaling. Like BRI, PRI has only one connection to the ISDN network, and the switch type must be specified for the configuration to function. An ISDN PRI T1 implementation has 23 B channels and a D channel. As with BRI, each of the B channels has 64-kbps bandwidth available. The D channel, however, is also a 64-kbps channel (unlike BRI).

In traditional T1 implementations, 24 time slots exist. Obviously, one of the 24 time slots (time slot 23, counting 0–23) is taken away for signaling and framing. With E1 PRI implementations, there are 30 B channels available and one D channel, all having 64-kbps bandwidth available.

In traditional E1 implementations, there are 30 time slots, leaving 2 time slots for signaling and framing. Time slot 0 is used for framing and time slot 16 is used for signaling (counting 0–31). E1 PRI uses this same principle. Time slot 16 is the D channel, and time slot 0 is used for framing information.

T1 is typically deployed in North America and Japan. E1 is utilized in Europe, Central/South America, and Asia Pacific. Figure 9-1 depicts T1 and E1 PRI.

Figure 9-1 *T1 and E1 PRI*

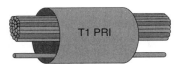 

23 x 64 kbps B channels   30 x 64 kbps channels
1 x 64 kbps D channel   1 x 64 kbps D channel (signaling)

ISDN Switch Type

The PRI installation procedure is similar to its BRI counterpart. A service call is placed, and then the demarcation point is determined and extended, if necessary. The carrier provides the basic information necessary for connectivity, but it will be necessary to configure the router with the appropriate switch type. Table 9-2 shows the Cisco-supported PRI switch types. (The BRI switch types are covered in Chapter 7.)

Table 9-2   *Cisco-Supported Primary Rate Switch Types*

Switch Type	Description
primary-4ess	AT&T 4ESS switch type for the U.S.
primary-5ess	AT&T 5ESS switch type for the U.S.
primary-dms100	Northern Telecom switch type for the U.S.
primary-net5	European switch type for NET5
primary-ni	National ISDN switch type for the U.S.
primary-ntt	Japanese switch type
primary-ts014	Australian switch type

Check with the provider for the appropriate switch type. A change of switch type requires a reload of the router.

T1 Framing and Line Coding

Although it is ISDN, PRI uses T1 framing and line coding. These technologies are based on the same model, represented in a number of 64-kbps channels.

The original use of digital facilities was to transport voice traffic. Because analog technologies were not adequate for long-distance transmission due to attenuation, another form of transmission—digitizing—was necessary. Digitizing the voice traffic for transmission enabled it to travel very long distances with no attenuation.

Once the data world was born, it became necessary to also transport data over long distances. Because the digital facilities were already available for voice traffic, it seemed a natural extension to use those facilities for data traffic as well. However, it proved to be something of a painful experience for a time. The history of voice and data transmission over T1 and E1 facilities followed the same growing pains.

T1 Framing

T1 specifies the physical coding of the signal on the wire, and DS1 specifies the framing of characteristics. So, T1 and DS1 are not the same thing after all, even though the two terms have been used interchangeably for years (and this book certainly is not going to stop that practice, but at least now you know the distinction).

A digital signal that is level 1 (DS1) consists of 24 DS0s. A DS0 is a 64-kbps channel. This channel is known as a *time slot*. One DS0 represents one voice call. The time slot is derived from the Nyquist theorem. Nyquist said that $f_s = 2(BW)$. Because the voice world had decided that 0–4000 Hz would be the supported range for voice circuits, the number 4000 was plugged into the formula in the BW position. Therefore, $f_s = 2(4000) = 8000$, which is the number of samples we should take of this analog wave per second.

To properly digitize (quantize) analog voice, it is necessary to take samples of the voice wave over time. If you sample too fast, you waste resources. If you sample too slowly, you allow for aliasing. Aliasing is a condition that occurs when two or more analog waves can match the coordinate points set forth by the samples (a little beyond our scope).

Each of the 8000 samples per second is represented by an 8-bit code word. Without going into too much depth, this code word simply defines the coordinates of the sample (polarity = 1 bit, segment = 3 bits, and step = 4 bits). Figure 9-2 depicts the sampling of the wave and the resulting code word.

The resulting throughput of 8000 eight-bit samples per second is 64,000 bps, or one DS0.

When one sample has been taken from each of the 24 time slots, a T1 frame is created. Because this is time division multiplexing (TDM), 8000 eight-bit samples are taken from each time slot every second. The result is 8000 T1 frames per second.

The telco provider specifies the type of framing that you should use when connecting to its facilities. The choices with T1 are SuperFrame (SF, also known as D4 framing) and Extended SuperFrame (ESF).

SF is the assembly of 12 T1 frames. Each of the T1 frames is separated from adjacent frames by a single framing bit (8000 T1 frames per second, each with an additional bit that is an additional 8000 bps of overhead).

ESF is the assembly of 24 T1 frames. Each frame is still separated by a delineating bit, but not all are used for framing: 2000 bps are used for framing, 2000 bps are used for CRC, and 4000 bps are used for data link control (this gives you many more management capabilities as compared to SF). Figure 9-3 depicts a SuperFrame and an Extended SuperFrame.

T1 Line Code

Once the framing has been configured, the next step is to configure the line coding. In North America, there are two types of line coding that are dominant: Alternate Mark Inversion (AMI) and Bipolar with 8 Zero Substitution (B8ZS).

Figure 9-2 *Sampling the Analog Wave*

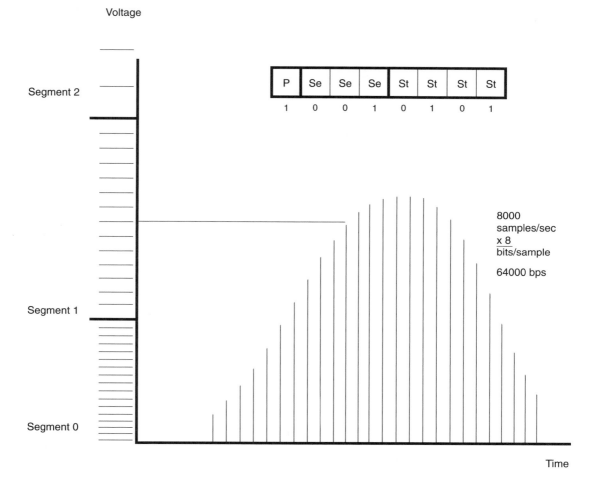

AMI is becoming increasingly rare in favor of B8ZS. AMI forces data bandwidth to 56 kbps due to the enforcement of a 1s density rule, which states that 12.5 percent of all bits transmitted must be 1s. To enforce the rule, AMI line-coded CSU/DSUs force every eighth bit (that is, the least significant bit of each time slot) to a 1. Effectively, this bit is lost. The rule may or may not actually change the bit, but effective throughput is reduced nonetheless. The end result is that there are still 8000 samples per second, but each sample has been reduced to 7 bits, thereby rendering 56,000 bits per second.

B8ZS has a more effective way of dealing with the enforcement of 1s density. It alters bits only when necessary, and then changes the affected bits back to their original values at the remote side.

Figure 9-3 *SF and ESF*

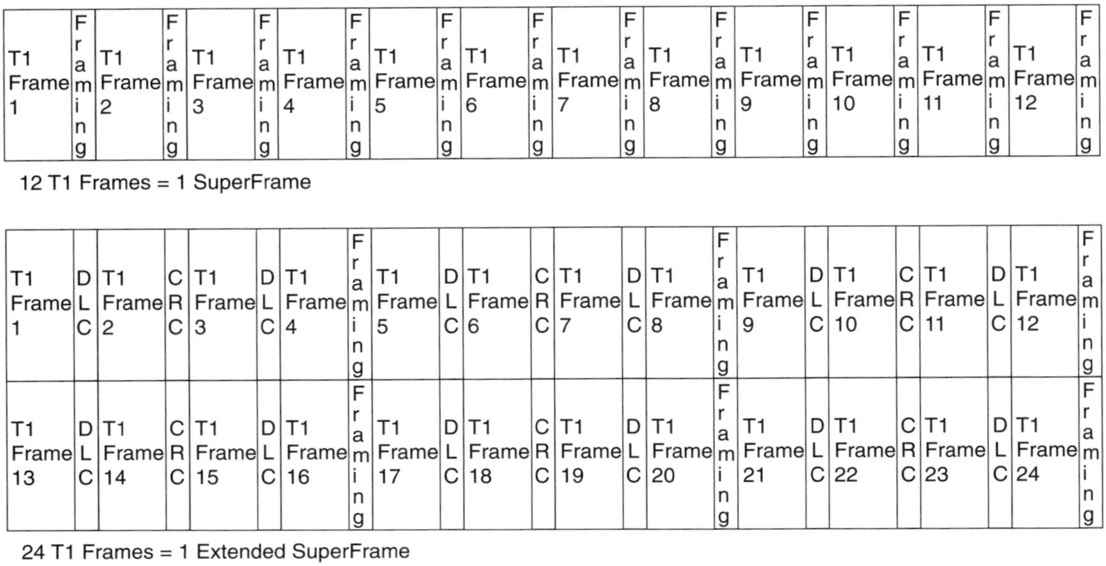

T1 Frame 1	Framing	T1 Frame 2	Framing	T1 Frame 3	Framing	T1 Frame 4	Framing	T1 Frame 5	Framing	T1 Frame 6	Framing	T1 Frame 7	Framing	T1 Frame 8	Framing	T1 Frame 9	Framing	T1 Frame 10	Framing	T1 Frame 11	Framing	T1 Frame 12	Framing

12 T1 Frames = 1 SuperFrame

T1 Frame 1	DLC	T1 Frame 2	CRC	T1 Frame 3	DLC	T1 Frame 4	Framing	T1 Frame 5	DLC	T1 Frame 6	CRC	T1 Frame 7	DLC	T1 Frame 8	Framing	T1 Frame 9	DLC	T1 Frame 10	CRC	T1 Frame 11	DLC	T1 Frame 12	Framing
T1 Frame 13	DLC	T1 Frame 14	CRC	T1 Frame 15	DLC	T1 Frame 16	Framing	T1 Frame 17	DLC	T1 Frame 18	CRC	T1 Frame 19	DLC	T1 Frame 20	Framing	T1 Frame 21	DLC	T1 Frame 22	CRC	T1 Frame 23	DLC	T1 Frame 24	Framing

24 T1 Frames = 1 Extended SuperFrame

To verify the configuration of the framing and line code currently being used, type the command **show controllers t1**. Example 9-1 shows a sample output of this command.

Example 9-1 **show controllers t1** *Command Output*

```
isdn-14#show controllers t1
  T1 0 is up.
    No alarms detected.
    Framing is ESF, Line Code is B8ZS, Clock Source is
      Line Primary.
    Data in current interval (676 seconds elapsed):
      0 Line Code Violations, 0 Path Code Violations
      0 Slip Secs, 0 Fr Loss Secs, 0 Line Err Secs,
      0 Degraded Mins
      0 Errored Secs, 0 Bursty Err Secs, 0 Severely Err Secs,
      0 Unavail Secs
    Total Data (last 46 15 minute intervals):
      0 Line Code Violations, 0 Path Code Violations,
      0 Slip Secs, 0 Fr Loss Secs, 0 Line Err Secs,
      0 Degraded Mins,
      0 Errored Secs, 0 Bursty Err Secs, 1 Severely Err Secs,
      0 Unavail Secs
```

E1 Framing and Line Coding

E1 has its roots in much the same technology as T1. The basic premise behind the use of each in a PRI scenario is virtually identical. E1 PRI uses E1 framing and line coding. The technologies are based on the same model, represented in a number of 64-kbps channels.

E1 Framing

E1 is based on the same basic foundation as T1. The concept of 64-kbps time slots created by 8000 eight-bit samples per second still holds true, and the sampling rates and methodologies between T1 framing and E1 framing are very similar. The differences lie in the assembly and multiplexing of the channels.

E1 frames are constructed of 30 time slots. Therefore, each E1 frame contains 30 eight-bit samples. When 16 E1 frames are assembled, a *MultiFrame* is created. MultiFrame is the dominant frame type in E1 implementations. Figure 9-4 depicts a MultiFrame.

Figure 9-4 *E1 MultiFrame*

E1 Frame 0	E1 Frame 1	E1 Frame 2	E1 Frame 3	E1 Frame 4	E1 Frame 5	E1 Frame 6	E1 Frame 7
E1 Frame 8	E1 Frame 9	E1 Frame 10	E1 Frame 11	E1 Frame 12	E1 Frame 13	E1 Frame 14	E1 Frame 15

16 E1 Frames = 1 MultiFrame

E1 Line Code

E1 deployments can implement AMI; however, the issues with AMI and data transmission still hold true: data transmissions are limited to 56 kbps. To remedy this, high-density bit level 3 (HDB3) was created. It operates similarly to B8ZS, but in a slightly more efficient manner. If a long string of 0s is detected, a number of them are changed to 1s for the duration of their trip across the provider network. They are then changed back to their original values at the remote CSU/DSU.

Because T1/E1 framing and line coding are not significant topics on the CCNP Remote Access Exam, they have not been discussed at length. However, they are important topics for an administrator to understand. For more information on these topics, check out Cisco.com. Search on keywords: "linecode", "AMI", "B8ZS" and "HDB3"

PRI Layers

PRI is based in the same technologies as BRI. In fact, PRI implements ISDN Q.921 (Layer 2) and Q.931 (Layer 3) in the same manner as BRI. In addition, the call setup messages are identical, as are the call release messages.

There are some basic differences between BRI and PRI, however. PRI relies on the assignment of a Terminal Endpoint Identifier (TEI). This TEI, however, is always 0 in Cisco's implementation.

Example 9-2 shows sample output of the **show isdn status** command. Notice the TEI and the fact that the state is MULTIPLE_FRAME_ESTABLISHED. This verifies the existence of Layer 2 connectivity.

Example 9-2   **show isdn status** *Command Output*

```
RouterA#show isdn status
 The current ISDN Switchtype = primary-ni
 ISDN Serial0:23 interface
     Layer 1 Status:
         ACTIVE
     Layer 2 Status:
         TEI = 0, State = MULTIPLE_FRAME_ESTABLISHED
     Layer 3 Status:
         No Active Layer 3 Call(s)
     Activated dsl 0 CCBs = 0
```

PRI Configuration

The configuration of the PRI service is quite simple. Although the command variations and options are very similar to that of its BRI counterpart, a PRI configuration has additional requirements.

To meet the needs of the PRI provisioning, the T1 or E1 (whichever is appropriate) must be configured to match telco requirements of framing and line code, as discussed in the preceding sections. The T1/E1 controller is actually an internal CSU/DSU. It must be told which time slots are included in the PRI configuration. For purposes of controller configuration, the time slot numbering starts at 1 (1–24 for T1, and 1–30 for E1). The command syntax is mercifully limited in the number of actual parameter choices available. Table 9-3 illustrates the options available for T1 and E1 configuration.

Table 9-3   *T1/E1 Framing and Line Code Options*

Options	Framing[a]	Line Code[a]
T1	SF (D4)	AMI
	ESF	B8ZS

Table 9-3 *T1/E1 Framing and Line Code Options (Continued)*

E1	CRC4	AMI
	NO-CRC4	HDB3
	CRC4 Australia	
	NO-CRC4 Australia	

[a] Framing and line code are telco-provided configuration parameters. If the controller configuration does not match what the telco has defined, the line does not function.

Once all the appropriate information is collected, the configuration can be completed. Example 9-3 illustrates a typical T1 controller configuration.

Example 9-3 *T1 PRI Configuration*

```
AS5300A(config)#isdn switch-type primary-ni
!
AS5300A(config)#controller t1 0/0
AS5300A(config-controller)#pri-group timeslots 1-24
AS5300A(config-controller)#framing esf
AS5300A(config-controller)#linecode b8zs
AS5300A(config-controller)#clock source line primary
!
AS5300A(config)#interface serial 0/0:23
AS5300A(config-if)#ip address 10.12.1.1  255.255.255.0
AS5300A(config-if)#isdn incoming-voice modem
```

Note that the switch type has been set. Again, this setting is based on telco-provided information. The **controller t1 0/0** command specifies the controller in slot 0, port 0. All 24 time slots are active in the configuration. The framing is ESF and the line code is B8ZS; both pieces of information are telco-provided. If this information is not provided by the telco, try using the configuration in Example 9-3.

ESF and B8ZS are the default (and most commonly deployed in North America) settings for the configuration in Example 9-3. For E1 implementations, the most common implementation is CRC4 and HDB3. If it doesn't work, change the line code and framing appropriately. There are a finite number of configuration variables. It is much less time consuming to experiment with the configuration and figure it out than it would be to call the telco and actually get to talk to someone who knows the appropriate settings for your installation.

Once the controller is configured, you must define the characteristics of the D channel. For controller t1 0/0, the D channel (as in Example 9-3) is interface serial 0/0:23. The last time slot (numbered 0–23 here) is the D channel in T1 PRI. The D channel in E1 PRI is time slot 15 (numbered 0–30).

The time slot numbering scheme has long been the subject of confusion. To aid in dispelling the confusion, the numbering scheme used at each point is specified. Example 9-4 illustrates the E1 equivalent configuration.

Example 9-4 *E1 PRI Configuration*

```
AS5300A(config)#isdn switch-type primary-ni
!
AS5300A(config)#controller e1 0/0
AS5300A(config-controller)#pri-group timeslots 1-30
AS5300A(config-controller)#framing crc4
AS5300A(config-controller)#linecode hdb3
AS5300A(config-controller)#clock source line primary
!
AS5300A(config)#interface serial 0/0:15
AS5300A(config-if)#ip address 10.12.1.1  255.255.255.0
AS5300A(config-if)#isdn incoming-voice modem
```

This interface, in this case serial 0/0:15, carries the protocol-specific configuration (that is, the IP address, the IPX network, and so forth) for protocols that need to traverse this link.

The configuration in Example 9-4 was captured from an AS5300 with eight PRI ports and two MICA modem blades with 120 modems each. The **isdn incoming-voice modem** command specifies that any inbound calls originating from modem users be directed to a MICA modem installed in this device rather than be treated as if an actual ISDN-capable device were issuing a call setup. This is not to say that a device with bearer capabilities cannot dial into this device for connectivity. It still can. The AS5300 detects the call type and treats it accordingly.

PRI Incoming Analog Calls on Digital Modems

Up to this point, the discussion has focused on data calls. In other words, the topics have centered on B channel to B channel calls.

In remote-access deployments, the end user dials into an access server. The incoming lines that provide connectivity from the end user to the access server are PRI implementations. These PRI lines are completely digital facilities. Figure 9-5 illustrates the typical deployment of an access server installation.

When an end user dials into the network access server (NAS), the router detects that the call is inbound from a modem. In other words, it sees the call as an incoming analog call. If it were a call from another B channel, the call would be completely digital; however, because the call originated from an analog modem, the NAS must answer back in the form expected by the modem. Using the **isdn incoming-voice modem** command, the router passes the call off to one of the internal MICA modems installed in the NAS.

Figure 9-5 *Network Access Server Deployment*

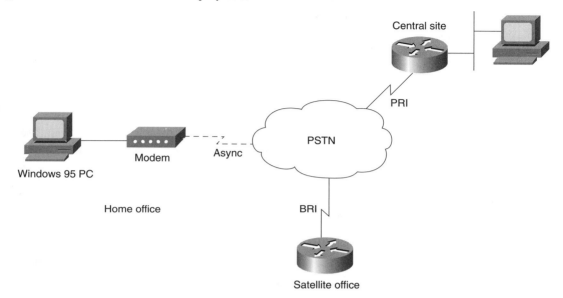

In a traditional modem-to-modem call setup, the call begins as digital communication between the PC and the modem. The modem converts the transmission to analog (that is, modulated) and passes it off to the edge CO switch. Once inside the PSTN, the transmission is again converted to digital format for its journey across the PSTN. Once the transmission arrives at the remote edge switch, it is converted back to analog only to be changed back to digital by the modem (that is, demodulated) at the remote site and forwarded to the receiving party. It all seems a bit redundant.

In the case of PRI incoming lines that are receiving these "voice" calls, the call process is the same—up to the point where the call is demodulated by the remote modem. In a NAS implementation, the demodulation is not necessary. It is taken, in digital form, and passed to a MICA modem where it is not demodulated, but left in digital form. The MICA modem negotiates the connection just as any other modem.

Once the connection is complete, the calling-party machine is assigned an IP address from the IP address pool configured on the NAS, or another configured source. Once an IP address and default gateway are assigned, the calling-party machine functions as if it were attached to the LAN on the remote side of the NAS.

Troubleshooting Multilink PPP and ISDN

Up to this point, the discussions have focused on the actual configuration and implementation of ISDN technologies. This section discusses Multilink PPP and its associated issues. Fortunately, there are some troubleshooting commands readily available. The commands in the following sections are useful in resolving any issues with your PPP connections. Each command is followed by sample output.

Also worthy of note at this point is the **show isdn status** command. It was covered earlier in this chapter. It constitutes one of the more useful commands in ISDN troubleshooting overall. Use it early and often when issues arise. Example 9-5 shows output from the **show isdn status** command.

Example 9-5   **show isdn status** *Command Output*

```
RouterA#show isdn status
The current ISDN Switchtype = basic-5ess
ISDN BRI0 interface
  Layer 1 Status:
        ACTIVE
  Layer 2 Status:
    TEI = 90, State = MULTIPLE_FRAME_ESTABLISHED
  Layer 3 Status:
        1 Active Layer 2 Call(s)
        Activated dsl 0 CCBs are 2, Allocated = 2
          callid=0, sapi=0, ces=2
          callid=8000, sapi=0, ces=1
```

You can easily see that the three layers of the ISDN model are in fact in good standing. The output shows the switch type as well as relevant information from each layer of the ISDN model.

show ppp multilink Command

Executing the **show ppp multilink** command displays the current status of Multilink PPP sessions. Example 9-6 shows sample output of a call in progress.

Example 9-6   **show ppp multilink** *Command Output*

```
RouterA#show ppp multilink
Bundle RouterA, 1 member, Master link is BRI 0
Dialer Interface is BRI0
  0 lost fragments, 0 reordered, 0 unassigned, sequence 0x0/0x0 rcvd/sent
  0 discarded, 0 lost received, 1/255 load

Member Link: 1 (max not set, min not set)
BRI0:1
```

Notice that Example 9-6, in the shaded areas, shows the physical interface being initialized and the B channel being used.

show dialer Command

Executing the **show dialer** command displays active calls and status information. Example 9-7 shows sample output of calls in session.

Example 9-7   **show dialer** *Command Output*

```
RouterA#show dialer
BRI0 - dialer type = ISDN
Dial String      Successes    Failures    Last called    Last status
2145552222       18           0           00:01:12       successful

0 incoming call(s) have been screened.

BRI0:1 - dialer type = ISDN
Idle timer (120 secs), Fast idle timer (20 secs)
Wait for carrier (30 secs), Re-enable (15 secs)
Dialer state is multilink member
Dial reason: ip (s=10.12.1.1, d=10.12.1.2)
Connected to 2145552222 (RouterB)

BRI0:2 - dialer type = ISDN
Idle timer (120 secs), Fast idle timer (20 secs)
Wait for carrier (30 secs), Re-enable (15 secs)
Dialer state is idle
 Idle timer (120 secs), Fast idle timer (20 secs)
Wait for carrier (30 secs), Re-enable (15 secs)
Dialer state is data link layer up
Time until disconnect 93 secs
Connected to 2145552223 (RouterB)
```

The **show dialer** command output is filled with information. It includes the number dialed and whether the attempt to reach that number succeeded or failed. Later in the output, you can see the state of each B channel. By looking at the last line of output under each B channel, it is evident that both B channels are connected and in use for this particular call. Also worthy of mention is the Idle timer. In the example, it shows 120 seconds. This is the countdown to disconnect. The Fast idle timer is the countdown to disconnect in the event that another call needs to be placed on this same interface to another destination.

debug ppp multilink Command

Executing the **debug ppp multilink** command monitors the PPP connect phase. Example 9-8 shows sample output of a **ping-**triggered call.

Example 9-8 **debug ppp multilink** *Command Output*

```
RouterA#debug ppp Multilink
*Apr 14 03:22:10.489: %LINK-3-UPDOWN: Interface BRI0:1, changed state to up
*Apr 14 03:22:10.497:%LINEPROTO-5-UPDOWN: Line protocol on Interface BRI0:1, changed state to up
*Apr 14 03:22:10.520%LINK-3-UPDOWN: Interface BRI0:2, changed state to up
*Apr 14 03:22:10.554: BR0:1 MLP: O seq 80000000 size 58
*Apr 14 03:22:10.558: BR0:2 MLP: O seq 40000001 size 60
*Apr 14 03:22:10.586: BR0:1 MLP: I seq 80000000 size 58
*Apr 14 03:22:10.590: BR0:2 MLP: I seq 40000001 size 60
*Apr 14 03:22:10.598: BR0:1 MLP: O seq 80000002 size 58
*Apr 14 03:22:10.598: BR0:2 MLP: O seq 40000003 size 60
*Apr 14 03:22:10.629: BR0:1 MLP: I seq 80000002 size 58
*Apr 14 03:22:10.629: BR0:2 MLP: I seq 40000003 size 60!!!
*Apr 14 03:22:10.630:Success rate is 94 percent (47/50), round-trip min/avg/max = 36/41/128 ms
*Apr 14 03:22:10.637: BR0:1 MLP: O seq 80000004 size 58
*Apr 14 03:22:10.641: BR0:2 MLP: O seq 40000005 size 60
%LINEPROTO-5-UPDOWN: Line protocol on Interface BRI0:2, changed state to up
*Apr 14 03:22:10.669: BR0:1 MLP: I seq 80000004 size 58
Apr 14 03:22:11.330:%ISDN-6-CONNECT:InterfaceBRI0:2 is now connected to 2145552223 RouterB
```

The output in Example 9-8 shows that BRI 0, B channel 1 was brought up and dialed out to a remote site. The load across that link was such that a second B channel was triggered and brought up. The traffic traversing the link is recorded in the output along with the interface and B channel being used for each transmission. Note that independent sequence numbers are used for each B channel to aid in re-sorting the traffic when it reaches the remote end.

debug dialer Command

There are many more commands and command outputs that are useful in troubleshooting the dial process in general. For instance, the **debug dialer** command is one of the best tools to use to figure out which traffic is attempting to traverse the ISDN link. Example 9-9 shows the **debug dialer** command output.

Example 9-9 **debug dialer** *Command Output*

```
RouterA#debug dialer
RouterA#ping 10.12.1.2

Type escape sequence to abort.
Sending 5, 100-byte ICMP Echos to 10.12.1.2, timeout is 2 seconds:
BRI0: Dialing cause ip (s=10.12.1.1, d=10.12.1.2)
```

Example 9-9 **debug dialer** *Command Output (Continued)*

```
BRI0: Attempting to dial 2145552222.
%LINK-3-UPDOWN: Interface BRI0:1, changed state to up
%LINEPROTO-5-UPDOWN: Line protocol on Interface BRI0:1, changed state to up.!!!
Success rate is 60 percent (3/5), round-trip min/avg/max = 36/41/52 ms
%ISDN-6-CONNECT: Interface BRI0:1 is now connected to 2145552222 RouterB
```

The output in Example 9-9 is fairly self-explanatory. It denotes the reason that the call is being dialed (i.e., IP traffic is defined as interesting and needs to traverse the link). Also of interest here is that the dial string is shown, as is the interface and B channel being initialized. Once the call is up, the interface can be seen in state change (i.e., changed state to up) and the **ping** succeeds.

debug isdn q921 Command

To view the processes occurring at the second layer of ISDN, the **debug isdn q921** command is useful. In the output of this command, you can find information such as TEI negotiation. Example 9-10 illustrates output from this command.

Example 9-10 **debug isdn q921** *Command Output*

```
RouterA#debug isdn q921
BRI0: TX -> IDREQ  ri = 65279  ai = 127
BRI0: RX <- UI sapi = 0  tei = 127 i = 0x0801FF0504038090A218018896250101
BRI0: TX -> IDREQ  ri = 61168  ai = 127
BRI0: RX <- IDASSN  ri = 61168  ai =64
BRI0: TX -> SABMEp sapi = 0  tei = 64
BRI0: RX <- UAf sapi = 0  tei = 64
BRI0: TX -> INFOc sapi = 0  tei = 64  ns = 0  nr = 0  i = x08017F5A080280D1
BRI0: RX <- RRr sapi = 0  tei = 64  nr = 1
BRI0: RX <- INFOc sapi = 0  tei = 64  ns = 0  nr = 1  i = x08007B963902EF01
BRI0: TX -> RRr sapi = 0  tei = 64  nr = 1
BRI0: RX <- INFOc sapi = 0  tei = 64 ns = 1  nr = 1 i = 0x8007B962201013201013B0110
BRI0: TX -> RRr sapi = 0  tei = 64  nr = 2
BRI0: TX -> RRp sapi = 0  tei = 64 nr = 2
BRI0: RX <- RRf sapi = 0  tei = 64  nr = 1
BRI0: TX -> RRp sapi = 0  tei = 64 nr = 2
BRI0: RX <- RRf sapi = 0  tei = 64  nr = 1
```

The following paragraphs provide a partial explanation of the output listed in Example 9-10. You should take the time to understand this section because the output gives a great deal of troubleshooting information. You may need to read it more than once to get it all straight.

The **ri** is a reference indicator. It provides the router and the switch a way to keep straight all the calls they may be processing. Notice in the *IDREQ* and the *IDASSN* that the *ri* value is the same. If the router sends an *IDREQ* and receives no response, it retries every two seconds. Each time the *ri* is different. The *ai* is an association indicator. *ai = 127* is the router's way of requesting a TEI from the switch. The switch reply is *ai = 64*. Therefore, 64 is the assigned TEI.

Notice that all remaining correspondence has *tei = 64* referenced. Once the router has a TEI, it sends a *SABME* (Set Asynchronous Balanced Mode Extended) message with *sapi = 0*. This means that this is a signaling connection (that is, this is all taking place over the D channel).

If no TEI is assigned, Layer 2 does activate and the output from the **debug isdn q921** command renders only *TX->IDREQ* lines. If all the Layer 2 processes are successful, you will see *MULTIPLE_FRAME_ ESTABLISHED* under the *Layer 2 Status* section in the output of the **show isdn status** command.

debug isdn q931 Command

The **debug isdn q931** command allows the real-time viewing of the operations at the third layer of the ISDN model. This is typically output showing call setup and teardown. Example 9-11 shows the beginning of a call setup. The output is from a **ping** to the remote side while the **debug isdn q931** command is active. Note the **ping** timeout (.), which is followed by a **ping** success (!) after the call setup.

Example 9-11 **debug isdn q931** *Command Output*

```
RouterA#debug isdn q931
RouterA#ping 10.12.1.2
Type escape sequence to abort.
Sending 5, 100-byte ICMP Echos to 10.12.1.2, timeout is 2 seconds:
ISDN BR0: TX -> SETUP pd = 8  callref = 0x0E
    Bearer Capability I = 0x8890
    Channel ID i = 0x83
    Keypad Facility i = 0x3935353532303032
ISDN BR0: RX <- SETUP_ACK pd = 8  callref = 0x8E
Channel ID i = 0x89
ISDN BR0: RX <- CALL_PROC pd = 8  callref = 0x8E
ISDN BR0: RX <- CONNECT pd = 8  callref = 0x8E
%LINK-3-UPDOWN:Interface BRI0:1, changed state to up
ISDN BR0: TX -> CONNECT_ACK pd = 8  callref = 0x0E
%LINEPROTO-5-UPDOWN: Line protocol on Interface BRI0:1, changed state to up..!!!
Success rate is 60 percent (3/5), round-trip min/avg/max = 36/36/36 ms
%ISDN-6-CONNECT: Interface BRI0:1 is now connected to 2145553000 RouterB
```

The ICMP traffic falls within the parameters of what has been defined as interesting traffic. The call is placed, and interface BRI 0, B channel 1 can be seen initializing and completing the call. The highlighted messages show the call setup procedure step by step.

The troubleshooting section of this chapter could continue on indefinitely. The commands described here are only those that are within the scope of the exam. For more information on other commands, go to http://www.cisco.com/univercd/cc/td/doc/product/software/ios113ed/dbook/index.htm and check out the **debug** command reference.

Foundation Summary

The Foundation Summary is a collection of information that provides a convenient review of many key concepts in this chapter. If you are already comfortable with the topics in this chapter, this summary can help you recall a few details. If you just read this chapter, this review should help solidify some key facts. If you are doing your final preparation before the exam, this section is a convenient way to review the day before the exam.

Table 9-4 summarizes the ISDN service offerings.

Table 9-4 *ISDN Services*

Service	B Channels	D Channel	Bandwidth
BRI	2 x 64 kbps	1 x 16 kbps	144 kbps
T1 PRI	23 x 64 kbps	1 x 64 kbps	1.544 Mbps
E1 PRI	30 x 64 kbps	1 x 64 kbps	2.048 Mbps

Table 9-5 summarizes ISDN protocols.

Table 9-5 *ISDN Protocols*

Layer	Protocol	Description
1	I.430/T1.601	This layer is the physical layer, which deals with connectivity. I.430 specifies framing between TE1 and NT1. T1.601 specifies framing between TE and the LE.
2	Q.921	Q.921 institutes an addressing scheme for ISDN.
3	Q.931	Q.931 is used between the TE and the local ISDN switch. Call setup is handled by Q.931 as well.

The offerings associated with ISDN PRI are quite similar to those offered with BRI implementations. The scale is somewhat larger, however. Typical implementations of PRI are deployed at central sites that expect moderate call volume from both dialup users and ISDN routers. The PRI interface can handle either type of call with relative ease. The base difference between the call types is simply a determination of whether the inbound call is digital signal (dial up) or digital data (from an ISDN host). Once the determination is made, the proper entity within the router can service the call and provide the proper resources.

As seen in the chapter, the configuration of PRI is quite similar to its BRI counterpart. The real differences come in configuring the T1 options, such as framing, line code, and time slots. The T1 controller is an integrated CSU/DSU. Therefore, an external CSU/DSU is not necessary.

ISDN is complex. However, Cisco has provided some of the most comprehensive (and easily read) **debug** and **show** commands available in any technology. These are vital to any implementation, because numerous issues can arise in an ISDN installation.

The first step in troubleshooting ISDN is to make sure the individual layers are properly connected. The **show isdn status** command is the best way to do that. This command shows, layer by layer, the status of each component in the ISDN stack.

A firm knowledge of **show** and **debug** commands will provide many answers to problems and issues surrounding the ISDN installation.

Q&A

The questions and scenarios in this book are more difficult than what you should experience on the actual exam. The questions do not attempt to cover more breadth or depth than the exam, but they are designed to make sure that you know the answer. Rather than enabling you to derive the answer from clues hidden inside the question, the questions challenge your understanding and recall of the subject. Hopefully, mastering these questions will help you limit the number of exam questions on which you narrow your choices to two options and then guess.

The answers to these questions can be found in Appendix A.

Refer to Figure 9-6 to answer the questions that follow.

Figure 9-6 *Network Diagram for Use with Q&A*

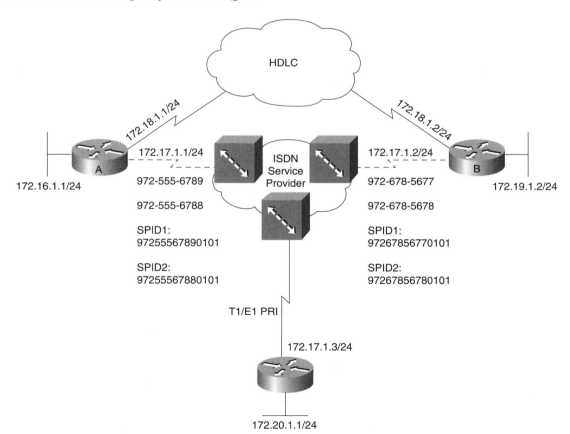

1. List the configuration commands necessary for router C to provide T1 PRI connectivity using B8ZS and ESF. Configure the appropriate IP addressing on interface S 0:23. It is not necessary to get into the PPP/DDR configurations.

2. Now assume that router C is being implemented in an E1 environment using the default settings for framing and line code. Because there is only one option for framing (MultiFrame), it is not necessary to enter the command. Make the appropriate configuration changes and list them in your answer.

3. Where is signaling information carried in T1 implementations?

4. Where is signaling information carried in E1 implementations?

5. What is the difference between SF and ESF?

6. To redirect calls to a MICA modem upon arrival at a NAS, what command can be issued on the NAS?

7. If an administrator were to feel the need to monitor call setup transactions, what command would be most useful?

8. To view the number of ISDN connections currently active in a router and the number of B channels in use, what command would be most useful? (Link: Troubleshooting Multilink PPP and ISDN)

PART IV: Broadband Access Methods to the Central Site

Chapter 10   Broadband Options to Access a Central Site

Chapter 11   Using DSL to Access a Central Site

This part of the book covers the following BCRAN exam topics:

- Configure DSL operation using Cisco IOS
- Design a solution of access control to meet required specifications
- Troubleshoot non-functional remote access systems

This chapter covers the following subjects:

- Broadband Background

- Cable Options

- Satellite Options

- Wireless Options

CHAPTER 10

Broadband Options to Access a Central Site

The CCNP Remote Access Exam requires you to have an in-depth understanding of various WAN technologies. In this chapter, the discussion focuses on the broadband options that are available currently. The recent emergence of broadband in the mainstream offerings of service providers has opened up a new world of options for remote and home users of these technologies. This chapter will serve, primarily, as an overview of the cable, satellite, and wireless alternatives currently on the market.

"Do I Know This Already?" Quiz

The purpose of the "Do I Know This Already?" quiz is to help you decide whether you really need to read the entire chapter. If you already intend to read the entire chapter, you do not necessarily need to answer these questions now.

The nine-question quiz, derived from the major sections in the "Foundation Topics" portion of the chapter, helps you to determine how to spend your limited study time.

Table 10-1 outlines the major topics discussed in this chapter and the "Do I Know This Already?" quiz questions that correspond to those topics.

Table 10-1 *"Do I Know This Already?" Foundation Topics Section-to-Question Mapping*

Foundation Topics Section	Questions Covered in This Section
Broadband Background	1
Cable Options	2–3
Satellite Options	4–5
Wireless Options	6–9

CAUTION The goal of self-assessment is to gauge your mastery of the topics in this chapter. If you do not know the answer to a question or are only partially sure of the answer, you should mark this question wrong for purposes of the self-assessment. Giving yourself credit for an answer that you correctly guess skews your self-assessment results and might provide you with a false sense of security.

1. Where is broadband typically implemented?

   a. Residence

   b. Large office

   c. Corporate enterprise

   d. Dialup solutions

2. Broadband cable technologies are based on which specification?

   a. 802.11a

   b. 802.3

   c. 802.2

   d. DOCSIS

3. How is a DOCSIS configuration file loaded onto a cable modem?

   a. FTP

   b. CLI entry

   c. SNMP

   d. TFTP

4. Which orbit scheme allows a satellite to remain over the same portion of Earth at all times?

   a. GEO

   b. LEO

   c. HEO

   d. SS

5. What is the typical round-trip time for a single data packet from ground to satellite back to ground?

   a. 1/8 second

   b. 1 second

   c. 1/4 second

   d. 1/10 second

6. Wireless LAN technologies are based on which technical specification?

   a. 802.11

   b. 802.10

    c. 802.2

    d. DOCSIS

7. Which 802.11 specification is most widely deployed?

    a. 802.11a

    b. 802.11b

    c. 802.11d

    d. 802.11g

8. Which 802.11 specifications are interoperable?

    a. 802.11a

    b. 802.11b

    c. 802.11d

    d. 802.11g

9. Which two are wireless authentication options?

    a. Open authentication

    b. Shared authentication

    c. Password authentication

    d. Challenge Handshake authentication

The answers to the "Do I Know This Already?" quiz are found in Appendix A, "Answers to the 'Do I Know This Already?' Quizzes and Q&A Sections." The suggested choices for your next step are as follows:

- **7 or fewer overall score**—Read the entire chapter. This includes the "Foundation Topics," "Foundation Summary," and "Q&A" sections.

- **8 or more overall score**—If you want more review on these topics, skip to the "Foundation Summary" section and then go to the "Q&A" section. Otherwise, move to the next chapter.

Foundation Topics

Broadband Background

Broadband can be delivered by a variety of technologies. As newer and more interesting ways to implement existing and new technologies are discovered, more options will become available. By no means should the battle for your Internet-access dollars be considered finished or won by any particular technology. The course of the battle changes with the wind.

In the end, the technology that is best is the one that can meet both the technological and financial needs of its customers. If a single technology is to prevail, it must be able to offer versatile, flexible, technologically sound options to its subscribers while not pushing itself into a cost-prohibitive state.

In general, broadband can be delivered via the following technologies:

- DSL
- Cable
- Satellite
- Wireless

In recent years, broadband options available to the average consumer have been offered in fierce competition with one another. The deployment of these technologies has been largely hit and miss. The overall battle has primarily (in most residential customer markets) come down to one of cable vs. DSL. DSL will be covered in Chapter 11, "Using DSL to Access a Central Site." Therefore, there will be little or no mention of it here.

Wireless technologies tend to be a bit more complex to implement due to security concerns. Until recently, the deployment of a wireless option was cost-prohibitive. This has changed drastically recently as more vendors attempt to exploit the home-networking market. As the cable vs. DSL battle rages on, the wireless networking camp seems to be finding a niche in providing home/office connectivity to a device running cable or DSL for broadband Internet connectivity.

Among the three technologies covered in this chapter, satellite is the least commonly utilized. Up to now, it has been a cost-prohibitive alternative due to increased network latency. This is not necessarily the case today. Now, there are less expensive technologies that make satellite a viable offering for the small office/home office (SOHO) world.

Wireless implementations are largely utilized in LAN environments rather than making them a true broadband access option. However, many planned communities have recently begun to station wireless access points at strategic points throughout a subdivision, allowing wireless access to all residents in the subdivision. The cost to the subscriber includes the wireless adapters for any machines connecting and, of course, a recurring subscription fee for the service.

Cable Options

Cable broadband implementations have been around since 1998 in larger cities. However, in many areas, local service providers are just beginning to offer cable broadband service.

Cable companies market their services as being in the multi-megabit bandwidth range. The actual service guarantee varies from provider to provider. Overall, customer reviews of cable as a SOHO solution have been mixed. Many people who were among the first in their area to get the service report that it was great until everyone figured out that it was available, after which latency became a problem.

Like any other technology, the satisfaction level of customers depends on the service provider's deployment and "oversubscription" strategy. When the product's viability and projected growth are grossly understated, it usually results in a diminished service and, appropriately, customer dissatisfaction. This leads customers to begin the search for the next great thing.

This search is what the cable companies—actually, all broadband providers—want to avoid. Toward that goal, broadband providers increasingly are listening to their customers, test marketing their products, and learning what makes the customers happy.

Telephone companies have experienced this very phenomenon. It's not enough anymore for a telco to simply provide dial tone. They must provide a wide array of dependable services to stay competitive. The broadband providers are simply going through the pains involved in figuring out this principle.

Cable Technology Background

Cable specifications are defined by a document known as Data Over Cable Service Interface Specification (DOCSIS). The current specification is known as DOCSIS 2.0. This specification defines the use of data over cable as well as sets for various functional details, some of which will be discussed in the following sections. Because this is an overview of the technology, the coverage focuses on the configuration of Cisco routers in cable implementations more so than the underlying technology.

DOCSIS Basics

DOCSIS defines technical specifications for equipment at both subscriber locations and cable operators' head ends. The use of DOCSIS accelerates the deployment and evolution of data-over-cable services. As is true for any technology, if all hardware vendors use the same standards and methods of constructing a technological offering, interoperability will be facilitated, thus easing the constraints and headaches involved in deploying newer technologies.

The DOCSIS specification is managed by CableLabs, a nonprofit research and development consortium that is dedicated to pursuing new cable telecommunications technologies. CableLabs was founded in 1988.

As a specification, DOCSIS has undergone three evolutions, beginning with version 1.0 and moving on to 1.1 and now 2.0. Most vendor implementations currently use DOCSIS 1.1. In the very near future, DOCSIS 2.0–capable devices will become available.

DOCSIS has several components that comprise its architecture:

- **Cable modem termination system (CMTS)**—A device that modulates the signal to the cable modem (CM) and demodulates the CM response. The CMTS usually resides in the head end.

- **Cable modem (CM)**—A CPE device that terminates as well as performs modulation and demodulation of signals to and from the CMTS. Typical transmission speeds for CMs range from 1.5 to 2.5 Mbps.

- **"Back office" services**—Services such as TFTP (for configuration file upload/download), DHCP (for dynamic IP addressing), ToD (for time-of-day log time-stamping), and others that provide vital tools for the maintenance of a CM installation.

Critical information for the configuration of CM hosts is carried in the DOCSIS configuration file. This is a file that contains information pertinent to all CM hosts that attach to the provider network. All DOCSIS-compliant configuration files include the following information elements:

- Radio Frequency Information
    - Downstream Frequency
    - Upstream Channel ID
    - Network Access Configuration
- Class of Service Information
    - Class of Service ID
    - Maximum Downstream Rate
    - Maximum Upstream Rate
    - Upstream Channel Priority
    - Minimum Upstream Rate

- — Maximum Upstream Channel Burst

- — Class of Service Privacy Enable

■ Vendor-Specific Options, including the vendor ID

■ SNMP Management

- — SNMP Write-Access Control and SNMP MIB Objects

■ Baseline Privacy Interface Configuration

- — Authorize Wait Timeout

- — Reauthorize Wait Timeout

- — Authorization Grace Timeout

- — Operational Wait Timeout

- — Rekey Wait Timeout

- — TEK Grace Time

- — Authorize Reject Wait Timeout

■ Customer Premises Equipment

- — Maximum Number of CPEs

- — CPE Ethernet MAC Address

■ Software Upgrade

- — TFTP Software Server IP Address

- — Software Image Filename

■ Miscellaneous

- — Concatenation Support

- — Use RFC2104 HMAC-MD5

- — CMTS Authentication

NOTE   The DOCSIS configuration file also contains fields for one-way cable modems that use telco-return; however, these fields do not apply to the Cisco uBR900 Series routers because they are two-way cable modems.

Cable transmissions are highly similar to wireless transmissions, with the obvious exception of the presence or absence of copper. Cable transmission uses the radio frequency (RF) band. The RF band comprises the frequencies above audio and below infrared.

For downstream transmission (cable company to CPE), cable uses the 55–750-MHz band. This same band is used for UHF and VHF transmissions as well. Upstream transmission (CPE to cable company) uses the 5–42-MHz band.

Cisco's implementation of the CMTS is a Universal Broadband Router (uBR) with features that enable it to communicate with a hybrid fiber-coaxial (HFC) cable network. HFC is a technology developed by cable vendors to provide high-speed, bidirectional data transmission using a combination of fiber optics and traditional coaxial cable. The Cisco cable-modem cards allow you to connect CMs on the HFC network to a Cisco uBR7200, uBR7100, or uBR10K in a head-end facility. The modem card provides an interface between the Cisco uBR PCI bus and the RF signal on the DOCSIS HFC network.

CM Initialization

Figure 10-1 illustrates a typical deployment of Cisco Cable Access products. This illustration provides a basis for the discussion of the remainder of this section.

Figure 10-1 *A Typical Cisco Cable Access Router Deployment*

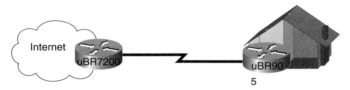

To establish a connection to the CMTS, the CM must initialize properly. On a uBR device, the command **show cable modem** can be used to show the status of individual connections. Example 10-1 shows output from this command.

Example 10-1 **show cable modem** *Command on a uBR Showing Modems Off Line*

```
sydney#show cable modem
Interface    Prim Online    Timing Rec   QoS CPE IP address    MAC address
             Sid  State     Offset Power
Cable2/0/U0 5    offline    2290   0.00  2   0   10.1.1.25     0050.7366.2223
Cable2/0/U0 6    offline    2811   0.00  2   0   10.1.1.22     0050.7366.1e01
Cable2/0/U0 7    offline    2810  -0.50  2   0   10.1.1.20     0030.96f9.65d9
Cable2/0/U0 8    offline    2810  -0.25  2   0   10.1.1.21     0030.96f9.6605
```

The preceding output shows that four modems are in the offline state. Obviously, to transfer data, the modems must be in operational state. The basic data transfer process is as follows:

1. Scan for a downstream channel and establish synchronization.

2. Obtain upstream parameters.

3. Make Ranging and Automatic Adjustments.

4. Establish IP connectivity (DHCP).

5. Establish Time of Day (ToD).

6. Transfer optional parameters.

7. Register with the CMTS.

8. Establish baseline privacy (optional).

The ranging process (Step 3) is used to calculate the necessary transmit power level to reach the CMTS at its desired input power level. Typically, transmit power is roughly 40–50 dBmV in a production network. After the transmit power level is calculated, the necessary adjustments are made to the power level.

After Step 7 is complete (and Step 8, if used), the CM is in operational state and can begin transferring traffic to and from the CMTS.

Once the data transfer process is complete, the **show cable modem** command on the uBR will show that the status of the modems is on line. Example 10-2 shows the state after initialization.

Example 10-2   **show cable modem** *Command Output on a uBR*

```
sydney#show cable modem

Interface     Prim Online    Timing Rec   QoS CPE IP address    MAC address
              Sid  State     Offset Power
Cable2/0/U0 5      online     2289   -0.25  5   0   10.1.1.25    0050.7366.2223
Cable2/0/U0 6      online     2811   -0.25  5   0   10.1.1.22    0050.7366.1e01
Cable2/0/U0 7      online     2811   -0.50  5   0   10.1.1.20    0030.96f9.65d9
```

CM Configuration

A DOCSIS configuration file is a "binary file" that contains the parameters for cable modems to come on line in accordance with what the ISP is provisioning, such as Maximum Downstream and Upstream Rates, Maximum Upstream Burst Rate, Class of Service or Baseline Privacy, MIBs, and many other parameters. This file can be loaded on the CM via TFTP or the CM can be manually configured.

For SOHO-type environments, Cisco offers the uBR900 Series routers. Figure 10-2 shows a picture of the uBR900.

Figure 10-2 *The Cisco uBR900 Series Router*

The router can act in one of two modes: bridging or routing. In bridging mode (the default), the transmission of data is performed based on the MAC address of the individual host(s). This is the default mode for most CM hardware.

Example 10-3 shows a sample configuration of a uBR900 Series router in bridging mode.

Example 10-3 *uBR900 in Bridging Mode*

```
UBR900(config)#

clock timezone - 0
ip subnet-zero
no ip routing
!
interface Ethernet0
 ip address 10.1.1.26 255.255.255.0
 no ip directed-broadcast
 no ip route-cache
 bridge-group 59
 bridge-group 59 spanning-disabled
!
```

Example 10-3 *uBR900 in Bridging Mode (Continued)*

```
interface cable-modem0
 ip address negotiated
 no ip directed-broadcast
 no ip route-cache
 cable-modem downstream saved channel 453000000 28 1
 cable-modem mac-timer t2 60000
 bridge-group 59
 bridge-group 59 spanning-disabled
!
ip default-gateway 10.1.1.10
!
ip classless
no ip http server
!
line con 0
 transport input none
!
line vty 0 4
!
end
```

The **no ip routing** command is sufficient, in this case, to place the uBR900 in bridging mode. Note that the traditional **bridge-group <group number>** commands are not present in the default configuration. These commands will be necessary if routing is enabled, then disabled. As mentioned, this is the default mode of forwarding for this device. This configuration was retrieved from a brand-new, out-of-the-box uBR905 upon achieving online status. This particular uBR905 was connected to a uBR7200. Example 10-4 shows the configuration of the uBR7200 used in this situation.

Example 10-4 *uBR7200 Configuration*

```
boot system flash ubr7200-ik1s-mz_121-2_T.bin
no logging buffered
enable password cisco
!
no cable qos permission create
no cable qos permission update
cable qos permission modems
!
ip subnet-zero
no ip domain-lookup
!
no lane client flush
!
interface Ethernet1/0
```

continues

Example 10-4 *uBR7200 Configuration (Continued)*

```
 ip address 172.17.110.139 255.255.255.224
!
interface Cable2/0
 ip address 10.10.1.1 255.255.255.0 secondary
 ip address 10.1.1.10 255.255.255.0
 no keepalive
 cable downstream annex B
 cable downstream modulation 64qam
 cable downstream interleave-depth 32
 cable downstream frequency 451250000
 cable upstream 0 frequency 28000000
 cable upstream 0 power-level 0
 no cable upstream 0 shutdown
 cable upstream 1 shutdown
 cable upstream 2 shutdown
 cable upstream 3 shutdown
 cable upstream 4 shutdown
 cable upstream 5 shutdown
 cable dhcp-giaddr policy
 cable helper-address 172.17.110.136
!
ip classless
ip route 0.0.0.0 0.0.0.0 172.17.110.129
no ip http server
!
line con 0
exec-timeout 0 0
 transport input none
line aux 0
line vty 0
 exec-timeout 0 0
 password cisco
 login
line vty 1 4
 password cisco
 login
!
end
```

In routing mode, the uBR900, unlike many vendor CMs, can act as a true IP router. The 900 Series can run RIP, RIPv2, IGRP, EIGRP, and static routing.

As part of the initialization phase, the CM makes contact with a DHCP server on the provider's network. The DHCP server provides the following information to the CM:

- IP address
- Subnet mask
- Default gateway
- TFTP server
- DHCP relay agent
- The complete name of the DOCSIS configuration file
- Address of ToD server
- Syslog server address

Once this information is obtained, the CM can issue a request to the ToD server to set its clock to the correct time. This facilitates syslog time stamps. At this point, also, the CM can issue a TFTP request to the TFTP server for its DOCSIS configuration file (discussed in the previous section).

To facilitate standardization of router software on client CMs the IOS images desired for use with the CMs can be stored on the TFTP server. The IOS version and filename can be specified in the DOCSIS configuration file to be downloaded at each power-on of the router. This takes several minutes, but it provides the service provider with some degree of control.

Additionally, the router configuration(s) can be stored on the TFTP server to be downloaded at each power-on as well.

These steps for IOS image storage are additional steps, because the Cisco IOS image and configuration can be stored on the router, as traditionally done in most routing environments. Storing the IOS image on a TFTP server makes the power-up sequence a much shorter process in the event of a router reload.

Obviously, this section simply scratches the surface of cable access methods and procedures. It is meant to be a high-level technological overview, as are the following, "Satellite Options" and "Wireless Options" sections. For more information on Cisco's cable product offerings and cable technologies in general, check out http://www.cisco.com. Search using the keywords "broadband cable."

Satellite Options

As mentioned, satellite service offerings are only just now becoming viable alternatives. Previously, the cost of hardware and the delay associated with satellite transmissions have presented major hurdles for broadband companies to overcome. This section discusses the basics of the technology as relevant to the CCNP Remote Access Exam.

Satellite Technology Background

Satellite technologies will have a difficult time competing for business in urban areas. In those markets where DSL and cable are available and service providers are highly competitive, satellite providers will have a difficult time gaining a foothold.

The same is not true in rural areas where DSL or cable is unlikely to be available anytime soon due to cost restraints. Because both DSL and cable are subject to physical distance limitations, they will be unavailable to many areas of the world for a long time to come. For example, a study published by Hughes Network Systems estimates that 37 percent of U.S. households will not be offered cable or DSL in the foreseeable future.

Satellite offers a solution to the lack of cable and DSL broadband availability in rural areas. However, it is relatively expensive. It requires the purchase of a satellite dish and adapters. The dish can cost around $500 typically, plus $200 or so for installation. The monthly subscription fee varies, but in early 2003, average pricing was around $70.

The satellites of some providers allow bidirectional access from 23,000 miles above Earth. Downstream speeds can reach 400 kbps in off-peak hours (150 kbps during peak hours) and upstream speeds ranging from 40 kbps to 128 kbps. Downstream and upstream transfer rates will vary based on numerous variables, ranging from traffic load to weather and sun conditions.

Satellite service providers have other hurdles to clear. The latency involved in having each packet travel 46,000 miles to get from point A to point B can be significant (roughly 1/4 second per round trip). Slow upstream rates and, of course, the cost of ownership will need to be overcome if there is hope of satellite technology competing with the DSL and cable markets.

Types of Orbits

This section provides definitions and descriptions of the commonly used satellite Earth orbits.

- **Geostationary orbit (GEO)**—Circular orbit focused on the plane of Earth's equator. A satellite in this orbit appears fixed over one spot on Earth's surface because it completes an orbit every 24 hours. The altitude to achieve this orbit effectively is 35,800 km.

- **Low earth orbit (LEO)**—Elliptical or circular orbit at an altitude of less than 2,000 km above the surface of Earth. The orbit period at these altitudes varies between 90 minutes and 2 hours.

- **Medium earth orbit (MEO)**—Circular orbit at an altitude of 10,000 km. The orbit period is about 6 hours. Also known as intermediate circular orbit (ICO).

- **Highly elliptical orbit (HEO)**—Typically uses a perigee altitude of 500 km and an apogee altitude as high as 50,000 km. The orbits are inclined at 63.4 degrees to provide communications services to locations at high northern latitudes. The orbit period varies from 8 to 24 hours.

- **Polar orbit (PO)**—Polar orbits are, in actuality, LEO orbits. They can be used to view only the poles or to view the same place on Earth at the same time each 24-hour day. They typically operate at an altitude of about 850 km, yielding an orbit period of roughly 100 minutes.

- **Sun-synchronous orbit (SSO)**—This orbit is a special case and highly coordinated of the polar orbit. In a sun-synchronous orbit, the satellite passes over the equator and each latitude of Earth at the same time every day.

Figure 10-3 illustrates various types of orbits utilized in satellite communications.

Figure 10-3 *Satellite Orbits*

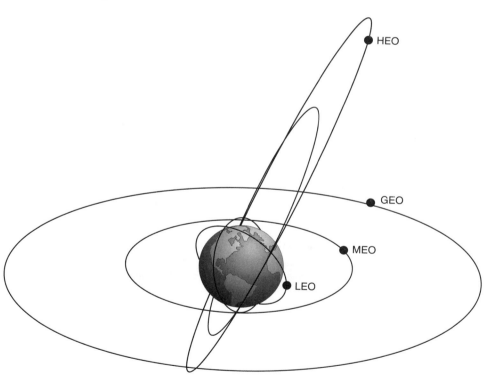

Each orbit has specific functions and capabilities. Larger satellite service providers that have numerous satellites deployed use several different orbits so that they can offer more services. A provider that has fewer satellites may be forced to use a higher altitude to provide a large enough coverage footprint. Consequently, the provider will be able to offer fewer services.

It may be some time before use of satellite broadband is widespread. Some estimates put the number of U.S. subscribers at around 600,000 in early 2003. For the time being, satellite broadband is a niche technology that utilizes specialized hardware. It is cost-inefficient in areas where other broadband technologies are present. However, in areas where those other technologies are absent, satellite broadband is a viable alternative.

Wireless Options

The world of wireless communications from a network perspective has been one of the fastest growing of all. The speed at which these technological offerings are evolving is simply stunning.

Wireless Technology Background

Wireless networking (aka *WiFi* from the term Wireless Fidelity) hardware is experiencing explosive growth and evolution at this time. Simply walking into the corner computer store makes that point evident. All manner of devices are available from a variety of vendors and in a wide price range. The technology is not so much a broadband offering for Internet access, as are DSL and cable, but a LAN technology.

Although some companies, and even communities, are using wireless technology advances to offer higher-speed Internet access, that market is not yet the main focus of vendors. Instead, vendors are focused mainly on the LAN niche. For those who wish to be freed from the need for network cabling at every turn, wireless may be the answer.

Several wireless offerings have made a great deal of commotion in recent years. Since the advent of IEEE 802.11, there has been a bit more of a semblence of interoperability in the market.

IEEE 802.11 provides for three variations: 802.11a, 802.11b, and 802.11g. The 11a and 11b offerings are widely accepted and in use. The 11g implementation is newer. Many market experts feel that 11g will win out over 11a and 11b in the coming months and years, primarily because of interoperability, price, and speed issues (discussed in the following sections).

IEEE 802.11

IEEE 802.11 is the specification that defines the rules for communciations in a wireless LAN. There are three primary offerings to 802.11: 802.11a, 802.11b, and the recent addition 802.11g. All three are discussed in this section.

802.11a

IEEE 802.11a operates in the 5-GHz band. The LAN system aims for a radio frequency in the the 5.15–5.25, 5.25–5.35, and 5.725–5.825-GHz unlicensed national information structure (U-NII) bands.

This allows the introduction of data transmission capabilities at 6, 9, 12, 18, 24, 36, 48, and 54 Mbps. The support of data rates at 6, 12, and 24 Mbps is mandatory. Note that these numbers indicate shared-bandwidth capabilities. Every vendor must support those speeds. The system uses 52 subcarriers (aka channels) that are modulated using binary or quadrature phase-shift keying.

In other words, the data transmission rates are achieved by using numerous simultaneous subchannels within a major channel. Each subchannel is monitored and maintained separately. This is similar to the DSL modulation techniques described in Chapter 12, Establishing a Frame Relay Connection.

802.11b

IEEE 802.11b tends to be implemented more often than 802.11a and 802.11g at this time. It utilizes slower transfer speeds, on average, than 802.11a. As noted previously, this is a radio frequency LAN system that aims for the 2.4–2.4835-GHz frequency range. This allows the introduction of data transmission capabilities at 1, 2, 5.5, and 11 Mbps.

802.11g

IEEE 802.11g is emerging as a viable alternative to 802.11a and 802.11b networks. 802.11g offers 54-Mbps data transfer rates.

In essence, 802.11g is an evolution of 802.11b. Thus, 802.11g-equipped devices provide a higher-speed, interoperable platform that can be easily migrated from 802.11b architectures (but not with 11a infrastructures). This is in stark contrast to the non-interoperability between 802.11a and 802.11b. Because 802.11b is the most widely deployed of the 802.11 specifications, the interoperability between 11b and 11g will ease the transition to the new 802.11g specification.

Wireless LANs

A typical wireless LAN will be logically similar to the old-standby star topology. The only difference is, of course, that there are no wires. A central device known as a wireless access point sits in a nonconspicuous space, physically attached to the LAN hub or switch.

Wireless adapters that are installed in network hosts home to the WAP and initiate a connection. There are some issues that can and do arise. Technologies can sometimes clash. If an 802.11b wireless adapter attempts to home to an 802.11a wireless access point, the result will be a failed connection. As mentioned earlier, these two specifications are incompatible. But, what else can clash with the network besides incompatible hardware?

Note that the 802.11b devices operate in the 2.4-GHz band. When installed in home offices, this can generate an interesting issue because many modern cordless phones also operate in the 2.4-GHz band. From time to time, the phone will seize a channel utilized, but idle, by a wireless client. The reverse can also occur. Because the access radius of the wireless access point varies based on physical impediments (i.e., walls and distance), this issue could affect neighboring homes as well.

Cisco has a fairly comprehensive product line for the wireless market in terms of both wireless access points and wireless adapters. Figure 10-4 shows the Cisco Aironet 1200 WAP.

Figure 10-4   *Cisco Aironet 1200 Wireless Access Points*

Figure 10-5 shows some additional components in the Aironet 350 Series. Both wireless access points and adapters are shown here. Note that there are both PCI and PCMCIA adapters available.

Figure 10-5 *Cisco Aironet 350 Series Wireless Access Points and Adapters*

Security Concerns

For many administrators as well as those who maintain home offices, security is a large issue. The thought of using radio-frequency transmissions for data brings such security concerns to the forefront. Blasting confidential or sensitive information out across the airwaves isn't something to be taken lightly.

With that in mind, several options have been developed to assist in making the transmissions secure. The first such step is known as Wired Equivalent Privacy (WEP).

WEP is meant to provide the first layer of security for wireless access point access. WEP uses unique keys assigned to registered users. The use of WEP keys can function as a type of access control because a client that lacks the correct WEP key cannot send data to or receive data from an access point. WEP, the encryption scheme adopted by the IEEE 802.11 committee, provides encryption with 40 bits or 104 bits of key strength.

When a wireless host attempts to connect to the WAP, an authentication process is initiated. This process is detailed in Figure 10-6.

Figure 10-6 *Wireless Client Authentication Process*

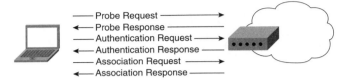

The 802.11 specification calls for two mechanisms to be used in authenticating wireless LAN clients: open authentication and shared key authentication. Two other mechanisms, the Service Set Identifier (SSID) and authentication by client MAC address, are also commonly used.

Open authentication is a null authentication algorithm. The access point grants any authentication request—essentially, it's an open door. This is useful in environments where bar-code scanners and other portable tools require access to the wireless network.

Shared key authentication requires the use of a client-configured static WEP key. If the WEP key is not present in the client configuration, the connection will be denied.

MAC authentication is not actually a part of the 802.11 specification; however, most vendors, including Cisco, use it to enhance security capabilities. This type of authentication checks the client MAC address against a configured list of allowed addresses. It is also possible to use an external authentication server for MAC authentication. MAC authentication supplements the open and shared key authentications and adds one more layer of security to the network.

The security measures just described do have some vulnerabilities. MAC addresses can be altered manually. Playback attacks are also a concern. These, and other issues, have been addressed by individual vendors in the form of proprietary security measures and protocols.

Cisco has created the Extensible Authentication Protocol (EAP). This protocol is also known as Light Extensible Authentication Protocol (LEAP). LEAP supports centralized, user-based authentication with the ability to generate dynamic WEP keys. LEAP, coupled with some additional augmentations to WEP such as Message Integrity Check (MIC), per-packet keying, and broadcast key rotation, makes Cisco wireless networks some of the most secure in the industry.

For more information on wireless access and security configuration, refer to http://www.cisco.com and search using the keyword "wireless" or "802.11."

Foundation Summary

This section is a collection of information that provides a convenient review of many key concepts in this chapter. If you are already comfortable with the topics in this chapter, this summary can help you recall a few details. If you just read this chapter, this review should help solidify some key facts. If you are doing your final preparation before the exam, this information is a convenient way to review the day before the exam.

Overall, the number of broadband options available to the general population today is increasing. Gone are the days of the traditional dialup-only service. To remain competitive and a dominant force in the market today, service providers are being forced to explore newer technologies while maintaining low prices for consumers. The market is highly volatile. Customer churn maintains all-time high numbers simply due to the options available.

DSL and cable are the current forerunners in the broadband market. Both use existing infrastructure. Whereas DSL uses phone lines, cable broadband uses the same cable over which television signals run. A provider can now offer consumers hundreds of TV channels. However, when none of those hundreds of channels has anything worth watching, the consumer can use the same cable to access the Internet. This is one step closer to the "single-vendor solution."

Cable and DSL installations are augmented in the home and small office by the use of WiFi equipment. Rather than running new wiring throughout a home or office, many people are opting to implement an 802.11 solution. Thus, wireless broadband has found its niche in the marketplace independent of the DSL vs. cable war.

Satellite communications remains a steady offering in places where no other broadband service is readily available. Bandwidth options for virtually all budgets can be deployed in virtually any corner of the globe.

Which technology will ultimately prevail in the market? The answer to that question is, at this time, unknown. Most likely, there will be no single winner. In fact, newer and faster methods of accessing information are evolving and will likely replace what is thought to be today's "leading-edge" technology.

Q&A

The questions and scenarios in this book are more difficult than what you should experience on the actual exam. The questions do not attempt to cover more breadth or depth than the exam, but they are designed to make sure that you know the answer. Rather than enabling you to derive the answer from clues hidden inside the question, the questions challenge your understanding and recall of the subject. Hopefully, mastering these questions will help you limit the number of exam questions on which you narrow your choices to two options and then guess.

The answers to these questions can be found in Appendix A.

1. Data over cable is defined in what specification? (Link: Cable Options)

2. What is the name of the organization that governs the cable specification? (Link: DOCSIS Basics)

3. Which DOCSIS component resides in the head end? (Link: DOCSIS Basics)

4. Which DOCSIS component is the CPE device? (Link: DOCSIS Basics)

5. What are the bands for downstream and upstream transmissions over cable? (Link: DOCSIS Basics)

6. Satellite transmissions can reach what downstream speed during off-peak hours? (Link: Satellite Technology Background)

7. What is the altitude necessary to reach geostationary orbit? (Link: Types of Orbits)

8. What is the amount of time necessary to complete one orbit in a medium earth orbit? (Link: Types of Orbits)

9. What is the top transmission speed offered in an 802.11a WiFi deployment? (Link: 802.11a)

10. What is the top transmission speed offered in an 802.11b WiFi deployment? (Link: 802.11b)

11. What is the protocol designed to provide security for Wireless Access Point devices? (Link: Security Concerns)

This chapter covers the following subjects:

- DSL Technology Background

- DSL Implementations

- PPP over Ethernet

- PPP over ATM

- Cisco 827 Series Router

- Troubleshooting DSL

- Troubleshooting at the Physical and Data Link Layers

CHAPTER 11

Using DSL to Access a Central Site

The CCNP Remote Access Exam requires you to have an in-depth understanding of various WAN technologies. In this chapter, the discussion focuses on DSL as a broadband option. As mentioned in Chapter 10, broadband offerings are becoming more common and competitive in offering options for remote and home users. This chapter will serve, primarily, as an overview of Digital Subscriber Line (DSL) offerings that are available on the market today.

"Do I Know This Already?" Quiz

The purpose of the "Do I Know This Already?" quiz is to help you decide whether you really need to read the entire chapter. If you already intend to read the entire chapter, you do not necessarily need to answer these questions now.

The 13-question quiz, derived from the major sections in the "Foundation Topics" portion of the chapter, helps you to determine how to spend your limited study time.

Table 11-1 outlines the major topics discussed in this chapter and the "Do I Know This Already?" quiz questions that correspond to those topics.

Table 11-1   *"Do I Know This Already?" Foundation Topics Section-to-Question Mapping*

Foundation Topics Section	Questions Covered in This Section
DSL Technology Background	1–6
PPP over Ethernet	7–8
PPP over ATM	9–10
Cisco 827 Series Router	11
Troubleshooting DSL	12–13

CAUTION   The goal of self-assessment is to gauge your mastery of the topics in this chapter. If you do not know the answer to a question or are only partially sure of the answer, you should mark this question wrong for purposes of the self-assessment. Giving yourself credit for an answer that you correctly guess skews your self-assessment results and might provide you with a false sense of security.

1. What is the distance limitation of ADSL utilizing 24-AWG cable?

   a. 2,500 ft

   b. 15,000 ft

   c. 18,000 ft

   d. 10,000 ft

2. Into which two general categories can DSL be broken?

   a. CAP

   b. DMT

   c. Asymmetric

   d. Symmetric

3. If running 1.5 Mbps over 26-AWG cable, what is the maximum allowable distance from the CO?

   a. 18,000 ft

   b. 15,000 ft

   c. 12,000 ft

   d. 9,000 ft

4. Which DSL modulation method is most prevalantly used today?

   a. CAP

   b. DMT

   c. DSL

   d. AMI

5. Which DSL modulation method utilizes a single channel for all downstream transmission?

   a. CAP

   b. DMT

   c. DSL

   d. AMI

6. How many channels does DMT utilize for downstream transmission?

   a. 128

   b. 256

  c. 512

  d. 1024

7. PPP authentication takes place after which of the following phases?

  a. Discovery

  b. Session

  c. Callback

  d. Call Setup

8. In a PPPoE call initiation, the two phases of the setup are what?

  a. Session

  b. Setup

  c. Discovery

  d. Transport

9. Which VCI is the first available for use in ATM end-user configurations?

  a. 5

  b. 16

  c. 32

  d. 18

10. ATM cells use how large a payload per cell?

  a. 53 bytes

  b. 50 bytes

  c. 5 bytes

  d. 48 bytes

11. The Cisco 827-4V differs from the Cisco 827H in that it:

  a. Has one Ethernet port and one ADSL port

  b. Has four voice ports

  c. Is Cisco IOS driven

  d. Supports PPPoE and PPPoA

12. A large percentage of DSL issues arise from the placement of what device?

    a. Router

    b. Switch

    c. DSL filter

    d. Phone

13. Which command will show DSL connection negotiation in real time?

    a. debug dsl events

    b. debug atm events

    c. debug ethernet events

    d. debug ppp authentication

The answers to the "Do I Know This Already?" quiz are found in Appendix A, "Answers to the 'Do I Know This Already?' Quizzes and Q&A Sections." The suggested choices for your next step are as follows:

■ **7 or fewer overall score**—Read the entire chapter. This includes the "Foundation Topics," "Foundation Summary," and "Q&A" sections.

■ **8–10 overall score**—Begin with the "Foundation Summary," then go to the "Q&A" section at the end of the chapter.

■ **11 or more overall score**—If you want more review on these topics, skip to the "Foundation Summary," then go to the "Q&A" section at the end of the chapter. Otherwise, move to the next chapter.

Foundation Topics

DSL Technology Background

Based on the expanding number of options currently and coming soon for the broadband market, competition for home and remote user dollars has reached a frenzied state. The deployment of broadband and similar technologies has involved quite a large amount of trial and error. The competition has seen the emergence of two primary services for widespread deployment. These are Cable and DSL. Other broadband offerings (cable, satellite, and wireless) are described in Chapter 10, "Broadband Options to Access a Central Site." This chapter is completely devoted to providing a basic overview of DSL as a technology.

Loosely defined, DSL is a technology that exploits unused frequencies on copper telephone lines to transmit traffic, typically at multimegabit speeds. DSL uses existing telephone wiring, without requiring any additional cabling resources. It has the capability to allow voice and high-speed data to be sent simultaneously over the same copper pair. The service is always available, so the user does not have to dial in or wait for call setup.

DSL technologies can be broken down into two fundamental classifications: asymmetric (ADSL) and symmetric (SDSL). As the name implies, ADSL uses higher downstream rates and lower upstream rates. In contrast, SDSL uses the same downstream and upstream rates. ADSL is the most commonly deployed DSL technology, and is the primary focus of the DSL portion of the CCNP Remote Access Exam. Therefore, although other available DSL implementations will be discussed briefly in this section, ADSL is the focus of the chapter.

Figure 11-1 illustrates the concepts that are discussed in this chapter overall.

Figure 11-1 *Typical SOHO DSL Implementation*

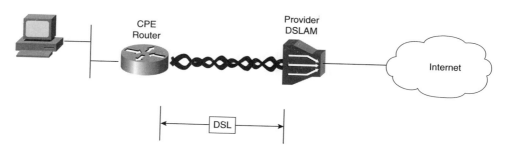

The figure represents a typical installation of DSL in a SOHO implementation. In this case, a Cisco 827 router has been placed at the site. The Ethernet interface has been connected either directly into the PC using a crossover cable or into a hub/switch providing connectivity to all network hosts. (The Cisco 827 router is discussed later in the chapter, in the section "Cisco 827 Series Routers.")

The copper pair between the CPE router and the DSL access multiplexer (DSLAM) is simply the same old connection that is used to get analog voice services to the premises. Very little, if any, additional wiring is necessary on the CPE side of the connection. Once the DSLAM receives the signal, it passes the data traffic on to the provider router to traverse the network to which it is connected—in this case, the Internet. Typically, the router is integrated into the DSLAM, as seen in many networks that use the Cisco 6400.

Questions typically arise regarding the misunderstandings associated with voice and data riding the same cable. Figure 11-2 alters the perception a bit by making a few changes to the picture presented previously. This figure illustrates the manner in which the passing of voice and data is accomplished. The voice and data signals are combined at differing frequencies, and then split back apart at the CO.

Figure 11-2 *Splitting Voice and Data Traffic*

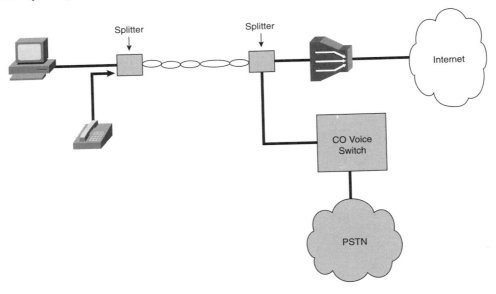

As can be seen in the figure, the use of DSL technologies involves the splitting of frequencies travelling across the wire. The actual division of space on the wire depends on the modulation type. Modulations types will be discussed shortly.

DSL Limitations

DSL is a highly distance-sensitive technology. As the distance from the CO increases, the signal quality and connection speeds decrease. ADSL service is limited to a maximum distance of 18,000 feet (5460 m) between the DSL CPE and the DSLAM, although many ADSL providers place an even lower limit on the distance to ensure quality.

The 18,000-foot distance limitation for DSL is not a limitation for voice telephone calls, but for data transmission. The telco uses small amplifiers, called loading coils, to boost voice signals. Loading coils have a nasty tendency to disrupt DSL data signals. This means that if there are loading coils in the loop between the CPE and CO, you probably are not within an area that can receive DSL service.

Factors that may potentially disqualify you from receiving ADSL include the following:

- **Fiber-optic cable**—ADSL signals cannot pass through the conversion from analog to digital to analog that occurs if a portion of the telephone circuit traverses fiber-optic cable in transit.

- **Bridge taps**—These are extensions between the CPE and the CO.

- **Loading coils**—Loading coils are used to extend the range of a local loop for voice operations. They're intended to function as inductors to compensate for parallel capacitance on the line. Loading coils significantly distort xDSL frequencies and must be removed for any DSL operation. They are often found at loops extending farther than 12,000 ft.

Table 11-2 outlines the distance limitations of some common DSL data-rate offerings.

Table 11-2   *DSL Distance Limitations*

Data Rate	Wire Gauge	Distance
1.5 or 2 Mbps	24 AWG	18,000 ft
1.5 or 2 Mbps	26 AWG	15,000 ft
6.1 Mbps	24 AWG	12,000 ft
6.1 Mbps	26 AWG	9,000 ft

As is evident from the table, DSL is offered in a wide range of transfer rates. The table does not represent all available rates, simply those that are most common.

POTS Coexistence

Plain old telephone service (POTS) has evolved greatly over the years. When Bell invented the telephone in 1876, he had no idea of what a profound effect it would have on the world. In fact, many potential investors he approached with his idea said that his invention had no commercial value whatsoever. Even the media was more than a little skeptical, stating that well informed people know that it is impossible to transmit voice over wires.

The modulation methods employed in bringing DSL to the CPE router simply exploit existing wires, making use of the untapped frequencies by setting aside channels or carriers for use by downstream and upstream data transfers.

ADSL Modulation

The ANSI standards for DSL define modulation types. The method used for individual installation is up to the carrier. Two choices are widely available: Carrierless Amplitude Phase (CAP) and Discrete MultiTone (DMT).

CAP

As shown in Figure 11-3, CAP divides the available space into three bands. The range from 0 to 4 kHz is allocated for POTS transmission. The range of 25 kHz to 160 kHz is allocated for upstream data traffic. The range of 240 kHz to 1.5 MHz is allocated for downstream data traffic.

Figure 11-3 *CAP Modulation*

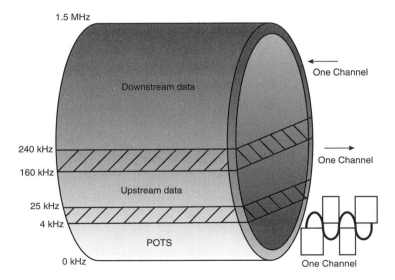

Figure 11-3 illustrates the breakdown of the available bandwidth of the wire itself. This figure effectively shows how the voice and downstream/upstream data are separated on the wire. Note that the range of frequencies available to downstream data is significantly wider than that available to upstream data or voice.

CAP is a variation of Quadrature Amplitude Modulation (QAM). QAM is outside the scope of the exam, and therefore this book. CAP is only used in ADSL implementations, because it offers significantly inferior performance, albeit at a reduced cost, compared to DMT. Unlike DMT, CAP is not an industry standard. CAP was, however, the de facto standard for xDSL deployments (deployed in 97 percent of xDSL installs) up until 1996, therefore it is still commonly encountered.

With the advent of DMT, CAP is rarely, if at all, used today in ADSL service offerings.

DMT

DMT describes a version of multicarrier DSL modulation in which incoming data is collected and then distributed over a large number of small individual carriers, each of which uses a form of QAM modulation.

Most of the ADSL equipment installed today uses DMT (see Figure 11-4). DMT divides signals into 256 separate channels (aka carriers), each of which is 4.3125-kHz wide. In other words, the available bandwidth on the line is divided into 256 equally sized pieces or channels. These channels can be independently modulated with a maximum of 15 bps/Hz. Each channel is monitored constantly. Should the quality become overly impaired, the signal will be reallocated to another channel. Signals are constantly reallocated in the search for the best-quality channels for transmission.

DMT has the capability to step up or down in 32-kbps increments to maintain quality, although the improved quality sometimes comes at the sacrifice of speed. This ability to adjust speed, correct errors, reallocate channels, etc. generates a significantly higher rate of power consumption to maintain it all.

DMT is more complex than CAP because of the processes and resources involved in monitoring and allocating information on the individual channels, coupled with the constant monitoring of the quality of all channels; however, DMT allows more flexibility than CAP. Until recently, the resources necessary to make DMT viable were cost prohibitive. Advances in technology and dropping prices have made DMT feasible.

Note the differences between Figures 11-3 and 11-4. Whereas CAP uses a single channel each for upstream and downstream data (Figure 11-3), DMT uses multiple channels for both upstream and downstream data (Figure 11-4). Both CAP and DMT use a single channel for POTS.

Figure 11-4 *DMT Modulation*

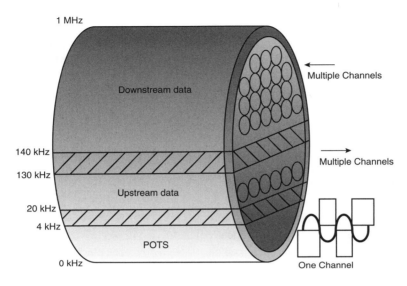

DSL Implementations

As mentioned, DSL is used in a number of forms. Generally, these forms can be broken into two categories:

- **Asymmetric implementations**—Utilize a significantly faster downstream transfer rate (to facilitate download requests) than upstream transfer rate.

- **Symmetric implementations**—Utilize matching download/upload transfer rates.

There are a number of "flavors" of DSL in both the asymmetric and symmetric offerings, as discussed in the following sections.

Asymmetric DSL Flavors

ADSL is most commonly deployed in the current broadband market where DSL is offered. The following are different flavors of DSL currently available:

- **ADSL**—The full-rate offering of ADSL, which can be configured to deliver from 1.5 to 9 Mbps downstream and 16 to 640 kbps upstream. ADSL enables voice and high-speed data to be sent simultaneously over the existing telephone line. ITU-T Recommendation G.992.1 and ANSI Standard T1.413-1998 specify full-rate ADSL.

- **G.lite ADSL**—ITU standard specifically developed to meet the "plug-and-play" requirements of the consumer market segment. G.lite is a medium-bandwidth version of ADSL that allows up to 1.5 Mbps downstream and up to 512 kbps upstream, and allows voice and data to coexist on the wire without the use of splitters. G.lite is a globally standardized (ITU-T G.992.2) interoperable ADSL system. Typical telco implementations currently provide 1.5 Mbps downstream and 160 kbps upstream.

- **RADSL (rate-adaptive DSL)**—A nonstandard version of ADSL that automatically adjusts the connection speed to adjust for the quality of the telephone line. This allows RADSL to function over longer distances than ADSL. Note, however, that standard ADSL also permits the ADSL modem to adapt speeds of data transfer.

- **VDSL (very-high-bit-rate DSL)**—Provides up to 26 Mbps, over distances up to 50 meters on short loops, such as from fiber to the curb. In most cases, VDSL lines are served from neighborhood cabinets that link to a central office via optical fiber. VDSL can also be configured in symmetric mode.

Symmetric DSL Flavors

While SDSL methodologies are not as widespread as those in the ADSL offerings, they are just as viable as broadband technologies. SDSL is available in the following forms:

- **SDSL (symmetric DSL)**—May include transfer rates, both downstream and upstream, ranging from as slow as 128 kbps to as fast as 2.32 Mbps. SDSL is a rather general term that encompasses a number of varying vendor implementations providing variable rates of service over a single copper pair.

- **SHDSL (symmetric high-data-rate DSL)**—An industry-standard SDSL offering. SHDSL equipment conforms to the ITU-T Recommendation G.991.2 (known as G.shdsl). SHDSL outperforms older SDSL versions with a 20 percent better loop-reach, less crosstalk into other transmission systems in the same cable, and promises vendor interoperability. HDSL systems operate in a range of transfer rates from 192 kbps to 2.3 Mbps. SHDSL is best suited to data-only applications that require higher upstream transfer rates than those typically available in DSL implementations.

- **HDSL (high-data-rate DSL)**—Created in the late 1980s, HDSL is meant to deliver symmetric service at upstream and downstream transfer rates up to 2.3 Mbps. Although it is available in 1.544 Mbps or 2.3 Mbps, this symmetric fixed-rate service does not allow for standard telephone service over the same copper pair.

- **HDSL2 (second-generation HDSL)**—Evolution of HDSL that allows 1.5 Mbps downstream and upstream transfer rates while still enabling the support of voice (non-POTS), data, and video using either ATM or other technology over the same copper pair. HDSL2 does not provide standard voice telephone service on the same wire pair. HDSL2 differs from HDSL in that HDSL2 uses one pair of wires to convey 1.5 Mbps, whereas ANSI HDSL uses two wire pairs.

- **IDSL (ISDN DSL)**—Supports downsteam and upstream transfer rates of up to 144 kbps using existing phone lines. It is unique in that it has the ability to deliver services through a DLC (digital loop carrier), a remote device that is typically located in remote terminals placed in newer housing develpments to simplify the distribution of wiring from the telco. IDSL differs from traditional ISDN in that it is an always-available service rather than a dial-up service. It is, however, capable of using the same TA used in traditional ISDN installations.

PPP over Ethernet

PPP over Ethernet (PPPoE) is, obviously, a twist on traditional PPP implementations. It is essentially a bridging architecture. Typical bridging implementations include wide-ranging security holes. Adding PPP architecture (using PAP or CHAP authentication) on top of this Ethernet bridging function alleviates the security holes and provides a well-known, robust platform.

PPP (RFC 1331) provides a standard method of encapsulating higher-layer protocols across point-to-point connections. It extends the High-Level Data Link Control (HDLC) packet structure with a 16-bit protocol identifier that contains information about the content of the packet.

The packet contains the following:

- **Link Control Protocol (LCP)**—Negotiates link parameters, packet size, or type of authentication
- **Network Control Protocol (NCP)**—Contains information about higher-layer protocols, including IP and IPX, and their control protocols (IPCP for IP)
- **Data frames**—Contain user data

PPP as a technology is covered in Chapters 6 and 7. For more information regarding PPP overall, refer to those chapters. For purposes of this discussion of PPPoE, Figure 11-5 serves as a reference point.

Figure 11-5 *PPPoE Reference Topology*

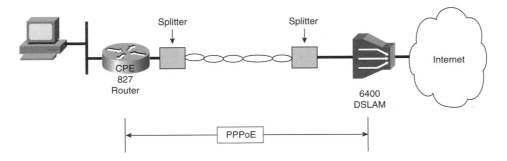

PPPoE, as defined in RFC 2516, provides the ability to connect a network of hosts over a simple bridging access device to a remote access concentrator, or in this discussion, a DSLAM. With this model, each router uses its own PPP stack and the user is presented with a familiar user interface. Access control, billing, and provision of service can be performed on a per-user, rather than a per-site, basis.

To provide a point-to-point connection over Ethernet, each PPP session must learn the Ethernet address of the remote peer and establish a unique session identifier. PPPoE includes a discovery protocol that provides this function.

PPPoE initialization has two distinct phases: a Discovery phase and a PPP Session phase. These phases are described next, in turn.

Discovery Phase

When a router wants to initiate a PPPoE session, it must first perform Discovery to identify the Ethernet MAC address of the peering device and establish a PPPoE SESSION_ID. Discovery is inherently a client/server relationship. During Discovery, a router discovers the provider DSLAM. Discovery allows the CPE router to discover all available DSLAMs, and then select one. When Discovery completes successfully, both the CPE router and the selected DSLAM have the information they will use to build their point-to-point connection over Ethernet.

The Discovery stage remains stateless until a PPP session is established. Once a PPP session is established, both the CPE router and the DSLAM *must* allocate the resources for a PPP virtual interface.

There are four basic steps in the Discovery phase:

1. The CPE router sends an initiation packet.
2. The DSLAM responds with an offer packet.
3. The CPE router continues to the Session phase.
4. The DSLAM continues to the Session phase.

As might be expected, the conversation takes place within the confines of an Ethernet frame payload. The structure of the Ethernet frame is typical for frames in LAN environments.

Figure 11-6 illustrates an Ethernet frame along with the PPPoE payload.

Figure 11-6 *PPPoE Framing Structure*

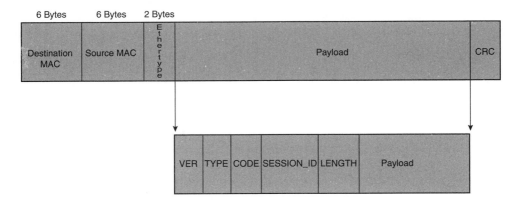

The Destination MAC address during Discovery is FF.FF.FF.FF.FF.FF, which is the Ethernet broadcast address. In contrast, the Source MAC address is that of the CPE router. The ETHER_TYPE field is set to either 0x8863 (Discovery phase) or 0x8864 (PPP Session phase).

Within the Ethernet Frame Payload rides the PPPoE structure. PPPoE requires the use of additional information. That information is contained within a sub-header. It breaks down as follows:

- The VER field is 4 bits and *must* be set to 0x1 for this version of the PPPoE specification.

- The TYPE field (not to be confused with the ETHER_TYPE field in the Ethernet header) is 4 bits and *must* be set to 0x1 for this version of the PPPoE specification.

- The CODE field is 8 bits. The value, during Discovery, is variable based on a given stage of the Discovery process. The PPPoE CODE *must* be set to 0x00 during the Session phase.

- The SESSION_ID field is 16 bits. It is an unsigned value in network byte order. Its value is variable based on a given stage of the Discovery process. The value, however, is fixed for a given PPP Session (it must use the value assigned during Discovery) and, in fact, defines a PPP session along with the Ethernet SOURCE_ADDR and DESTINATION_ADDR. A value of 0xffff is reserved for future use and *must not* be used.

- The LENGTH field is 16 bits. The value, in network byte order, indicates the length of the PPPoE payload. It does not include the length of the Ethernet or PPPoE headers.

During the Discovery Phase, the CODE and SESSION_ID values will change based on the chain of events. The discovery phase encompasses Initiation, Offer, Request, Session-confirmation and Termination operations. Both values will be constant during the Session Phase.

PPP Session Phase

Once the PPPoE Session phase begins, PPP data is sent as in any other PPP encapsulation. All Ethernet frames are unicast. The ETHER_TYPE field, in the Ethernet header, is set to 0x8864. The PPPoE CODE field *must* be set to 0x00. The SESSION_ID field *must not* change for that PPPoE Session and *must* be the value assigned in the Discovery stage. The PPPoE payload contains a PPP frame. The frame begins with the PPP Protocol-ID.

Once the session stage is complete, the PPP LCP options can engage. As mentioned previously, the Session is stateless until the PPP connection is negotiated, including authentication, and any other configured LCP options are negotiated. For more information on the PPP negotiation parameters, refer to Chapters 6 and 7.

PPP over ATM

PPPoA is similar in operation to PPPoE. In fact, both implementations use RFC 1483 (obsoleted by RFC 2364) functions. PPPoA uses ATM adaption layer 5 (AAL5) framing along with SNAP encapsulation on virtual circuits. Both private virtual circuits (PVCs) and switched virtual ciruits (SVCs) are possible in PPPoA installations; however, only PVC implementations are addressed at this time.

An overall discussion of ATM would seem out of place in this chapter, and rightly so. However, it is prudent to take a look at some of the basics behind ATM.

ATM uses a 53-byte cell as its framing structure; 5 bytes are header and the remaining 48 bytes constitute the payload. Figure 11-7 illustrates the encapsulation process for ATM cell production.

As this figure shows, ATM is simply another method of Layer 2 encapsulation. The only real difference is the added step of segmentation and reassembly (SAR). Once the segmentation is complete, ATM headers can be added to the newly created SAR PDUs to complete the creation of ATM cells.

ATM uses virtual circuits that are identified by unique connection identifiers. Each connection identifier is a pair of numbers denoting both a virtual path identifier (VPI) and a virtual circuit identifier (VCI). Valid VPI/VCI pairs vary based on the equipment in use. The valid range of VPIs, supported by the ATM cell header, is 0–255. The valid range of VCIs supported by the UNI cell header is 0–65535. VCIs 0–15 are reserved for use by the ITU and 16–31 are reserved for use by the ATM Forum. Therefore, 32 is the first valid VCI for end-user configurations. The service provider will specify the VPI and VCI for each virtual circuit to be provisioned.

PPPoA, as is the case with PPPoE, simply carries additional overhead to facilitate the PPP connectivity. A CPE device encapsulates the PPP session based on RFC 2364 for transport across the ADSL loop and the DSLAM.

Figure 11-7 *ATM Encapsulation*

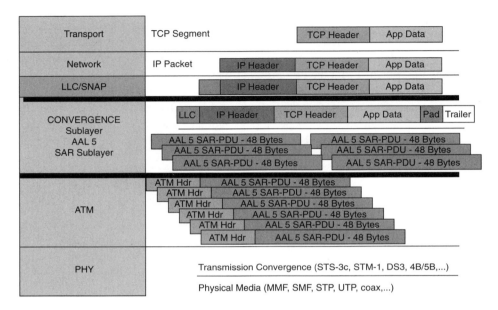

Cisco 827 Series Routers

Now that the basics of the DSL technologies have been covered, a discussion of router configuration is in order. The current DSL router of choice for Cisco is the 827 Series router.

The 827 Series routers look similar to the 700 Series and the other models in the 800 Series line. Figure 11-8 shows the 827 Series router.

Figure 11-9 shows the rear view of the 827 router.

There are two flavors available for the 827 router: the 827-4V and the 827H. Here are the high points that the two flavors have in common:

- ADSL router
- Cisco IOS driven
- Recommended for up to 20 users
- Business-class security with integrated stateful firewall and support for IPSec 3DES for VPNs
- Differentiated classes of service

Figure 11-8   *Cisco 827 DSL Router*

Figure 11-9   *Cisco 827 DSL Router Rear View*

- Mission-critical reliability
- PPPoE, PPPoA support
- NAT/PAT
- SNMP, Telnet, and Console configuration access
- Can be shipped to customer premises preconfigured
- Include the Cisco Router Web Setup tool to allow setup by nontechnical personnel

The Cisco Router Web Setup (CRWS) tool is a web-based configuration tool for simplified installation and setup. To configure the product, users simply point a web browser to the IP address of the router and follow a few simple steps. Figure 11-10 shows the CRWS home page.

The 827-4V is built with IP telephony in mind. It comes standard with four voice ports and is an H.323 standards-based Voice over IP (VoIP) gateway. It also supports standards-based H.323 with Registration, Admission, and Status (RAS) protocol support, providing gateway-to-gatekeeper functionality.

Figure 11-10 *Cisco Router Web Setup Tool*

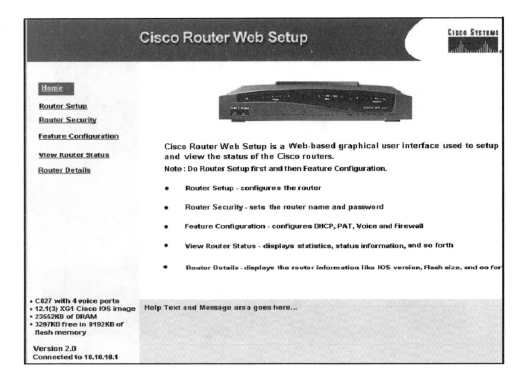

The 827H is built with classical routing in mind rather than focusing on IP telephony. It has an integrated four-port hub to aid multiuser connectivity. Much attention has been given to QoS in the form of queuing, compression, and other means of manipulating traffic flows.

Queuing choices include the classic options of Weighted Fair Queuing (WFQ), Custom Queuing, and Priority Queuing. Newer queuing applications such as Low-Latency Queuing (LLQ) and Class-Based Weighted Fair Queuing (CBWFQ) provide added flexibility.

The 827 has the ability to allow per-circuit traffic shaping and queuing. When coupled with Weighted Random Early Detection (WRED), these methodologies allow optimal control of traffic flow. ATM circuits can be classified as constant bit rate (CBR), variable bit rate–real time (VBR-RT), or unspecified bit rate (UBR), depending on the type of traffic they are to carry.

For more information on ATM traffic types, check out http://www.cisco.com and search for the following keywords: CBR, VBR, and UBR.

Support for both IP and IPX protocol suites has been included in the 827's capability package. When routing IP, various routing protocols are available. These include RIP, RIPv2, EIGRP, IGRP, GRE, IRB, L2TP, and IP Multicast (up to 10 PVCs).

The maximum receive unit (MRU) option on either side of the link must not negotiate to a size larger than 1492; Ethernet's maximum payload size of 1500 octets coupled with the PPPoE header's 6 octets and the PPP protocol ID's 2 octets dictates that the PPP maximum transmission unit (MTU) must not be greater than 1492. This can be achieved by configuring **IP mtu 1492** for PPPoE virtual-template interfaces.

Example 11-1 details a PPPoE and NAT configuration on the 827 router.

Example 11-1 *PPPoE Sample Configuration with NAT*

```
vpdn enable
no vpdn logging                    ←--default
!
vpdn-group pppoe
 request-dialin                    ←--This client is requesting session establishment
 protocol pppoe
!
interface Ethernet0
 ip address 10.92.1.182 255.255.255.0
 ip nat inside
!
interface ATM0                     ←--This is the DSL interface
 no ip address
 no atm ilmi-keepalive
 bundle-enable
 dsl operating-mode auto
 hold-queue 224 in
interface ATM0.1 point-to-point
pvc 0/35                ←-- A sample VPI/VCI. Must match provider VPI/VCI
   pppoe-client dial-pool-number 1      ←--Ties this sub-if to a dialer interface
!
interface Dialer1
 ip address negotiated
 ip mtu 1492                    ←--1500 by default, but must be set to 1492 (Ethernet+PPP)
 ip nat outside
 encapsulation ppp
 dialer pool 1
 ppp authentication chap callin    ←--Specify PPP authentication method
 ppp chap hostname <username>
 ppp chap password <password>
!
ip nat inside source list 1 interface Dialer1 overload    ←-- NAT Config
ip classless
ip route 0.0.0.0 0.0.0.0 dialer1        ←--Default Route
no ip http server
!
access-list 1 permit 10.92.1.0 0.0.0.255    ←--For NAT
```

Example 11-2 details the configuration of the 827 router for PPPoA deployment.

Example 11-2   *PPPoA Configuration*

```
vpdn enable
no vpdn logging ←--default
!
vpdn-group pppoa
 request-dialin                    ←--This client is requesting session establishment
 protocol pppoa
!
interface Ethernet0
 ip address 192.168.1.1 255.255.255.0
 no ip directed-broadcast
!
interface ATM0
 no ip address
 no ip directed-broadcast
 no atm ilmi-keepalive
 bundle-enable
!
interface ATM0.1 point-to-point
 no ip directed-broadcast
 pvc 1/35              ←-- A sample VPI/VCI. Must match provider VPI/VCI
  encapsulation aal5mux ppp dialer        ←--Define the ATM PVC encapsulation
  dialer pool-member 1 ←--Ties this sub-if to a dialer interface
!
interface Dialer1
 ip address negotiated
 no ip directed-broadcast
 encapsulation ppp
 dialer pool 1
!
ip route 0.0.0.0 0.0.0.0 Dialer1            ←--Default Route
```

Troubleshooting DSL

DSL troubleshooting is really no different than troubleshooting in other technologies. To be successful, there must be a method to the madness. If nothing is outwardly incorrect, a good approach is to use the OSI reference model. Start from the physical layer and work upward through each layer from there. Check each item that corresponds to each layer. The OSI reference model was created with troubleshooting methodologies in mind. No higher-layer function can operate successfully without proper operation of the lower-layer functions.

Start with the cabling. Ask a few key questions, "Is this the right cable for the job?" and "Is this cable faulty?" Replace the cable or verify that it is indeed a functional cable by connecting it to a known-good device. Once the physical medium is verified as good, the next layer can be verified, and so on up the OSI reference model stack.

The most common errors in DSL implementations occur at the customer premises. You simply need to use some logic to figure out the issues in many cases. Table 11-3 outlines some common issues.

> **NOTE**   A large percentage of DSL-related issues tie back to the installation at the customer premises. DSL requires the placement of filters between the wall jack and any phone/fax device that will use the shared line. The omission or misinstallation of this filter is the most common culprit in DSL training-, line-, and noise-related issues.

Table 11-3   *Common DSL Symptoms and Problems*

Symptom	Problem
DSL trains okay, and then retrains once the telephone handset is picked up	Excessive noise on the line when the phone is in use. This is typically a telco splitter issue and should be resolved by the carrier.
DSL functions properly, but there is static in the phone handset	Most likely the filter was either omitted or placed between the wall jack and the DSL modem rather than between the wall jack and phone. DSL and voice can work together, but the filters must be in place for any phone/fax on the shared line.
DSL not training to advertised speeds for upstream/downstream transmission	Typically, this is one of two issues. The most common is that the circuit on the telco end has been misprovisioned. Contact the telco to remedy the issue. The second possibility is that the customer premises is outside the distance limitations of DSL. Service will be inconsistent at best in this case.

Granted, there are many typical scenarios and even more solutions. The liberal application of common sense is usually enough to resolve the issues. Other times, it may require some aging and loss of hair.

There are a number of useful **show** and **debug** commands that should be a standard part of any troubleshooting scenario. These include: **show running-config, show version, show processes cpu**, and **show diags**, to name a few.

Issues pertaining specifically to DSL are wide ranging. Because several technologies are at work behind the scenes of DSL, troubleshooting may not seem very straightforward.

Troubleshooting at the Physical and Data Link Layers

Troubleshooting typically begins at Layer 1. ADSL connectivity issues can easily arise from physical connectivity faults. Here are some quick items to double-check:

- ADSL uses pins 3 and 4 between the ADSL interface and the demarc. Ensure that the cable being used is of high quality (Category 5) and properly terminated.

- After you verify the cable, ensure that the CD LED on the router is lit and green.

- Check the router configuration to ensure that the proper VPI/VCI pair is used, according to the documentation provided by the carrier.

- Verify PPP PAP/CHAP authentication settings. The connection will obviously fail if the username and password combination is incorrect.

- Use the **show interface** command to display the status of all physical ports (Ethernet and ATM) and logical interfaces on the router. Example 11-3 illustrates the **show interface atm 0** command. Significant messages in the command output are highlighted.

Example 11-3 show interface atm 0 *Output*

```
820-uut2#show interface atm0
ATM0 is up, line protocol is up
Hardware is PQUICC_SAR (with Alcatel ADSL Module)
Internet address is 14.0.0.16/8
MTU 1500 bytes, sub MTU 1500, BW 640 Kbit, DLY 80 usec,
reliability 40/255, txload 1/255, rxload 1/255
Encapsulation ATM, loopback not set
Keepalive not supported
Encapsulation(s):AAL5, PVC mode
10 maximum active VCs, 1 current VCCs
VC idle disconnect time:300 seconds
Last input 01:16:31, output 01:16:31, output hang never
Last clearing of "show interface" counters never
Input queue:0/75/0 (size/max/drops); Total output drops:0
Queueing strategy:Per VC Queueing
5 minute input rate 0 bits/sec, 0 packets/sec
5 minute output rate 0 bits/sec, 0 packets/sec
512 packets input, 59780 bytes, 0 no buffer
Received 0 broadcasts, 0 runts, 0 giants, 0 throttles
0 input errors, 1024 CRC, 0 frame, 0 overrun, 0 ignored, 0 abort
426 packets output, 46282 bytes, 0 underruns
0 output errors, 0 collisions, 2 interface resets
0 output buffer failures, 0 output buffers swapped out
```

Example 11-3 shows an example of a properly functioning interface. Because the interface is up and the line protocol is up, it is evident that the link is functional. There are other potential values for the interface and line protocol status:

- **ATM0 is down, line protocol is down**—The interface is hard down. This could be indicative of an unplugged cable, lack of carrier detected on the wire, or a simple lack of configuration on the interface.

- **ATM0 is administratively down, line protocol is down**—The interface has been shut down by an administrator. Activate the interface by issuing the **no shutdown** command at the interface configuration prompt.

- **ATM0 is up, line protocol is down**—The interface is properly configured and trying to initialize, but is not receiving carrier on the wire. This is typically, but not always, a carrier problem.

Another useful command is **show atm interface atm 0**, as shown in Example 11-4. In this output, the router lists circuit-specific information. Again, the points of interest are highlighted.

Example 11-4   show atm interface atm 0 *Command Output*

```
tw_820#show atm int atm 0
Interface ATM0:
AAL enabled: AAL5 , Maximum VCs:11, Current VCCs:0
Maximum Transmit Channels:0
Max. Datagram Size:1528
PLIM Type:INVALID - 640Kbps, Framing is INVALID,
DS3 lbo:short, TX clocking:LINE
0 input, 0 output, 0 IN fast, 0 OUT fast
Avail bw = 640
Config. is ACTIVE
```

In the output of this command, there seems to be some problem. There are 0 active Current VCCs (Virtual Circuit Connections). This interface has not been configured properly or is not in an up/up state (as was the interface in Example 11-3). The configuration of the interface is active and there is 640 kbps of bandwidth available to the interface, once the circuit is established.

Use the **debug atm events** command to display ATM events. Example 11-5 provides output from this command. This command is useful for diagnosing problems in an ATM network by logging events on the ATM processor. If the interface is successfully in communication with the DSLAM, the modem state will show 0x10. If the interface is not communicating with the DSLAM, the modem state will show 0x8.

Example 11-5 **debug atm events** *Command Output*

```
00:02:57: DSL: Send ADSL_OPEN command.
00:02:57: DSL: Using subfunction 0xA
00:02:57: DSL: Using subfunction 0xA
00:02:57: DSL: Sent command 0x5
00:02:57: DSL: Received response: 0x26
00:02:57: DSL: Unexpected response 0x26
00:02:57: DSL: Send ADSL_OPEN command.
00:02:57: DSL: Using subfunction 0xA
00:02:57: DSL: Using subfunction 0xA
00:02:57: DSL: Sent command 0x5
00:03:00: DSL: 1: Modem state = 0x8
00:03:02: DSL: 2: Modem state = 0x10
00:03:05: DSL: 3: Modem state = 0x10
00:03:07: DSL: 4: Modem state = 0x10
00:03:09: DSL: Received response: 0x24
00:03:09: DSL: Showtime!
00:03:09: DSL: Sent command 0x11
00:03:09: DSL: Received response: 0x61
00:03:09: DSL: Read firmware revision 0x1A04
00:03:09: DSL: Sent command 0x31
00:03:09: DSL: Received response: 0x12
00:03:09: DSL: operation mode 0x0001
00:03:09: DSL: SM: [DMTDSL_DO_OPEN -> DMTDSL_SHOWTIME]
```

At 00:03:00, the modem state shows 0x8, indicating a lack of communication with the DSLAM. Two seconds later, it changes to 0x10, indicating that it has reached the DSLAM. In Example 11-6, this is not the case. The DSLAM is unreachable.

Example 11-6 *DSLAM Unreachable*

```
00:02:57: DSL: Send ADSL_OPEN command.
00:02:57: DSL: Using subfunction 0xA
00:02:57: DSL: Using subfunction 0xA
00:02:57: DSL: Sent command 0x5
00:02:57: DSL: Received response: 0x26
00:02:57: DSL: Unexpected response 0x26
00:02:57: DSL: Send ADSL_OPEN command.
00:02:57: DSL: Using subfunction 0xA
00:02:57: DSL: Using subfunction 0xA
00:02:57: DSL: Sent command 0x5
00:03:00: DSL: 1: Modem state = 0x8
00:03:00: DSL: 1: Modem state = 0x8
00:03:00: DSL: 1: Modem state = 0x8
00:03:00: DSL: 1: Modem state = 0x8
00:03:00: DSL: 1: Modem state = 0x8
00:03:00: DSL: 1: Modem state = 0x8
```

Based on the output in Example 11-6, there is a problem. To resolve the problem, your first step is to go back through the **debug** and **show** commands in this section.

In the event that an exact cause of the issue cannot be found in this section, please refer to the CCO and either perform a manual search or open a formal case with the TAC.

Foundation Summary

This section is a collection of information that provides a convenient review of many key concepts in this chapter. If you are already comfortable with the topics in this chapter, this summary can help you recall a few details. If you just read this chapter, this review should help solidify some key facts.

Overall, there isn't much in the way of "new" technology with regard to DSL. It relies on PPP, ATM, Ethernet, and other technologies to make it work. PPP, ATM, and Ethernet are well founded and well evolved technologies. They provide a sound base for what ends up being a relatively new application of an old principle.

The basics of PPPoE, PPPoA, and their configuration are relatively easy to understand and implement.

The Cisco 827 router has a very small footprint but a very large feature set for a box its size. DHCP, NAT/PAT, and VPN technologies, along with firewall capabilities, make it a good all-around SOHO router. With the CRWS tool, virtually anyone can configure the router and get it to a functional state.

Q&A

The questions and scenarios in this book are more difficult than what you should experience on the actual exam. The questions do not attempt to cover more breadth or depth than the exam, but they are designed to make sure that you know the answer. Rather than enabling you to derive the answer from clues hidden inside the question, the questions challenge your understanding and recall of the subject. Hopefully, mastering these questions will help you limit the number of exam questions on which you narrow your choices to two options and then guess.

The answers to these questions can be found in Appendix A.

1. What are three things that can adversely affect DSL signals?

2. If 26-AWG cable is deployed to support a DSL order for 1.5 Mbps downstream, what is the distance limitation from the CO?

3. If 24-AWG cable is deployed to support a DSL order for 6 Mbps downstream, what is the distance limitation from the CO?

4. CAP modulation divides voice from upstream and downstream data transmission. List the ranges of frequency for each of the three traffic types.

5. DMT modulation divides the signals into how many separate channels?

6. If there is signal degradation or other quality impairments on the line, what will DMT do to correct the situation?

7. What are the two general categories of DSL implementations and what is the basic difference between them?

8. What is the range of bandwidths available with ADSL offerings?

9. What is G.lite and what are its advantages?

10. In the establishment of a PPPoE session, what options are typically implemented to overcome the security issues brought about in a traditional bridged environment?

11. In the PPP architecture, which portion of the protocol stack deals with link negotiation, packet size, and authentication?

12. What is the purpose of the Discovery phase in PPPoE session initiation?

13. During the Discovery phase, what is the address in the Destination MAC address field of the PPPoE frame?

14. PPPoA uses what RFC to define operations for VC encapsulation?

15. List at least three features of a Cisco 827 router.

16. What are the two flavors of 827 generally available?

17. A user has had DSL installed in his home. The DSL line trains to the advertised speeds and functions properly. The line is shared for voice and data. When the user lifts the handset, there is a great deal of static on the line. What is likely the cause of the static?

18. In the event that a show interface is issued and shows the status of the interface as up, line protocol down, what is likely the issue?

PART V: Establishing a Dedicated Frame Relay Connection and Control Traffic Flow

This part of the book covers the following BCRAN exam topics:

- Describe traffic control methods used to manage traffic flow on WAN links
- Configure frame relay operation and traffic control on WAN links
- Configure access control to manage and limit remote access
- Design a Cisco frame relay infrastructure to provide access between remote network components
- Plan traffic shaping to meet required quality of service on access links
- Troubleshoot traffic control problems on a WAN link

This chapter covers the following subjects:

- Understanding Frame Relay

- Frame Relay Topologies

- Frame Relay Configuration

CHAPTER 12

Establishing a Frame Relay Connection

The CCNP Remote Access Exam requires you to have an in-depth understanding of various WAN technologies. This chapter discusses the basics of Frame Relay and how to tweak it to maximize traffic control and throughput.

Although Frame Relay is not a new technology by any means, it is still widely implemented around the world. Even with the advent of newer (and faster) broadband technologies, Frame Relay continues to remain popular in the workplace.

Frame Relay is a high-performance WAN protocol that operates at Layer 2 of the OSI reference model. Frame Relay originally was designed for use with ISDN interfaces. It is now used over a variety of other network interfaces as well, primarily those that need to support multiple protocols and traffic types, such as data, voice, and video.

By nature, Frame Relay is a nonbroadcast multiaccess (NBMA) network. In an NBMA, broadcasts are not allowed inside the network itself. Instead, for any two points to communicate, there must be a specific connection between them. In other words, for broadcasts to propagate through the Frame Relay network, they must traverse virtual circuits. In contrast, broadcast multiaccess (BMA) networks, such as Ethernet, require that transmissions be placed on the wire for all stations to process.

As a packet-switched network (PSN), Frame Relay enables the dynamic sharing of network resources. Most of today's popular LANs, such as Ethernet and Token Ring, are PSNs.

In many circles, Frame Relay is often described as a streamlined version of X.25 because it offers fewer robust capabilities, such as windowing and retransmission of lost data, than does X.25. Frame Relay typically operates over WAN facilities that offer more reliable connection services.

"Do I Know This Already?" Quiz

The purpose of the "Do I Know This Already?" quiz is to help you decide whether you really need to read the entire chapter. If you already intend to read the entire chapter, you do not necessarily need to answer these questions now.

The nine-question quiz, derived from the major sections in the "Foundation Topics" portion of the chapter, helps you to determine how to spend your limited study time. Table 12-1 outlines the major topics discussed in this chapter and the "Do I Know This Already?" quiz questions that correspond to those topics.

Table 12-1 *"Do I Know This Already?" Foundation Topics Section-to-Question Mapping*

Foundation Topics Section	Questions Covered in This Section
Understanding Frame Relay	1–3
Frame Relay Topologies	4–7
Frame Relay Configuration	8–9

CAUTION The goal of self-assessment is to gauge your mastery of the topics in this chapter. If you do not know the answer to a question or are only partially sure of the answer, you should mark this question wrong for purposes of the self-assessment. Giving yourself credit for an answer that you correctly guess skews your self-assessment results and might provide you with a false sense of security.

1. Which of the following is a characteristic of Frame Relay?

    a. Connectionless

    b. Connection oriented

    c. IP-based

    d. ATM-based

2. What are the two flavors of Frame Relay virtual circuits?

    a. Soft virtual circuit

    b. Switched virtual circuit

    c. Permanent virtual circuit

    d. Private virtual circuit

3. Frame Relay virtual circuits are logically defined by a DLCI. What is the range of valid DLCIs for user traffic?

    a. 1–15

    b. 16–1024

    c. 16–1007

    d. 0–1023

4. The Frame Relay star topology is also known as what?

    a. Full mesh

    b. Hub and spoke

    c. Partial mesh

    d. NBMA

5. What is an advantage of a partial-mesh network?

    a. High cost, full redundancy

    b. Full-circuit redundancy, low cost

    c. Lower cost, while still providing redundancy

    d. Higher cost with no redundancy

6. Split horizon can cause reachability issues in Frame Relay networks. Which two ways allow you to deal with split horizon problems?

    a. Relegate the frame split to two horizons

    b. Configure the subinterface

    c. Create multiple point-to-point interfaces to connect sites

    d. Disable split horizon

7. With what two different personalities can Frame Relay subinterfaces be created?

    a. Point to point

    b. Point to multipoint

    c. Serial

    d. Ethernet

8. What mechanism is used to provide dynamic mapping of DLCIs?

    a. ARP

    b. Inverse ARP

    c. RFC 1483

    d. RARP

9. What command is issued to disable LMI traffic on an interface?

   a. **no frame-relay lmi-type**

   b. **no frame-relay lmi-traffic**

   c. **no keepalive**

   d. **no cdp enable**

The answers to the "Do I Know This Already?" quiz are found in Appendix A, "Answers to the 'Do I Know This Already?' Quizzes and Q&A Sections." The suggested choices for your next step are as follows:

■ **5 or fewer overall score**—Read the entire chapter. This includes the "Foundation Topics," "Foundation Summary," and "Q&A" sections.

■ **6 or 7 overall score**—Begin with the "Foundation Summary" section, and then go to the "Q&A" section.

■ **8 or more overall score**—If you want more review on these topics, skip to the "Foundation Summary" section and then go to the "Q&A" section. Otherwise, move to the next chapter.

Foundation Topics

Understanding Frame Relay

Frame Relay is a connection-oriented, Layer 2 networking technology. It operates at speeds from 56 kpbs to 45 Mbps. It is very flexible and offers a wide array of deployment options.

Frame Relay operates by statistically multiplexing multiple data streams over a single physical link. Each data stream is known as a virtual circuit (VC).

Frame Relay VCs come in two flavors, permanent (PVCs) and switched (SVCs). PVCs are, as the name implies, permanent, nailed-up circuits. They don't tear down or reestablish dynamically. SVCs are just the opposite. With SVCs, a data connection is made only when there is traffic to send across the link. Frame Relay SVCs are established dynamically and can reroute around network failures. Frame Relay PVC services are used in almost every deployment. For a short time, a limited number of carriers tested the feasibility of deploying SVCs but found little market or acceptance for it. Cisco IOS Software has supported Frame Relay SVCs since the beginning of the 11.2 train.

> **NOTE**   Because Frame Relay SVCs are beyond the scope of this book (and the exam), they are not covered in detail.

Each VC is tagged with an identifier to keep it unique. The identifier, known as a data-link connection identifier (DLCI), is determined on a per-leg basis during the transmission. In other words, it is locally significant. It must be unique and agreed upon by two adjacent Frame Relay devices. As long as the two agree, the value can be any valid number, and the number doesn't have to be the same end to end (that is, from router to router across a telco network).

For ANSI LMI, valid DLCI numbers are 16 to 1007. For DLCI purposes, 0 to 15 are reserved, as are 1008 to 1023. The DLCI also defines the logical connection between the Frame Relay (FR) switch and the customer premises equipment (CPE). DLCIs are a constant subject of discussion throughout this chapter.

Device Roles

Frame Relay devices fall into one of two possible roles, data terminal equipment (DTE) or data circuit-terminating equipment (DCE). DCE is sometimes known as data communications equipment as well. Both terms are correct.

It is important to understand that the DTE/DCE relationship is a Layer 2 (data link layer) relationship. DTE and DCE relationships are normally electrical (that is, Layer 1). The DTE/DCE relationship at Layer 1 is independent of that at Layer 2. In other words, just because a router is a Layer 1 DCE doesn't mean it is also the Layer 2 DCE.

DTE devices are generally considered to be terminating equipment for a specific network and are located at the customer premises. The customer typically owns the DTE devices. Examples of DTE devices are terminals, personal computers, routers, and LAN switches.

DCE devices are carrier-owned internetworking devices. DCE provides clocking and switching services in a network; DCE devices are the devices that actually transmit data through the WAN. In most cases, the devices are packet switches.

Figure 12-1 depicts the roles of Frame Relay devices as discussed to this point.

Figure 12-1 *Frame Relay Device Roles*

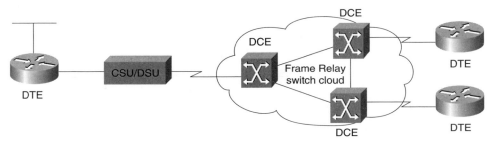

Frame Relay LMI

Local Management Interface (LMI) is the means by which Frame Relay edge devices maintain keepalive messages. The Frame Relay switch is responsible for maintaining the status of the CPE device(s) to which it is attached. LMI is the communication by which the switch monitors status.

LMI implements a keepalive mechanism that verifies connectivity between DCE and DTE and the fact that data can flow. An LMI multicast capability, in conjunction with an LMI multicast addressing mechanism, enables attached devices to learn local DLCIs and provide global, rather than local, significance to those DLCIs. Finally, LMI provides a status indicator that is constantly exchanged between router and switch.

The LMI setting is configurable using the **frame-relay lmi-type [type]** command; however, the router still tries to figure out the type on its own. (This statement is true as of Cisco IOS Software Release 11.2, prior to which the LMI setting was manually configured based on telco requirements.) This is known as lmi-autosense. It can be disabled in the router quite easily.

There are three supported types of LMI (can you guess the default?):

- **Cisco**—Created by the "gang of four," this type was defined by a joint effort between Cisco, StrataCom, Nortel, and DEC. Cisco LMI uses DLCI 1023. Cisco LMI is the default LMI type.
- **ANSI**—This type is also known as Annex D. (Actually, the full version of the name is ANSI standard T1.617 Annex D.) ANSI LMI uses DLCI 0.
- **Q933a**—This type, defined by the ITU, is known as Annex A and uses DLCI 0. (Its full name is actually ITU-T Q.933 Annex A.)

Figure 12-2 depicts LMI communication between the Frame Relay switch and the CPE router.

Figure 12-2 *LMI Exchange*

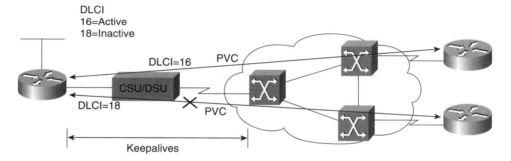

Frame Relay Topologies

Frame Relay supports connectivity of remote sites through one of three topological strategies. Each has its own advantages and disadvantages, as pointed out in the following list:

- **Hub and spoke**—Also known as the star topology, this is the dominant method of deploying Frame Relay. It consists of a single central site acting as a connection point for all remote offices. Routing between two satellite offices is accomplished through the central site. Routing through the central site tends to be the low-cost solution; however, it is also the least redundant (that is, fault tolerant) strategy.
- **Full mesh**—Also called "full mess" due to its resemblance to a spider web, this topology has a large number of connections (because each site is connected to every other site) and is very expensive to operate; however, it is the most fault tolerant. The number of connections that are required is derived through the following formula, where n is the number of devices you wish to connect: $n(n-1)\div2$. For example, if you have 20 routers to connect, you would need $20(20-1)\div2 = 190$ connections to provide a VC from each site to every other site.

- **Partial mesh**—This implementation deploys hub and spoke with redundancy. It avoids the cost of full mesh and minimizes the lack of fault tolerance of hub and spoke. Although a central site is used, redundant connections are installed between critical sites. In essence, it is possible to create a backup central site. This is particularly useful in networks in which delay reductions are necessary, because getting to a destination without traversing a central router can decrease delay significantly.

Figure 12-3 depicts the three topologies.

Figure 12-3 *Frame Relay Topologies*

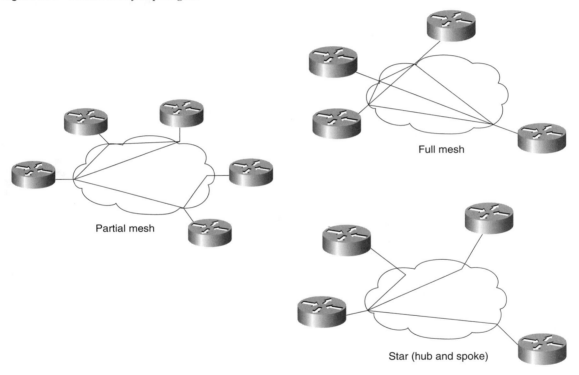

Full mesh

Partial mesh

Star (hub and spoke)

A topology has some effect on the manner in which routers are configured. By default, Frame Relay encapsulated interfaces are multipoint in nature. In environments in which the connection is a single end-to-end PVC with no other connections, there should be no problems. However, in hub-and-spoke or partial-mesh environments, routing update problems can arise.

Issues When Connecting Multiple Sites Through a Single Router Interface

When a single physical interface is used on a central router to connect multiple remote sites, routing problems arise. These problems are caused by *split horizon*. Split horizon is a rule in routing protocol operation that is designed to eliminate routing loops by not allowing routing updates to be sent out of the interfaces through which they were received.

Consider the situation in which one serial interface serves multiple remote sites. In this scenario, split horizon effectively shuts down the passing of routing updates regarding networks on the far side of the remote sites. Although the central site can receive the updates through Serial 0, process them, and then make appropriate changes to the routing table, when the time comes to send them back out Serial 0 to other remote sites, split horizon does not allow it. The end result is that the central site knows all routes, but the remote sites are unable to reach each other because the central site is not allowed to send updates to them. Figure 12-4 illustrates the concept of split horizon.

Figure 12-4 *Split Horizon*

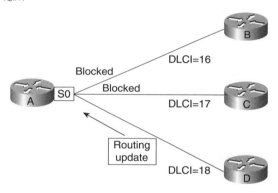

Another problem that arises on a single interface that services multiple VCs is the issue of broadcast traffic. NBMA networks do not enable the propagation of broadcasts through the network. Therefore, the broadcast must be transmitted over each individual VC. In other words, the broadcast goes into a broadcast queue and is sent one time for each circuit being serviced (for example, ten VCs results in ten broadcasts). These broadcasts can consume large amounts of bandwidth in a short time, depending on the volume of broadcast traffic being sent.

Many Frame Relay deployments begin as hub and spoke and then evolve into a partial mesh. Based on traffic patterns and utilization of links, you can add additional connections between remote sites and increase the bandwidth available to each site. This can help you deal with broadcast traffic and other high-volume traffic types.

Resolving Split Horizon Problems

To solve the problems created by split horizon, the first impulse is to turn it off. This is not, however, the most recommended action to take, because turning off split horizon can be difficult. There are ways of dealing with it by overriding the behavior of routing process through distribution lists; however, such tasks should not be undertaken lightly.

In fact, IP is usually the only protocol that allows split horizon to be disabled. By default, IPX and AppleTalk don't allow split horizon to be disabled; however, with EIGRP as the routing protocol for IPX and AppleTalk, it is possible (but problematic) to disable split horizon. Unfortunately, once split horizon is disabled, routing loops can easily occur and cause routes to be erroneously advertised.

The easy way out of the split horizon problem is through the use of subinterfaces. A subinterface is a logical division of a physical interface (hereafter known as a major interface). Theoretically, almost any number of subinterfaces can be placed on a single major interface. The limit lies in the number of Interface Descriptor Blocks (IDBs) available to the router. This number varies depending on the router series and Cisco IOS Software release.

A logical subinterface should be treated almost the same as a major interface. You can configure it for multiple protocols, shut it down, or do anything else to it that is common on other interfaces—with one notable exception: you cannot set encapsulation on a subinterface. Encapsulation must be defined at the major interface.

The configuration of subinterfaces solves the split horizon issue by creating multiple logical interfaces where before existed only one major interface. Split horizon has no problem with updates leaving through interfaces other than the one through which they were received. Example 12-1 shows the necessary commands for creating a subinterface.

Example 12-1 *Creating a Frame Relay Subinterface*

```
RouterA(config)#interface serial 0
RouterA(config-if)#encapsulation frame-relay
RouterA(config-if)#interface serial 0.1 point-to-point
RouterA(config-subif)#ip address 10.1.1.1 255.255.255.0
RouterA(config-subif)#interface serial 0.2 point-to-point
RouterA(config-subif)#ip address 10.1.2.1 255.255.255.0
RouterA(config-subif)#interface serial 0.3 point-to-point
RouterA(config-subif)#ip address 10.1.3.1 255.255.255.0
```

Figure 12-5 depicts the same network scenario from Figure 12-4, but with subinterfaces implemented.

Figure 12-5 *Frame Relay Subinterfaces*

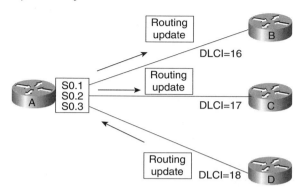

Note that the routing updates can now flow easily. However, using subinterfaces involves a trade-off. In exchange for the proper functioning of split horizon and the passing of routing updates, additional subnets are necessary. In addition, each interface has to have its own unique subnet, no matter which protocols are configured.

In configuring a subinterface, you must specify whether it is point-to-point or multipoint. Point-to-point subinterfaces establish a single PVC between two endpoints. Each interface is its own subnet and has a single DLCI configured. Broadcasts do not present an issue here because the routers treat the subinterface as a dedicated circuit between the two points.

Multipoint subinterfaces can be used with multiple PVC configurations on a single subinterface. All participating PVC connections are members of a common subnet. Multiple DLCIs would be configured here. However, split horizon dictates that no routing updates can pass in from and then out of the same subinterface.

Frame Relay Configuration

The basic configuration of Frame Relay is quite simple. In many cases, the configuration can be as simple as setting the encapsulation and putting an IP address on the interface. This enables Inverse ARP to dynamically configure the DLCI and discover neighboring routers across the cloud. However, configurations are rarely that simple. Although basic functionality can be achieved in this manner, more complex procedures are necessary for hub-and-spoke subinterface configurations that deal with point-to-multipoint implementations.

Configuration of Frame Relay can be accomplished in a few steps, as follows:

Step 1   Determine the interface to be configured.

Step 2   Configure Frame Relay encapsulation.

Step 3   Configure protocol-specific parameters.

Step 4   Configure Frame Relay characteristics.

Step 5   Verify Frame Relay configuration.

Step 1: Determine the Interface to Be Configured

The first step is to decide which interface should be configured for Frame Relay functionality. This should be a fairly easy decision. The interface that interfaces the Frame Relay network is obviously the one that needs the configuration. Once the interface has been selected, you should change to the appropriate interface configuration mode in the router.

Now is the time to decide whether subinterfaces should be implemented. For a single point-to-point implementation, it might not be necessary to use subinterfaces; however, this implementation does not scale. If future sites are planned, it is best to use subinterfaces from the beginning.

To create a subinterface, simply enter the command to change to the desired interface, and the interface is created. For example, to create subinterface 1 on Serial 0, use the command **interface serial 0.1**. Once this command is entered, the interface is created and the router prompt is **Router(config-subif)#**.

You must also determine the nature, or *cast type*, of the subinterface to be created. In other words, you must decide whether the subinterface acts as a point-to-point connection or a point-to-multipoint connection. The subinterface, in Cisco IOS Software releases prior to 12.0, defaulted to a multipoint connection. However, as of Cisco IOS Software Release 12.0, the router will force the specification of cast type.

To specify the cast type, simply add the keywords **point-to-point** or **multipoint** to the end of the interface designation when it's created. For example, **interface serial0.1 point-to-point** creates a point-to-point subinterface and **interface serial0.1 multipoint** creates a point-to-multipoint subinterface.

Step 2: Configure Frame Relay Encapsulation

To enable Frame Relay on the interface, simply issue the command **encapsulation frame relay**. The encapsulation of the interface determines the way it should act because each encapsulation is technology-specific. Note that, by default, the Cisco-specific Frame Relay encapsulation is used. If connecting to a non-Cisco device on the remote end, it is necessary to use the IETF standard Frame Relay encapsulation. This is done by entering the command **encapsulation frame-relay ietf**.

The encapsulation specified at this point dictates the Layer 2 framing characteristics of the packet passed to this specific interface from Layer 3. Once the Layer 2 framing is established, the resulting frame can be passed down to the physical layer for transmission.

Step 3: Configure Protocol-Specific Parameters

For each protocol to be passed across the Frame Relay connection, you must configure appropriate addressing. This addressing must be planned in advance.

For point-to-point connections, each individual circuit should have its own subnetwork addressing and two available host addresses. In the instance of IP, each subinterface is assigned a separate (and of course, unique) IP subnet. For IPX, each subinterface must have a unique IPX network number, and so on. As with any other addressing scheme, each side of the link must have a unique host address.

For point-to-multipoint connections, each subinterface also must have unique addressing. However, a point-to-multipoint connection can (by its very nature) connect to multiple remote sites. Thus, all sites sharing the point-to-multipoint connection are members of the same subnetwork, no matter the number of connections or the protocol.

The cast type of the interface also dictates the manner in which DLCIs are assigned to the Frame Relay interface. The next section covers this topic in detail.

Step 4: Configure Frame Relay Characteristics

You must define specific parameters for Frame Relay operation. The parameters include LMI and DLCI configuration.

If you're using a release of Cisco IOS Software earlier than Release 11.2, you must specify the LMI type that is being implemented. The Frame Relay service provider, or telco, should provide the LMI information. For Cisco IOS Software Release 11.2 and later, you need not configure the LMI type. To disable LMI completely, use the **no keepalive** command to cease to transmit and receive LMI. However, keepalives must also be disabled at the switch.

At this point, you can configure address mapping, if necessary. In the case of point-to-point connections, mapping of protocol addresses to DLCIs is dynamic and requires no intervention (using Inverse ARP). However, if point-to-multipoint connections are in use, manual mapping is necessary.

Mapping is quite the same from protocol to protocol, so IP is the only one discussed in this section of the chapter. Figure 12-6 depicts a sample topology.

Figure 12-6 *Configuration Topology Example*

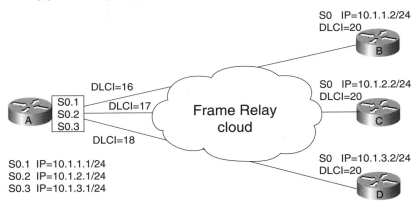

Figure 12-6 shows three point-to-point subinterfaces that require the creation of three individual subnets. The central router in this configuration is router A.

Although Example 12-1 covered the basic configuration for router A, the PVCs still need to be defined. In addition, because Example 12-1 already uses point-to-point interfaces, the only thing lacking is the DLCI, which the configuration in Example 12-2 provides.

Example 12-2 *Frame Relay Subinterfaces Configuration (Point-to-Point)*

```
RouterA(config)#interface serial 0
RouterA(config-if)#encapsulation frame-relay
RouterA(config-if)#interface serial 0.1 point-to-point
RouterA(config-subif)#ip address 10.1.1.1 255.255.255.0
RouterA(config-subif)#frame-relay interface-dlci 16
RouterA(config-fr-dlci)#interface serial 0.2 point-to-point
RouterA(config-subif)#ip address 10.1.2.1 255.255.255.0
RouterA(config-subif)#frame-relay interface-dlci 17
RouterA(config-fr-dlci)#interface serial 0.3 point-to-point
RouterA(config-subif)#ip address 10.1.3.1 255.255.255.0
RouterA(config-subif)#frame-relay interface-dlci 18
```

Example 12-3 details the same basic configuration. The difference is that the interfaces were created as multipoint interfaces. In other words, each subinterface is capable of connecting to more than one remote location. This was not the case in the previous example.

Example 12-3 *Frame Relay Subinterface Configuration (Multipoint)*

```
RouterA(config)#interface serial 0
RouterA(config-if)#encapsulation frame-relay
RouterA(config-if)#interface serial 0.1 multipoint
RouterA(config-subif)#ip address 10.1.1.1 255.255.255.0
RouterA(config-subif)#frame-relay map ip 10.1.1.2 16 broadcast
RouterA(config-subif)#interface serial 0.2 multipoint
RouterA(config-subif)#ip address 10.1.2.1 255.255.255.0
RouterA(config-subif)#frame-relay map ip 10.1.2.2 17 broadcast
RouterA(config-subif)#interface serial 0.3 multipoint
RouterA(config-subif)#ip address 10.1.3.1 255.255.255.0
RouterA(config-subif)#frame-relay map ip 10.1.3.2 18 broadcast
```

Note in Example 12-3 that the command defining the circuit has changed. In addition, although Example 12-2 specifies the DLCI and nothing else, Example 12-3 creates a static mapping that associates the next-hop IP address with the local DLCI that has been created by the telco. The **frame-relay map** command is the same as for other protocols. The command structure for **frame-relay map** is

```
Router(config-if)#frame-relay map protocol protocol-address dlci [broadcast][ietf |
cisco]
```

Protocols supported in the **frame-relay map** command include IP, IPX, AppleTalk, CLNS, DECnet, XNS, and Vines, to name just a few. The *protocol-address* in the command is the next-hop logical address for the router on the remote end of the connection. The *dlci* argument represents the *local* DLCI, not the DLCI of the remote end. You should always map the local DLCI to the next-hop address.

As is the nature of NBMA networks, broadcasts are not allowed. In the **frame-relay map** command, the **broadcast** keyword specifies that routing updates traverse the network through this circuit. Without this keyword, no routing updates will traverse the link.

The final option in the command specifies which Frame Relay implementation to use in communications with the remote router. When communicating with a Cisco device on the remote side, the default value (**cisco**) can be used. This is enabled by simply entering the command **encapsulation frame-relay** at the major interface. However, when communicating with non-Cisco gear on the remote end, it can be necessary to specify that the IETF implementation of Frame Relay be used, by issuing the command **encapsulation frame-relay ietf**.

Step 5: Verify Frame Relay Configuration

The most useful method of verifying configurations, aside from a good old-fashioned ping, is through the use of the **show** and **debug** commands. The examples in the following subsections show sample command output.

show frame-relay pvc Command

Example 12-4 shows output from the **show frame-relay pvc** command. This command is useful for viewing the status of statically or dynamically defined PVCs.

Example 12-4   **show frame-relay pvc** *Command Output*

```
RouterA#show frame-relay pvc
PVC Statistics for interface Serial0/0 (Frame Relay DTE)

                Active    Inactive    Deleted      Static
   Local          2          0           0            0
   Switched       0          0           0            0
   Unused         9          6           0            0

DLCI = 16, DLCI USAGE = LOCAL, PVC STATUS = ACTIVE, INTERFACE = Serial0/0.102

   input pkts 1              output pkts 2211        in bytes 34
   out bytes 489614          dropped pkts 0          in FECN pkts 0
   in BECN pkts 0            out FECN pkts 0         out BECN pkts 0
   in DE pkts 0              out DE pkts 0
   out bcast pkts 2211        out bcast bytes 489614
   pvc create time 21:15:39, last time pvc status changed 21:00:59


DLCI = 17, DLCI USAGE = LOCAL, PVC STATUS = ACTIVE, INTERFACE = Serial0/0.103

   input pkts 2101           output pkts 2220        in bytes 461204
   out bytes 492080          dropped pkts 0          in FECN pkts 0
   in BECN pkts 0            out FECN pkts 0         out BECN pkts 0
   in DE pkts 0              out DE pkts 0
   out bcast pkts 2220        out bcast bytes 492080
   pvc create time 21:14:39, last time pvc status changed 21:14:39


DLCI = 18, DLCI USAGE = UNUSED, PVC STATUS = ACTIVE, INTERFACE = Serial0/0

   input pkts 0              output pkts 0           in bytes 0
   out bytes 0              dropped pkts 0          in FECN pkts 0
   in BECN pkts 0            out FECN pkts 0         out BECN pkts 0
   in DE pkts 0              out DE pkts 0
   out bcast pkts 0          out bcast bytes 0          Num Pkts Switched 0
   pvc create time 21:32:09, last time pvc status changed 18:44:30
```

Note in the output that each PVC is detailed. The highlighted portion shows the DLCI of the circuit being detailed, the status of the PVC (ACTIVE, INACTIVE, or DELETED), and the interface with which the particular PVC is associated.

The output also gives for each circuit information that specifies the receipt or transmission of FECN/BECN packets. Because FECN (Forward Explicit Congestion Notification) and BECN (Backward

Explicit Congestion Notification) packets provide notification that congestion exists in the Frame Relay network, a low number is preferable (0 is the best). The output also details the number of Discard Eligible (DE) packets received. Again, the lower the number, the better.

show frame-relay lmi Command

Along with checking the status of individual PVCs, you can monitor the communication status between the router and the switch. Example 12-5 shows the output from the **show frame-relay lmi** command, which shows the number of LMI messages sent and received across the link between the router and the switch.

Example 12-5 **show frame-relay lmi** *Command Output*

```
RouterA#show frame-relay lmi

LMI Statistics for interface Serial0 (Frame Relay DTE) LMI TYPE = CISCO
  Invalid Unnumbered info 0        Invalid Prot Disc 0
  Invalid dummy Call Ref 0         Invalid Msg Type 0
  Invalid Status Message 0         Invalid Lock Shift 0
  Invalid Information ID 0         Invalid Report IE Len 0
  Invalid Report Request 0         Invalid Keep IE Len 0
  Num Status Enq. Sent 8060        Num Status msgs Rcvd 8061
  Num Update Status Rcvd 0         Num Status Timeouts 0

LMI Statistics for interface Serial1 (Frame Relay DTE) LMI TYPE = ANSI
  Invalid Unnumbered info 0        Invalid Prot Disc 0
  Invalid dummy Call Ref 0         Invalid Msg Type 0
  Invalid Status Message 0         Invalid Lock Shift 0
  Invalid Information ID 0         Invalid Report IE Len 0
  Invalid Report Request 0         Invalid Keep IE Len 0
  Num Status Enq. Rcvd 6711        Num Status msgs Sent 6711
  Num Update Status Sent 0         Num St Enq. Timeouts 2
```

The shaded lines highlight an important aspect of this output: the LMI type can be specified differently for each interface, so the type is specified in the output.

Another critical piece of this output is the LMI input/output information. This is shown in the second highlighted line. If the number of sent inquiries is incrementing, but the number of received messages remains at 0, LMI is not being received from the switch. As long as both numbers are greater than 0 and continue to increment on a regular basis (every few seconds), LMI is being exchanged. The output also shows timeouts, errors, and so on.

debug frame-relay lmi Command

Probably the most useful tool you can use to verify and troubleshoot Frame Relay is the **debug frame-relay lmi** command, as demonstrated in Example 12-6.

Example 12-6 **debug frame-relay lmi** *Command Output*

```
RouterA#debug frame-relay lmi
Frame Relay LMI debugging is on
Displaying all Frame Relay LMI data
1d18h: Serial1(in): StEnq, myseq 85
1d18h: RT IE 1, length 1, type 1
1d18h: KA IE 3, length 2, yourseq 86, myseq 85
1d18h: Serial1(out): Status, myseq 86, yourseen 86, DTE up
1d18h: Serial0(out): StEnq, myseq 162, yourseen 161, DTE up
1d18h: datagramstart = 0x3001754, datagramsize = 13
1d18h: FR encap = 0xFCF10309
1d18h: 00 75 01 01 01 03 02 A2 A1
1d18h:
1d18h: Serial0(in): Status, myseq 162
1d18h: RT IE 1, length 1, type 1
1d18h: KA IE 3, length 2, yourseq 162, myseq 162
1d18h: Serial1(in): StEnq, myseq 86
1d18h: RT IE 1, length 1, type 1
1d18h: KA IE 3, length 2, yourseq 87, myseq 86
1d18h: Serial1(out): Status, myseq 87, yourseen 87, DTE up
1d18h: Serial0(out): StEnq, myseq 163, yourseen 162, DTE up
1d18h: datagramstart = 0x34D25B4, datagramsize = 13
1d18h: FR encap = 0xFCF10309
1d18h: 00 75 01 01 00 03 02 A3 A2
```

Using the **debug frame-relay lmi** command enables you to watch the real-time communication between the router and the switch. Each request sent from the router to the switch is noted as *myseq*, and the counter is incremented by 1 with each request. LMI messages sent from the switch to the router by the telco are noted as *yourseen* and also are incremented by 1 with each request.

It is important to see inbound and outbound activity, as highlighted in Example 12-6. Status and StEnq messages show *myseq* and *yourseen* values greater than 0, along with *DTE up*. In the event that the link was malfunctioning, DTE status will bounce repeatedly from up to down and back again. Also, the *myseq* value will increment while the *yourseen* value will remain at 0.

show frame-relay map Command

The **show frame-relay map** command is used to view the DLCI mappings that have been created. They can be static or dynamic and are noted as such in the command output. Example 12-7 shows the output from this command.

Example 12-7 *show frame-relay map Command Output*

```
RouterA#show frame-relay map
Serial0.1 (up): point-to-point dlci, dlci 16(0x10,0x400), broadcast
          status defined, active
Serial0.2 (up): point-to-point dlci, dlci 17(0x0A,0x401), broadcast
          status defined, active
Serial0.3 (up): point-to-point dlci, dlci 18(0x0B,0x402), broadcast
          status defined, active
```

Foundation Summary

This section is a collection of information that provides a convenient review of many key concepts in this chapter. If you are already comfortable with the topics in this chapter, this summary can help you recall a few details. If you just read this chapter, this review should help solidify some key facts.

Frame Relay is a highly versatile technology. It supports data in varying degrees and speeds, and it supports voice traffic. In addition, it can tell the difference between the two traffic types.

Table 12-2 provides a review of the Frame Relay LMI types that are supported by Cisco routers.

Table 12-2   *LMI Types*

LMI Type	Also Known As	Defined by
Cisco	Gang of Four	Cisco, StrataCom, Nortel, and DEC
ANSI	Annex D	T1.617 Annex D
Q933a	Annex A	Q.933 Annex A

Table 12-3 provides review information regarding Frame Relay topologies.

Table 12-3   *Frame Relay Topologies*

Topology	Description
Hub and spoke (also known as star)	This is the dominant method of deploying Frame Relay. It consists of a single central site that acts as a connection point for all remote offices. Routing between two satellite offices is accomplished through the central site. This tends to be the lowest-cost solution; however, it is also the least redundant (that is, fault tolerant) strategy.
Full mesh	This topology consists of a large number of connections. It is very expensive to operate; however, it is the most fault tolerant. Because each site is connected to every other site, the number of connections can quickly grow and become cost prohibitive. The formula for deriving the number of required connections is $n(n-1) \div 2$, where n is the number of devices you wish to connect.
Partial mesh	This implementation is hub and spoke with redundancy. The cost of full mesh is avoided and the lack of fault tolerance of hub and spoke is minimized. A central site is still used; however, redundant connections are installed between critical sites. In essence, it is possible to create a backup central site. This is particularly useful in networks in which delay reductions are necessary, because the capability to get to a destination without traversing a central router decreases delay significantly.

Table 12-4 *Useful Frame Relay* **show** *and* **debug** *Commands*

Command	Function
show frame-relay pvc	Displays status information for PVCs, including the DLCI, LMI counts, FECN/BECN counts, and PVC state (ACTIVE, INACTIVE, or DELETED).
show frame-relay lmi	Displays LMI traffic statistics for both inbound LMI packets and outbound LMI packets.
show frame-relay map	Displays the protocol to DLCI mappings for PVCs and indicates whether the mapping is static or dynamic.
debug frame-relay lmi	Enables the real-time logging and monitoring of LMI packets sent and received. It also monitors the state of the Frame Relay connection (DTE up or DTE down). This is arguably the most valuable troubleshooting command for new Frame Relay connections.

Q&A

The questions and scenarios in this book are more difficult than what you should experience on the actual exam. The questions do not attempt to cover more breadth or depth than the exam, but they are designed to make sure that you know the answer. Rather than enabling you to derive the answer from clues hidden inside the question, the questions challenge your understanding and recall of the subject. Hopefully, mastering these questions will help you limit the number of exam questions on which you narrow your choices to two options and then guess.

The answers to these questions can be found in Appendix A.

1. What are the two types of virtual circuits and what are the common attributes of each?

2. What is meant in the description of DLCIs as being *locally significant*?

3. Frame Relay devices fall into one of two possible roles. What are they?

4. What are the three supported LMI types for Cisco routers?

5. If the lmi-type is not set on the Frame Relay interface, what will happen, by default?

6. What are three typical Frame Relay topologies?

7. In a fully meshed Frame Relay environment, how many circuits will be necessary to connect 40 routers?

8. Which Frame Relay topology offers the lowest delay overall for traffic that is traversing between remote sites?

9. How can issues regarding split horizon be avoided or remedied in a Frame Relay point-to-multipoint connection?

10. When creating a subinterface, what happens if the cast type is not specified?

11. What is the function of Inverse ARP in a Frame Relay network?

12. If connecting to a non-Cisco device on the remote end, what command must be entered to make the two routers communicate?

13. What command would be used to map the next-hop address of 172.16.214.89 to the local DLCI set at 135?

14. What keyword added to the command entered in the answer to question 13 will augment the functionality by allowing routing updates to traverse the link? Restate the command to allow routing updates.

15. Which command will allow the viewing of a PVC with the DLCI 135?

16. Which command will allow the viewing of the real-time conversation between the router and the Frame Relay switch?

17. In the output of the command **debug frame-relay lmi**, which pieces of output are the most important in ensuring that the link is functional?

This chapter covers the following topics that you will need to master the BCRAN exam:

- Frame Relay Traffic Shaping

- Frame Relay Traffic Shaping Configuration

CHAPTER 13

Frame Relay Traffic Shaping

Frame Relay traffic shaping enables you to exercise a high degree of control over traffic flow across a particular interface or PVC. Frame Relay is somewhat unique in the WAN world because it allows the implementation of not only point-to-point connections (such as PPP or HDLC) and point-to-multipoint connections, but also a speed mismatch. This means that opposing sides of a particular PVC need not have the same amount of allocated bandwidth. This is particularly useful in hub-and-spoke topologies where a central site (hub) has been configured with high bandwidth and branch sites (spoke) have been configured with lower-bandwidth connections.

In such cases, the hub site could easily overrun the spoke sites with traffic. The resulting congestion could have dramatic, sometimes unpredictable, repercussions on the network.

Frame Relay traffic shaping is a methodology that enables you to govern traffic leaving a particular interface or subinterface. Traffic shaping can be applied to a major interface, subinterface, or individual PVC. The shaping parameters can be applied to either inbound or outbound traffic flow.

"Do I Know This Already?" Quiz

The purpose of the "Do I Know This Already?" quiz is to help you decide whether you really need to read the entire chapter. If you already intend to read the entire chapter, you do not necessarily need to answer these questions now.

This five-question quiz, derived from the major sections in the "Foundation Topics" portion of the chapter, helps you to determine how to spend your limited study time.

Table 13-1 outlines the major topics discussed in this chapter and the "Do I Know This Already?" quiz questions that correspond to those topics.

Table 13-1 *"Do I Know This Already?" Foundation Topics Section-to-Question Mapping*

Foundation Topics Section	Questions Covered in This Section
Frame Relay Traffic Shaping Fundamentals	1–2
Frame Relay Traffic Shaping Configuration	3–5

> **CAUTION**   The goal of self-assessment is to gauge your mastery of the topics in this chapter. If you do not know the answer to a question or are only partially sure of the answer, you should mark this question wrong for purposes of the self-assessment. Giving yourself credit for an answer you correctly guess skews your self-assessment results and might provide you with a false sense of security.

1. In Frame Relay traffic shaping, which of the following is the speed at which you may transmit during noncongestive periods?

   a. MIR

   b. CIR

   c. MinCIR

   d. Bc

2. If CIR is 64,000 bps, what should typically be the value of MinCIR?

   a. 32,000 bps

   b. 128,000 bps

   c. 16,000 bps

   d. 64,000 bps

3. In map class configuration mode, what command enables the router to respond to BECN requests?

   a. enable becn

   b. frame-relay adaptive-shaping becn

   c. frame-relay becn enable

   d. frame-relay adaptive-becn

4. In map class configuration mode, what command specifies the CIR if you want CIR set to 512,000 bps?

   a. cir 512,000

   b. mincir 512,000

   c. frame-relay cir 512,000

   d. frame-relay mincir 512,000

5. In periods of congestion, what is the percentage drop of throughput experienced with each BECN?

    a. 10%

    b. 25%

    c. 40%

    d. 50%

The answers to the "Do I Know This Already?" quiz are found in Appendix A, "Answers to the 'Do I Know This Already?' Quizzes and Q&A Sections." The suggested choices for your next step are as follows:

- **4 or fewer overall score**—Read the chapter. This includes the "Foundation Topics" and "Foundation Summary" sections, and the "Q&A" section at the end of the chapter.

- **5 overall score**—If you want more review on these topics, skip to the "Foundation Summary" section and then go to the "Q&A" section at the end of the chapter. Otherwise, move to the next chapter.

Foundation Topics

Frame Relay Traffic Shaping Fundamentals

Frame Relay traffic shaping is a means of controlling the output of traffic across the Frame Relay network. Whether the goal is to meet service contract obligations or to control output speed to slower links, traffic shaping can provide granular control of outbound data. Traffic shaping can provide per–virtual circuit (VC) rate enforcement, Backward Explicit Congestion Notification (BECN) support, and queuing (weighted fair queuing [WFQ], priority queuing [PQ], or custom queuing [CQ]) at the VC level.

Frame Relay traffic shaping is supported only on fast-switching and process-switching paths. Therefore, to use it, other switching methods must be disabled on all interfaces that send traffic to the serial interface.

> **NOTE** Frame Relay traffic shaping can be applied to a major interface, subinterface, or PVC. However, if the **frame-relay traffic-shaping** command has not been entered at the major interface, none of the traffic shaping parameters applied to subinterfaces or PVCs residing under that major interface will respond to traffic shaping. No error message will be given. It will simply not work.

Frame Relay Traffic Parameters

To understand the concepts of traffic shaping, it is important to have a firm grasp of the various traffic parameters in the Frame Relay network. In particular, you should know that some (such as committed information rate [CIR] and excessive burst [Be]) are commonly used but misunderstood. Table 13-2 details the traffic parameters.

Table 13-2 *Frame Relay Traffic Parameters*

Parameter	Description
CIR (Committed Information Rate)	The average rate at which you want to transmit. This is generally not the same as the CIR provided by the telco. This is the rate at which you want to send in periods of noncongestion.
Be (Excessive Burst)	The amount of excess data allowed to be sent during the first interval once credit is built up. Transmission credit is built up during periods of nontransmission. The credit is the burst size. Full credit is typically CIR / 8.

Table 13-2 *Frame Relay Traffic Parameters (Continued)*

Parameter	Description
Bc (Committed Burst)	The amount of data to send in each Tc interval.
Tc (Committed Rate Measurement Interval)	The Bc / CIR time interval. The time interval shouldn't exceed 125 ms (almost always 125 ms).
MinCIR (Minimum CIR)	The minimum amount of data to send during periods of congestion. This is usually what you get from the telco. MinCIR defaults to one-half of CIR.
PIR (Peak Information Rate)	The highest possible rate of transmission on a given interface.
MIR (Minimum Information Rate)	The slowest rate of transmission on a given interface.
Interval	Bc / CIR. The maximum is 125 ms, or 1/8 second.
Byte Increment	Bc / 8. This value must be greater than 125.
Limit	Byte Increment + Be / 8 (in bytes).

The information in Table 13-2 can be easily misunderstood. For instance, consider the details of a 128-kbps Frame Relay link:

- The CIR would have a value of 128,000 bps, but that's not necessarily the guaranteed throughput value provided by the telco.

- MinCIR is usually the guaranteed value and it defaults to one-half of CIR, so MinCIR would be 64,000 bps.

- The Bc is CIR / 8, so it would be 16,000 bps.

- The byte increment is Bc / 8, so it should be 2000 bps.

- Finally, the Tc would be 125 ms, which is where it should normally sit.

All parameters might or might not be utilized in the course of traffic shaping. The parameters are more related to BECN response to network congestion. BECN is explained more thoroughly in the next section. Forward Explicit Congestion Notification (FECN) is not configurable on the router, so it is not mentioned in particular detail.

FECN and BECN

Frame Relay traffic shaping relies largely on its capability to detect congestion. To that end, FECN and BECN are implemented in today's Frame Relay networks.

If a Frame Relay switch senses congestion in the network, it sets the FECN bit to 1 in the Frame Relay header for traffic moving toward the destination device. This number indicates a congestive situation. Once received, the destination device flips the BECN bit in return traffic to the source. This informs the source device of the congestion in the network and that it should reduce the transmission rate.

When congestion is experienced, any traffic moving through the network in violation of the negotiated CIR that has been flagged as Discard Eligible (DE) can be dropped. Retransmission of dropped traffic is left to the Layer 4 protocol of the end devices (for example, to TCP).

If the router receives BECNs during the current time interval, it decreases the transmission rate by 25 percent. The rate continues to drop with each BECN (the limit is one drop per time interval) until the traffic rate gets to the minimum acceptable incoming or outgoing committed information rate (MinCIR). At this point, the decline in throughput is halted.

Once the traffic rate has declined involuntarily, it takes 16 time intervals without the receipt of BECNs to start to increase traffic flow again. Traffic increases by (Be + Bc) / 16, or, more accurately, the byte limit that shows up in the output of the **show frame-relay pvc** command is divided by 16.

It takes significantly longer to get back up to CIR than it did to drop. To shorten the length of time, set Be to a value seven times the value of Bc. Continuing the example following Table 13-2, note that the Bc is 16,000 bps. If the Be is set to 7(16,000) = 112,000, the traffic increase is (Be + Bc) = 16, or (112,000 + 16,000) / 16 = 8000, bps per time interval. This forces it back to CIR (128,000 bps) immediately after the 16 (16(8000)) time intervals with no BECN.

This behavior occurs only when Frame Relay traffic shaping is active. If traffic shaping is not active, the transmission increment is fixed even though BECNs are not being received.

Using Frame Relay Traffic Shaping

Frame Relay traffic shaping can be useful in many situations. For instance, it can be useful if your network consists of high-bandwidth links exclusively, or if your network is a mixed-bandwidth environment. In addition, any environment in which Voice over Frame Relay (VoFR) is being implemented requires the use of traffic shaping to adequately configure the network for voice traffic.

In mixed-bandwidth environments, traffic shaping can be used to protect the lower-speed links. For example, a T1 link transmitting data to a site in which the bandwidth is only 56 kbps can be forced into a congestive state quite easily. If traffic shaping is implemented on the faster side, specifically on the VC directing traffic to that specific site, congestion can be stopped before it begins.

Frame Relay Traffic Shaping Configuration

Frame Relay traffic shaping is accomplished through the creation of a map class, which can be associated with one or more PVCs. The map class defines the traffic parameters for any circuits to which it is applied. The command structure for defining the map class is as follows:

```
RouterA(config)# map-class frame-relay name
```

The *name* parameter is an arbitrary value. This is the parameter that is used to tie the map class to one or more PVCs.

After you enter the **map-class** command, the prompt changes. At this point, it is time to define the traffic parameters. You can configure the average and peak transmission rates at this point and define whether the router should respond to BECN requests. It is also possible to define queues to prioritize PVCs. The command structure for defining peak and average rates is as follows (the peak rate is optional):

```
RouterA(config-map-class)# frame-relay traffic-rate average [peak]
```

The average rate is measured in bps and should be set to the contracted CIR. The peak rate is also measured in bps. Do not use the **frame-relay traffic-rate** command if you are enabling the **adaptive-shaping becn** command. Instead, you should enable a BECN response. If no values are specified for these rates, the router assumes that all values are set to the clock speed of the interface and that all available bandwidth is usable as needed.

To specify that the router should respond to BECN requests for throughput reduction, use the **frame-relay adaptive-shaping becn** command, the command structure for which is as follows:

```
RouterA(config-map-class)# frame-relay adaptive-shaping becn
```

There are no configurable options; you simply issue the command. Use this command instead of the **frame-relay traffic-rate** command whenever possible. In addition, note that the **frame-relay adaptive-shaping becn** command makes the **frame-relay becn-response-enable** command obsolete.

The preceding commands do not address the issues of defining CIR, Bc, Be, and MinCIR. As you probably guessed, each parameter has an associated command. The command structure for the **frame-relay cir** command for the map class is as follows:

```
RouterA(config-map-class)# frame-relay cir [in |out] bits
```

The rate in the **frame-relay cir** command is expressed in bps and should be the rate at which transmission should be sent during periods with no congestion.

Use the **frame-relay bc** command to define the committed burst size for the map class:

```
RouterA(config-map-class)# frame-relay bc [in |out] bits
```

The Bc is the amount to be transmitted per interval in bytes (usually CIR / 8).

Use the **frame-relay be** command to define excessive burst for a map class:

```
RouterA(config-map-class)# frame-relay be [in |out] bits
```

The Be is the additional amount to be sent in the first interval. If CIR = port speed, set Be to 0, because no additional bandwidth is available for a burst.

Use the **frame-relay mincir** command to specify the MinCIR for the map class:

```
RouterA(config-map-class)# frame-relay mincir [in |out] bits
```

Note that the MinCIR in this command is the CIR that was negotiated with the telco. It is usually one-half the actual CIR.

Example 13-1 brings it all together in a configuration that implements all the commands.

Example 13-1 *Frame Relay Traffic Shaping*

```
RouterA(config)# map-class frame-relay EM&AM
RouterA(config-map-class)# frame-relay adaptive-shaping becn
RouterA(config-map-class)# frame-relay cir 128000
RouterA(config-map-class)# frame-relay bc 16000
RouterA(config-map-class)# frame-relay be 0
RouterA(config-map-class)# frame-relay mincir 64000
RouterA(config-map-class)# exit
RouterA(config)# interface serial 0
RouterA(config-if)# encapsulation frame-relay
RouterA(config-if)# frame-relay traffic-shaping
RouterA(config-if)# interface serial 0.1 point-to-point
RouterA(config-subif)# ip address 10.1.1.1 255.255.255.0
RouterA(config-subif)# frame-relay interface-dlci 16
RouterA(config-fr-dlci)# class EM&AM
```

The preceding configuration provides a number of functions for the PVC. The **map-class** is defined and applied to the individual circuit using the **class** command. The class could have been applied to the major interface, subinterface, or PVC definition.

As mentioned throughout this section, Frame Relay traffic shaping can provide granular, per-VC flow control. However, it can also provide per-interface flow control. If applied to an interface rather than a specific circuit, it shapes all circuits defined on that interface. It can be placed on the major interface or the subinterface, or both.

Example 13-2 shows the same configuration as in Example 13-1, but applied to the major interface.

Example 13-2 *Frame Relay Traffic Shaping on the Interface*

```
RouterA(config)# map-class frame-relay EM&AM
RouterA(config-map-class)# frame-relay adaptive-shaping becn
RouterA(config-map-class)# frame-relay cir 128000
RouterA(config-map-class)# frame-relay bc 16000
RouterA(config-map-class)# frame-relay be 0
RouterA(config-map-class)# frame-relay mincir 64000
RouterA(config-map-class)# exit
RouterA(config)# interface serial 0
RouterA(config-if)# encapsulation frame-relay
RouterA(config-if)# frame-relay traffic-shaping
RouterA(config-if)# frame-relay class EM&AM
RouterA(config)# interface serial 0.1 point-to-point
RouterA(config-subif)# ip address 10.1.1.1 255.255.255.0
RouterA(config-subif)# frame-relay interface-dlci 16
```

To verify the operation of the Frame Relay traffic shaping configuration, use the **show frame-relay pvc** command as demonstrated in Example 13-3.

Example 13-3 **show frame-relay pvc** *Command Output Verifies the Operation of Frame Relay Traffic Shaping*

```
RouterA# show frame-relay pvc
PVC Statistics for interface Serial0.1 (Frame Relay DTE)
DLCI = 16, DLCI USAGE = LOCAL, PVC STATUS = ACTIVE, INTERFACE =
Serial0.1
  input pkts 0            output pkts 0          in bytes 0
  out bytes 0            dropped pkts 0          in FECN pkts 0
  in BECN pkts 0          out FECN pkts 0        out BECN pkts 0
  in DE pkts 0            out DE pkts 0
  out bcast pkts 0          out bcast bytes 0
  Shaping adapts to BECN
  pvc create time 23:34:33, last time pvc status changed 23:34:33
  cir 128000      bc 16000      be 0      limit 10000   interval 125
  mincir 64000      byte increment 1000   BECN response yes
  pkts 0          bytes 0          pkts delayed 0        bytes delayed 0
  shaping inactive
  Serial0.1 dlci 50 is first come first serve default queueing

  Output queue 0/40, 0 drop, 0 dequeued
```

With traffic shaping turned on, all configured parameters are listed. Other useful commands include **show traffic-shape** and **show traffic-shape statistics**. Example 13-4 illustrates output from the **show traffic-shape** command.

Example 13-4   *The* **show traffic-shape** *Command*

```
RouterA# show traffic-shape

access       Target Byte    Sustain   Excess    Interval Increment Adapt
I/F    list   Rate  Limit  bits/int bits/int (ms)     (bytes)   Active
S0     101                 1000000  23437     125000   125000    63   7813   -
S1                         5000000  87889     625000   625000    16   9766   -
```

As the output in Example 13-4 indicates, the **show traffic-shape** command identifies the current traffic shaping configuration, interface by interface. Note how the output has changed dramatically as compared with the listing in Example 13-3. In Example 13-4, all that is shown is the sustained and excess throughput. Example 13-3 has a much more dramatic display.

Two other options are available when utilizing the **show traffic-shape** command: **show traffic-shape statistics** and **show traffic-shape queue**. Example 13-5 shows the output from the **show traffic-shape statistics** command.

Example 13-5   *Output from the* **show traffic-shape statistics** *Command*

```
RouterA# show traffic-shape statistics
         Access Queue   Packets   Bytes   Packets   Bytes  Shaping
I/F      List  Depth   Delayed  Delayed                    Active
Et0      101    0         2        180      0         0      no
Et1             0         0        0        0         0      no
```

This command shows the amount of traffic affected by traffic shaping. Queue depth and delayed packet counts are important to watch in maintaining a balanced traffic shaping configuration. Note that traffic shaping is not active on either interface. It is interesting to note that access-list 101 is on Ethernet 0. The remaining fields illustrate a count of the effects of the traffic shaping in the form of delay. It is likely that the delayed traffic is due to the access list applied to the interface rather than traffic shaping.

Example 13-6 shows the output from the **show traffic-shape queue** command.

Example 13-6   *Output from the* **show traffic-shape queue** *Command*

```
routerA# show traffic-shape queue Serial1/1 dlci 16
Traffic queued in shaping queue on Serial1.1 dlci 16
Queueing strategy: weighted fair
Queueing Stats: 1/600/64/0 (size/max total/threshold/drops)
Conversations 0/16 (active/max total)
```

Example 13-6 *Output from the* **show traffic-shape queue** *Command (Continued)*

```
Reserved Conversations 0/2 (active/allocated)
(depth/weight/discards) 1/4096/0
Conversation 5, linktype: ip, length: 608
source: 172.21.59.21, destination: 255.255.255.255, id: 0x0006, ttl: 255,
TOS: 0 prot: 17, source port 68, destination port 67
```

From the output, it is evident that Weighted Fair Queuing is active on this interface. Source and destination addressing and source and destination port numbers are included as well. As the queuing strategy on the interface is altered, the output of the command, too, will be altered.

Foundation Summary

This section is a collection of information that provides a convenient review of many key concepts in this chapter. If you are already comfortable with the topics in this chapter, this summary can help you recall a few details. If you just read this chapter, this review should help solidify some key facts. If you are doing your final preparation before the exam, these tables are a convenient way to review the day before the exam.

Traffic shaping in general is one of the most misunderstood concepts of Frame Relay implementations. This is unfortunate, because the traffic shaping configuration can have a significant effect, both positive and negative, as a software-based process.

For the exam, you should understand the finer points of traffic shaping and its use. Reread this chapter and Chapter 12 to ensure that you understand traffic shaping adequately.

Table 13-3 revisits the topic of Frame Relay traffic shaping. This table is a near duplicate of Table 13-2 and is placed here for review purposes.

Table 13-3 *Frame Relay Traffic Parameters*

Parameter	Description
CIR	The average rate you want to transmit. This is generally not the same as the CIR provided by the telco. This is the amount you want to send in periods of noncongestion.
Be	The amount of excess data allowed to be sent during the first interval once credit is built up. Transmission credit is built during periods of no transmission. The credit is the burst size. Full credit is typically CIR / 8.
Bc	The amount of data to send in each Tc interval.
Tc	The Bc / CIR time interval. The time interval shouldn't exceed 125 ms (almost always 125 ms).
MinCIR	The minimum amount of data to send during periods of congestion. This is usually what you get from the telco. MinCIR defaults to one-half of CIR.
PIR	The highest possible rate of transmission on a given interface. Also known as the clocking speed.
MIR	The slowest rate of transmission on a given interface.
Interval	Bc / CIR. The maximum is 125 ms, or 1/8 second.
Byte Increment	Bc / 8. This value must be greater than 125.
Limit	Byte Increment + Be / 8 (in bytes).

Table 13-4 reviews the commands to implement Frame Relay traffic shaping.

Table 13-4 *Frame Relay Traffic Shaping Commands*

Command	Function
frame-relay traffic-shaping	Enables traffic shaping on a Frame Relay interface. This command should be issued at the major interface.
map-class frame-relay *name*	Used to define a profile for the traffic parameters for any circuits to which it is applied. The *name* is case-sensitive when applied to a circuit.
frame-relay traffic-rate *average* [*peak*]	Defines average and peak transmission rates for any circuit to which the map class containing this command is applied.
frame-relay adaptive-shaping becn	Enables the router to respond to inbound frames with BECN markers. Once a BECN frame is received, the transmission rate is reduced.
frame-relay cir [in | out] *bits*	Defines the CIR for a map class.
frame-relay bc [in | out] *bits*	Defines the Bc for a map class.
frame-relay be [in | out] *bits*	Defines the Be for a map class.
frame-relay mincir [in | out] *bits*	Defines the MinCIR for a map class.
class *name*	Associates a map class with a specific PVC or subinterface.
frame-relay class *name*	Associates a map class with a major interface.

Table 13-5 provides a review of the **show** and **debug** commands mentioned in the chapter for Frame Relay verification.

Table 13-5 *Useful Frame Relay* **show** *and* **debug** *Commands*

Command	Function
show traffic-shape	Displays general traffic shaping information and statistics.
show traffic-shape statistics	Displays only traffic shaping statistics.
show traffic-shape queue	Displays interface- and DLCI-specific traffic shaping information.

Q&A

The questions and scenarios in this book are more difficult than what you will experience on the actual exam. The questions do not attempt to cover more breadth or depth than the exam, but they are designed to make sure that you know the answer. Rather than enabling you to derive the answer from clues hidden inside the question itself, the questions challenge your understanding and recall of the subject.

Hopefully, mastering these questions will help you limit the number of exam questions on which you narrow your choices to two options and then guess.

The answers to these questions can be found in Appendix A.

1. List the three possible locations that a Frame Relay traffic shaping definition can be applied.

2. A Frame Relay traffic shaping definition has been applied to a PVC on a subinterface. However, the shaping parameters are inactive. The class definition has been verified. What would keep a properly configured and applied traffic shaping definition from working?

3. The parameter that specifies the minimum guaranteed rate of traffic throughput across the carrier network is known as what?

4. If the command **frame-relay adaptive-shaping becn** has not been entered, how will the router respond to BECN requests on that interface or PVC?

5. If the CIR = 128,000 bps, MinCIR = 64,000 bps, and Bc = 8000 bps, what is the Tc and how long, in seconds, is the amount of time that must elapse once BECN requests have ceased before traffic can begin to step back up?

PART VI: Backup and Network Management Methods

Chapter 14   Enabling a Backup to the Permanent Connection

Chapter 15   Managing Network Performance with Queuing and Compression

This part of the book covers the following BCRAN exam topics:

- Describe traffic control methods used to manage traffic flow on WAN links
- Plan a Cisco ISDN solution for remote access or primary link back-up
- Troubleshoot non-functional remote access systems
- Troubleshoot traffic control problems on a WAN link

This chapter covers the following subjects:

- Dial Backup

- Alternative Backup Strategies

CHAPTER 14

Enabling a Backup to the Permanent Connection

The CCNP Remote Access Exam requires you to have an in-depth understanding of various WAN technologies. Among these is included a significant background in ISDN technologies. To provide for backup service in the event of a primary link failure, backup interfaces can be established and kept in reserve.

Backup interfaces are not specific to ISDN, though it is common to see the association made. This chapter discusses the intricacies of creating a backup connection to facilitate data transmission during an outage suffered by a primary link.

"Do I Know This Already?" Quiz

The purpose of the "Do I Know This Already?" quiz is to help you decide whether you really need to read the entire chapter. If you already intend to read the entire chapter, you do not necessarily need to answer these questions now.

The four-question quiz, derived from the major sections in the "Foundation Topics" portion of the chapter, helps you to determine how to spend your limited study time. Table 14-1 outlines the major topics discussed in this chapter and the "Do I Know This Already?" quiz questions that correspond to those topics.

Table 14-1 *"Do I Know This Already?" Foundation Topics Section-to-Question Mapping*

Foundation Topics Section	Questions Covered in This Section
Dial Backup	1–2
Alternative Backup Strategies	3–4

> **CAUTION** The goal of self-assessment is to gauge your mastery of the topics in this chapter. If you do not know the answer to a question or are only partially sure of the answer, you should mark this question wrong for purposes of the self-assessment. Giving yourself credit for an answer that you correctly guess skews your self-assessment results and might provide you with a false sense of security.

1. Which command implements dial backup 5 seconds after failure of the primary interface, and keeps the backup interface up for 30 seconds following the return of the primary interface?

   a. **backup load 5 30**

   b. **backup delay 5 30**

   c. **backup load 30 5**

   d. **backup delay 30 5**

2. Which command specifies BRI1 as a dial backup interface to Serial0?

   a. **interface serial 0**

      backup interface bri1

   b. **interface bri1**

      backup interface serial0

   c. **interface bri1**

      backup-pool 1

      interface serial 0

      backup-group 1

   d. **interface serial 0**

      dial-backup interface bri1

3. Which command configures IGRP or EIGRP to use any route that has a metric within the range of one to ten times the value of the metric of the best route in the routing table for a given destination?

   a. **variance 10**

   b. **variance 1 10**

   c. **variance 1**

   d. **variance 100**

4. Which command will create a backup route to the 192.168.1.0/24 network that will only be utilized in case of the loss of the dynamic route from the routing table?

   a. **ip route 192.168.1.0 255.255.255.255 10.1.1.1 200**

   b. **ip route 192.168.1.0 255.255.255.0 10.1.1.1**

   c. **ip route 192.169.1.0 0.0.0.255 10.1.1.1 200**

   d. **ip route 192.168.1.0 255.255.255.0 10.1.1.1 200**

The answers to the "Do I Know This Already?" quiz are found in Appendix A, "Answers to the 'Do I Know This Already?' Quizzes and Q&A Sections." The suggested choices for your next step are as follows:

- **1 or 2 overall score**—Read the entire chapter. This includes the "Foundation Topics," "Foundation Summary," and "Q&A" sections.

- **3 or 4 overall score**—If you want more review on these topics, skip to the "Foundation Summary" section and then go to the "Q&A" section. Otherwise, move to the next chapter.

Foundation Topics

Dial Backup

The purpose of dial backup is to provide redundancy for critical WAN links. Although the bandwidth that ISDN provides may not be comparable to that of the primary link, ISDN can provide a maintenance pathway so that remote devices can be accessed if the primary link fails. Note that the failure need not be catastrophic—the backup mechanism can be configured to act even for link overloads.

Figure 14-1 illustrates a network in which dial backup could be utilized. The primary data pathway across the WAN exists between each router's serial 0 interface.

Figure 14-1 *Dial Backup Scenario*

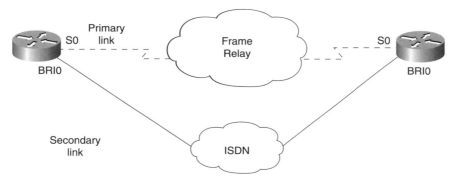

Dial backup can be implemented to provide service in either of two situations:

■   When a primary link fails
■   When a primary link is overloaded

Primary Link Failure

The most obvious use for dial backup is to provide service when a primary link fails. This occurs when a "down" condition is detected on the primary interface, and then the secondary, or backup, link is changed to an "up" state and a connection is established. During the time that the backup interface is out of service, it cannot be used for any other purpose. Once the condition has cleared, the primary interface is placed back in service. The backup interface will be subject to configured parameters regarding when it should be placed back into an idle state.

In Example 14-1, notice the **backup delay 5 60** command. It is possible that the primary link has suffered a temporary outage for whatever reason. If the link were to simply bounce, the backup link might not be necessary. Therefore, a specific amount of time can be specified before bringing up (or back down) the backup link. This command specifies that if there is a failure, the system should wait 5 seconds to initialize the backup link. Once the failure has passed, the system should wait 60 seconds to bring the backup link back down. In other words, the timers exist to compensate for an interface that drops momentarily and then comes right back up.

Example 14-1 *Dial Backup Configuration*

```
RouterA(config)#isdn switch-type basic-5ess
!
RouterA(config)#interface serial 0
RouterA(config-if)#ip address 10.14.1.1 255.255.255.0
RouterA(config-if)#backup interface BRI0
RouterA(config-if)#backup delay 5 60
RouterA(config-if)#backup load 90 5
!
RouterA(config)#interface BRI0
RouterA(config-if)#ip address 10.12.1.1 255.255.255.0
RouterA(config-if)#encapsulation ppp
RouterA(config-if)#dialer idle-timeout 180
RouterA(config-if)#dialer map ip 10.12.1.2 2145552222
RouterA(config-if)#dialer-group 1
!
RouterA(config)#dialer-list 1 protocol ip permit
```

Primary Link Overload

The backup functionality available with Cisco IOS is not simply for redundancy in the case of a failure of a primary link. In situations where a WAN link approaches saturation, the ISDN service can be initialized until the period of congestion has passed. The configuration enables the use of a load setting both for the initialization of the link and for the termination of the link after the condition is clear.

In Example 14-1, the **backup load 90 5** command specifies that the router should monitor the load on the primary interface and bring the link up when the load across the primary link is particularly heavy. The numbers represent the load on the interface, as shown by the **show interface s0** command.

The load on an interface is represented by a number between 1 and 255. In the **backup load 90 5** command, **90** is the percentage load at which the backup link is activated (in this case, 230/255).

The second number (in this case, **5%**) is a measurement of aggregate load. Once the backup link has been initialized, the router continues to monitor the load. Once the load of both interfaces combined reaches a value of 13/255, the secondary link is terminated.

So, although dial backup was designed for link redundancy to partially compensate for primary link failure, it can also provide load-sharing capabilities to alleviate congestion on the WAN link.

Alternative Redundancy Strategies

Dial backup is not the only method of providing redundancy. In some implementations, ISDN is not available or viable. In such cases, using alternative methods may be the only option. It may not always be feasible to use dial backup in the form discussed up to this point in the chapter. Because the backup interface is taken out of service, many choose an alternate method rather than expend resources on an idle interface. It is possible to use a dynamic or a static backup scenario (or both) without placing the backup interface in standby mode. This section discusses these two additional redundancy strategies.

Dynamic Redundancy

If multiple links are available, standard routing protocol operations automatically load-balance across equal-cost, redundant paths. This load balancing usually requires no configuration. From time to time, such as with IPX RIP, it is necessary to define the number of alternative pathways that should be allowed from a specific source to a specific destination.

IGRP and EIGRP have a configuration option known as a *variance*. These two Cisco proprietary routing protocols can load-balance over a maximum of six redundant pathways. The difference between these and other routing protocols is that the redundant pathways do not have to be equal-cost pathways. The only real rules in the selection are that the next hop must be closer to the destination (that is, it cannot go back to go forward), and the metric of any suboptimal pathway must be within a multiple of x (where x is the variance configured) of the metric of the best route. For example, if the metric of the best route is calculated to a value of 20 and the variance is configured to a value of 4 (for example, by issuing the **variance 4** command at the routing protocol configuration mode), the suboptimal routes must have a metric within the range of $20 \times 4 = 80$ or less to be considered for load balancing.

The variance factor also determines the amount of traffic to send across these suboptimal routes. For example, using a variance of 4 tells the router to send four times more data over the best route than eligible suboptimal routes.

Variance is calculated based on the documentation of your network. It should be evident from the examination of network topological maps exactly how many pathways are available from a particular source to a particular destination.

Static Redundancy

Static routes that are used for redundancy purposes are usually implemented, and known, as floating static routes. By default, static routes are the most preferred routes because an administrator defines them. Being administrator defined, to a router, means that the information about that particular destination is undeniable truth and therefore to be used over any other information learned about that same destination.

This concept of one route being more preferred than another is known as *administrative distance.* Depending on how it was derived, a particular route (whether static or dynamic) can be more believable, from the router's perspective, than another route derived by a less sophisticated method.

Static routes have a default administrative distance of 0 if they are defined with an outbound interface, or 1 if a next-hop address is defined. This makes them highly believable and dependable routes to the router. It is possible to alter administrative distance to make a route less preferred (or believable) than routes that are dynamically derived.

Administrative distance is a number between 0 and 255. The higher the distance, the less preferred the route. When the administrative distance of a static route is altered to the point where it is less preferred than the dynamic routes derived by a dynamic routing protocol (which are typically less preferred), it becomes a "floating" static route. Example 14-2 illustrates how to configure a floating static route.

Example 14-2 *Floating Static Route*

```
RouterA(config)#ip route 10.13.1.0 255.255.255.0 10.12.1.2 254
```

The number **254** at the end of the line defines the static route as having an administrative distance of 254. If the dynamic routing protocol being used is RIP (default administrative distance = 120), the static route is now less preferred than the dynamic route. Should the RIP route be lost for some reason, the floating static route becomes the preferred route until the RIP route returns. Table 14-2 displays the administrative distances of common routing protocols.

> **NOTE**   An administrative distance of 255 specifies that the destination is unreachable. Therefore, you should not use 255 as the administrative distance for a floating static route, because the route will not be used under any circumstances, even if no other path is available.

Table 14-2 *Administrative Distances*

Routing Protocol	Administrative Distance
Connected	0
Static Route	1
EIGRP Summary	5
External BGP	20
Internal EIGRP	90
IGRP	100
OSPF	110
IS-IS	115
RIP	120
EGP	140
External EIGRP	170
Internal BGP	200
Unknown/unreachable	255

Foundation Summary

This section is a collection of information that provides a convenient review of many key concepts in this chapter. If you are already comfortable with the topics in this chapter, this summary can help you recall a few details. If you just read this chapter, this review should help solidify some key facts.

Overall, providing the backup for a primary link is a fairly simple operation. You must decide only the manner in which the primary link will be backed up. If you use a traditional dial backup scenario, the backup interface itself is placed into standby mode. Once in standby mode, the interface is unable to be used for any other purpose. In many cases, this is not an acceptable use of resources, so alternate methods are used to back up the primary links.

The use of dynamic and/or static redundancy options is a widely used alternative for backing up critical links. The use of multiple routing protocols, especially those with variance capabilities, provides an additional layer of redundancy.

Using floating static routes allows all interfaces to be used both in day-to-day routing and if an outage of a primary link occurs.

Q&A

The questions and scenarios in this book are more difficult than what you should experience on the actual exam. The questions do not attempt to cover more breadth or depth than the exam, but they are designed to make sure that you know the answer. Rather than enabling you to derive the answer from clues hidden inside the question, the questions challenge your understanding and recall of the subject. Hopefully, mastering these questions will help you limit the number of exam questions on which you narrow your choices to two options and then guess.

The answers to these questions can be found in Appendix A.

Use Figure 14-2 to answer the following questions.

Figure 14-2 *Network Diagram for Use Questions*

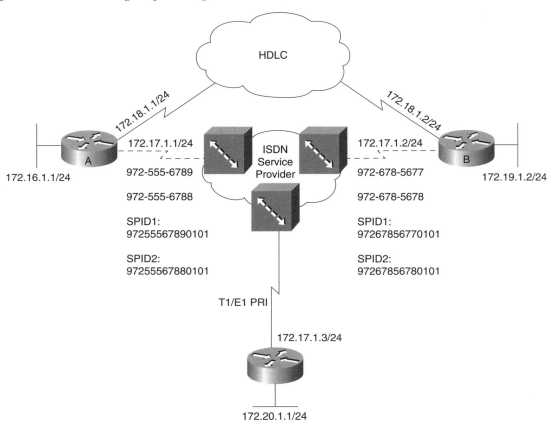

1. Dial backup, in the traditional sense, can be accomplished based on which two criteria points?

2. In the command **backup delay 60 30**, what do 60 and 30 represent?

3. Configure router A and router B so that the ISDN link is activated only in cases in which the HDLC link is down or has reached 85 percent capacity. The backup timers for failure are at your discretion.

4. To configure an IP routing protocol to support load balancing over multiple equal-cost pathways, what commands must be entered?

5. Explain the rules behind the use of the **variance** command.

6. Remove the dial backup configuration from routers A and B, and then implement an alternative configuration using the methods described in this chapter to back up the HDLC link.

7. If a router is running multiple routing protocols (RIP, OSPF, EIGRP, and IBGP) and each protocol has a route to a particular destination, which route will be selected to forward a packet to that destination? Why?

This chapter covers the following subjects:

- Queuing Overview

- Introduction to Queuing

- Class-Based Weighted Fair Queuing (CBWFQ)

- Low-Latency Queuing (LLQ)

- Compression Techniques

CHAPTER 15

Managing Network Performance with Queuing and Compression

The CCNP Remote Access exam requires you to have an in-depth understanding of various WAN technologies. In this chapter, the discussion focuses on some of the advanced queuing techniques offered in Cisco IOS. The latter part of this chapter also discusses compression techniques that are possible from Cisco routers.

There are various opinions on whether queuing is needed in a router, or in a network. Normally, there are ways to justify the need for queuing, and the type of queuing required. This chapter discusses the concepts behind queuing, when to use queuing, and which type of queuing is best for a particular situation.

"Do I Know This Already?" Quiz

The purpose of the "Do I Know This Already?" quiz is to help you decide whether you really need to read the entire chapter. If you already intend to read the entire chapter, you do not necessarily need to answer these questions now.

This ten-question quiz, derived from the major sections in the "Foundation Topics" portion of the chapter, helps you determine how to spend your limited study time.

Table 15-1 outlines the major topics discussed in this chapter and the "Do I Know This Already?" quiz questions that correspond to those topics.

Table 15-1   *"Do I Know This Already?" Foundation Topics Section-to-Question Mapping*

Foundation Topics Section	Questions Covered in This Section
Queuing Overview	1–2
Introduction to Queuing	3–4
Class-Based Weighted Fair Queuing	5–6
Low-Latency Queuing	7–8
Compression Techniques	9–10

> **CAUTION**   The goal of self-assessment is to gauge your mastery of the topics in this chapter. If you do not know the answer to a question or are only partially sure of the answer, you should mark this question wrong for purposes of the self-assessment. Giving yourself credit for an answer you correctly guess skews your self-assessment results and might provide you with a false sense of security.

1. Which network conditions justify the use of queuing? (Select two.)

   a. High-bandwidth interfaces

   b. Congested interfaces

   c. Low-speed interfaces

   d. LAN interfaces

   e. Underutilized interfaces

2. Which effects does queuing have on a router? (Select two.)

   a. Increases router performance

   b. Decreases CPU load

   c. Increases CPU load

   d. Increases the bandwidth on an interface

   e. Decreases router performance

3. Which queuing strategy uses the IP type of service (ToS) bits to help determine egress priority?

   a. First-In, First-Out queuing

   b. Fair Queuing

   c. Weighted Fair Queuing

   d. Priority Queuing

4. How are packets sequenced when using FIFO queuing?

   a. The shortest packets always go to the front of the queue.

   b. The longest packets always go to the front of the queue.

   c. The packets are sequenced based on when each respective first bit arrives on the egress interface.

   d. The packets are sequenced based on when each packet arrives entirely on the egress interface.

5. Which Cisco IOS command is used to create a list of packets that match one or more criteria?

    a. **class-map**

    b. **policy-map**

    c. **service-policy**

    d. **class-list**

6. Which Cisco IOS command determines how much bandwidth a particular flow should get during congested conditions?

    a. **class-map**

    b. **bandwidth**

    c. **service-policy**

    d. **policy**

7. Which Cisco IOS command determines how much bandwidth a particular flow should get at all times?

    a. **class-map**

    b. **bandwidth**

    c. **service-policy**

    d. **policy**

8. What is the difference between CBWFQ and LLQ?

    a. There is no difference because they use the same IOS commands.

    b. CBWFQ defines a priority queue that is used at all times whereas LLQ is used only during congestion.

    c. LLQ defines a priority queue that is used at all times whereas CBWFQ is used only during congestion.

    d. CBWFQ has more configuration options than LLQ.

9. Which of the following compression methods can be used only on point-to-point links? (Select two.)

    a. TCP header compression

    b. Stac

    c. Predictor

    d. MPCC

    e. IP header compression

10. Which of the following compression methods is Cisco-proprietary?

   a. TCP header compression

   b. Stac

   c. Predictor

   d. MPCC

The answers to the "Do I Know This Already?" quiz are found in Appendix A, "Answers to the 'Do I Know This Already?' Quizzes and Q&A." The suggested choices for your next step are as follows:

- **6 or fewer overall score**—Read the chapter. This includes the "Foundation Topics," "Foundation Summary," and the "Q&A" section.

- **7 or 8 overall score**—Begin with the "Foundation Summary" section and then go to the "Q&A" section.

- **9 or more overall score**—If you want more review of these topics, skip to the "Foundation Summary" section and then go to the "Q&A" section. Otherwise, move to the next chapter.

Foundation Topics

Queuing Overview

Queuing is the process of sequencing packets before they leave a router interface. Normally, packets leave the router in the order they arrived. This first-in, first-out (FIFO) process does not give any special attention to voice or mission-critical traffic through the router. Today's networks may require special sequencing to ensure that important packets get through the router in a timely fashion. Cisco routers have a variety of queuing techniques that may be used to improve traffic throughput.

Along with a discussion of traffic queuing, this chapter also addresses the topic of compression. Compression is a somewhat misunderstood tool. Although compression has a number of situations in which it is useful, it has just as many circumstances in which it is detrimental.

The misconception that queuing is a necessary part of any router configuration is a topic that needs to be dealt with up front. As mentioned, any queuing strategy results in higher delay in the network, because of a higher per-packet processor requirement. In other words, each traffic type must be sorted out and dealt with according to the defined parameters of the queue. This is the trade-off for assuring that your critical traffic passes through the router. In an oversimplified view, queuing is simply sorting packets into some new sequence before they leave any particular interface.

Queuing is only necessary when the existing traffic flow is having problems getting through the router. If all traffic is going through properly and no packet drops are occurring, leave it alone. Simply put, in the absence of congestion, do not implement a queuing strategy and leave the default setting alone. Depending on the interface type and speed, a queuing strategy might already be in place. Again, if it works, do not change it. That point cannot be stressed enough.

It is also important to remember that regardless of the queuing method that is employed, in most cases, it never actually functions unless the egress interface is busy. If an interface is not stressed, and there is no outbound packet congestion, then the queuing strategy is not applied (LLQ is the exception to this rule). It you want the queuing policy to work at all times, you must adjust the outbound hardware buffers to make it appear that the interface is always busy.

The concept of queuing is shown in Figure 15-1. In this diagram, packets are arriving at an interface at various intervals. Some are considered more important than others, but the router is not capable of distinguishing this by itself. Also, the flow of packets toward the interface is greater than the interface can empty out on the other side.

Figure 15-1   *Queuing Concepts*

Figure 15-1 shows that the voice packet arrived last, yet exits first. Also, small, interactive packets such as Telnet packets have the next highest priority. And finally, the generic web packets are sent through the router. Without a defined queuing mechanism, packets would be sent FIFO. In Figure 15-1, FIFO would not be a good option, because the voice and Telnet packets would suffer.

There are two advanced types of queuing discussed in detail later in this chapter:

- Class-Based Weighted Fair Queuing (CBWFQ)
- Low-Latency Queuing (LLQ)

Before CBWFQ is explored, the concepts leading up to it need to be reviewed. Thus, First-In, First-Out (FIFO queuing, Fair Queuing (FQ), and Weighted Fair Queuing (WFQ) are briefly covered. This background information makes it much easier to understand CBWFQ. LLQ is a natural follow-on to, and actually an extension of, CBWFQ.

Queuing is most effectively implemented on WAN links. Bursty traffic and low data rates can combine to create a congestive situation that can require administrative oversight to correct. Depending on the maximum transmission units (MTUs) of the surrounding media, queuing is most effective when applied to links with T1 (1.544 Mbps) or E1 (2.048 Mbps) bandwidth speeds or lower. In fact, any serial interfaces on a Cisco router use WFQ by default if the throughput (clockrate) is less than or equal to 2 Mbps.

If congestion is temporary, queuing can be a proper remedy to the situation. If the congestion is chronic, queuing can compound the issue by introducing additional delay. If congestion is a constant issue, then it might be time to accept the fact that a bandwidth upgrade (and possibly a router upgrade) is in order. Although a circuit or hardware upgrade will cost considerably more than implementing a policy change, there are times when there is no other choice.

The establishment of a queuing policy assists the network administrator with handling individual traffic types. The goal, typically, is to maintain the stability of the overall network, even in the face of numerous traffic needs and types. Unfortunately, a lot of time can be spent supporting traffic types that are not in line with company goals. Some administrators will transport all traffic, regardless of whether it is really necessary. Sometimes, it might be difficult to create or enforce a policy of policing traffic (throwing out stuff that does not belong). Thus, queuing is necessary to sequence the important traffic first, and maybe leave the less important stuff to the back of the line.

Queuing is an organization policy. It decides the order that packets leave any given interface. Queuing does not increase bandwidth. It simply works within the parameters of an interface and best utilizes those parameters. Note that different queuing strategies have different opinions on the term "best."

Once the decision has been made to implement a queuing strategy, you must decide which queuing strategy should be utilized. Figure 15-1 serves as a fundamental map to assist in that decision. As shown in the figure, you must determine whether the level of congestion constitutes a condition that requires queuing. Once you make that determination, another decision awaits. How strictly should the control of the queuing policy be enforced? Are the defaults OK, or should a more granular approach be applied?

Introduction to Queuing

Cisco routers support a wide variety of queuing methodologies. Some have been around quite some time. Others are more modern, and can be quite complex and difficult to understand. Due to the complexity of more modern queuing technologies, it is difficult to describe and understand them without first understanding the queuing basics that lead up to the more complex methods.

This section describes the following three queuing methods that lead up to the complex queuing methods discussed later:

- First-In, First-Out (FIFO) Queuing
- Fair Queuing (FQ)
- Weighted Fair Queuing (WFQ)

First-In, First-Out Queuing

FIFO queuing is the most basic of strategies. In essence, it is the first-come, first-served approach to data forwarding. In FIFO, packets are transmitted in the order in which they are received. Keep in mind that this process occurs on each interface in a router, not in the router as a whole.

On high-speed interfaces (greater that 2 Mbps), FIFO is the default queuing strategy on a router. Normally, such high-bandwidth interfaces do not have problems getting traffic out the door.

Figure 15-2 displays the basic model of FIFO. Notice that there are three different sizes of packets. One potential problem of FIFO is that the small packets must wait in line for the larger packets to get dispatched. In the figure, the smallest packet is actually ready to leave before the largest packet is finished arriving. However, because the largest packet started to arrive at the interface first, it gets to leave the interface first. This actually causes gaps between data on the wire, which decreases efficiency.

Figure 15-2 *FIFO*

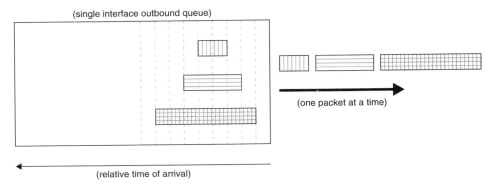

FIFO is not really queuing; it is more along the lines of buffering. The packets are routed to the interface and stored (queued) in router memory until transmittal. The transmission order is based on the arrival order of the first bit of the packet, even though the last bit may be still far away. Essentially, the outbound packet buffer is selected as soon as its outbound interface is selected.

Fair Queuing

FIFO queuing does not offer any way to permit packets that are "ready" to be transmitted to leave before packets that are still "preparing" to be transmitted. As was demonstrated in Figure 15-2, large packets, based on arrival time, can clog an outbound interface because their first bit was first to arrive on the interface.

Fair Queuing is a methodology that allows packets that are ready to be transmitted to leave, even if they started to arrive after another packet. Note that FQ is not an option in Cisco routers, but understanding FQ will help you to understand WFQ.

Using the same example as before, the effects of FQ are shown in Figure 15-3. The same data flow is sent to the egress interface, only this time the smallest packets are allowed to leave first because they are ready to leave before the larger packet.

FQ allows smaller packets to "cut the line" in front of larger packets that are still in the process of arriving. This process solves the FIFO problem of gaps between packets on the wire caused by the blocking by the large packets.

Figure 15-3 *Fair Queuing*

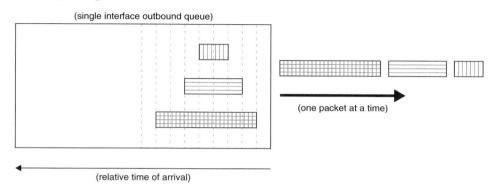

(single interface outbound queue)

(one packet at a time)

(relative time of arrival)

Weighted Fair Queuing

As mentioned, FIFO is often not the ideal queuing method on low-bandwidth interfaces. Different data patterns may suffer in a FIFO environment. Consider Telnet and FTP competing for the same egress interface. With FIFO, the small Telnet packets must wait behind the large FTP packets. With FQ, the small Telnet packets are allowed to leave once each packet has completely arrived at the interface. When a large FTP packet is ready to go, it is dispatched. Then, while another large FTP packet is building in the buffer, multiple Telnet packets are sent.

However, FQ does not take into account any parameters stored within the packet, such as type of service (ToS). Some small packets, such as voice, should have a higher priority than other small packets, such as Telnet. If size were the only delimiter (FQ), then small voice packets would be considered the "same" as small Telnet packets. This could cause delay and jitter in the voice quality.

WFQ starts by sorting traffic that arrives on an egress interface into conversations or flows. The router determines what the actual flows are, and the administrator cannot influence this decision. Basically, the conversations are based on a hash (combination) of the source and destination IP addresses, protocol number, ports, MAC addresses, DLCI numbers, etc. Not all values may be used to determine any flow. The ToS is not used to determine flow.

The administrator can define the maximum number of flows possible. The router performs the flow selection. WFQ dispatches packets from the front of any given flow only. Thus, a packet in the middle of flow #2 cannot be dispatched until all the packets at the front of flow #2 are sent. In other words, each flow is handled in FIFO order.

WFQ differs from FQ because it uses the ToS bits that travel within each IP header. Remember that FQ looks at when a packet finished arriving (relative time) to determine when it actually is dispatched. Thus, the priority of the packet specified in the ToS bits becomes a "weight" when dispatching packets through an egress interface.

WFQ multiplies this relative time by a mathematical variation of the ToS to determine the new "when to dispatch" number. For this description, and to simplify the math, ToS 7 = multiplier 1, ToS 6 = multiplier 2, down through ToS 0 = multiplier 8. In reality, the multiplier numbers are much larger, but on a similar scale.

Figure 15-4 shows how the WFQ system works. Three packets have arrived on this egress interface. The router, configured for FQ on this interface, has determined that there are three different flows. The administrator cannot impact the flow selection process. The relative arrival time is shown below the queue.

Figure 15-4   *Weighted Fair Queuing*

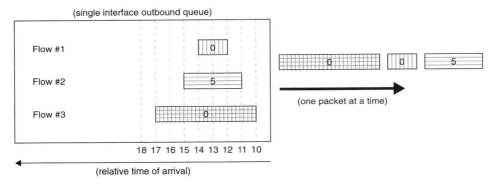

For FIFO, the largest packet would be dispatched first, followed by the medium one, followed by the smallest. FQ corrects this by sending the smallest first, then the medium one, then the largest. But in this new example, the medium packet has a much higher priority (ToS = 5) than the small packet (ToS = 0). Thus, WFQ adjusts the dispatch accordingly.

Remember that all values shown here for the "multiplier" are adjusted for simple mathematical examples. Real numbers are much larger, but on a similar scale.

The large packet starts arriving at time 10, but finishes at time 17. With a ToS of 0, the multiplication factor is 8. Thus, $17 \times 8 = 136$. The medium packet starts arriving at time 11, but finishes at time 15. Its ToS of 5 has a multiplication factor of 3. Thus $15 \times 3 = 45$. And finally, the small packet starts arriving at time 12, however it finishes at time 14. ToS 0 = multiplier 8, thus $14 \times 8 = 112$.

Table 15-2 takes all these potentially confusing numbers and arranges them logically.

Table 15-2   *Weighted Fair Queuing*

Packet	Start	Finish	ToS	Multiplier (based on ToS)	Dispatch (finish × multiplier)
Small	12	14	0	8	112
Medium	11	15	5	3	45
Large	10	17	0	8	136

So, the medium packet is dispatched first, followed by the small packet, followed by the large one. So it seems that WFQ solves the problems of getting small packets out first and ensuring that higher-priority packets get fair usage of the bandwidth. However, because the administrator cannot control the selection of the conversations (or flows), WFQ does have a few issues. Consider Figure 15-5.

Figure 15-5   *WFQ #2*

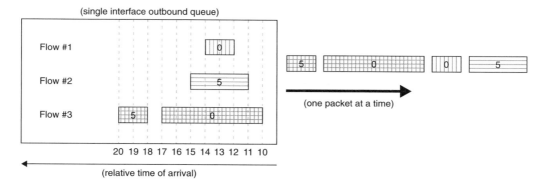

In this example, the third flow has two packets. However, the second packet is a high-priority packet (ToS = 5). It is quite possible to have packets of various ToS in a single flow. Remember that dynamic flow selection is not based on ToS.

The problem here is that the high-priority packet in flow #3 cannot be dispatched until after the large packet in front of it (same flow) leaves. Packets within a flow are handled FIFO. The WFQ algorithm only works with the first packets in each of the dynamically created flows. And as mentioned, the administrator has no control over how packets get sorted into the flows.

Thus, in the scenario shown, although it would be nice (and probably desired) to have the high-priority packets leave first, it is not the case. The high-priority packet in flow #3 is actually the last one out the door.

Class-Based Weighted Fair Queuing

Because all the problems associated with getting the proper packets out first have not been addressed (thus far), additional queuing methods have been developed. The basic building block of WFQ offers a nice starting point for additional queuing strategies. WFQ separates the packets into flows and applies a weight to high-priority packets so that they can leave first, but as the previous section shows, the potential shortcoming of WFQ is the lack of administrator control.

CBWFQ adds a level of administrator control to the WFQ process. The same WFQ dispatch process is followed. The difference now is that the administrator can control how packets are divided into the conversations or flows.

Thus far, FIFO and WFQ really do not need much configuration. FIFO is really the lack of WFQ, and WFQ is on by default for interfaces that are less than 2 Mbps. There are a few commands to tweak WFQ, but there are no commands to control WFQ. CBWFQ, on the other hand, can be controlled. Figure 15-6 shows how CBWFQ tames WFQ.

Figure 15-6 *Class-Based Weighted Fair Queuing*

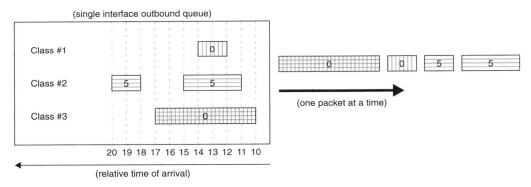

In this example, the administrator has decided that all high-priority traffic should reside in the same flow, regardless of any other conditions that might place them into separate flows. The administrator-defined flows are called classes. The WFQ algorithm is still at work, but the queue definition is under control now. Table 15-3 shows that although the second high-priority packet arrived well after the large packet, it still goes out second in line.

CBWFQ allows the administrator to define the various flows needed to classify traffic into unique conversations. In addition to this separation of traffic, CBWFQ can be used to guarantee that flows receive adequate bandwidth (defined by the administrator).

Table 15-3   *CBWFQ Uses WFQ*

Packet	Start	Finish	ToS	Multiplier (based on ToS)	Dispatch (finish × multiplier)
Small #1	12	14	0	8	112
Medium	11	15	5	3	45
Large	10	17	0	8	136
Small #2	18	20	5	3	60

CBWFQ has three basic components. The first part is defining the flows for specific traffic patterns (**class-map** command). There are many different ways to determine such flows. The second part is deciding how to handle each flow (**policy-map** command). Normally, minimum and/or maximum bandwidth requirements are set on each flow. And the final part is to assign this policy to the interface (**service-policy** command). CBWFQ can also be assigned to a Frame Relay DLCI. The following three sections describe each of these components in turn. The actual configuration and verification commands are then described.

The class-map Command

The first configuration part of CBWFQ is to define the individual flows that are to pass through the queuing system. The **class-map** command, which is used to create these flows, selects specific traffic to be put into the CBWFQ. It is possible to have many **class-map** commands, and each one can have up to 64 matching conditions within. Example 15-1 shows how to create a class map.

Example 15-1   *The **class-map** Command*

```
class-map match-all bcran-class
```

The **class-map** command, as shown in Example 15-1, defines a named class (using *bcran-class* as a name) that is used to select traffic. There are two options used when a class map is defined. The preceding command uses the **match-all** option. This means that all **match** commands within the class map must be true for this class to succeed. Thus, this is a logical AND condition. The alternate is the **match-any** command. This states that any one of the **match** commands causes this class to succeed. This is the logical OR condition.

Within the class map, **match** commands are used to find packets for this class. Example 15-2 shows a class map with a single **match** command.

Example 15-2 *The* **match** *Command*

```
class-map match-all bcran-class
  match access-group 101
```

In Example 15-2, any packets that are permitted in IP access list 101 are put into the class map *bcran-class*. Because only a single match statement is used, the class map could be either **match-all** or **match-any**.

In Example 15-3, only packets that are permitted in both IP access lists 101 and 102 are entered into the class map.

Example 15-3 *The* **match-all** *Command*

```
class-map match-all bcran-class
  match access-group 101
  match access-group 102
```

In Example 15-4, packets that are permitted by either IP access list 101 or 102 are put into the class map. The difference this time is the use of the **match-any** command when defining the class map.

Example 15-4 *The* **match-any** *Command*

```
class-map match-any bcran-class
  match access-group 101
  match access-group 102
```

The **match** command can be used to examine a wide variety of different criteria. As has been shown, IP traffic in access lists can be examined. Also, the IP precedence value, IP DSCP value, IP RTP ports, COS bits, QoS group number, MPLS experimental bits, and protocol values can be matched in a **class-map**.

The policy-map Command

A class map consists of one or more **match** commands to select packets for the class. A **policy-map** collects one or more **class-maps** and defines the actions that are taken for each **class-map**. Thus, for a **policy-map** command to properly function, a **class-map** must already exist. Example 15-5 shows how a **policy-map** is created.

Example 15-5 *The* **policy-map** *Command*

```
policy-map bcran-policy
  class bcran-class
    bandwidth 48
```

Example 15-5 first defines a **policy-map** named *bcran-policy*. The **policy-map** then maps the **class-map** named *bcran-class* (created earlier). And, all packets that are officially a member of the **class-map** are given a minimum bandwidth of 48 kbps. The bandwidth option states that the **class-map** is guaranteed 48 kbps. Note that the guarantee of bandwidth is not enforced unless the interface is congested.

In reality, the **class-map** may use more bandwidth if it is available, but if the interface where this policy is applied is busy, this particular **class-map** will get 48 kbps.

Example 15-6 shows the same **policy-map** named *bcran-policy*, but this time, there are three different **class** statements used.

Example 15-6 *A Complete* **policy map** *Configuration*

```
policy-map bcran-policy
  class bcran-class
    bandwidth 48
  class other-class
    bandwidth 24
  class class-default
    fair-queue
```

Two of the **class** statements reference specific class maps that have already been defined. The first class, called *bcran-class*, gets a minimum of 48 kbps. The second one, called *other-class*, gets a minimum of 24 kbps. And everything else that passes through the interface where this policy is applied uses WFQ. The function of the *class-default* is to catch any traffic that does not match any of the class maps within the policy map.

The preceding configuration example allocates a specific amount of bandwidth to each **class-map**. Bandwidth can also be allocated to a percentage of the total available bandwidth on an interface, or as a percentage of the remaining bandwidth not claimed by any other **class-maps**. Other configuration options include policing traffic (throwing out) to either a percentage of bandwidth or to a specific bandwidth value; shaping traffic (buffering); setting various markers; and adjusting the queue limits to avoid tail drops.

The service-policy Command

Now that the CBWFQ policy has been constructed, it must be applied to an interface. The **service-policy** command is used to map an existing policy map to an interface. Note that CBWFQ policies can be applied to either incoming or outgoing traffic flows.

Example 15-7 shows how to apply a prebuilt **policy-class** to an interface.

Example 15-7 *The* **service-policy** *Command*

```
interface serial 0/0
  service-policy output bcran-policy
```

Only one **policy-class** can be applied to an interface in one direction. Normally, the policy is applied for egress (output) traffic, because the low-bandwidth region is outside the interface.

The completed configuration that has been discussed piece-by-piece throughout this chapter thus far is shown in Example 15-8.

Example 15-8 *The Complete CBWFQ Configuration*

```
! ACL 101 permits telnet from 172.16.1.0/24 to 192.168.1.0/24
access-list 101 permit tcp 172.16.1.0 0.0.0.255 192.168.1.0 0.0.0.255 eq telnet

! ACL 102 permits priority 5 traffic from 172.16.2.0/24 to 192.168.2.0/24
access-list 102 permit ip 172.16.2.0 0.0.0.255 192.168.2.0 0.0.0.255 precedence critical

! ACL 103 permits priority 5 traffic from 172.16.3.0/24 to 192.168.3.0/24
access-list 103 permit ip 172.16.3.0 0.0.0.255 192.168.3.0 0.0.0.255 precedence critical

! class-map bcran-class1 matches anything from either ACL 101 or 102
class-map match-any bcran-class
  match access-group 101
  match access-group 102

! class-map bcran-class2 matches anything from ACL 103
class-map match-any other-class
  match access-group 103

! policy-map bcran-policy allows class-map bcran-class 48Kbps,
! class-map other-class 24Kbps, and all other traffic is WFQ
policy-map bcran-policy
  class bcran-class
    bandwidth 48
  class other-class
    bandwidth 24
  class class-default
    fair-queue

! policy-map bcran-policy is applied to outbound traffic on serial 0/0
interface serial 0/0
  service-policy output bcran-policy
```

CBWFQ Verification

Once CBWFQ has been configured, the individual pieces can be examined from the command-line interface (CLI). The first thing that should be examined is the interface queuing policy. CBWFQ is an upgrade to WFQ. Thus, the queue examination between WFQ and CBWFQ are quite similar. Example 15-9 shows an interface configured for WFQ.

Example 15-9 *The* **show queue** *Command*

```
Router# show queue serial 0/0
  Input queue: 0/75/0/0 (size/max/drops/flushes); Total output drops: 0
  Queueing strategy: weighted fair
  Output queue: 0/1000/64/0 (size/max total/threshold/drops)
    Conversations  0/0/256 (active/max active/max total)
    Reserved Conversations 0/0 (allocated/max allocated)
    Available Bandwidth 1158 kilobits/sec
! Next, the same interface is shown when the CBWFQ policy is applied:
Router# show queue serial 0/0
  Input queue: 0/75/0/0 (size/max/drops/flushes); Total output drops: 0
  Queueing strategy: weighted fair
Output queue: 0/1000/64/0 (size/max total/threshold/drops)
    Conversations  0/1/256 (active/max active/max total)
    Reserved Conversations 2/2 (allocated/max allocated)
    Available Bandwidth 1086 kilobits/sec
```

At first glance, it may appear that these two queue displays are identical. Both claim that the interface is configured for WFQ. However, closer examination shows that the second display has two reserved conversations. These reservations represent the two **class-map** references from the policy map that is applied to this interface. However, there is no specific reference to which policy map may be applied to this interface. Thus, the actual **policy-map** must be displayed to see the actual **class-maps** within.

In Example 15-10, the **policy-map** shows that there are three class statements.

Example 15-10 *The* **show policy-map** *Command*

```
Router# show policy-map
  Policy Map bcran-policy
    Class other-class
      Weighted Fair Queueing
          Bandwidth 24 (kbps) Max Threshold 64 (packets)
    Class bcran-class
      Weighted Fair Queueing
          Bandwidth 48 (kbps) Max Threshold 64 (packets)
    Class class-default
      Weighted Fair Queueing
          Flow based Fair Queueing
          Bandwidth 0 (kbps) Max Threshold 64 (packets)
```

In this example, *other-class* allocates 24 kbps to packets, *bcran-class* gives 48 kbps to packets, and the *class-default* class does not promise any bandwidth to the remaining packets. All other packets are handled via WFQ. However, packets that match any of the displayed class maps are only known by examining the **class-maps**.

In Example 15-11, the contents of both class maps are shown.

Example 15-11 *The* **show class-map** *Command*

```
Router# show class-map
 Class Map match-any other-class (id 3)
   Match access-group  103

 Class Map match-any class-default (id 0)
   Match any

 Class Map match-any bcran-class (id 2)
   Match access-group  101
   Match access-group  102
```

class-map *other-class* has a single **match** statement and looks at only ACL 103. **class-map** *bcran-class* has two **match** statements for two different ACLs. The ACLs are "OR'd" together, due to the **match-any** statement. The *class-default* simply matches everything that has not been matched thus far.

The access lists that are actually the basis for the matching are shown in Example 15-12.

Example 15-12 *The* **show access-list** *Command*

```
Router# show access-lists
Extended IP access list 101
    permit tcp 172.16.1.0 0.0.0.255 192.168.1.0 0.0.0.255 eq telnet
Extended IP access list 102
    permit ip 172.16.2.0 0.0.0.255 192.168.2.0 0.0.0.255 precedence critical
Extended IP access list 103
    permit ip 172.16.3.0 0.0.0.255 192.168.3.0 0.0.0.255 precedence critical
```

As previously shown in Example 15-8, ACL 101 permits a particular Telnet session. ACL 102 permits a particular series of packets with the priority set to 5. And ACL 103 also deals with priority 5 packets, but this time for a different packet stream.

Low-Latency Queuing

Low-Latency Queuing (LLQ) is really just an extension of CBWFQ. In fact, the only real difference between the two is how the bandwidth is allocated to the class maps in the policy map.

In the examples shown thus far, the **bandwidth** command was used to allocate a certain amount of bandwidth to any given class map. Remember that the **bandwidth** command has an effect in the queuing strategy only if the interface is congested. Thus, if the interface is not filled up, there is no real guarantee that any particular class map will get the requested amount of bandwidth.

LLQ uses the **priority** command instead of the **bandwidth** command to request bandwidth. The **priority** command guarantees that the requested bandwidth is available whether the interface is busy or not. Because this bandwidth is always available, the class map that uses the **priority** command is guaranteed low latency through the interface (thus the name, LLQ). This is also called a strict priority queue.

It is important to remember that any packets that exceed the requested bandwidth (using the **priority** command) when the interface is busy are discarded (policed). During low interface utilization, the class map may use more bandwidth than requested by the **priority** command. But the class map will get the required bandwidth at all times.

The policy-map Command

LLQ is configured the same as CBWFQ. The difference is how the bandwidth is requested in the policy map. Example 15-13 shows the use of the **priority** command.

Example 15-13   *The* **policy-map** *Command*

```
policy-map bcran-policy
  class bcran-class
    priority 48
```

The difference here is that **class-map** *bcran-class* is absolutely guaranteed 48 kbps of bandwidth at all times, regardless of how busy the interface is.

LLQ Verification

Because LLQ is nearly identical to CBWFQ, most of the verification screens are the same. The one place where the difference can be seen is when the policy map is examined. Example 15-14 examines the **policy-map** built for LLC.

This time, **class-map** *bcran-class* is shown with a strict priority of 48 kbps. This verifies that it is guaranteed the requested bandwidth under all circumstances.

Example 15-14 *The **show policy-map** Command*

```
Router# show policy-map
  Policy Map bcran-policy
    Class other-class
      Weighted Fair Queueing
            Bandwidth 24 (kbps) Max Threshold 64 (packets)
    Class bcran-class
      Weighted Fair Queueing
            Strict Priority
            Bandwidth 48 (kbps) Burst 1200 (Bytes)
    Class class-default
      Weighted Fair Queueing
            Flow based Fair Queueing
            Bandwidth 0 (kbps) Max Threshold 64 (packets)
```

As shown in Figure 15-7, the flow of packets through the LLQ is almost identical to that of the flow through the CBWFQ. The only real difference is that the priority traffic in the LLQ is always guaranteed its prescribed bandwidth. The CBWFQ is only in operation when the interface is congested.

Figure 15-7 *Low-Latency Queuing*

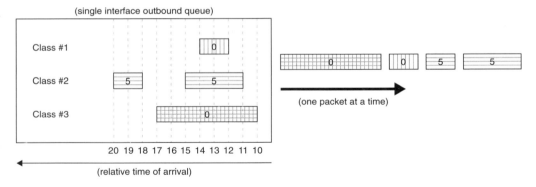

Compression Techniques

Various types of compression algorithms are in use in the world today.

For compression, a scope needs to be set ahead of time. There are compression methods for data (entire files), links (data that travels between routers), hard drives (data stored on a hard drive), and so on. This section of the chapter focuses on compression across WAN links (links).

It is also true that too much compression is a bad thing. If data is already compressed when WAN links begin to process it, the ability of the router to further compress that data is affected. Data that is already compressed can actually become larger by recompressing it. The discussion in this chapter focuses on what happens at the WAN interface, regardless of the type of data being transported.

Compression is only one technique for squeezing every possible bit of bandwidth from an existing internetwork deployment. Compression, like queuing, is meant to provide critical time to plan and deploy network upgrades and to reduce overall utilization of a WAN link. However, nothing is free. The execution of the compression algorithm adds a significant number of CPU cycles. Unfortunately, the additional load on the CPU might not be something it can handle.

With compression enabled, CPU utilization of the router increases considerably. On the bright side, the WAN link utilization drops considerably. Thus, compression is a trade-off, because all that has been accomplished is the displacement of utilization from the WAN to the router. Obviously, the effects of compression vary based on the algorithm implemented.

As technology advances, compression will move from a software function to a hardware function. This is already a reality in some router models, with the addition of newly available modules specifically geared toward performing data compression in hardware. Not only is this much faster than software compression, it is less costly for the CPU (generally).

The effects of compression must be taken into account prior to any implementation. If the routers are already running at 80 percent or more CPU utilization (**show cpu process** command), it is not a good idea to implement compression. Doing so can result in the router literally running out of CPU to do any further processing.

Data compression makes efficient use of bandwidth and increases WAN throughput by reducing the size of the frame being transported. Compression is best utilized on slower WAN links. There comes a point when the router can send the data faster if it is uncompressed than if the router compresses the data, sends it, and then decompresses the data at the other end.

Cisco supports a number of compression types:

- Link
- Payload
- TCP Header
- Microsoft Point-to-Point

Microsoft Point-to-Point compression, which is an algorithm, is beyond the scope of this book and thus is not discussed further.

Figure 15-8 illustrates where various types of compression make transmission more efficient.

Figure 15-8 *Compression Methods*

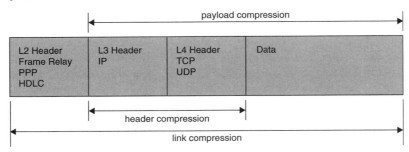

Link Compression

Link compression (also known as *per-interface compression*) compresses the entire frame (Layer 2 through Layer 7) as it leaves the interface. In other words, both the header and the data are compressed. Because the entire frame is compressed, it must be uncompressed immediately upon receipt at the other end of the link so that the header information can be used to further forward the frame. Thus, a link-compressed frame is only compressed for the trip across one link.

Link compression is not dependent on any particular protocol function. Every frame that leaves the interface that is configured for compression is reduced in size—no questions asked, no exceptions to the rule. Cisco supports two algorithms on its router chassis to compress traffic: Stac and Predictor. For HDLC links, Stac is the only available choice.

Because the header and data are unusable after being compressed, link compression should be used only for data transmission over point-to-point dedicated connections.

It is also important to remember that if compression is used on one side of a link, compression must also be enabled on the other side, and the same compression algorithm must be used at both ends. Compression can be compared to a language. If English is spoken on one end, then English must be present on the other end to decipher the communication.

Stac

Stac is based on an algorithm known as Lempel-Ziv (LZ), which searches the data stream for redundant strings and replaces them with a token. The token is an information pointer that is significantly shorter than the string it replaces. If LZ cannot find any duplicated strings in the data, no compression occurs and transmission occurs as if the link had no compression activated. Stac is an open-standard compression algorithm and is used by many different vendors.

There are cases, such as the sending of encrypted data or data that has already been compressed, in which compression actually expands the size of a transmission. In such cases, the original transmission is sent untouched. The Stac compression algorithm tends to be quite CPU intensive and should not be implemented on routers with an already high CPU utilization. Stac might also be a poor selection on smaller routers that do not have much CPU to begin with.

Predictor

The Predictor compression method is rightly named. This Cisco-proprietary algorithm attempts to predict the incoming character sequences by implementing an indexing system that is based on a compression dictionary. It is essentially a code book that is based on possible data sequences. If a character string is found that matches an entry in the dictionary, the string is replaced with the dictionary entry. That entry is a much shorter sequence of characters. At the remote end, the incoming characters are compared to the data dictionary once again to be decoded. The incoming dictionary strings are replaced with the appropriate (and original) information.

The Predictor compression method is like sign language. Rather than spelling out each individual word (no compression), a single hand motion utilizes an entire word or concept (compression). Because both parties understand the hand motions, successful communication occurs. Conversely, when one of the people involved in the communication does not understand sign language, communication does not occur.

Predictor-like algorithms are used in some voice-compression standards. For example, G.729 and G.729a (CSA-CELP) implementations compress a 64-kbps voice stream into an 8-kbps data stream. These implementations are directly based on the code book/dictionary prediction methodology. One big difference between Predictor (link compression) and voice-compression algorithms (payload compression) is that the voice-compression routines compress only the voice data (payload), not the entire frame.

Remember that Stac is CPU intensive. Predictor, on the other hand, tends to be extremely memory intensive. If the router has not been outfitted with a good amount of RAM, Predictor should not be implemented. However, if RAM is plentiful, Predictor is a compression consideration that can be beneficial.

Payload Compression

Payload compression is exactly what its name implies. Also known as per-VC compression, payload compression compresses only the data portion of the transmission. All L2 headers are left intact.

It cannot be assumed that customer WAN links are all dedicated point-to-point connections (PPP or HDLC). For such circuits, link compression can be used because the provider's WAN switches do not examine any portion of the data being transmitted.

However, payload compression is needed if the WAN switches must examine the data sent from a customer location. WAN technologies such as Frame Relay require that the L2 header information be untouched so that the provider's switches can read it and make forwarding decisions based on it. Any implementation of VCs disallows link compression. In these cases, payload compression is appropriate.

TCP Header Compression

RFC 1144 defines the Van Jacobson algorithm. In doing so, it also defines the algorithm for TCP/IP header compression. The 20-byte IP header and the 20-byte TCP header combination (a total of 40 bytes) is compressed to 2 or 4 (typically 4) bytes to reduce overhead across the network. The L2 header remains intact so that it can be utilized by the appropriate L2 transport.

This type of compression is most beneficial when used with implementations that transmit small packets, such as Voice over IP, Telnet, and so forth. This type of compression can be done on just about any WAN implementation (X.25, Frame Relay, ISDN, and so on).

TCP header compression, as suggested in the name, compresses only the TCP and IP headers. If the data payload is 1000 bytes, then the total package (excluding the L2 frame) would be 1000 + 40 (data + TCP + IP) bytes. TCP header compression would bring this down to 1000 + 2 bytes. However, if the payload is 20 bytes, then 20 + 40 becomes 20 + 2 (a big improvement). Table 15-4 summarizes the benefits. This table does not consider the L2 headers.

Table 15-4   *TCP Header Compression*

Data	TCP Header	IP Header	Total Without Compression	% Overhead	Total With Compression	% Overhead
1000	20	20	1040	3.8%	1002	.2%
20	20	20	60	66.7%	22	9.1%

Note that for packets with larger data portions, the compression provides noticeable improvement (3.8 percent overhead compared to .2 percent). However, for smaller data portions, the improvement is dramatic (66.7 percent overhead compared to 9.1 percent).

As with other forms of compression, TCP header compression must be configured on both ends of the link to ensure a connection. Because the L2 headers are not compressed, TCP header compression can be used on any serial interface, and across WAN clouds that must be able to read the L2 headers during transit.

If any form of compression is used in a Cisco router, the exact same form of compression must be implemented on the other end of the link. Failure to apply the same compression algorithm on each causes all data to fail across the link.

Compression Issues

Compression is not a feature that is simply turned on or off. When selecting the algorithm that is to be utilized for a particular deployment, you should consider the following:

- **Modem compression**—Some modems implement compression. Modems that use MNP5 and V.42bis are not compatible. Although each offers 2 and 4 times compression, they cannot communicate with each other. If you use modem compression, make sure that the modems at both ends of the connection are using a common protocol. If compression is being performed by the modem, do not attempt to configure compression at the router level.

  If modem compression is successfully enabled, then data compression (from the router for example) should not be enabled. Remember that compressing a compressed string might increase the size. Conversely, if compression is performed on the router, then the modem should not attempt any further compression.

- **Data encryption**—Encryption occurs at the network layer where compression is an L2 function. The main purpose of encryption is security. Encryption removes common patterns in data streams. In other words, when Stac tries to find redundant strings, there are none. When Predictor looks into the dictionary for common patterns, there are none. Therefore, the compression is unsuccessful and can actually expand the traffic it was attempting to compress. In such a case, the traffic is sent uncompressed.

- **CPU and memory**—Some algorithms are memory intensive and some are CPU intensive. Thus, before you plan or implement compression, you must know the physical configuration of your router (that is, its RAM and CPU) before ordering additional hardware.

Configuring Compression

To configure compression, there are several commands. Most are technology-specific and fairly intuitive. The **compress** configuration command is used at the interface level (normally a slow serial interface) to select the link-compression algorithm. Remember to configure the same compression type on both ends of the point-to-point link.

```
Router(config-if)# compress [predictor | stac | mppc]
```

For Frame Relay connections, use the **frame-relay payload-compress** interface-level configuration command to enable Stac compression on an interface or a subinterface (payload compression). There are no additional configuration parameters for use with this command, as shown by the following command structure:

```
Router(config-if)# frame-relay payload-compress
```

To enable TCP header compression for a given interface, use the **ip tcp header-compression** command. The command structure is as follows:

```
Router(config-if)# ip tcp header-compression [passive]
```

The **passive** keyword at the end of the command specifies that compression be performed only if packets received on that interface are compressed on arrival.

Foundation Summary

This section is a collection of information that provides a convenient review of many key concepts in this chapter. If you are already comfortable with the topics in this chapter, this summary can help you recall a few details. If you just read this chapter, this review should help solidify some key facts. If you are doing your final preparation before the exam, these tables are a convenient way to review the day before the exam.

Table 15-5 summarizes the various advanced queuing techniques discussed in this chapter.

Table 15-5 *Queuing Summary*

FIFO	Class-Based Weighted Fair	Low-Latency
No configuration	Define flows (**class-map**), policy per flow (**policy-map**), and assign to an interface (service-policy)	Same configuration as CBWFQ, but add a priority queue for delay-sensitive traffic
No priority traffic	Administrator-defined policies	High-priority traffic has its own priority queue—guarantee of service
Traffic dispatched on first-come, first-served basis	Traffic dispatched using WFQ between flows, FIFO within flows	Priority queue is sent first, then remaining queues are WFQ, with FIFO within a queue

Table 15-6 summarizes the various queuing commands discussed in this chapter.

Table 15-6 *Queuing Command Summary*

Command	Function
class-map { **match-all** | **match-any** } *class-map-name*	Creates a data structure to select specific traffic. **match-all** is an AND of all conditions within the **class-map**. **match-any** is an OR of the conditions within the **class-map**.
match	Matches specific traffic within a **class-map** (defined below).
access-group {*number* | *name*}	Matches a numbered or named IP access list.
any	Matches all traffic.
class-map *class-map-name*	Creates a nested **class-map**.

Table 15-6 *Queuing Command Summary (Continued)*

Command	Function
cos *IP-TOS*	Matches the IP ToS bits.
destination-address mac *MAC-address*	Matches a specific destination MAC address.
input-interface *interface*	Matches the interface the traffic arrived on.
ip {**dscp** *value* | **precedence** *value* | **rtp** *start-port port-range*}	Matches various IP header values.
mpls experimental *value*	Matches the MPLS experimental bits.
protocol *value*	Matches any given protocol.
qos-group *value*	Matches traffic from a specific QoS group.
source-address mac *MAC-address*	Matches a specific source MAC address.
policy-map *policy-map-name*	Creates a data structure to reference one or more **class-maps** and is assigned to an interface.
class *class-map-name*	Maps the **class-map** (defined earlier) to the **policy-map**. There are many parameters (below) to reference only specific traffic within the class map.
bandwidth {*Kbps-value* | **percent** *value*}	Defines how traffic is handled during congested situation (CBWFQ).
priority *Kbps-value*	Defines how traffic is handled at all times (LLQ).
queue-limit *#-packets*	Defines how many packets may reside in a particular queue.
service-policy *policy-map-name*	Creates nested policy maps.
shape {**average** *bps-value* | **max-buffers** *buffer-value* | **peak** *bps-value*}	Defines traffic shaping (buffering) parameters.
police *bps-value*	Defines traffic policing (discarding) parameters.
set {**cos** *value* | **ip** *value* | **mpls experimental** *value* | **qos-group** *value*}	Allows marking of various parameters.
service-policy { **input** | **output** } *policy-map-name*	Assigns a policy map to an interface. Packet queuing is normally done outbound.

Table 15-7 summarizes the various advanced queuing techniques discussed in this chapter.

Table 15-7 *Compression Summary*

Link	Stac	Predictor	Payload	TCP Header
Compresses OSI Layers 2–7	Very CPU intensive	Memory intensive	Compresses OSI Layers 3–7	Compresses OSI Layers 3–4
Two algorithms = Stac and Predictor	Replaces redundant strings with tokens	Replaces text with smaller codes		Compresses ONLY IP and TCP headers
	Does not expand encrypted or compressed data (no redundant strings)	Could possibly expand compressed data		Good for very small data packets
	Open standard	Cisco proprietary	Open standard	
Used across point-to-point circuits only	Can be used on both PPP and HDLC links	Can be used on PPP links only	Can be used on HDLC, PPP, and Frame Relay links	Can be used on any links

Q&A

The questions and scenarios in this book are more difficult than what you will experience on the actual exam. The questions do not attempt to cover more breadth or depth than the exam, but they are designed to make sure that you know the answer. Rather than enabling you to derive the answer from clues hidden inside the question itself, the questions challenge your understanding and recall of the subject.

Hopefully, mastering these questions will help you limit the number of exam questions on which you narrow your choices to two options and then guess.

The answers to these questions can be found in Appendix A.

1. Where on a router is queuing implemented?

2. When should queuing be considered a viable implementation?

3. Should a queuing strategy be implemented on all WAN interfaces?

4. When is WFQ enabled by default?

5. How does CBWFQ differ from WFQ?

6. What is the Cisco IOS command to select and sort traffic into various flows in CBWFQ?

7. What is the Cisco IOS command to assign a policy to one or more flows?

8. What makes LLQ more detailed than CBWFQ?

9. What command is used to create LLQ from a CBWFQ configuration?

10. What is the actual Cisco IOS command to match all traffic from subnet 10.1.1.0 /24 to network 192.168.1.0 /24?

11. What are the actual Cisco IOS commands to match the access list in question 10 into a single group or flow?

12. What are the actual Cisco IOS commands to apply a policy that states that "traffic will get 48 kbps during congestion" to the previous flow?

13. What are the actual Cisco IOS commands used to apply the policy in question 12 to interface serial 0/0?

14. List the types of compression supported by most Cisco routers.

15. When should link compression be implemented?

16. Which type of compression should be utilized on VC-based WAN deployments?

17. What are the two link-compression algorithms, and which one is considered an open standard?

18. When is TCP header compression most effective?

19. When can TCP header compression be implemented?

20. What compression options are possible across a Frame Relay link?

Part VII: Scaling Remote Access Networks

This part of the book covers the following BCRAN exam topics:

- Describe the process of Network Address Translation (NAT)
- Configure access control to manage and limit remote access
- Configure Network Address Translation (NAT)

This chapter covers the following subjects:

- Characteristics of NAT

- Simple NAT Translation

- Overloading

- Overlapping Networks

- TCP Load Distribution

- NAT Definitions

- NAT Configurations

- Verification of NAT Translation

- Port Address Translation

CHAPTER 16

Scaling IP Addresses with NAT

It is imperative for a CCNP candidate to understand the use of NAT. This information is needed in today's network environment as well; NAT is a standard deployment for almost all enterprise networks.

During the late 1990s, much ado was given to IP version 6 (IPv6) as a way to alleviate the current IP version 4 (IPv4) address limitations. IPv6 proposes the use of 128 bits for address space, compared to the current IPv4 space of 32 bits.

The prolific use of NAT has diminished the need for transitioning to this larger address space. Most companies now embrace the idea of using the private address space, defined in RFC 1918, and using NAT to access the Internet.

The use of NAT enables a large corporation to use its own selected address space and still gain access to the Internet. Regardless of which address space is used on the inside of a private network, NAT can provide the necessary numbering for Internet access in a much more efficient manner.

Overloading an IP address enables a private company to use a single legitimate address as a proxy for hundreds and thousands of private addresses. This topic is relevant not only to obtaining a CCNP or CCDP, but also to internetworking in a real-world situation.

"Do I Know This Already?" Quiz

The purpose of the "Do I Know This Already?" quiz is to help you decide whether you really need to read the entire chapter. If you already intend to read the entire chapter, you do not necessarily need to answer these questions now.

The 15-question quiz, derived from the major sections in the "Foundation Topics" portion of the chapter, helps you to determine how to spend your limited study time.

Table 16-1 outlines the major topics discussed in this chapter and the "Do I Know This Already?" quiz questions that correspond to those topics.

Table 16-1 *"Do I Know This Already?" Foundation Topics Section-to-Question Mapping*

Foundation Topics Section	Questions Covered in This Section
Characteristics of NAT	1–2
Simple NAT Translation	3
Overloading	4–5
Overlapping Networks	6–8
TCP Load Distribution	9
NAT Definitions	10–11
NAT Configurations	12
Verification of NAT Translation	13
Port Address Translation	14–15

CAUTION   The goal of self-assessment is to gauge your mastery of the topics in this chapter. If you do not know the answer to a question or are only partially sure of the answer, you should mark this question wrong for purposes of the self-assessment. Giving yourself credit for an answer you correctly guess skews your self-assessment results and might provide you with a false sense of security.

1.   Which of the following is not a benefit of NAT?

   a. Address conservation

   b. Address flexibility

   c. Address accountability

   d. Overlap dysfunction

2.   Which two of the following are disadvantages of NAT?

   a. Increased latency

   b. Greater accountability

   c. Application dysfunction

   d. Address conservation

3.   Using simple NAT translation, the NAT software alters what TCP header information?

   a. The destination IP address

   b. The source IP address

    c. The destination IP and socket address

    d. The source IP and socket address

4. What TCP header information is altered by using NAT overload?

    a. Source IP address, subnet mask, and source port

    b. Destination IP address and destination port

    c. Source IP address and source port number

    d. Source IP address only

5. What does it mean when a NAT translation is overloaded?

    a. The same IP address is used at multiple PC workstations.

    b. The NAT table is too small.

    c. The translation is tracked by PC source port numbers.

    d. The router needs to be reset.

6. What Class B private address space is available from RFC 1918?

    a. 172.16.0.0–172.16.255.255

    b. 172.16.0.0–172.31.255.255

    c. 172.16.0.0–172.32.0.0

    d. 172.16.0.0–192.168.0.0

7. When should NAT overlapping be deployed?

    a. Never

    b. When two similarly numbered networks are merged

    c. To ensure a common remote numbering system with multiple "remote" offices

    d. Only when overloading is being used

8. What NAT translation type is generally used for overlapped networks?

    a. Simple NAT

    b. Overload NAT

    c. Port translation

    d. NAT table lookup

9. Which of the following describes the use of NAT TCP load distribution?

   a. Load distribution uses a small pool of addresses to "share" the translation among many users.

   b. Load distribution advertises a single address that represents a pool of devices.

   c. Load distribution requires port address translation.

   d. Load distribution advertises multiple pseudo-device addresses that are resolved to a single device.

10. Which of the following four NAT address descriptions is incorrect?

   a. Inside local addresses are unique to the host inside the network, but are not globally significant.

   b. Inside global addresses are assigned by the IANA or service provider and are globally significant.

   c. Outside local addresses are presented to the local network and are globally significant.

   d. Outside global addresses are globally routable on the Internet and unique to the local network.

11. An inside local address is translated to what in a simple NAT translation?

   a. Inside global address

   b. Outside global address

   c. Outside local address

   d. It is not translated

12. What are four types of NAT translations or configurations?

   a. Simple, overload, complex, TCP load distribution

   b. Overload, simple, TCP load distribution, overlap

   c. Simple, TCP load distribution, pooled, static

   d. Table lookup, overlap, TCP load distribution, simple

13. What command is used to erase all current NAT-translated sessions?

   a. **ip clear nat ***

   b. **clear ip nat ***

   c. **clear ip nat translation ***

   d. **ip clear nat translation ***

14. Port address translation is used on what router series only?

    a. Cisco 600 Series

    b. Cisco 700 Series

    c. Cisco 2500 Series

    d. Cisco 2600 Series

15. What is the maximum number of port handler addresses that can be used on a Cisco 700 Series router?

    a. 32

    b. 16

    c. 15

    d. 10

The answers to the "Do I Know This Already?" quiz are found in Appendix A, "Answers to the 'Do I Know This Already?' Quizzes and Q&A sections." The suggested choices for your next step are as follows:

- **6 or fewer overall score**—Read the entire chapter. This includes the "Foundation Topics" and "Foundation Summary" sections, the "Q&A" section, and the scenarios at the end of the chapter.

- **7, 8, or 9 overall score**—Begin with the "Foundation Summary" section and then go to the "Q&A" section and the scenarios at the end of the chapter.

- **10 or more overall score**—If you want more review on these topics, skip to the "Foundation Summary" section and then go to the "Q&A" section and the scenarios at the end of the chapter. Otherwise, move to the next chapter.

Foundation Topics

Characteristics of NAT

NAT enables nonregistered IP addresses, or the RFC 1918 private address space, to be used inside a private network and to gain access to a public network, such as the World Wide Web. The edge router connected to the public network uses NAT to translate the private network addresses to a registered public address. The translation can be statically or dynamically done.

In the case of a simple translation, each nonregistered IP address is translated to a unique public address. This enables access from networks that are using nonregistered addressing (or a private address space) to the web. In this scenario, the administrator first has to find an Internet service provider (ISP) to supply a block of addresses for use. This may be monetarily difficult for all but the largest of companies.

To conserve the use of address space, a private space can be "overloaded" to a single or small number of addresses by using the source IP address plus the source port of the packet to further distinguish the sending address. Figure 16-1 illustrates the packet header.

Figure 16-1 *Packet Header Information*

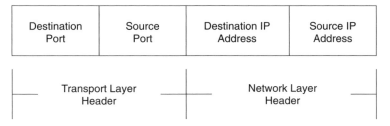

The disadvantages of using a NAT implementation are the increased latency, the address accountability, and the loss of certain application functionality, as described in the following list:

- **Latency**—An increased latency is due to the introduction of a translation step (a Layer 7 application used for the translation) in the switching path.

- **Accountability**—Some may perceive the hiding of internal addresses from the external world as advantageous. However, this can be problematic when you are trying to determine which internal IP address is responsible for what traffic. Constantly monitoring the NAT connections or providing *only* static NAT translations would help your workload, but would also detract from the ease of use provided by a dynamic NAT implementation.

- **Functionality**—Some applications that require a specific source port or source address would not be able to function in a NAT environment that provides randomly selected address and port assignments. For example, a specialized database that uses IP addresses for access to specific records would not function at all. Functionality could be restored, however, by using statically mapped translations, but again the dynamic functionality of NAT would be lost.

- **Embedding issues**—The last reason that a specific source port or source address would not be able to function in a NAT environment is that some applications embed IP address information at the application layer, in addition to the IP packet addressing; when this happens, NAT is unable to identify the situation that is producing a mismatch between the information included in the IP packet and the information included at the application layer. Oracle and other relational databases are common examples of applications that embed IP address information.

The advantages of using a NAT implementation are that NAT conserves legal addresses, reduces overlap dysfunction, increases Internet flexibility, and eliminates network renumbering in a changed environment, as described in the following list:

- **Conservation**—Legally registered addresses can be conserved using the private address space and NAT to gain access to the Internet.

- **Overlap dysfunction**—In an overlapped network situation, NAT can enable immediate connectivity without renumbering. In the case in which two companies have merged and are both using the same private address space, overlap dysfunction can be temporarily alleviated with NAT. This solution is not a design example but a bandage for a quick resolution of the problem. In addition, if a service provider has connectivity to multiple clients that are using the same private address space, it may be necessary to allow connection to multiple clients that have elected to use the same private address space.

- **Flexibility**—Connecting to an ISP or changing ISPs (which is not uncommon) can be accomplished with only minor changes to the NAT configuration. With NAT, changing ISPs is simply a matter of changing the pool of addresses that have been assigned. Because the NAT function occurs at the edge of the network, the router is the only device that requires a reconfiguration. If the customer accepts a nonprivate block of addresses from a provider and uses those addresses on the inside network, changing ISPs would require renumbering the entire network.

- **Eliminated renumbering**—As network changes are made, the cost of immediate renumbering can be eliminated by using NAT to allow the existing address scheme to remain. The renumbering effort can be gradually implemented or relegated to a DHCP server in an incremental fashion rather than all at once.

Simple NAT Translation

NAT translation (in its original form) replaced the source IP address with a publicly legitimate address. The replacement address came from a pool of addresses that were defined on the NAT device. These replacement addresses were, of course, publicly valid in the Internet address space. NAT is an application layer process that inserts the legitimate address into the packet header and maintains a table of translated addresses, as shown in Figure 16-2.

Figure 16-2   *NAT in Operation*

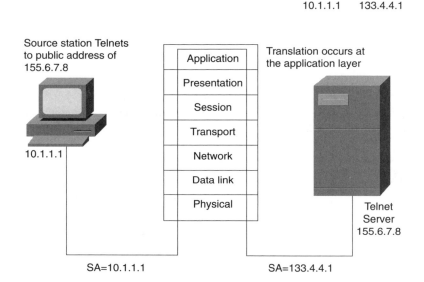

NAT Application has the address range of 133.4.4.1 through 133.4.4.254

Overloading

Overloading uses the source port to further distinguish which sending station is transmitting. In this fashion, a single legitimate IP address can be used for many senders. The source port is a number greater than 1024 and is a software-addressable port at the transport layer. The first 1024 port numbers are well-known ports, which are assigned by RFC 1400.

The terms "socket" and "port" are often used interchangeably. This use is incorrect. A socket is the *IP address:port number* pair that is unique to an IP-addressable device. The port refers to a numbered entity that is addressable by software. For example, every device has a port number of 23 for Telnet (regardless of whether it is in use). In contrast, only one device has the socket 122.5.7.8:23. In other words, the socket refers to a specific location on the network, whereas a port is simply a reference point that could exist on any device.

The overloading feature of NAT uses the entire socket to track the sender; thus, the same IP address can be substituted for many sending addresses, as illustrated in Figure 16-3.

Figure 16-3   *Overloading of Substitute Addresses*

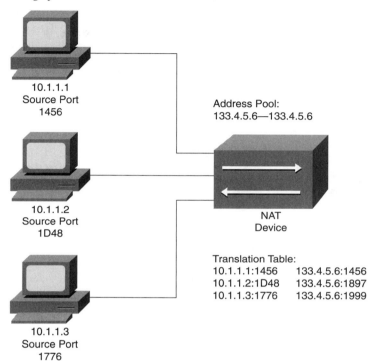

10.1.1.1
Source Port
1456

Address Pool:
133.4.5.6—133.4.5.6

10.1.1.2
Source Port
1D48

NAT
Device

Translation Table:
10.1.1.1:1456   133.4.5.6:1456
10.1.1.2:1D48   133.4.5.6:1897
10.1.1.3:1776   133.4.5.6:1999

10.1.1.3
Source Port
1776

Each device that is sending through the NAT device in Figure 16-3 is translated and given a new socket number. The new socket number has a unique port number (known by the router or NAT device and a common IP address) and new subnet mask for each translation. In this fashion, only one legitimate address is required for the translation. The use of the port to make the translation unique is called *Port Address Translation (PAT)*. With PAT, the entire socket is replaced.

Overlapping Networks

Another use of NAT occurs when two networks are overlapped, or using the same numbering scheme. If they are merged, the IP address scheme fails because of the overlap of network addresses. This NAT function is *not* something that should be designed into a network.

The NAT overlap function aids the administrator when a merger occurs because NAT can translate between like-numbered end stations. The two entities, without the renumbering of each end station, can be consolidated. In this fashion, the administrator can focus on putting a renumbering plan in place.

Overlapping networks can occur for a number of reasons, such as a merger, the consolidation of company resources that are tied with newly installed WAN components, and so on. To reduce the impact of mergers and consolidations, many companies have chosen to use the private address space defined by RFC 1918, which reserves the address ranges for the private network space shown in Table 16-2.

Table 16-2   *Private Address Ranges*

Class	Range	Number of Networks
A	10.0.0.0–10.255.255.255	1
B	172.16.0.0–172.31.255.255	16
C	192.168.0.0–192.168.255.0	255

The overlapping of network numbering will probably continue to be a problem due to the extensive use of the private address space in the private sector and the current trend toward inter- and intra-company connectivity. You can merge two companies using the same private address space by using the NAT overlapping network feature; essentially, each network is translated to the other. This double translation can take place on a single router.

The use of the limited number of addresses in the private space increases the odds dramatically that an overlap will occur if two private networks are merged. It is with that in mind that most design guidelines dictate that if your company is using the private space, you should *not* start with the 10.1.0.0 network because many other companies are likely to do just that. The recommended practice is to start in the middle, such as 10.128.0.0, and work from there.

The drawback to this restriction is that most technical people read the same literature and go to the same classes and talk to the same pundits. Therefore, the next time a merger occurs, they will not have to worry about the overlap of the 10.1.0.0 network; they will have to worry about the overlap of the 10.128.0.0 network.

Another area in which overlapping can occur is when a company elects to use a nonprivate address for its own purposes with the idea that it will never connect to the Internet. This is a very bad assumption in today's e-commerce-driven world. Common sense dictates that an Internet connection eventually will be required in this electronic age and, consequently, renumbering will be needed. With NAT, you have an interim fix for overlap.

TCP Load Distribution

NAT can be used for *TCP load distribution*. This works in a form that is somewhat reversed from other translations. In the other uses of NAT, the sender uses a nonlegitimate source address in a packet destined for the outside world. In contrast, load distribution takes advantage of the NAT function by allowing a site to advertise an address but when you send a packet to the advertised address, it is rerouted to another set of addresses.

To understand how load distribution occurs, consider an example. A large hardware company has multiple mirrored servers on its internal web site and has advertised through DNS that to access its server, you must attach to 122.7.7.128. In reality, however, the server is addressed as 122.7.7.1, 122.7.7.2, and so on. In this fashion, as each request comes in, it is sent in a rotary or round-robin fashion to each of the mirrored servers. Figure 16-4 shows an example of this configuration.

Cisco offers the Local Director software product, which can accomplish the same load distribution, but in a much more resilient fashion. Although the use of NAT for load distribution may be considered a low-budget solution, it can provide a cost-effective solution for small shops.

Figure 16-4 *TCP Load Distribution Using NAT*

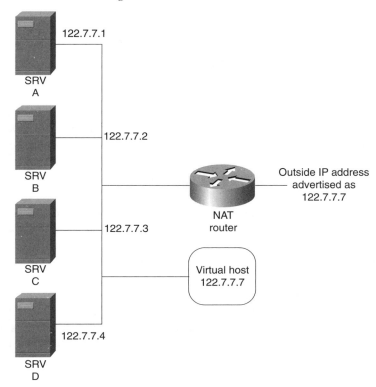

The ubiquitous use of the private space and the proficiency of NAT and PAT have greatly reduced the short supply of address space available on the Internet. This has not stopped the development of IPv6 (or IP Next Generation IPNG), but has slowed the implementation of it dramatically.

NAT Definitions

The addresses used for NAT can be summed up in four categories:

- **Inside local**—IP addresses that are unique to the host inside the network, but not globally significant. They are generally allocated from RFC 1918 or randomly picked.
- **Inside global**—IP addresses that are assigned by the IANA or service provider. They are legitimate in the global address space or Internet. The Inside Local addresses are translated to the Inside Global addresses for Internet use.
- **Outside local**—IP addresses of a host on an outside network that is presented to the inside network and that is legitimate to the local network. These addresses *do not* have to be globally significant. They are generally selected from RFC 1918 or randomly picked.
- **Outside global**—IP addresses that are globally routable on the Internet space.

To make the thought process easier, consider the following definitions:

- **Inside**—Addresses that are inside my network
- **Outside**—Addresses that are outside my network
- **Local**—Addresses that are legitimate inside my network
- **Global**—Addresses that are legitimate outside my network

Simple NAT translation replaces the inside local IP address with an inside global address. To say it another way, addresses that are neither legal nor RFC 1918 addresses are converted to legal Internet-routable addresses, where both the global and local addresses are valid inside my network. In the previous scenario, "inside my network" is a point of perspective.

The use of overloading is the same as simple NAT translation; however, the same inside global address is used over and over by maintaining the translation using the port address. For TCP load distribution, "my network" presents an inside global address to the Internet. When Internet users address this global address, it is translated to an inside local address.

The need for the "outside local address" category occurs when two networks are using the same IP address space. In the case of overlapping network numbering, the network that is using an outside global address is translated to an outside local address. In addition, the outside address could be the same as the address that is being used on the inside, because the outside global address is, from my perspective, not on my network but okay where it is.

Because this network address is okay where it is but, in the case of overlapping networks, not okay on my network, it must be translated to an outside local address. This address is outside my network but okay when it gets in.

Figure 16-5 shows each category of address and its location relative to "my network." The terms "inside" and "outside" are relative to the network being discussed; hence, what is outside my network is inside to the far side.

Figure 16-5   *Overlapping Address Definitions*

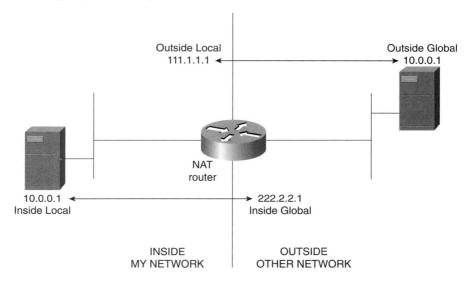

In Figure 16-5, both networks are using the 10.0.0.0/24 network. "My Network" is being translated to the 222.2.2.0/24 network, and the "Other Network" is being translated to the 111.1.1.0/24 network.

NAT Configurations

Five general configurations are used for NAT: simple, static, overload, overlap, and load distribution. In all cases, you should recognize that the general syntax is essentially the same for each configuration. In addition, though, you should pay particular attention to the arguments that are added to indicate which configuration is being used. As a sample configuration, assume that you need to convert a simple translation to an overloaded translation. To do this, you would add the keyword **overload** to the end of the NAT translation statement.

Overall, the same steps are used for each of the configurations described in the sections that follow:

Step 1   Declare the address pool that will be used for the translation.

Step 2   Define the translation.

Step 3   Define the interfaces that will participate in NAT.

Step 4   Define the addresses that will be translated.

Again, the successful CCNP candidate should review each of the configurations presented. While reviewing the configurations here, it can be helpful to identify each of the four steps in the configurations.

Simple Dynamic NAT Configuration

The simplest form of configuration is a one-to-one translation in which the IP address of the Inside Local address in the network header is replaced by an Inside Global address. The replacement can be done statically or dynamically. Example 16-1 shows a simple NAT translation with the assignments done dynamically.

Example 16-1 *Simple NAT Translation*

```
!define what addresses are to be converted
access-list 1 permit 10.0.0.1 0.0.0.255

!define the pool of addresses to use for translation and
!what interfaces and addresses to use
ip nat pool simple-nat-pool 123.123.123.1 123.123.123.254 netmask 255.255.255.0
ip nat inside source list 1 pool simple-nat-pool

!declare inside interfaces
Interface ethernet0
  ip address 10.0.0.1 255.255.255.0
  ip nat inside

!declare outside interface
interface serial0
  ip address 144.144.144.1 255.255.255.0
  ip nat outside
```

The access list defines what addresses to translate using the **permit** statement. The two key commands are **ip nat pool** and **ip nat inside**. The **ip nat pool** statement can be read as

> **ip nat** uses the **pool** called **simple-nat-pool**, which has the addresses **123.123.123.1–123.123.123.254** and which uses a network mask of **255.255.255.0**.

Each address that matches the criteria stipulated by the access list can use the pool of addresses specified in the previous statement. To decide which addresses are to be translated, the **ip nat inside** (or **outside**) statement is used. This statement can be read as

> **Perform an ip nat translation**, if a packet enters the router on an interface that is declared as **inside**, and the **source** address of a packet matches the **access-list 1**, then use the **pool** called **simple-nat-pool** to replace the IP address if the traffic destination is located beyond an interface that has been declared **outside**. Note that if a packet comes in an interface that

is **inside** and is exiting on an interface that is **inside** or undeclared then no translation occurs.

The following conditions dictate the use of NAT translation:

■ *Only* on interfaces that are declared inside or outside can packets be translated.

■ *Only* traffic from an **outside** to an **inside** interface, or from an **inside** to an **outside** interface is translated.

■ Packets received on an outside interface destined for an outside interface *are not* translated.

■ Packets received on an inside interface destined for an inside interface *are not* translated.

The definition of inside and outside can be arbitrary. Declaring the Serial0 interface to be an inside interface with the Ethernet0 being the outside interface can be done. The **ip nat inside** command is simply changed to **ip nat outside**. The question, then, would be, why? The answer is that maintaining the concept of inside and outside as it is used with the address definitions lends itself to using the correct declarations of inside and outside.

A key concept to keep in mind is that *only* traffic from an inside to an outside (or vice versa) is translated. A packet that is inbound to an inside interface and that has as a routed destination an outside interface is a candidate for translation. The command **ip nat inside source list 1 pool simple-nat-pool** then states that if the source address is on list 1, the declared pool should be used. The selection of inside versus outside and source versus destination is up to the administrator. The examples in subsequent sections of this chapter use inside and outside in relation to the owned network, which is the preferred methodology.

Static NAT Configuration

It is possible, and sometimes desirable, to configure NAT statically. A classic example of this configuration would be a resource on the inside of a network that must be accessed from the outside world at a specific location. In this situation, the advertised location of the resource is propagated to the world through DNS, and the inside resource must *always* carry in the outside world the same translated address and *always* be reachable at the same Inside Global address.

Static translation is done using the following command:

```
ip nat inside source static 10.0.0.1 108.77.2.1
```

This command says the following:

> **ip nat**, if the packet is inbound to a NAT **inside** interface destined for a NAT **outside** interface, always (**statically**) changes the address **10.0.0.1** to the address **108.77.2.1**.

If a group of requestors is being translated using a pool and one of the internal devices is a resource (10.0.0.1), the configuration from Example 16-1 is changed to that shown in Example 16-2.

Example 16-2 *Static NAT Configuration*

```
access-list 1 permit 10.0.0.0 0.0.0.255

ip nat pool natpool 222.12.12.2 222.12.12.254 netmask 255.255.255.0
ip nat inside source static 10.0.0.1 222.12.12.1
ip nat inside source list 1 pool natpool

!declare inside interfaces
interface e0
  ip address 10.0.0.1 255.255.255.0
  ip nat inside

!declare outside interface
interface s0
  ip address 144.14.14.1 255.255.255.0
  ip nat outside
```

Note that the range of available addresses does not contain the statically assigned address. The resource has a uniquely defined address in the outside world. The 222.12.12.0 network is legitimate in the Internet community and would be advertised there. The 222.12.12.1 inside address is addressable and entered into the DNS tables for the Internet community. In this way, the device that is statically (and *always*) translated to the 222.12.12.1 address is available to the outside world.

NAT Overloading Configuration

To convert the configuration for simple NAT translation to overload, the administrator must use the **overload** argument. Overloading an Inside Global address uses the same syntax as the simple NAT translation, but with the extra argument, the router knows to track the port numbers for the translation table.

The configuration in Example 16-3 extends simple NAT translation to an overload implementation.

Example 16-3 *NAT Overload Implementation*

```
!define what addresses are to be converted
access-list 1 permit 10.0.0.1 0.0.0.255

!define the pool of addresses to use for translation and
!what interfaces and addresses to use
ip nat pool natpool 123.123.123.1 123.123.123.2 netmask 255.255.255.0
ip nat inside source list 1 pool natpool overload
```

Example 16-3 *NAT Overload Implementation (Continued)*

```
!declare inside interfaces
interface e0
  ip address 10.0.0.1 255.255.255.0
  ip nat inside

!declare outside interface
interface s0
  ip address 144.14.14.1 255.255.255.0
  ip nat outside
```

The change to the configuration is extremely minor; an extra argument was added to the simple NAT translation. However, in an overload configuration, only a single IP address is needed to front for a large number of clients.

NAT Overlapping Configuration

NAT can deal with overlapping networks, even though it is not desirable to create an overlapped network. The overlapping of networks typically occurs during a merger of two companies that are using the same private address space. The overlap configuration is put in place as a stopgap while renumbering takes place.

Example 16-4 uses the addresses designated as Outside Global and Outside Local with reference, albeit arbitrary, to one or the other network. One network is declared as the inside space and one is declared as the outside space.

Figure 16-6 shows a scenario in which two networks that are both using the 10.0.0.0 address space are merged using an overlap configuration. It should be pointed out that the same overall effect could be accomplished by doing a simple translation on the edge router and leaving each of the networks intact; however, with the overlap configuration, the translation is done on one router platform only. This provides a single point for the configuration and a single point for maintenance of the address space.

The configuration in Example 16-4 declares that all addresses beginning with 10.1 be translated. The key is which pool is used. For those source addresses that arrive on an outside interface and that are destined for an inside interface, the translation uses the pool called **coming-in**. The source addresses that arrive on an inside interface destined for the outside interface use the pool called **going-out**. The access list that dictates which addresses are matched and must use the designated pool is the same for both because all 10.1 addresses require translation before crossing from an inside to an outside interface, or vice versa.

Figure 16-6 *Overlapped Networks*

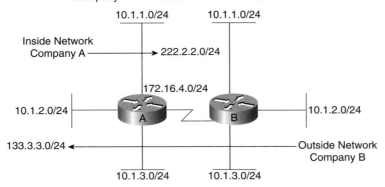

Company A is translated to the 222.2.2.0/24 Network
Company B is translated to the 133.3.3.0/24 Network

Router A handles both translations.

Example 16-4 accomplishes the double translation on Router A.

Example 16-4 *Overlapping Network NAT Implementation*

```
!declare the address pools
ip nat pool coming-in 133.3.3.1 133.3.3.254 prefix-length 24
ip nat pool going-out 222.2.2.1 222.2.2.254 prefix-length 24

!declare the translations
ip nat outside source list 1 pool coming-in
ip nat inside source list 1 pool going-out

!specify which addresses will use the pool
access-list 1 permit 10.1.0.0 0.0.255.255

!specify the interfaces
interface serial 0
  ip  address 172.16.4.1 255.255.255.0
  ip nat outside
!
interface ethernet 0
  ip address 10.1.1.1 255.255.255.0
  ip nat inside
!
interface ethernet 1
  ip address 10.1.2.1 255.255.255.0
  ip nat inside
!
```

Example 16-4   *Overlapping Network NAT Implementation (Continued)*

```
interface ethernet 2
  ip address 10.1.3.1 255.255.255.0
  ip nat inside
```

NAT TCP Load Distribution Configuration

NAT can be used as a simple tool for TCP load balancing. Figure 16-7 illustrates a classic example for TCP load balancing. In the figure, Company A has four mirrored web servers. They advertise that users can download beta copies of their software for testing at www.companya.com, which is found at 188.88.88.88 on the Internet. The address 188.88.88.88 is a legitimate address that Company A obtained from its service provider. NAT translates incoming requests for 188.88.88.88 in a round-robin or rotary fashion to balance the requests across the mirrored servers.

Figure 16-7   *NAT TCP Load Distribution*

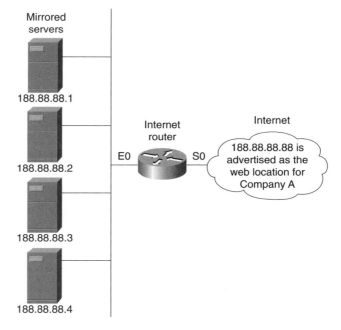

The configuration is straightforward. Any packet that arrives at Company A's Internet router, which has a destination for the 188.88.88.88 host, is translated in a rotary fashion to one of the four mirrored servers. The configuration in Example 16-5 shows the syntax for this implementation.

Note that the declaration statement for the translation specifies that the destination address should be checked against list 1, not the source address as in previous configurations. In addition, the argument **rotary** is placed at the end of the declaration. In this fashion, each incoming packet is

Example 16-5 *NAT TCP Load Distribution Implementation*

```
!declare the pool
ip nat pool company-A 188.88.88.1 188.88.88.4 prefix-length 24

!declare the translation
ip nat outside destination list 1 pool company-A rotary

!declare the access-list for translation candidates
access-list 1 permit 188.88.88.88 0.0.0.0

!declare the interfaces
interface Serial0
  ip nat outside

interface Ethernet0
  ip nat inside
```

translated to one of the pool members in a recurring sequential fashion; thus, a load distribution is achieved over the four servers.

Also note that the router does not keep track of the availability of the destination addresses assigned to it in the "pool"; hence, any change to the number of rotary members or the internal configuration *must* be reflected in the router definitions.

Verification of NAT Translation

There are two commands to verify and troubleshoot the NAT configuration: **show ip nat translation** and **show ip nat statistics**. The translation table is the same format for simple, overload, overlapped, and load distribution. The information provided is different depending upon the configuration. Example 16-6 shows the output for a simple translation.

Example 16-6 *Verifying NAT Translation*

```
Router#show ip nat translation
Pro    Inside global    Inside local    Outside local    Outside global
---    156.8.34.1       10.15.0.1       ---              ---
---    156.8.34.2       10.15.0.2       ---              ---
---    156.8.34.3       10.15.0.3       ---              ---
```

Because this is a simple translation, only the information that is relevant is put into the table. The concept of outside local and outside global is not used and therefore not presented when a simple NAT translation is configured. If an overloaded translation has been configured, the output from the **show ip nat translation** command would be as demonstrated in Example 16-7.

Example 16-7 *NAT Overloaded Translation Output*

```
Router#show ip nat translation
Pro    Inside global      Inside local     Outside local    Outside global
tcp    143.4.23.1:1098    10.1.0.1:1098    73.4.5.6:23      73.4.5.6:23
tcp    143.4.23.1:1345    10.1.0.2:1345    73.4.5.6:23      73.4.5.6:23
tcp    143.4.23.1:1989    10.1.0.3:1989    73.4.5.7:21      73.4.5.7:21
```

Notice that the Outside Local address and the Outside Global address are the same. Because the router is not performing an overlapped configuration, the Outside Global address is not known.

When an overlapping configuration is being used, the router has knowledge of the Outside Global address, so the output from a **show ip nat translation** command would appear as demonstrated in Example 16-8.

Example 16-8 *NAT Overlapping Translation Output*

```
Pro    Inside global      Inside local     Outside local    Outside global
tcp    133.3.3.1:1098     10.1.0.1:1098    173.4.5.6:23     10.1.0.23:23
tcp    133.3.3.2:1345     10.1.0.2:1345    173.4.5.6:23     10.1.0.23:23
tcp    133.3.3.3:1989     10.1.0.3:1989    173.4.5.7:21     10.2.0.45:21
```

Because the router is performing both translations, the Outside Global address is known.

The **show ip nat statistics** command is also useful in troubleshooting a NAT installation, as demonstrated in Example 16-9.

Example 16-9 *Troubleshooting NAT Installation with* **show ip nat statistics**

```
Router#show ip nat statistics
Total translations: 1 (0 static, 1 dynamic; 0 extended)
Outside interfaces: Serial0Inside interfaces: Ethernet0Hits: 1  Misses: 0
Expired translations: 2Dynamic mappings:-- Inside Source
access-list 1 pool my-pool refcount 2 pool my-pool: netmask 255.255.255.0
        start 172.3.4.1 end 172.3.4.7
        type generic, total addresses 7, allocated 1 (14%), misses 0
```

The **show ip nat statistics** command displays which interfaces are inside and which are outside, the pool name, and the addresses that are with the mask. The hits and misses refer to the number of times a translation lookup succeeded or failed.

To troubleshoot NAT, you can use the **debug ip nat** command. The output from this command shows which addresses were translated and, for a TCP connection, what the transaction numbers are. The output in Example 16-10 shows a sample output from a NAT debug.

Example 16-10 *Troubleshooting a NAT Installation with* **debug ip nat**

```
Router#debug ip nat
NAT: s=10.1.0.1->12.1.3.2, d=155.5.5.5 [1]
NAT: s=155.5.5.5, d=12.1.3.2->10.1.0.1 [1]
NAT: s=10.1.0.1->12.1.3.2, d=155.5.5.5 [2]
NAT*: s=155.5.5.5, d=12.1.3.2->10.1.0.1 [2]
!Additional output omitted...........
```

The translation is shown clearly from the source address to the destination and the reverse communications. The * indicates that the translation was done in the fast path or by using cache. To watch and debug this output in real time would be daunting at best. The number in brackets indicates the sequencing number for a TCP session that could be useful for debugging a protocol analyzer trace of the session.

The administrator can shut down a translated session using the **clear** command for **ip nat**. The syntax for clearing a simple NAT translation is as follows:

```
clear ip nat translation inside global-ip-address local-ip-address
```

The administrator must type the addresses without error to clear the correct translation session. Any typographical error in the command syntax can clear the wrong session! It is also possible to clear *all* current translated sessions on the router by using this command:

```
clear ip nat translation *
```

The use of the asterisk (*) as a wildcard clears *all* currently established NAT sessions. The use of this command might be needed on a periodic basis to clear out any hung NAT sessions. It is common practice at some sites to clear all translations at the end of Friday to allow all tables a chance to reset.

Port Address Translation

Port address translation (PAT) is a form of NAT in which the port is also replaced at the translating device. PAT is the only address-translation feature for the Cisco 700 Series router. Only a minor treatment of the PAT syntax was discussed in both the CMTD, Cisco Maintenance and Troubleshooting Dial-Up, and BCRAN course material. Note that additional 700 Series commands will be discussed here.

The concept behind PAT is the same as for NAT. A pool of addresses is not needed because only one address services all devices. The two commands that are needed for the 700 to use PAT are

```
set ip pat on
set ip pat porthandler port ip-address
```

where *port* is the transport layer port for the application and *ip-address* is the local address of the device.

Once you enter the **set ip pat** *on* command, the single address that is used for the translation is included in the port-handler assignment. The port handler is unique to the 700 Series router. The port handler declares which ports are translated. Earlier, the chapter explained how an access list declares which traffic will be translated for routers that are based on Cisco IOS software. In our current situation, however, the selection is done on a port basis; up to 15 port-handler statements can be on a 700 Series router. Figure 16-8 shows the port handler in use.

Figure 16-8   *Using the Port Handler for PAT*

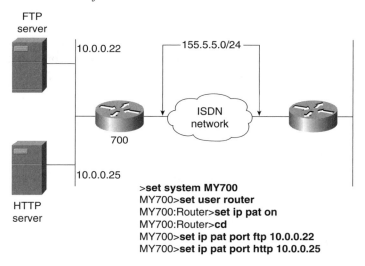

The FTP and HTTP servers are translated when they are sent using the router profile. The address to which they are translated is the address of the interface that is in use at the time. In the example in Figure 16-8, FTP packets from the outside world that are destined for 155.5.5.2 (the 700 Series router's ISDN interface address) are translated to 10.0.0.22—the inside FTP server. Likewise, HTTP packets addressed to the 155.5.5.2 address are translated to 10.0.0.25—the HTTP server.

Turning PAT on is a system-wide command to the 700 Series router. The definition for the port-handler function is done within a profile. There are three limitations that must be addressed while using this technology:

- **ping** from an outside host ends at the router. Hence, end-to-end connectivity testing is not possible.

- Only one inside web server, FTP server, Telnet server, and so forth is supported, because *all* port traffic is defined by a single **ip porthandler** command.

- Only 15 port handlers are supported in a single configuration.

The limitations specified should not be a deterrent to the use of PAT on a 700 Series router. You should remember the market positioning of this device and realize that small remote offices can take advantage of the translation function to share resources on a larger network.

The two commands associated with PAT on the 700 Series router are **set ip pat on**, which is a global command that requires no arguments, and **set ip pat porthandler**, which has the following arguments:

```
default | telnet | ftp | smtp | wins | http | port ip-address | off
```

The **telnet**, **ftp**, **smtp**, **wins**, and **http** arguments declare the well-known ports for those protocols. The key arguments are **default** and *port ip-address*. The **default** argument specifies any port that is not declared by another (there are up to 15) **set ip pat porthandler** command. The *port ip-address* is used when the administrator must specify a port other than the defined ports—Telnet, FTP, SMTP, WINS, and HTTP.

The limiting numbers for the 700 Series router are as follows:

- 400 PAT entries are allocated for sharing among the inside machines.

- Only 15 port handler addresses can be used.

- 1500 maximum MAC addresses can be supported.

The bottom line is that the 700 Series router can be configured for a lot more than a 128-kbps ISDN line can handle. The limitation is not what the device can do, but what can be done on the resource that the device uses.

Foundation Summary

The Foundation Summary is a collection of information that provides a convenient review of many key concepts in this chapter. If you are already comfortable with the topics in this chapter, this summary can help you recall a few details. If you just read this chapter, this review should help solidify some key facts. If you are doing your final preparation before the exam, this section is a convenient way to review the day before the exam.

The addresses used for NAT translation can be summed up in four categories:

- **Inside local**—IP addresses that are unique to the host inside the network, but not globally significant. They are generally allocated from RFC 1918 or randomly picked.

- **Inside global**—IP addresses that are assigned by the IANA or service provider. They are legitimate in the global address space or Internet. The inside local addresses are translated to the inside global addresses for Internet use.

- **Outside local**—IP addresses of a host on an outside network that is presented to the inside network and that is legitimate to the local network. These addresses *do not* have to be globally significant. They are generally selected from RFC 1918 or randomly picked.

- **Outside global**—IP addresses that are globally routable on the Internet space.

To make the thought process easier, consider the following definitions:

- **Inside**—Addresses that are inside my network

- **Outside**—Addresses that are outside my network

- **Local**—Addresses that are legitimate inside my network

- **Global**—Addresses that are legitimate outside my network

Table 16-3 *Private Address Space Ranges*

Address Class	Range	Number of Networks
A	10.0.0.0	1
B	172.16.0.0–172.31.255.255	16
C	192.168.0.0–192.168.255.0	255

Q&A

The questions and scenarios in this book are more difficult than what you should experience on the actual exam. The questions do not attempt to cover more breadth or depth than the exam, but they are designed to make sure that you know the answer. Rather than enabling you to derive the answer from clues hidden inside the question, the questions challenge your understanding and recall of the subject. Hopefully, mastering these questions will help you limit the number of exam questions on which you narrow your choices to two options and then guess.

The answers to these questions can be found in Appendix A.

1. What are the benefits of NAT?

2. The outside global address is converted to which NAT address class?

3. Why is accountability listed as a disadvantage of NAT?

4. Using overlapped NAT translation, what TCP header information is altered?

5. How many Class B private address spaces are available from RFC 1918?

6. What does it mean when a NAT translation is overloaded?

7. Which two commands would you use to define an overloaded NAT translation using a defined pool of addresses called **transpool** for outbound traffic?

8. When should NAT overlap be deployed?

9. What type of NAT translation is generally used for overlapped networks? Why?

10. What command would show which interfaces have been declared as outside or inside?

11. Briefly describe the use of NAT TCP load distribution.

12. An inside local address is translated to what in a simple NAT translation?

13. What is the most common type of NAT translation? Why?

14. What is the function of the port handler for the 700 Series router?

15. Can an inside local address be selected from a globally routable address pool?

16. What command is used to erase all currently established NAT translated sessions?

17. Port address translation is used *only* on what router series?

18. Given the following output, what type of translation is being used on this router?

```
Pro    Inside global    Inside local    Outside local    Outside global
tcp    103.32.32.1:1098   10.1.0.1:1098   13.43.5.6:23     13.43.5.6:23
tcp    103.32.32.1:1345   10.1.0.2:1345   13.43.5.6:23     13.43.5.6:23
tcp    103.32.32.1:1989   10.1.0.3:1989   13.43.5.7:21     13.43.5.7:21
```

19. Given the following router configuration information, what addresses will be dynamically translated?

```
access-list 1 permit 10.0.0.0 0.0.0.255

ip nat pool natpool 222.12.12.2 222.12.12.10 netmask 255.255.255.0
ip nat inside source static 10.0.0.1 222.2.2.1
ip nat inside source list 1 pool natpool
```

20. What differentiates PAT from NAT?

Scenarios

> **NOTE**   With all of the translation possibilities available, there is generally no one absolute way
> to do all translations. The examples that you will encounter in this part of the chapter have been
> crafted to lend themselves to simple, overlapped, or overloaded.

The following scenarios and questions are designed to draw together the content of the chapter and
exercise your understanding of the concepts. There is not necessarily a right answer to each scenario.
The thought process and practice in manipulating each of the concepts is the goal of this section. In
addition, the constant reminder of RAS is always syntax, syntax, and more syntax.

Each of the scenarios listed describes a situation, some of the changes planned, and a small amount
of insight into the company or companies involved. As with all types of design and consulting work,
much more information would be needed to provide a solution that would minimize any future
ramifications.

The reader should use these to develop a strategy to answer NAT design issues and to become
proficient at capturing all the needed syntax to create a useful NAT solution.

Scenario 16-1

Your company, a medium-sized law firm, has been dialing up from individual PCs to receive
information from a data warehouse service.

It has recently been decided to network the PCs, which are running Windows 98 or 95, to gain access
to the data through the Internet. You have contacted a local ISP and will maintain a leased line to its
POP. You have approximately 15 lawyers and 20 support staff members with which to deal. Internet
usage will be tolerated only for the lawyers on staff and certain research assistants.

The ISP has given you a single IP address—187.202.4.6. Based on this information, answer or
complete the following questions and tasks.

1. What router would you select for the office?

2. What would be your IP address scheme?

3. Create the NAT configuration that would be used for this connection.

4. Describe your solution to the Internet access policy that is described for the lawyers and office
    staff.

Scenario 16-2

Your company has merged with a smaller entity. You will provide its Internet access over a newly installed T1 facility. Its IP address scheme uses three private Class C addresses: 192.168.11.0/24, 192.168.22.0/24, and 192.168.33.0/24. You are currently using the 10.0.0.0 network.

The newer, smaller company currently has no Internet access. Your provider has given you a CIDR block of 103.112.8.24/29. You are currently using 103.112.8.25–103.112.8.29 for addresses on your DMZ. You have been using 103.112.8.30 for your 10.0.0.0 NAT translation. Based on this information, answer or complete the following questions and tasks:

1.   What can you do to enable translation of the new company's address space?

2.   Create the NAT configuration that would be used for this connection.

3.   What recommendation would you have for the consolidation of address space?

Scenario 16-3

Your company has merged with another company of equal size and you have both been using the 10.0.0.0 network as a base for your internal network numbering. Management has promised a bonus if you can get minimal communication between the ABCServer and the XYZServer by this weekend. The ABCServer is on your network, and the XYZServer is on the other network. The address in your space for the ABCServer is 10.1.0.1/24, and the address in the new company's space is 10.1.0.18/24.

Users in the ABC network should be able to talk to the XYZServer, and the users in the XYZ network should be able to talk to the ABCServer. For simplicity, assume that all addresses are 10.1.0.x/24. Based on this information, answer or complete the following questions and tasks:

1.   Explain what you will do to quickly complete the overall task.

2.   Create the NAT configuration that would be used for this connection.

3.   What considerations, other than NAT, must be addressed to allow the configuration to happen?

4.   What is your long-term recommendation for the configuration and how can you implement it?

Scenario Answers

The answers provided in this section are not necessarily the only possible correct answers. They merely represent one possibility for each scenario. The intention is to test your base knowledge and understanding of the concepts discussed in this chapter.

Should your answers be different (as they likely will be), consider the differences. Are your answers in line with the concepts of the answers provided and explained here? If not, go back and read the chapter again, focusing on the sections related to the problem scenario.

Scenario 16-1 Answers

1. Given the fact that only 15 or so people would be using the connection at a given time can lead you to select a 1600 Series router. However, some consideration should be given to using a 3620, which would provide a higher degree of scalability for the situation.

2. Any IP address scheme would work in this situation; however, strictly adhering to the private address space number would be recommended. Given the size of the office, you can choose a Class C address space and use a 24-bit mask to keep it simple.

3. The following NAT configuration could be used, given a selection of 192.168.1.0/24 as the internal addresses used:

```
access-list 1 permit 192.168.1.0 0.0.0.255

ip nat pool lawpool 187.202.4.6 187.202.4.6 netmask 255.255.255.0
ip nat inside source list 1 pool lawpool overload

!declare inside interface
interface ethernet0
  ip address 192.168.1.1 255.255.255.0
  ip nat inside

!declare outside interface
interface serial0
!address assigned to the interface by the ISP
  ip address 112.18.23.2 255.255.255.250
  ip nat outside
```

4. There are a number of ways to allow only the lawyers and certain others to use this connection. One way would be to apply an access list on the inbound Ethernet to block unwanted users from routing through the router. This would be highly CPU-intensive, but with such light usage, it might not be a problem. After all, the only time that these users would try to get through the router is when they were trying to do something that they were not authorized to do anyway.

It would also be possible to use different portions of the Class C address for the lawyers and those that could use the Internet, and then translate only that group of addresses. An access list could be placed on the outbound side of the serial port to block all nontranslated addresses. Although this would be easier to accomplish from a CPU perspective than would the previously discussed solution, either way would work.

Scenario 16-2 Answers

1. To allow translation of the new addresses, additional match criteria can be added to the NAT translation access list. This scenario is simply an addition of more addresses for translation. Because the companies were not using the same address space, nothing else needs to be done.

2. The following NAT configuration could be used:

```
access-list 1 permit 10.0.0.0 0.0.0.255
access-list 1 permit 192.168.11.0 0.0.0.255
access-list 1 permit 192.168.22.0 0.0.0.255
access-list 1 permit 192.168.33.0 0.0.0.255

ip nat pool bigpool 103.112.8.30 103.112.8.30 netmask 255.255.255.0
ip nat inside source list 1 pool bigpool overload

!declare inside interface
interface e0
  ip address 10.0.0.1 255.255.255.0
  ip nat inside

!declare outside interface
interface s0
!address assigned to the interface by the ISP
  ip address 156.108.213.2 255.255.255.250
  ip nat outside
```

3. Not enough information is given to lead one to believe that anything should be done to consolidate address space. As it stands, both companies are using the private space, which is easily controlled and routed. As they say, if it ain't broke, don't fix it.

Scenario 16-3 Answers

1. To provide immediate connectivity, you can use the overlap feature in NAT. This would enable the ABC and XYZ companies to coexist during a transition.

2. The following NAT configuration could be used, given a selection of 192.168.1.0/24 as the internal addresses used:

```
ip nat pool XYZ-in 192.168.1.2 192.168.1.254 prefix-length 24
ip nat pool ABC-out 192.168.2.2 192.168.2.254 prefix-length 24

!declare the translations
ip nat outside source list 1 pool XYZ-in
```

```
ip nat inside source list 1 pool ABC-out
!declare the static translation so the servers can be reached
!these lines give an constant 'known' translation to the
!server addresses
ip nat inside source static 10.1.0.1 192.168.1.1
ip nat outside source static 10.1.0.18 192.168.2.1
!specify which addresses will use the pool
access-list 1 permit 10.1.0.0 0.0.255.255

!specify the interfaces
interface serial 0
  ip  address 172.16.4.1 255.255.255.0
  ip nat outside
!
interface ethernet 0
  ip address 10.1.0.2 255.255.255.0
  ip nat inside
```

3. The primary consideration, other than NAT, is the sharing of the server address information between the two entities. The static NAT declarations provide the capability for the two companies to have unique addresses in each other's space for their servers; however, it would be necessary to provide a DNS service for the users to be able to contact the other side easily.

4. The long-term recommendation would be to implement some sort of IP renumbering and then remove the translation between the companies.

This chapter covers the following subjects:

- Using AAA to Secure and Scale Access Control in an Expanding Network

- AAA Overview

- AAA Definitions

- Security Protocols Used for AAA Services

- Router Access Modes and Interfaces Types

- Security Servers and Options

- Cisco Secure Access Control Server (CS-ACS) Overview

- Enabling AAA Globally on the Device

Using AAA to Scale Access Control in an Expanding Network

This chapter covers some of the initial steps to securing your network. Before you can stop someone from hacking your network, you need to decide who can access the network and what they can do on the network, and then you need to keep track of the information so that you can tell when traffic is not part of normal operations on the network and possibly who has performed the task. This can be accomplished in part by using authentication, authorization, and accounting (AAA) security services.

The chapter explores the different components that make up AAA services, what devices can perform AAA services, and what protocols transport this information. The text also looks at the Cisco Systems AAA server called Cisco Secure Access Control Server (CS-ACS).

The Remote Access exam will cover all the areas discussed in this chapter. It is essential that any good network administrator be aware of the pros and cons to the different AAA configurations and services offered on networks today.

"Do I Know This Already?" Quiz

The purpose of the "Do I Know This Already?" quiz is to help you decide whether you really need to read the entire chapter. If you already intend to read the entire chapter, you do not necessarily need to answer these questions now.

The 16-question quiz, derived from the major sections in the "Foundation Topics" portion of the chapter, helps you to determine how to spend your limited study time.

Table 17-1 outlines the major topics discussed in this chapter and the "Do I Know This Already?" quiz questions that correspond to those topics.

Table 17-1   *"Do I Know This Already?" Foundation Topics Section-to-Question Mapping*

Foundation Topics Section	Questions Covered in This Section
Using AAA to Secure and Scale Access Control in an Expanding Network	1–2
AAA Definitions	3–4
Security Protocols Used for AAA Services	5–9
Router Access Modes and Interface Types	10–11
Cisco Secure Access Control Server (CS-ACS) Overview	12
Enabling AAA Globally on the Device	13–16

CAUTION   The goal of self-assessment is to gauge your mastery of the topics in this chapter. If you do not know the answer to a question or are only partially sure of the answer, you should mark this question wrong for purposes of the self-assessment. Giving yourself credit for an answer you correctly guess skews your self-assessment results and might provide you with a false sense of security.

1. What three options does AAA give you?

    a. Accounting

    b. Access lists

    c. Authorization

    d. Authentication

    e. Accumulative rights

2. What are some of the combinations of the three services from AAA that you can implement?

    a. Authentication, authorization

    b. Authentication, authorization, accounting

    c. Authorization, accounting

    d. Authentication, accounting

    e. a, b, d

3. Authentication identifies what?

    a. Devices

    b. Port(s) being used

    c. Users

    d. Protocol

4. Authorization can be used by itself. True or False?

    a. True

    b. False

5. What are the two primary security protocols for AAA services?

    a. IPSec

    b. IP

    c. ESP

    d. RADIUS

    e. TACACS

6. What standard protocol/port does TACACS use?

    a. TCP 49

    b. UDP 49

    c. UDP 69

    d. TCP 23

    e. UDP 1645

7. What part(s) of the packet does TACACS+ encrypt?

    a. Password only

    b. Entire payload

    c. Entire packet

    d. Username and password

    e. Username and password and vendor-specific information

8. RADIUS supports what type of communication?

    a. Client/server

    b. Bidirectional

    c. Both a and b

    d. Point-to-point

9. RADIUS uses what protocol at the transport layer?

   a. TCP

   b. RTP

   c. UDP

   d. ESP

10. What are the two primary access modes?

   a. Packet

   b. Character

   c. Privileged

   d. User

11. An async port can be configured for what type of access mode?

   a. Character

   b. Packet

   c. Privileged

   d. Both a and b

   e. All of the above

12. Cisco Secure Access Control Server supports which protocols for AAA services?

   a. TACACS

   b. RADIUS

   c. IPSec

   d. SNMP

   e. Both a and b

13. The AAA commands:

   a. Are always enabled

   b. Need to have the **aaa** command entered

   c. Need to have the **aaa new-model** command entered

   d. Are turned on by the AAA server

14. Authentication can support what option(s) for checking a username database?

   a. TACACS

   b. RADIUS

   c. None

   d. Enable

   e. All of the above

15. If you turn on authentication, what other AAA options must also be turned on?

   a. Accounting

   b. Authorization

   c. None

   d. Encryption

16. What method(s) are available for writing account records?

   a. **start-stop**

   b. **wait-start**

   c. **stop-only**

   d. All of the above

   e. a and c only

The answers to the "Do I Know This Already?" quiz are found in Appendix A, "Answers to the 'Do I Know This Already?' Quizzes and Q&A Sections." The suggested choices for your next step are as follows:

- **10 or fewer overall score**—Read the chapter. This includes the "Foundation Topics," "Foundation Summary," and the "Q&A" sections.

- **11, 12, or 13 overall score**—Begin with the "Foundation Summary" section and then go to the "Q&A" section.

- **14 or more overall score**—If you want more review of these topics, skip to the "Foundation Summary" section and then go to the "Q&A" section. Otherwise, move to the next chapter.

Foundation Topics

Using AAA to Secure and Scale Access Control in an Expanding Network

Today's network administrators must be able to control access to and monitor the information that end users can see and manipulate. Doing so could directly result in a company's success or failure. With this in mind, AAA is an excellent way to start locking down what end users are capable of doing on the network. You can force authentication of the user, authorize what they are allowed to do, and account changes as they happen in the network. As you can tell, security is of the utmost importance.

With this level of control, it is easier to securely implement and manage your network scenario. You can define roles for specific users, give them the exact commands they need to complete their tasks, and keep track of changes throughout the network. With event-based logging capability, you can make sure the appropriate adjustments have taken place.

All of these components are necessary to maintain the health and security of your network. From the information you gather, you can predict essential upgrades in a timely manner. Whether it be the need for securing data, increasing bandwidth, or tracking when problems started on the network, AAA services are essential.

AAA Overview

AAA provides a network administrator with vital information for the health and security of their network. It can provide authentication of end users so that you can guarantee each user's identity. Once you know a user's identity, you can limit the scope (authorization) of what that user can do. As the user uses the network, you also need to keep track (accounting) of what they do. The three parts to AAA, authentication, authorization, and accounting, are separate entities and you can use some or all of the services as necessary to help with the scalability and security of your network.

AAA can be used to gather information from most of the devices in your network. You can turn on AAA services in routers, switches, firewalls, VPN devices, servers, and other common devices in the network.

AAA Definitions

AAA services are broken down into three sections, authentication, authorization, and accounting. It is imperative that you understand the subtle differences between authentication and authorization and how they work together. It is also important to understand the different types of accounting records that can be written. The following three sections describe the differences between the three components that make up AAA.

Authentication

Authentication identifies users. During the authentication process, the user login (name) and password are checked against the AAA database. Also, depending on the protocol, AAA supports encryption of at least the username and password.

Authentication determines who the user is (example: I am user TAMMY and my password EnDuSeR01 validates me). Passing the authentication test enables access to the network. This process is only one of the components for user control with AAA. Once the userid and password are accepted, AAA can be used to define what the user is then authorized to do.

Authorization

Authorization enables the administrator to control authorization on a one-time, per-service, per–user list, per-group, or per-protocol basis. AAA lets the administrator create attributes that describe the functions that the user is allowed to use. Therefore, you must have the user authenticate before you can assign authorization to them.

AAA authorization works by assembling a set of attributes that describe what the user is authorized to perform. (For example, I can access server OTTAWA_SALES with FTP.) These attributes are compared to the information contained in a database for a given user and the result is returned to AAA to determine the user's actual capabilities and restrictions. This requires that the database be in constant communication with the AAA server during the connection to the RAS device.

Accounting

Accounting enables the administrator to collect information such as start and stop times for user access, executed commands, traffic statistics, and resource usage and then store that information in the relational database management system (RDBMS). In other words, accounting enables the tracking of services and resources that are "consumed" by the user. For example, user TAMMY accessed the OTTAWA_SALES server with FTP five times. The key point to accounting is that it enables the administrator to proactively track and predict service and resource usage. This information can then be used for client billing, internal billing, network management, or audit trails.

Security Protocols Used for AAA Services

There are two primary security protocols used for AAA services, Terminal Access Control Access Control System (TACACS) and Remote Authentication Dial-In User Service (RADIUS). Both protocols have proprietary versions or attributes. An example of a proprietary version of TACACS is the Cisco version TACACS+, which is backward compatible with TACACS. RADIUS has proprietary extensions that allow a vendor to add its specific information to be carried by RADIUS.

TACACS or RADIUS is used from a device such as a network access server (NAS) to the AAA server. Consider a remote dialup client as an example (see Figure 17-1). The user dials in from their laptop to an NAS. The NAS prompts the user for their authentication information. From the laptop to the NAS, the protocol is PPP, so a protocol such as CHAP or PAP is used to transport the authentication information. The NAS passes the information to the AAA server for authentication. It is carried by either the TACACS or RADIUS protocol.

Figure 17-1 *Where Security Protocols Reside in the Network*

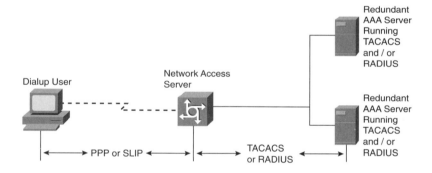

TACACS Overview

TACACS is a standards-based protocol that uses TCP for connection-oriented communication. TACACS has a well-known port number of 49 in TCP. Some of the advantages of TACACS are the following:

- With the receipt of a reset (RST) packet in TCP, a device can tell immediately if the other end device has crashed during communication.

- TCP is more scalable because of some forms of built-in error recovery. It can adapt to growing, as well as congested, networks with the use of sequence numbers for retransmission.

- The entire payload is encrypted with TACACS+ with the use of a shared secret key. TACACS+ marks a field in the header to specify if encryption is used, because it is optional for debugging purposes.

- TACACS+ encrypts the entire body of the packet with the use of a shared secret but leaves a standard TACACS header. Within the header is a field that indicates whether the body is encrypted or not. For debugging purposes, it is useful to have the body of the packets unencrypted. However, during normal operation, the body of the packet is fully encrypted for more secure communications.

- TACACS+ is broken down into three sections, authentication, authorization, and accounting. With this modular approach, you can use other forms of authentication and still use TACACS+ for authorization and accounting. Using Kerberos authentication and TACACS+ authorization and accounting is a common example in a one-time password scenario.

- TACACS+ supports a variety of protocols.

- With TACACS+ you can use two methods to control the authorization of router commands on a per-user or per-group basis. The first method is to create privilege levels with certain commands, and the user is verified by the router and TACACS+ server for the specified privilege level. The second method is to create specific TACACS+ server command lists, on a per-user or per-group basis, with the allowed commands.

TACACS is usually used in an enterprise environment. It offers many advantages and works well for managing everyday network needs. If you need enhanced accounting capabilities for billing or tracking network usage, you should consider RADIUS.

NOTE   To troubleshoot your TACACS server if you suspect it is down, try telneting to the AAA server IP address on port 49 where TACACS should be running. If you get a connection and a blank Telnet screen, then you know that the TACACS service is responding on the AAA server and that routing through the network is working. If you get any other response, check your routing between the device and the TACACS server and check the TACACS server itself.

TIP   You can use the following router command to test whether your TACACS server is accessible:

```
telnet 10.1.1.1:49
```

RADIUS Overview

RADIUS is a client/server-based network security protocol. It uses UDP for a transport protocol. The RADIUS server is typically run on a computer. The clients are any type of device that is responsible for passing user information to designated RADIUS servers and then acting on the response that is returned. Transactions between the client and RADIUS server are authenticated through the use of a shared secret, which is never sent over the network. Some of the advantages of RADIUS are the following:

- RADIUS has less packet overhead because it uses UDP.

- With source code format distribution, RADIUS is a fully open protocol format. The user can modify it to work with any security system currently available on the market.

- RADIUS offers enhanced accounting functionality.

RADIUS is often used to do billing based on resource usage. An example would be an ISP that bills a user for connection charges. You can implement RADIUS accounting without using RADIUS for authentication and authorization. The enhanced accounting functionality of RADIUS allows data to be sent at the start and end of services, which allows you to keep track of usage of the resource (time, packets, bytes, etc.) during the session.

Router Access Modes and Interface Types

Determining the access method and type of port a user can access the network on is essential. This is the basis to configuring AAA properly.

There are two primary access modes, character based and packet based. Character mode is used on the TTY, VTY, AUX, and CON ports and usually involves configuring the device. Packet mode is used on the async, group-async, BRI, PRI, serial, dialer profiles, and dialer rotaries. These are the communication ports on the router and usually mean you are trying to communicate to another device. An example would be a PPP dialup session to an ISP, in which you are trying to communicate to web servers on the Internet through the async port.

The key thing to keep in mind is packet versus character mode, not the physical port itself. The AUX port, for instance, can be used in both modes. After enabling AAA, each attachment to the router, whether it is character or packet mode, must be declared for authentication. Failure to declare a method for a connection results in a failed authentication.

Security Servers and Options

In today's ever-expanding networking world, there are many choices as to which AAA server you should use. The best way to decide which server is right for your network is to sit down and make a list of features that are needed to support your network and then compare the offerings to your criteria. There are many flavors of freeware TACACS or RADIUS servers, but you have to be careful in your choice. The following are some questions that you should ask yourself when considering a particular AAA server:

- Do I know who wrote the code for this AAA server and are there holes or back doors I have to be concerned about? If you use a freeware version, you have no idea who wrote the code or whether it has been tested from a security standpoint. Many hackers are willing to give you a free product, but there could be back doors or poor encryption on the user database that undermines the entire security of your network.

- Does this AAA server support both TACACS and RADIUS for the same user database?

- Do I have a user-friendly interface for configuration or will I have to train staff to use this software?

- Can I support enhanced features like wireless access authentication and Voice over IP (VoIP)?

- Can I support centralized or distributed logging?

- Can I support authentication forwarding?

Cisco Secure Access Control Server (CS-ACS) Overview

CS-ACS is the Cisco offering for AAA services. It provides many enhanced features, such as:

- Provides AAA services to network devices that function as AAA clients, such as NASs, PIX Firewalls, VPN 3000 Concentrators, or routers and switches.

- Optional centralized access control and accounting on one database, in addition to controlling specific router and switch configuration levels.

- Local or remote network administrators can quickly administer accounts, with the ability to change levels of service offerings for entire groups of users.

- CS-ACS optionally supports many popular external user database repository implementations.

- Uses one username database with support for TACACS+ and RADIUS protocols to provide AAA services that ensure a secure environment for all devices running either protocol.

- Can authenticate against many popular token servers.

- Downloadable per-user access control lists (ACLs)

- Customizable shared network access restrictions (NARs)

- Multiple or individual devices included in AAA client configuration

- User-defined RADIUS vendor-specific attributes (VSAs)

CS-ACS is an extremely robust AAA server. It is built in a modular approach comprising seven modules:

- CSAdmin

- CSAuth

- CSMon

- CSTacacs

- CSRADIUS

- CSDBSync

- CSLog

Each module can be started and stopped individually from within the Microsoft Service Control Panel or as a group from within the CiscoSecure ACS browser interface. CS-ACS relies on the

CSMon or the monitoring module to make sure that all other services are running. If CSMon detects one of the modules is not responding, you can have CSMon do one of three options:

- Restart the specific service
- Restart all services
- Reboot the server

CS-ACS is managed by an HTML/JAVA-based web page. The web-based interface is used to view and edit user and group information. It allows you to restart services, add remote administrators, change NAS information, and back up the system. The interface has predefined reports that are viewable from anywhere on the network. These reports track connection activity, show which users are currently logged in, list the failed authentication and authorization attempts, and show administrators' recent tasks.

You can configure and perform almost all functions for CiscoSecure ACS through the user interface, including:

- Adjust or review group profiles
- Adjust or review user profiles
- Update NAS and server information, including network device groups (NDGs)
- Stop and start the CiscoSecure ACS services
- Back up the system information (using CS-UTIL)
- Restore the system backup
- Configure the user interface
- Use local and remote administrator configuration
- Utilize Distribute system logs or settings
- Configure how unknown users are to be handled
- Troubleshoot
- Replication databases
- Use server information mirroring/synchronization
- Utilize extensive reports and activity
- Use in-depth online documentation

Access to CS-ACS is done in one of two ways:

- From the browser at the server on which CiscoSecure ACS is installed, as follows:

  `http://127.0.0.1:2002`

- From a browser on a remote workstation, as follows:

  `http://`*Windows NT Server IP address*`:2002`

Enabling AAA Globally on the Device

You first have to enable AAA and then you can configure it. AAA configuration is implemented in three steps:

Step 1   Enable AAA Configuration on the router. During the declaration of AAA, the router must be told whether it will be "speaking" with a TACACS server or a RADIUS server.

Step 2   Define who will be authenticated, what they are authorized to do, and what will be tracked in the database.

Step 3   Enable or define the method on the interface.

The following subsections detail how to turn on AAA (Step 1), how to define the methods for authentication, authorization, and accounting (Step 2), and how to declare AAA on an interface (Step 3). For brevity, in the following configurations, Steps 2 and 3 have been combined.

It should be noted that once AAA is turned on for a router, any interface and connection method must be defined or access is not permitted. Therefore, it is important to leave a "back door" or local access method available during initial deployment to guard against loss of router access due to coding mistakes. This is discussed in the upcoming sections on authentication for each of the access methods: **login**, **enable**, **ppp**, **arap**, and **nasi**.

Step 1: Enabling AAA

To enable AAA on the router, use this command:

```
router (config)# aaa new-model
```

The **no** form of this command disables AAA on the router. Once AAA is enabled, the router must point to the source of the AAA server. For a TACACS server, the command is as follows:

```
router (config)# tacacs-server host ip-address [single-connection]
```

The *ip-address* parameter designates the location of the CiscoSecure server or another TACACS server. The optional **single-connection** parameter tells the router to maintain a single connection for the duration of the session between the router and the AAA device. The alternative is to open and close a TCP connection for each session. The opening and closing of a connection is the default. Cisco recommends the single-connection feature for improved performance.

A shared password is used between the access router and the AAA server for security. The command to establish this password on the router is as follows:

```
router (config)# tacacs-server key cisco
```

The password must be configured on the AAA server also. The passwords are case sensitive.

The first steps for the configuration of AAA used on a RADIUS server are similar to the TACACS implementation: **tacacs** is replaced by **radius**. The following example is the initial command set for a RADIUS implementation:

```
router (config)# aaa new-model
router (config)# radius-server host 192.168.1.1
router (config)# radius-server key radiuskey
```

In the command set, the IP address is 115.55.43.1 and the shared password is **radiuskey**.

Step 2 and Step 3: Authentication, Authorization, and Accounting

After you "turn on" the AAA commands, you have access to many specific commands to deal with authentication, authorization, and accounting. The following sections will discuss each of the three areas of AAA security in detail and provide general configuration guidelines.

AAA Authentication

Once AAA has been enabled on the router, the administrator must declare the methods by which authentication can take place. The key issue is to ensure that the administrator has a way to gain access to the router if the AAA server is down. Failure to provide a backdoor interface can result in lost communications to the router and the necessity to break in through the console port. Care should be taken to always configure a local access method during any implementation of AAA.

The syntax for configuring AAA on the router can be daunting at first glance. Breaking it down keeps it simpler. Each of the modes listed (**login**, **enable**, **arap**, and so on) is a method by which a user might gain access to or through the router.

Recall the packet and character mode designation from the previous section. The global configuration commands enable the administrator to declare the method that is used for authentication, regardless of the access mode being used. These methods, which are shown later, include **enable**, **line**, **local**, **none**, and so on and are checked in the order in which they are specified in the command. The generic form for the **authentication** command is as follows:

```
router (config)# aaa authentication [login | enable | arap | ppp | nasi] method
```

This example does not include specifics for the method by which the access is evaluated. It is clearer to show each of the commands and then discuss the method that can be added to the command.

Each command in the following list can stand alone and each declares a command definition for the **authentication** command. In addition, each command is used for a specific access purpose.

■ **aaa authentication login**—This command answers this question: How do I authenticate the login dialog?

■ **aaa authentication enable**—This command answers this question: Can the user get to the privileged command prompt?

■ **aaa authentication arap**—This command answers this question: Does the AppleTalk Remote Access Protocol (ARAP) user use RADIUS or TACACS+? (One must be selected.)

■ **aaa authentication ppp**—This command answers this question: What method should be used if a user is coming over a PPP connection?

■ **aaa authentication nasi**—This command answers this question: What method should be used if a user is coming over NASI (NetWare Asynchronous Services Interface)?

AAA Authentication Login

What method of authentication is going to be used during the login procedure? The answer to this question is defined by this interface command:

```
router (config)# aaa authentication login [default | listname]
```

The declaration of **default** tells the router what to do if no listname has been declared on the interface. If a listname has been declared, that listname controls the login. For example, the global command

```
router (config)# aaa authentication login salesgroup argument argument argument …
```

declares how the **salesgroup** list is interpreted. On each interface that is declared to use authentication **salesgroup**, one or more of the following arguments is used for the authentication:

```
[enable | line | local | none | tacacs+ | radius | guest]
```

Each of the previous arguments declares a method of authentication, and they can be listed one after another on the command line. Example 17-1 shows this concept.

Example 17-1 *Declaring a Method of AAA Authentication*

```
Router(config)#aaa authentication login salesgroup tacacs+ radius local
Router(config)#aaa authentication login default tacacs+
Router(config)#line 1 12
Router(config-line)#login authentication salesgroup  - Part of Step 3
```

The first statement declares that list **salesgroup** use TACACS+, and then RADIUS, and then local username/password pairs for authentication. The fourth statement declares on lines 1 to 12 that anyone attempting to log in to these interfaces is authenticated using the order specified in the list **salesgroup**. Note that if someone attaches to the console port, they are authenticated by TACACS+ only because that is the default and because there is not a login authentication statement on the console port.

The term *listname* (defined as **salesgroup** in Example 17-1) refers to the list of methods that will be used, not to a list of people that will be authenticated. In Example 17-1, the term can be interpreted as "my people will use this list for authentication."

The order of the authentication arguments is important. In Example 17-1, if the *user* fails authentication with TACACS+, that user is denied access. If the *router* fails to access TACACS+, the router tries to contact a RADIUS server. The key issue is that a secondary method is used only if a previous method is unavailable to the router.

This key issue is important to remember because if **tacacs+** is the only option to verify a login and the TACACS+ service is unavailable or down, *nobody* can log in. If the authentication methods were set as **tacacs+** and **local**, administration username/password pairs could be placed on the router so that even if TACACS+ were down, an administrator could still gain access to the router.

It is important to maintain a proper order for the methods. You should make **local** a last resort method so that access to the router is maintained by at least a local username/password pair.

The following list describes each of the methods for login authentication. You should memorize this list for the exam.

- **line**—This method specifies to use the password that is on the line that is being attached to. This is done using the line command **login** (ask for a password) and the command **password** *xxx*, where *xxx* is the password for the line.
- **enable**—This method specifies to use the **enable** password for authentication on the interface. The authentication is compared against the **enable** password on the router.
- **local**—This method specifies to use the **username** *yyyy* **password** *xxxx* pairs that are on the router for authentication.
- **none**—This method specifies to not use an authentication method.
- **tacacs+**—This method specifies to use the TACACS+ server declared by the **tacacs-server host** *ip-address* statement on the router.
- **radius**—This method specifies to use the RADIUS server declared by the **radius-server host** *ip-address* statement on the router.

AAA Authentication Enable

What method is used if a user tries to access privileged mode on the router? If no AAA methods are set, the user must have the enable password. This password is demanded by Cisco IOS Software. If AAA is being used and *no* default is set, the user also needs the enable password for access to privileged mode.

The construct for AAA is similar to the login authentication commands, as shown in the following code:

```
Router(config)#aaa authentication enable thefolks tacacs+ enable
```

This command declares that to gain access to privileged mode, TACACS+ is checked first, and only if TACACS+ returns an error or is unavailable is the enable password then used. With all the lists that are set for AAA, the secondary methods are used only if the previously listed methods return an error or are unavailable. If the returned message is a "fail," the router does not try to authenticate using the subsequent method in the list.

The following list describes each of the methods for enabling authentication. You should memorize this for the exam.

- **enable**—This method says to use the enable password for authentication on the interface. The authentication is compared against the enable password on the router.

- **line**—This method says to use the password that is on the line that is being attached to. This is done using the line command **login** (ask for a password) and the command **password** *xxx*, where *xxx* is the password for the line.

- **none**—This method says to not use an authentication method.

- **tacacs+**—This method says to use the TACACS server declared by the **tacacs-server host** *ip-address* statement on the router.

- **radius**—This method says to use the RADIUS server declared by the **radius-server host** *ip-address* statement on the router.

AAA Authentication ARAP

The **aaa authentication arap** command is used in conjunction with the **arap authentication** line configuration command. This describes the methods that are tried when ARAP users attempt to gain access to the router. Example 17-2 shows the configuration.

Example 17-2 *Declaring AAA Authentication with ARAP*

```
Router(config)#aaa authentication arap applefolk tacacs+ local
Router(config)#line 1 12
Router(config-line)#arap authentication applefolk   - part of step 3
```

The first statement declares that the authentication is first TACACS+ and then local username/ password pairs if TACACS+ returns an error or is unavailable. On lines 1 through 12, the list points back to the AAA declaration in the first statement.

The following list describes each of the methods for authentication using AAA for ARAP. You should memorize this for the exam.

- **line**—This method says to use the password that is on the line that is being attached to. This is done using the line command **login** (ask for a password) and the command **password** *xxx*, where *xxx* is the password for the line.

- **local**—This method says to use the **username** *yyyy* **password** *xxxx* pairs that are on the router for authentication.

- **tacas+**—This method says to use the TACACS server declared by the **tacacs-server host** *ip- address* statement on the router.

- **guest**—This method says to allow a login if the username is guest. This option is only valid using ARAP.

- **auth-guest**—This method says to allow the guest login only if the user has already logged in to the EXEC process on the router and has now started the ARAP process.

Note that, by default, guest logins through ARAP are disabled when you initialize AAA. The **aaa authentication arap** command with either the **guest** or **auth-guest** keyword is required for guest access when using AAA.

AAA Authentication PPP

The **aaa authentication ppp** command is used in conjunction with the **ppp authentication** line configuration command to describe the methods that are tried when Point-to-Point Protocol (PPP) users attempt to gain access to the router. Example 17-3 shows this configuration.

Example 17-3 *Declaring AAA Authentication with PPP*

```
Router(config)#aaa authentication ppp pppfolk tacacs+ local
Router(config)#line 1 12
Router(config-line)#ppp authentication pppfolk  - part of step 3
```

The same type of syntax is used throughout all AAA commands. With the **ppp** command set, the interface command is **ppp authentication** *option(s)*, where the options are the standard non-AAA options of **pap**, **chap**, **pap chap**, **chap pap**, or **ms-chap**. In addition, the AAA command methods can be used. In the previous example, the authentication is first TACACS+ and then local username/ password pairs if TACACS+ is unavailable or returns an error.

The following list describes each of the methods for authentication using AAA for PPP. You should memorize this for the exam.

- **local**—This method says to use the **username** *yyyy* **password** *xxxx* pairs that are on the router for authentication.

- **none**—This method says to not use an authentication method.

- **tacacs+**—This method says to use the TACACS server declared by the **tacacs-server host** *ip-address* statement on the router.

- **radius**—This method says to use the RADIUS server declared by the **radius-server host** *ip-address* statement on the router.

- **krb5**—This method says that the Kerberos 5 method is available only for PPP operations, and communications with a Kerberos security server must be established. Kerberos login authentication works with PPP Password Authentication Protocol (PAP) only. The name Kerberos comes from Greek mythology and is the name of the three-headed dog that guarded the entrance of Hades.

- **if-needed**—This is another PPP-only option. It stops authentication if the user has been authenticated previously on the TTY line.

AAA Authentication NASI

The **aaa authentication nasi** command is used with the **nasi authentication** line configuration command to specify a list of authentication methods that are tried when a NASI user attempts to gain access to the router. Example 17-4 shows this configuration.

Example 17-4 *Declaring AAA Authentication with NASI*

```
Router(config)#aaa authentication nasi novellfolk tacacs+ local
Router(config)#line 1 12
Router(config-line)#nasi authentication novellfolk  - part of step 3
```

As with the other access methods, when a user is using NASI, this example would require TACACS+ authentication and then would use the username/password pair if TACACS+ was unavailable.

The following list describes each of the methods for authentication using AAA for NASI. You should memorize this for the exam.

- **line**—This method says to use the password that is on the line that is being attached to. This is done using the line command **login** (ask for a password) and the command **password** *xxx*, where *xxx* is the password for the line.

- **enable**—This method says to use the enable password for authentication on the interface. The authentication is compared against the enable password on the router.

- **local**—This method says to use the **username** *yyyy* **password** *xxxx* pairs that are on the router for authentication.

- **none**—This method says to not use an authentication method.

- **tacacs+**—This method says to use the TACACS server declared by the **tacacs-server host** *ip-address* statement on the router.

When AAA is turned on, all lines and ports on the router use AAA; hence, the default group should be configured for any access method that the router will see.

AAA Authorization

Once a user has been authenticated, they can be further restricted in what they are allowed to do. This is done using the **aaa authorization** command. These restrictions can be applied to activities or services offered on the router.

As with authentication, it is easier to see an example before diving into each option available. The syntax is quite simple and declares which activity or service (network, EXEC, command level, config-commands, and reverse-access) is being attempted and which method of authorization is to be used (**local**, **none**, **radius**, **tacacs+**, or **krb5**). Example 17-5 demonstrates the syntax for AAA authorization.

Example 17-5 *Applying Restrictions with AAA Authorization*

```
Router(config)#aaa new-model
Router(config)#aaa authentication login myfolk tacacs+ local
Router(config)#aaa authorization exec tacacs+ local
Router(config)#aaa authorization command 1 tacacs+ local
Router(config)#aaa authorization command 15 tacacs+ local
```

In the example, AAA is turned on with **aaa new-model**, and the authentication method is declared for the list called "myfolk." The third line declares that if one of the logged-in users wants to gain access to the EXEC mode, TACACS+ is contacted to see whether the user is allowed to perform that function.

The last two lines are similar. The logged-in user is tested against the TACACS database for authorization to run level 1 and level 15 commands; the router IOS commands are either level 1 or level 15 commands. It is possible to change the level of each command on the router to allow for a more controlled access environment for the users.

AAA has power, but the administrative overhead to use this power can be daunting to most administrators. In addition, this level of control can be unnecessary for most installations. As an example of this overhead, consider a common scenario in which AAA is set up so that subadministrators can have access to configuration mode, but with the ability to use only a subset of the commands. Although possible, the configuration on the router to change the level for each command can become less than productive.

The generic form of the authorization command is as follows:

```
aaa authorization do-what? check-how?
```

The *do-what?* arguments can be any of the following:

- **network**—This argument uses the *check-how?* method for authorization to perform all network-related service requests, that is, SLIP, PPP, and ARAP protocol.

- **exec**—This argument uses the *check-how?* method for authorization to determine if the user is allowed to create and run the router EXEC shell. If TACACS+ or RADIUS is being used, it is possible that the database could return autocommand information to the user.

- **command level**—This argument uses the *check-how?* method for authorization of all commands at the specified privilege level. The level can be set to values of 1 to 15.

- **reverse-access**—This argument uses the *check-how?* method for authorization of reverse access connections such as reverse Telnet.

The *check-how?* arguments are the same as those used for authentication. *check-how?* simply points to where the authentication should be done. The *check-how?* arguments can be any of the following:

- **tacacs+**—In this argument, TACACS+ authorization is done by associating attribute-value (AV) pairs to individual users. The AV pair associates a function that the user is authorized to do. When a user attempts to do a *do-what?*, the TACACS database is checked.

- **if-authenticated**—In this argument, if the user has been authenticated, they are allowed to perform the function. Notice that you are not checking authorization, but whether the user is in the database and is valid.

- **none**—In this argument, the router does not request authorization information for the *do-what?*. Authorization is not performed and a query is not sent to the database.

- **local**—In this argument, the router or access server consults its local database, as defined by the use of the username/password pairs that are configured in global configuration mode on the router.

- **radius**—In this argument, RADIUS authorization is done by associating attributes to a username on the RADIUS server. Each username and the associated attributes are stored within the RADIUS database.

- **krb5-instance**—In this argument, the router queries the Kerberos server for authorization. The authorizations are stored on the Kerberos server.

In general, authorization can be implemented in many ways. The issue is finding which database or resource has the AV pair or attribute or map to provide the router with the answer to the authorization query.

AAA Accounting

AAA accounting can supply information concerning user activity back to the database. This concept was especially helpful in the early days of Internet service when many ISPs offered 20 or 40 hours per week at a fixed cost and hourly or minute charges in excess of the specified timeframe. Today it is much more common for the ISP charge to be set for an unlimited access time. This does not, however, minimize the power of accounting to enable the administrator to track unauthorized attempts and proactively create security for system resources. In addition, accounting can be used to track resource usage to better allocate system usage.

Accounting is generally used for billing and auditing purposes and is simply turned on for those events that are to be tracked. The commands follow this general syntax:

```
aaa accounting what-to-track how-to-track where-to-send-the-information
```

The *what-to-track* arguments are as follows:

- **network**—With this argument, network accounting logs the information, on a user basis, for PPP, SLIP, or ARAP sessions. The accounting information provides the time of access and the network resource usage in packet and byte counts.

- **connection**—With this argument, connection accounting logs the information about *outbound* connections made from the router or RAS device, including Telnet and rlogin sessions. The key word is outbound; it enables the tracking of connections made from the RAS device and where those connections were established.

- **exec**—With this argument, EXEC accounting logs the information about when a user creates an EXEC terminal session on the router. The information includes the IP address and telephone number, if it is a dial-in user, and the time and date of the access. This information can be particularly useful for tracking unauthorized access to the RAS device.

- **system**—With this argument, system accounting logs the information about system-level events. System-level events include AAA configuration changes and reloads for the device. Again, this information would be useful to track unauthorized access or tampering with the router.

- **command**—With this argument, command accounting logs information regarding which commands are being executed on the router. The accounting record contains a list of commands executed for the duration of the EXEC session, along with the time and date information.

As you can see, the amount of information that can be tracked is substantial. It is important that the administrator track only information that is useful. Tracking unwanted information can create a large overhead on the network resource.

The *how-to-track* argument can be any of the following:

- **start-stop**—This option sends an accounting record when the process begins. This is sent as a background process, and the user request is begun without delay. When the user process is completed, the stop time and information is sent to the AAA database. This option is needed when an elapsed time of usage is required.

- **stop-only**—This option sends aggregated information based on the *what-to-track* argument at the end of the user process. This option can be used when only the *what-to-track* information is needed.

- **wait-start**—As mentioned, this option does not allow the user process to start until an acknowledgement is received from the accounting database engine by the RAS device. **wait-start** is particularly important when the tracked event can cause a loss of connectivity with the accounting database.

The last piece of information needed for the router or RAS is where to send the information that is being tracked. The *where-to-send-the-information* argument can be either of the following locations:

- **tacacs+**—When this option is used, the information is sent to the TACACS+ server defined by the **tacacs-server host** *ip-address* command.

- **radius**—When this option is used, the information is sent to the RADIUS server database defined by the **radius-server host** *ip-address* command. The current Cisco implementation does not support the command accounting feature.

Example 17-6 shows a simple accounting setup.

Example 17-6   *AAA Accounting Setup*

```
Router(config)#aaa accounting command 15 start-stop tacacs+
Router(config)#aaa accounting connection start-stop tacacs+
Router(config)#aaa accounting system wait-start tacacs+
```

In the first line, accounting has been activated for all level 15 commands to show when the command began and when it ended for the user that initiated the command. The second line logs to the database when the user's connection began and when it ended. In the last statement, any system-level events, such as a reload or configuration change, are tracked by start and end time.

The **wait-start** argument assures that the logging of the start of the system event is acknowledged before the event is allowed to start. The key issue here is that if the event is a reload of the router, it is imperative that the event be logged and acknowledged before the router reloads. If the message is missed or lost in transmission, the event would go unrecorded.

The basics of accounting are that the accounting records are sent to a TACACS+ server or a RADIUS server. In addition, the records that are to be tracked should be recorded to the router with the AAA accounting commands.

Accounting is a powerful tool for proactive management of network resources; however, it is a double-edged sword. The more accounting, the more resources are used to accomplish the accounting. It is generally recommended that the **stop-only** argument be used if an elapsed time is not needed.

The format of accounting records depends on the AAA software that is being used. The treatment of AAA within the confines of the BCRAN class is intended to give the student a basic understanding of AAA. All AAA software engines can provide the same or similar functionality; it is impossible to describe the intricacies of an individual software suite as the standard for AAA.

Foundation Summary

This section is a collection of information that provides a convenient review of many key concepts in this chapter. If you are already comfortable with the topics in this chapter, this summary can help you recall a few details. If you just read this chapter, this review should help solidify some key facts.

By this point, you should be aware of the importance of AAA services in a network. You should be aware of each individual section of AAA, authentication (who a user is), authorization (what a user can do), and accounting (keeping track of the resources used).

AAA information is transported by one of two protocols, TACACS or RADIUS, from the network device to the AAA server. TACACS is said to offer a more reliable service because it uses TCP as its transport protocol. TACACS also has enhanced features such as packet payload encryption, compared to RADIUS, which uses UDP and only encrypts the username and password as defined by the current RFC. The most common reason for a network administrator to use RADIUS is the extensive accounting capability. Usually, TACACS is used in an enterprise environment and RADIUS is used only when IP billing or enhanced accounting features are necessary.

One of the toughest concepts to grasp from this chapter is the access method that a user is connecting with. This chapter discussed Character mode versus Packet mode and the different types of interfaces that they run on. The key point is that a Character mode (sending each character one by one) access is usually done on an interface that is used for configuration of the device—for example, a console (CON) port. It is used to specifically configure the device, and it sends the information on a character-by-character basis. Packet mode is usually done on an interface you use to communicate through to other parts of the network—for example, a serial interface. What you need to take away from this book is not what the different interface types are (because some interfaces could be used in both facets, such as an async serial interface), but rather the general overview of Packet versus Character mode.

A common AAA server is CS-ACS. It offers many enhancements over most freeware AAA servers, the most useful of which is a common username and password database for both TACACS and RADIUS. This is useful in today's networks because the current VPN 3000 Concentrator Series uses only RADIUS. If network administrators already have some AAA services running, they are usually transported by TACACS. CS-ACS was created in a modular fashion. It relies on CSMon to poll the other six services to make sure everything is functioning. If one module fails, the rest should be okay; for example, if the TACACS service were to fail, you could still use the RADIUS service on the CS-ACS server because of the modular functionality of CS-ACS.

Q&A

The questions and scenarios in this book are more difficult than what you will experience on the actual exam. The questions do not attempt to cover more breadth or depth than the exam, but they are designed to make sure that you know the answer. Rather than enabling you to derive the answer from clues hidden inside the question itself, the questions challenge your understanding and recall of the subject.

Hopefully, mastering these questions will help you limit the number of exam questions on which you narrow your choices to two options and then guess.

The answers to these questions can be found in Appendix A.

1. What advantages does an AAA server have over a local router database?

2. What is authorization used for and how is it assigned?

3. Why are accounting records important?

4. Between what devices would TACACS or RADIUS be used?

5. List a couple of reasons why TACACS is said to be more secure than RADIUS.

6. What is Character-based mode?

7. Why would you not necessarily want to use a freeware AAA server?

8. What is the name the module of CS-ACS that checks whether the other modules are still functioning and what options does it offer you if one module is down?

9. Why must you turn on authentication if you want to have authorization for services on your network?

10. Why would a network administrator choose to run both RADIUS and TACACS+ on a network?

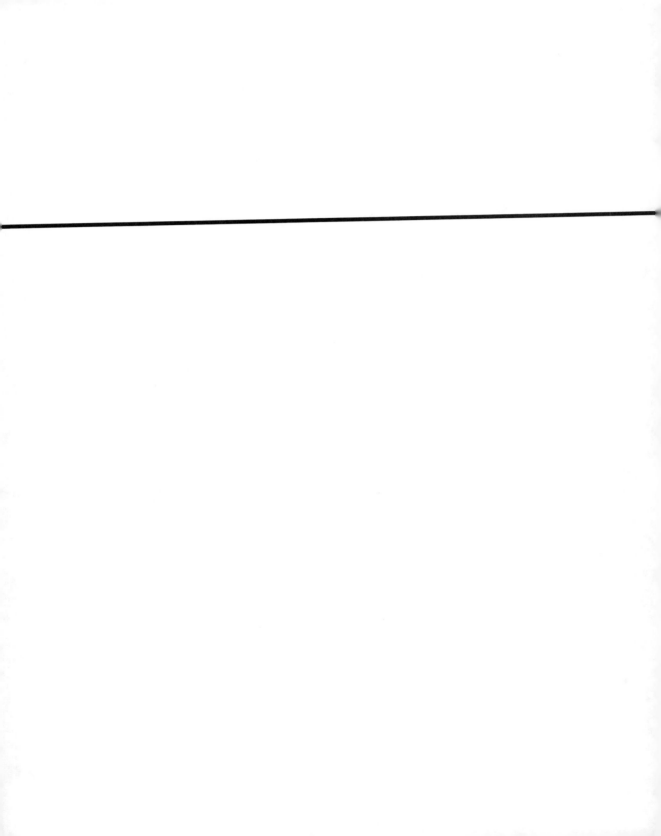

Part VIII: Securing Remote Access Networks

Chapter 18   Securing Remote Access Network Connections

This part of the book covers the following BCRAN exam topics:

- Explain the operation of remote network access control methods
- Describe the structure and operation of virtual private network technologies
- Configure access control to manage and limit remote access
- Design a solution of access control to meet required specifications
- Troubleshoot a VPN system

This chapter covers the following subjects:

- VPN Overview

- Encryption Algorithms

- IPSec Overview

- Preparing for IKE and IPSec

- Testing and Verifying Configuration

Securing Remote Access Network Connections

As the need for real-time information becomes more and more critical, remote access to corporate data is a must for many employees, regardless of whether they are on the other side of town from their office or on the other side of the country or world.

The biggest issue regarding remote access is how to ensure that the data can be accessed securely. This issue raises many questions. For example, if the data is posted on a web page, how can the company track who has seen it? Or if the user is dialing in to the network, how can the user prove that they are a valid user? Or if a user wants to work from home and connect to the office over a public infrastructure such as the Internet, how does the company guarantee that no one can see the information being transmitted? These types of problems are the driving force for today's vast market of VPN products. These products are designed to help provide secure, authenticated, remote access to data, independent of media or connection type. You will learn about these products in this chapter.

"Do I Know This Already?" Quiz

The purpose of the "Do I Know This Already?" quiz is to help you decide whether you really need to read the entire chapter. If you already intend to read the entire chapter, you do not necessarily need to answer these questions now.

The 15-question quiz, derived from the major sections in the "Foundation Topics" portion of the chapter, helps you to determine how to spend your limited study time.

Table 18-1 outlines the major topics discussed in this chapter and the "Do I Know This Already?" quiz questions that correspond to those topics.

Table 18-1 *"Do I Know This Already?" Foundation Topics Section-to-Question Mapping*

Foundation Topics Section	Questions Covered in This Section
VPN Overview	1–5
Encryption Algorithms	6–7
IPSec Overview	8–13
Preparing for IKE and IPSec	12–15

> **CAUTION** The goal of self-assessment is to gauge your mastery of the topics in this chapter. If you do not know the answer to a question or are only partially sure of the answer, you should mark this question wrong for purposes of the self-assessment. Giving yourself credit for an answer you correctly guess skews your self-assessment results and might provide you with a false sense of security.

1. What are the three things a VPN network should provide?

   a. Cost-effective access

   b. Reliable connection

   c. Secure communication

   d. Virus protection

2. What are the three OSI layers at which encryption is usually performed?

   a. Application layer

   b. Data link layer

   c. Session layer

   d. Network layer

   e. Physical layer

3. What is a common application layer encryption standard?

   a. SSL

   b. IPSec

   c. CET

   d. DES

4. What drawback with regard to routing do you get when you encrypt at the data link layer?

   a. None

   b. IP header is encrypted so you can't route

   c. Serial connections won't pass encrypted frames

   d. Only proprietary routing protocols can be used

5. What are three components that you get from a good VPN network?

   a. Authentication

   b. Authorization

    c. Accounting

    d. Integrity

    e. Payload encryption

6. The same key is used to encrypt and decrypt in a symmetrical encryption algorithm.

    a. True

    b. False

7. Hashing algorithms give what type of output?

    a. Fixed length

    b. Variable length

    c. User-defined length

    d. A or B

8. Diffie-Hellman helps with what part of IPSec?

    a. Session Key Exchange

    b. Security associations

    c. Sets encryption algorithms

    d. Diffie-Hellman is not used with IPSec

9. What are the two primary protocols in the IPSec standard?

    a. AH and RSA

    b. RSA and SSL

    c. SSH and SSL

    d. AH and ESP

    e. ESP and RSA

10. What protocol number is AH?

    a. 6

    b. 17

    c. 443

    d. 51

    e. 50

11. What protocol number is ESP?

    a. 6

    b. 17

    c. 443

    d. 51

    e. 50

12. What is the default mode for Cisco VPN routers to send ESP packets?

    a. Tunnel

    b. Transport

    c. GRE

    d. Compressed

13. IKE is enabled by default on Cisco routers.

    a. True

    b. False

14. Transform sets can have how many AH option sets?

    a. One

    b. Two

    c. Three

    d. Four

15. How many crypto maps can be applied to an interface?

    a. One

    b. Two

    c. Three

    d. Depends on how many neighbors you have

The answers to the "Do I Know This Already?" quiz are found in Appendix A, "Answers to the 'Do I Know This Already?' Quizzes and Q&A Sections." The suggested choices for your next step are as follows:

■ **10 or fewer overall score**—Read the entire chapter. This includes the "Foundation Topics," "Foundation Summary," and the "Q&A" sections.

■ **11 or 12 overall score**— Begin with the "Foundation Summary" section and then go to the "Q&A" section.

■ **13 or more overall score**—If you want more review on these topics, skip to the "Foundation Summary" section and then go to the "Q&A" section. Otherwise, move to the next chapter.

Foundation Topics

VPN Overview

As a CCNP candidate, you will be forced to come up with solutions for remote access that are secure, reliable, and cost effective. This chapter helps you to understand the process Cisco Systems uses to create VPN networks with its line of products and IPSec. Cisco has a dedicated VPN product line, the VPN 3000 Concentrator, but other devices such as routers or PIX Firewalls also have very similar capabilities.

This section covers a general overview of Cisco's VPN solutions, focusing on a router-based VPN implementation.

With today's data networks, there is an ever-increasing need to transport information from one area of the network to another, whether it is within one office building or between branch sites. A network could have remote sales office people who need access to data stored at the head office, just like a bank would do when checking with a central credit bureau.

With this need for remote access to data comes the worry about what would happen if the information were compromised. For example, what if company A spends millions of dollars on research and development of its new product and then company B is able to access the data and create a competitive product, but doesn't have to spend the money on R&D? Company A would have to recoup in the price of its product the R&D money that it spent, whereas company B would be able to sell the product cheaper because it doesn't have the initial costs of the R&D. With this in mind, network administrators are very cautious about sending data across any type of public or insecure network.

There are many different approaches to securing data as it crosses a network. You could secure it at the application layer, the network/transport layers, or the data link layer.

An example of an application layer implementation would be almost any web banking scenario. You need to be able to access your web banking from any PC in the world, so you create an SSL connection between two applications and transport your data. As long as the web browser you are using and the web server have the same standard implementation of SSL, it should work. A downfall of this solution is that the encryption is usually software based, which can add processing time and use valuable CPU cycles on your PC.

Another solution is to implement encryption at the data link layer. This solves the problem of using CPU cycles on the PC, but it does not allow you to scale to an ISP-sized environment very easily.

When doing encryption at the data link layer, everything from Layer 2 through Layer 7 in the OSI model is encrypted, including the network address. This makes it impossible to route the packet until you decrypt the information.

If encryption is done at the data link layer, the IP header will also be encrypted, which means you must encrypt the frame as it comes out of the router, transport it, and then decrypt it before it gets to the next router. There is no possible way to do this if you are crossing any type of a public WAN link through a service provider's cloud, because of the vast number of devices in its network. The only solution would be to create a private WAN network everywhere you need to go.

Another option is to use encryption at the network and transport layers of the OSI model. There are many examples of this type of encryption, such as Cisco Encryption Technology (CET) and IPSec. The problem with using CET or any other proprietary encryption method is that you are limited to one vendor's equipment. This is why most people use the IPSec protocol in VPN networks today. It is a standards-based protocol that provides for a multivendor solution to your VPN needs. Three necessary components to a good VPN network are authentication, integrity, and payload encryption. IPSec enables you to select any or all these components, allowing for a speed versus security trade-off.

NOTE   Confidentiality (encryption), integrity, and authentication are commonly referred to as CIA.

Encryption Algorithms

Many different types of algorithms are used within the IPSec protocol suite. Two common types of algorithms used for encryption are synchronous and asynchronous. A third type of algorithm used within the IPSec protocol suite is a hashing algorithm to provide authentication and integrity for the data. This section looks at the advantages of each type of algorithm and how to use the Diffie-Hellman key exchange to exchange the keys used in each of the processes.

Some of the qualities you should look for in a good encryption algorithm are the following:

- Security against cryptographic attacks
- Scalable, variable key lengths
- Any change to the clear-text input should result in a large change to the encrypted output
- No restrictions on import or export

Symmetrical and Asymmetrical Algorithms

A *symmetrical* algorithm is loosely defined as a shared key algorithm that is used to encrypt and decrypt a message. Symmetrical algorithms use the same key to encrypt and decrypt the message. See Figure 18-1.

Figure 18-1 *A Symmetrical Algorithm Encrypts Traffic*

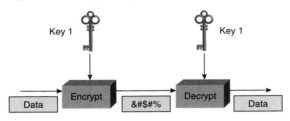

An *asymmetrical* algorithm is loosely defined as an algorithm that uses a pair of keys to securely encrypt and decrypt a message. Asymmetrical algorithms use one key to encrypt and a different, but related, key to decrypt. See Figure 18-2.

Figure 18-2 *An Asymmetrical Algorithm Encrypts Traffic*

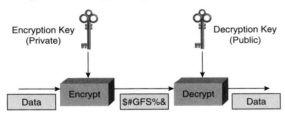

Some common symmetrical algorithms are the 56-bit Data Encryption Standard (DES), the 168-bit 3DES, and the 128- or 256-bit Advanced Encryption Standard (AES). All of these algorithms use the same key to encrypt and decrypt the information.

Advantages of symmetrical algorithms include the following:

- They are very fast at encrypting bulk amounts of information.
- The key length is usually 40 to 168 bits.
- Mathematical computations are easy to implement in hardware, so offloading the processing can be done cheaply and easily.
- The sender and receiver share the same passwords. The problem with shared passwords is how to get the key from one device to the other. If the key is sent across an untrusted network, you run the risk of it being sniffed and captured by a hacker. If you phone the technician at the other end, you run the risk of phone tapping. As you progress through this chapter, you will see that key management can be a major concern for security.

Asymmetrical algorithms do not usually have as many problems with key management. One key is usually kept private and the other key is public and given to everyone that needs to decrypt the data.

Asymmetrical algorithms are usually called private and public key algorithms or public key systems. Some typical asymmetrical algorithms are RSA, ElGamal, and elliptic curves.

The following are some advantages of asymmetrical algorithms:

- They are great for use in authentication because one key is always private (you are the only one with that key).

- Key management is easier (one key is public to everyone).

- They can be used for digital signatures, authenticated key exchanges, e-mail, or small amounts of data.

- They are based on very hard mathematical equations.

The disadvantage to the public key system is that it is usually very slow encrypting information compared to symmetrical encryption. Therefore, it is used to encrypt session keys and small amounts of data, such as e-mail messages.

Hashing Algorithms

A hashing algorithm is loosely defined as a one-way algorithm that produces a fixed-length output no matter what size the input variable is. Hashing algorithms are used for integrity assurance. They are based on some type of one-way hashing function.

Consider the following analogy of a hashing algorithm. You get a standard blender, three small oranges, and three big oranges. You put all the oranges in the blender and make juice out of them. When you pour it into a cup, you get one glass of juice. If your neighbor were to get the same blender, three small oranges, and three big oranges and do the same process, they would also get one glass of juice.

A hashing algorithm takes any input and massages it until it gets a fixed-length output. As long as you use the same input (the oranges) and the same algorithm (blend oranges after putting them into the blender), you always get the same output. You can never reverse-engineer the answer to get the original input, just as you can't put together the orange juice to determine that three big and three small oranges went into the blender to make the glass of juice.

Two common hashing algorithms are MD5, which gives you a fixed-length 128-bit output, and SHA-1, which gives you a fixed-length 160-bit output.

These are the qualities you want to look for in a good hashing algorithm:

- It has high resistance to cryptographic attack.

- Any change to the clear-text input results in a large change to the encrypted output.

- The probability of collision (two different inputs giving the same output) is low.

MD5 is considered OK for today's environments, but SHA-1 is preferred because it is less likely to result in a collision.

Diffie-Hellman Key Exchange

In a VPN network, fast, strong, encryption is a must. That is why most implementations use a symmetrical algorithm to do payload encryption. As discussed earlier, the problem with symmetrical algorithms is key management. The Diffie-Hellman key exchange can help to solve this. It is used for automatic secure key exchange of symmetrical keys (and other types of keys) across an insecure network for the IPSec protocol suite.

A very simplified view of how Diffie-Hellman works is as follows (also see Figure 18-3): Tammy has a paint can and puts 1 liter of her favorite color in it. Bob has a paint can and puts 1.5 liters of his favorite color in it. A shared color is chosen and both parties add 1.1 liters of the shared color to their paint can. The paint cans are exchanged and both parties add their original favorite colors in the same quantity to the other person's paint can. Both paint cans now have the same color: 1 liter of Tammy's color plus 1.1 liters of the shared color plus 1.5 liters of Bob's color. For a detailed description of the Diffie-Hellman key exchange, see RFC 2412.

Figure 18-3 *Simplified Diagram of the Diffie-Hellman Exchange*

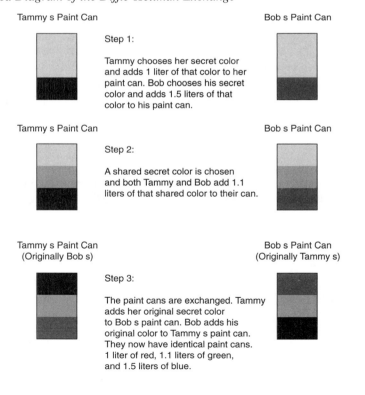

Current Cisco IOS software supports a Diffie-Hellman key size of 768 bits or 1024 bits. Larger key sizes are being added in future revisions of Cisco IOS code.

IPSec Overview

IPSec was designed to work at Layers 3 and 4 of the OSI model. With the different options that IPSec offers, you can authenticate, check for data integrity, and encrypt the payload portion of an IP packet. IPSec's main goals are data confidentiality, data integrity, and origin authentication between a pair of gateways, pair of hosts, or a host and its gateway. Optionally, if the receiver checks for antireplay, IPSec will also provide replay protection services.

There are two primary protocols in the IPSec standard: protocol 51 is Authentication Header (AH) and protocol 50 is Encapsulating Security Protocol (ESP). The next few sections will help describe what makes up the IPSec protocol suite.

Authentication Header

AH is used to provide data integrity and authentication. It does not provide any form of encryption to the payload of the packet. AH uses a keyed one-way hash function (also called an HMAC) such as MD5 or SHA-1 to guarantee the integrity and origin of the packet. Optionally, it can provide antireplay protection.

When you use the AH functionality, the entire IP packet is put through a one-way hash function. This includes the IP header, which could lead to problems. Any field that changes in transit, such as the TTL field, must be zeroized to give a "standard header" so that both sides will be able to use it as a standard input in the one-way hash function. The hash output is used to create a new AH header for the packet, and the new packet can now be transmitted (see Figure 18-4).

Figure 18-4 *Creation of an AH Header*

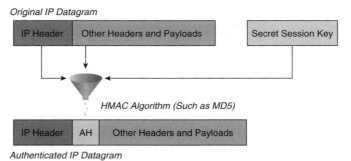

Encapsulating Security Payload

ESP is primarily used to provide payload encryption. With the current revisions of the RFC for ESP, it also includes the ability to provide authentication and integrity.

Because ESP can do all the services needed in a secure VPN network (including optional AHs services), most implementations do not include any AH options. When the IPSec standard was created, its developers took into account the need for increased security. Therefore, IPSec can use different algorithms for payload encryption, such as DES to give you 56-bit encryption or 3DES to give you 168-bit encryption. As the need for stronger payload encryption arises, the standard will allow vendors to implement other algorithms.

Tunnel Mode Versus Transport Mode

Both ESP and AH can operate in two different modes (see Figures 18-5 and 18-6): tunnel mode (default for Cisco) or transport mode. In tunnel mode, the original packet is put through the ESP and/or AH options and then a new IP header is created for the new packet, which is a combination of the original packet plus ESP and/or AH information plus a new IP header. In transport mode, the original packet is put through the ESP and/or AH options and then the original IP header is reused with the packet, which would be the original packet plus added information from ESP and/or AH.

Figure 18-5 *AH Header in Tunnel or Transport Mode*

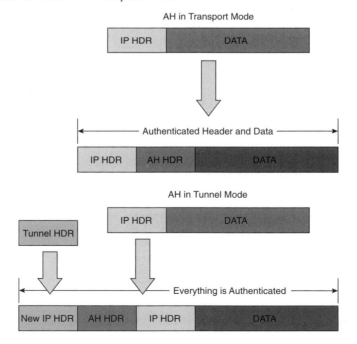

Figure 18-6 *ESP Header in Tunnel or Transport Mode*

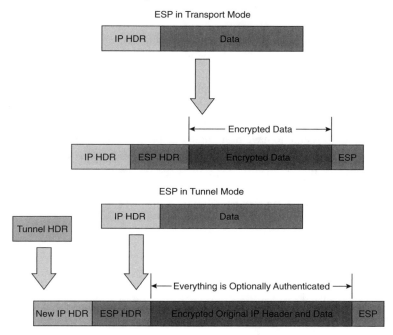

If a packet is sent in transport mode, the current IP header has been used in the hashing algorithm and therefore cannot be changed from sender to receiver. If the packet goes through any device that performs something such as NAT or PAT, then a portion of the current IP header is changed and you will never have the same hash output, because you have different inputs at the sender and receiver ends. Therefore, the packet will never be validated at the receiving end.

Transport mode should be used only if you have control of the network from end to end and can guarantee that no IP packet header manipulation will take place. When in tunnel mode, a new IP header is used from gateway device to gateway device and the original packet is tunneled inside. Once the receiving end receives the packet, it pops off the new header and runs the decryption and hashing with the original header; therefore, the new tunnel header can get manipulated throughout the network without affecting the tunneled payload.

Security Associations

To this point, you have looked at some of the different pieces that make up the IPSec protocol suite. When you make an IPSec connection between different devices, there are many parts that have to be looked after such as what type of encryption you will be using, checking for authentication and integrity, how long do your keys last, and many other options. Before an IPSec tunnel can be created, all of these parameters must be negotiated and kept track of.

In every VPN device, you need to have some form of a security policy database (SPD). This information is referred to as a Security Association (SA).

An SA is a single connection and all the parameters associated with it that are agreed upon by the two devices participating in the exchange. Each SA is unidirectional, so you will always have at least two SAs in your SPD: one SA from device A to device B and the reciprocal SA from device B to device A. It is quite possible to have more than one peer in a VPN network, such as a VPN concentrator at the head office and many clients traveling the world, so you also need to identify each individual SA so that its specific characteristics are verified for each packet. Each SA gets a unique 32-bit Security Parameter Index number that is sent in every packet pertaining to the specific SA. The SA is made up of the SA database and the SPD and keeps track of general information such as the following:

- Source IP address
- Destination IP address
- IPSec protocols used
- SPI number
- Encryption and authentication algorithms
- Key lifetime (sets the amount of time and/or byte count that a key is valid for; the longer the time, the more vulnerable your data is)

Internet Key Exchange

Internet Key Exchange (IKE) is used to establish all the information needed for a VPN tunnel. Within IKE, you negotiate your security policies, establish your SAs, and create and exchange your keys that will be used by other algorithms such as DES.

IKE is broken down into two phases, described next.

Phase One of IKE

Phase one is used to negotiate policy sets, authenticate peers, and create a secure channel between peers.

A standard policy set would look like the information in Table 18-2.

Table 18-2 *Policy Set in Phase One*

Parameter	Strong	Stronger
Encryption algorithm	DES	3DES
Hash algorithm	MD5	SHA-1
Authentication method	Preshared	RSA signatures
Key exchange	Diffie-Hellman group 1	Diffie-Hellman group 2
IKE SA lifetime	86,400 seconds	less than 86,400 seconds

IKE phase one can happen in one of two modes, main mode or aggressive mode. The major difference is that in main mode, three different and distinct exchanges take place to add to the security of the tunnel, whereas in aggressive mode everything is sent in a single exchange.

Phase Two of IKE

IKE phase two is used to negotiate the IPSec security parameters (such as the IPSec transform sets), establish SAs, and optionally perform additional Diffie-Hellman exchanges. IKE phase two has only one mode, called quick mode, which happens only after IKE phase one has completed.

Preparing for IKE and IPSec

There are five basic steps to setting up an IPSec tunnel:

Step 1   Define interesting traffic that should be protected.

Step 2   Perform IKE phase 1—negotiate the security policy, etc.

Step 3   Perform IKE phase 2—negotiate SAs, etc.

Step 4   Transfer data—encrypt interesting traffic and send it to peer devices.

Step 5   Tear down the tunnel.

If you are considering running IPSec on some of your network devices, it is strongly recommended that you plan your implementation thoroughly before you proceed. Here are some of the questions you will need to answer:

■ Do my current access lists applied to my interfaces allow ESP, AH, and IKE to terminate on the router?

■ What interesting traffic needs to be encrypted?

- What IKE phase one policies can I support?
- What IKE phase two policies will be implemented?
- Does the network route properly before I add encryption services? (Can I ping?)

Setting Up IKE

Once you have gathered the background information, you are ready to configure IKE on your routers. Here are the basic steps:

Step 1   Enable or disable IKE.

Step 2   Create IKE policies.

Step 3   Configure your ISAKMP identity.

Step 4   Configure preshared keys.

Step 5   Verify the IKE configuration.

By default, IKE is enabled in Cisco IOS software. If it was turned off manually, then you need to enable it. This can be done as a global configuration command:

```
R1(config)#crypto isakmp enable
```

You then create your isakmp policies. The lower the number of the policy, the more preferred it is. You might have many policies on one device because each remote peer could have a different security profile created. For example, your R&D lab would probably have high security settings applied, such as 3DES for payload encryption and SHA-1 for authentication and integrity. A shipping office might only have MD5 authentication and integrity checking turned on and no payload encryption, because it may not matter whether your competitors know how many items you are shipping. These are the router commands to create a policy:

```
R1(config)#crypto isakmp policy {policy number}
```

You are now in an isakmp subconfiguration mode and you can apply all options for your phase one IKE policy:

```
R1(config-iskamp)#
```

Your options for an isakmp policy are shown in Table 18-3.

Table 18-3 *Options for an isakmp Policy*

Option	Value (one choice from each section)
Peer authentication	Preshare, RSA nonces, or RSA signatures
Encryption algorithm	DES or 3DES
Integrity and authentication algorithm	SHA-1 or MD5
Key exchange parameters	Group 1 or group 2
Lifetime	Time in seconds

Next, you need to configure your identity for use when authenticating peers during IKE phase one. Decide whether you want to use IP addresses or host names and use them consistently throughout your entire network configurations.

> **CAUTION**   If you use host names and your DNS fails to resolve the host name, your tunnels may fail! You have two options to overcome this:
>
> 1. Use the actual IP addresses of all devices.
> 2. Create a local hosts table and assign a local IP to name resolution.

Here is the router command to set the identity of the router in a VPN scenario:

```
R1(config)#crypto isakmp identity {address | hostname}
```

After you have set your crypto identity, you must specify preshared keys if this is the option you have chosen in your security policy.

Here is the router command to set the key to be used with a specific VPN peer:

```
R1(config)#crypto isakmp key {key} address {ip address}
```

or

```
R1(config)#crypto isakmp key {key} hostname {name}
```

Now that you have configured the IKE parameters, you should double-check your configuration.

Here is the router command to display all isakmp policies or a specific one:

```
R1#show crypto isakmp policy {policy number}
```

Setting Up IPSec

After you have IKE configured, you only have to worry about what traffic you are sending across the VPN tunnel and how it is protected. The three basic steps for configuring IPSec are as follows:

Step 1   Configure the transform sets to be used.

Step 2   Configure the global IPSec SA lifetimes (optional).

Step 3   Create your crypto access lists to specify interesting traffic.

After you complete those basic steps, you need to tie the whole configuration together with a crypto map and then apply it to the appropriate interface.

Creating Transform Sets

The transform set defines the type of authentication, integrity, and payload encryption you will be using for your VPN tunnel. Depending on your security policy, you can choose what type of algorithms will be applied to the data for a specific connection. You could choose just authentication and integrity by selecting only AH, or you could choose payload encryption, authentication, and integrity by selecting two ESP options, or you could have the strongest security by adding AH and ESP options.

When you create your transform sets, you have the options that are outlined in Table 18-4.

Table 18-4   *Options Available to Create a Transform Set for the VPN Tunnel*

Transform Type	AH Transform (Pick up to one)	ESP Encryption Transform (Pick up to one)	ESP Authentication Transform (Pick up to one)
Allowed Transform Options	ah-md5-hmac ah-sha-hmac	esp-des esp-3des esp-null	esp-md5-hmac esp-sha-hmac

Here is the router command to create an IPSec transform set:

```
R1(config)#crypto ipsec transform-set {transform-set-name} {transform1} [transform2
[transform3]]
```

Specifying SA Lifetimes

The next step, which is optional, is to specify a global SA lifetime that will be used by every crypto map that you do not specifically enter these values for.

Here is the router command to set a security lifetime in seconds or kilobytes:

```
R1(config)#crypto ipsec security-association lifetime {seconds seconds | kilobytes
kilobytes}
```

Specifying Crypto Access Lists

At this point, you have configured how all of the traffic will be encrypted and transported and what your peers will use as session keys. All that is left is to specify "interesting traffic" to be encrypted by your tunnel. This is done by using extended access lists.

The crypto access list does not "permit" or "deny" traffic as a normal access list does; it is to define what is encrypted "permit" or not encrypted "denied" in your VPN tunnel. All traffic still flows from device to device unless a different access list is applied with the **access-group** command on an interface.

The crypto access lists must be mirror images of each other. For example, if router A encrypts all TCP traffic to router B, router B must encrypt all TCP traffic back to router A.

Here is the router command to create an "interesting traffic" access list:

```
R1(config)# access-list {access-list-number} permit {protocol} {source-address}
{wildcard-mask}[port] {destination-address} {wildcard-mask} [port]
```

Here is an example of it in use:

```
R1(config)#access-list 101 permit tcp 10.1.1.0 0.0.0.255 10.2.2.0 0.0.0.255
```

Crypto Maps

Now that you have all the required information to create your VPN tunnel, you need to pull everything together and apply it to an interface. You use a crypto map to do this. The crypto map specifies:

- The traffic protected (crypto access list)
- Where the IPSec traffic should be sent (peer statement)
- The IPSec transform set used (transform-set)
- Use of manual or IKE exchanged keys, etc. (stated in the crypto map type)
- The Security Association lifetime (optional)

There are a few types of crypto map statements. For this exam, we cover an ipsec-isakmp crypto map for automatic key exchanges. There are other crypto maps if you want to do key exchanges manually or to a dynamic client, etc. Refer to the article, "IPSec (IP Security Protocol)" at Cisco.com for more detailed information on the types of crypto maps available.

Here is the router command to create a crypto map:

```
R1(config)#crypto map {map-name} {seq-num} {ipsec-isakmp}
```

Here is an example of it in use:

```
R1(config)#crypto map to-branch-office 10 ipsec-isakmp
```

This takes you into a crypto map subconfiguration mode, in which you can enter the specifics pertaining to this crypto map:

```
R1(config-crypto-map)#match address {access-list-number}
R1(config-crypto-map)#set peer {ip-address | hostname}
R1(config-crypto-map)#set transform-set name
R1(config-crypto-map)#set pfs {group1 | group2}
R1(config-crypto-map)#set security-association lifetime
```

After you have specified all the needed information in your crypto map, you need to apply it to the outgoing interface. If you have multiple remote sites, you can apply only one crypto map per interface. Therefore, you must make a single crypto map with different sequence numbers.

Here are the router commands to create a multisite VPN connection:

```
R1(config)#crypto map multi-site 10 ipsec-isakmp
R1(config-crypto-map)#set peer address-for-site1
R1(config)#crypto map multi-site 20 ipsec-isakmp
R1(config-crypto-map)#set peer address-for-site2
```

You can then apply the crypto map to the specific interface.

Here are the router commands to apply the crypto map to an interface:

```
R1(config)#interface ethernet 1/1
R1(config-if)#crypto map multi-site
```

Testing and Verifying Configuration

Once you have finished your configuration, it is extremely important to test and verify that the proper information is being encrypted and transmitted. Some of the common troubleshooting commands are described next.

The **show crypto isakmp policy** command shows you all the configured policies that you will try to negotiate and then the default policy settings at the end.

> **TIP** Always organize your policies from most secure to least secure. Assign your most secure policy the lowest policy value, because any device trying to connect will match on the first possible policy.

The **show crypto ipsec transform-set** command shows you every transform set that you have created on the router.

The **show crypto ipsec sa** command shows you the settings used by current security associations.

The **show crypto map** command shows you all the crypto maps configured on the router so that you can see what transform sets, peer devices, and crypto access lists are used.

Every IPSec packet processed by the router will generate output with the **debug crypto ipsec** command.

When you are having problems with SA establishment and peer authentication, the **debug crypto isakmp** command can be very helpful, because it shows you information about every packet dealing with IKE phase one or two.

Foundation Summary

This section is a collection of information that provides a convenient review of many key concepts in this chapter. If you are already comfortable with the topics in this chapter, this summary can help you recall a few details. If you just read this chapter, this review should help solidify some key facts. If you are doing your final preparation before the exam, these tables and figures are a convenient way to review the day before the exam.

This chapter covered the basic configuration of a site-to-site VPN router configuration. This is a very popular implementation because anyone who currently has remote offices can quickly bring up a VPN tunnel and remove the cost of expensive, dedicated WAN links. The important things to remember when creating a VPN connection are as follows:

- An IPSec tunnel will not work if routing is not functioning properly. Test your connection between the two devices with a ping.

- An IPSec session must be able to terminate on the router, so any inbound access lists must be modified to allow for the appropriate IPSec protocols to enter the router. Examine the following code:

```
R1 (config)#access-list 101 permit udp host 1.1.1.1 eq isakmp host 2.2.2.2 eq isakmp
R1 (config)#access-list 101 permit esp host 1.1.1.1 host 2.2.2.2
R1 (config)#access-list 101 permit ah host 1.1.1.1 host 2.2.2.2
```

- ISAKMP is enabled on all interfaces by default. If it has been explicitly turned off, you need to re-enable it on the specific interface or globally on the entire router. These commands enable IKE/ISAKMP on the router:

```
R1(config)# crypto isakmp enable
R1(config)# crypto isakmp identity address
```

- You must create an identical ISAKMP policy on both devices, using the following:

```
R1(config)# crypto isakmp policy 110
R1(config-isakmp)# authentication pre-share
R1(config-isakmp)# group 1
R1(config-isakmp)# encryption 3des
rP(config-isakmp)# hash md5
rP(config-isakmp)# lifetime 86400
```

- You must assign the preshared key to the peer device, using the following:

```
R1(config)# crypto isakmp key THEKEY address 2.2.2.2
```

- You must decide on the transform set parameters and the tunnel mode. (Refer to Table 18-4 for the options in the transform set.)

```
R1(config)# crypto ipsec transform-set ESPDESONLYEXAMPLE esp-des
R1(cfg-crypto-trans)# mode tunnel
```

- You must define the interesting traffic to encrypt, using the following:

```
R1(config)# access-list 100 permit ip 10.1.0.0 0.0.0.255 10.2.0.0 0.0.0.255
```

■   After you have configured all the options, you must pull all the pieces together in a crypto map
statement and apply it to the outgoing interface:

```
R1(config)# crypto map DEVICE2DEVICE 10 ipsec-isakmp
R1(config-crypto-map)# match address 100
R1(config-crypto-map)# set transform-set ESPDESONLYEXAMPLE
R1(config-crypto-map)# set peer 2.2.2.2
R1(config)# interface Ethernet 0/0
R1(config-if)# crypto map DEVICE2DEVICE
```

After your configuration is complete, be sure to double-check to ensure your important data is truly
being encrypted.

Q&A

The questions and scenarios in this book are more difficult than what you will experience on the actual exam. The questions do not attempt to cover more breadth or depth than the exam, but they are designed to make sure that you know the answer. Rather than enabling you to derive the answer from clues hidden inside the question itself, the questions challenge your understanding and recall of the subject.

Hopefully, mastering these questions will help you limit the number of exam questions on which you narrow your choices to two options and then guess.

The answers to these questions can be found in Appendix A.

1. What options (and how many) would be used in a very strong transform set?

2. What are three common things provided by a VPN network?

3. Who could use a VPN solution?

4. What is a common trade-off in VPN networks?

5. What is the primary motivation for the use of IPSec?

6. Why should you order your isakmp policies from strongest to weakest?

7. When creating a hub-and-spoke VPN network topology, how do you configure the hub device to distinguish different traffic to be sent to different peers when you can apply only one crypto map per interface?

Answers to the "Do I Know This Already?" Quizzes and Q&A Sections

Chapter 1

"Do I Know This Already?" Quiz

1. Who is usually considered to be using remote access?

   Answer: d

2. What are some common considerations for remote access usage?

   Answer: e

3. What are the two main categories for Cisco's product lineup?

   Answers: a, c

4. Where does the Cisco 800 Series router fit into the product lineup?

   Answers: a, b

5. Where does the Cisco 2600 Series router fit into the product lineup?

   Answers: b, c

6. Where does the PIX 501 Firewall fit into the product lineup?

   Answers: a, d

7. What is the most common dedicated WAN connection?

   Answer: e

8. What is the typical maximum speed of an asynchronous dialup connection?

   Answer: d

9. What are three emerging WAN technologies?

   Answers: b, c, d

10. What are typical network growth estimates at a head office site?

    Answer: e

11. To save costs, fixed-configuration devices are used at the branch-office level.

    Answer: a

12. At home office or small office sites, what is the predominant deciding factor when choosing the connection type?

    Answer: c

13. What is the default interface queuing option on serial interfaces?

    Answer: b

14. What is a common problem with Priority Queuing?

    Answer: d

15. How many user-definable queues are available with Custom Queuing?

    Answer: d

Q&A

1. What are some of the considerations for remote access networks?

   Answer: Common considerations are availability of the desired technology, the monthly recurring cost versus the bandwidth available, reliability, and the need for backup. All of these are common considerations, but cost versus speed is the primary deciding factor.

2. Why are modular chassis preferred over a fixed configuration?

   Answer: With a fixed-configuration device, you are forced to do a "forklift" upgrade, where you completely remove the old device and replace it with something that supports the new technology.

3. What is the difference between traffic shaping and traffic policing?

Answer: Traffic policing actually drops traffic above a certain rate, whereas traffic shaping simply limits the flow of traffic.

4. How does Custom Queuing work?

Answer: The administrator can configure up to 16 different queues and then specify how many bytes are sent from each. Each queue is serviced in a round-robin format.

5. Why is queuing only put on links that spike to 100 percent utilization and not on every single link?

Answer: If a link is at 100 percent utilization, queuing does not give you more bandwidth; the only solution is to increase the speed of the link. A link that never hits 100 percent utilization transfers all traffic all the time, so there is no need for queuing. Only links that spike to 100 percent utilization for short periods of time need queuing to smooth out the traffic.

6. What advantages does using wireless WAN links offer the designer?

Answer: Wireless networking overcomes the limitations of copper/fiber wires. Wireless is easy to deploy and you do not need to own the "right of way" between two points to connect the networks together.

Chapter 2

"Do I Know This Already?" Quiz

1. Which of the following best describes some telecommunications parameters for a central office?

Answer: b. Redundancy is normally required at a central site, because being off line is costly and not optional.

2. Which of the following link connection speeds is considered appropriate for a remote office?

Answer: d. With 100 users, a smaller connection would be inadequate. And a large connection with too few users is expensive.

3. Which of the following terms describes whether a service provider is capable of providing a service in your area?

Answer: c. Availability defines whether a service or connection option is offered by any local carrier.

4. How does QoS affect the flow of packets?

Answer: a. QoS is where the administrator defines which traffic gets to leave the router first.

5. Which connection option guarantees consistent bandwidth availability all the time?

Answer: b. A leased line offers a steady amount of bandwidth all the time. Even Frame Relay with a high CIR cannot guarantee traffic flow through the cloud.

6. What is the maximum speed of an ISDN BRI connection?

Answer: b. An ISDN BRI connection has a maximum of two bearer channels, which is 2×64 kbps, or 128 kbps.

7. Which of the following WAN connection methods establishes connections with an ISP instead of with another site?

Answer: d. DSL, like a cable modem, offers a connection directly to an ISP, and not to any specific destination.

8. What type of VPN link creates a tunnel between a PC and a router?

Answer: b. A VPN client is used to create an encrypted tunnel from a PC to a remote site (router, firewall, or VPN concentrator).

Q&A

1. Which type of site has the most diverse forms of WAN connections?

Answer: A central office needs to be able to terminate any type of connection from any ROBO or SOHO.

2. How is redundancy defined?

Answer: Redundancy is the ability to have a secondary connection to another site. Redundancy may also involve the duplication of equipment and services to ensure that connectivity is not disrupted.

3. What is the most important selection criteria at a SOHO?

   Answer: Cost is often the primary consideration at a SOHO.

4. Which design selection criteria adds cost yet reduces throughput?

   Answer: Security, such as access lists and encryption, increases cost due to additional equipment and configuration, but also reduces throughput because packets must now survive access list and/or be encrypted.

5. How many leased-line circuits can terminate on one router serial port?

   Answer: A leased line has a single circuit to a single destination.

6. The term "packet switching" describes which WAN access method?

   Answer: Frame Relay is a form of packet switching.

7. Which WAN access methods actually place phone calls from one location to another?

   Answer: ISDN is a digital calling option. Also, asynchronous dialup uses normal analog phone lines to place a call to a remote location.

8. Why is encryption important for a SOHO?

   Answer: Encryption (VPN tunnels) is a way to ensure that if the data falls into the wrong hands, it cannot be read, played back, or modified.

9. What is a host-to-host VPN?

   Answer: A host-to-host VPN is a VPN in which the routers/firewalls encrypt only specific streams of data between sites.

10. What type of connection technologies are more likely to require VPNs?

    Answer: A cable modem and DSL are permanent connections to an ISP, and thus a secure connection to a remote office or central office is needed.

Chapter 3

"Do I Know This Already?" Quiz

1. Which of the following routers is best used as a central-site router?

   Answer: d. 7206 has the CPU and slots available for many terminations.

2. Which of the following routers best serves as a small office or home office (SOHO) router for telecommuters?

    Answer: a. The 804 is a good SOHO router, with a four-port Ethernet hub and an ISDN WAN connection.

3. Which Cisco 800 Series router has a built-in DSL port?

    Answer: d. The 827 is the only 800 series router that is DSL-ready.

4. Which of the following Cisco SOHO/ROBO routers can use one or more WIC modules and has at least one network module (select 2)?

    Answers: b and e. The 3620 has two network modules that can accept WIC modules, and the 2621 can accept two WIC modules and one network module.

5. What type of port on a Cisco router is used to connect to a Frame Relay provider?

    Answer: b. A serial port is used for both Frame Relay and leased-line connections.

6. Which of the following WAN connection types use an Ethernet port to connect to the provider (select 2)?

    Answers: c and e. DSL uses an Ethernet port of a router to connect to the WAN provider. It could also use an integrated DSL interface on some routers. Cable modems use an Ethernet port of a router to connect to the WAN provider. They could also use an integrated F-connector interface on some routers.

7. Which of the following connection technologies use an RJ-45 port for connectivity (select 2)?

    Answers: b and d.

8. What does the DTR indicator on a serial interface mean?

    Answer: b.

9. When looking at the **show interfaces** display for a serial interface, which of the following conditions would cause the interface to be up/down?

    Answer: c. On a serial interface, up/down could be caused by a mismatched encapsulation, a missing clock rate, or an overclocked DCE.

10. Which Cisco IOS command is used to verify the encapsulation type on any interface?

    Answer: b. The Cisco IOS command show interfaces **displays many interface parameters, including the encapsulation type.**

Q&A

1. At a central site where LAN and WAN access and hundreds of dialup ports are required, which type of routers works best?

   Answer: A 5400 offers hundreds of dialup ports, as well as both LAN and WAN access.

2. Which central-site router comes with 2 10/100-Mbps auto-sensing Ethernet ports built into the chassis?

   Answer: The 3662 has two built-in 10/100-Mbps Ethernet ports.

3. If a 3640 router is procured for use at a central site, but no modules are initially purchased, how can the router be used?

   Answer: The only ports that a 3640 comes with are the console and auxiliary interfaces. The router does not have any network connectivity by default.

4. Which SOHO router can be rack-mounted?

   Answer: The 1760 is the only 1700 Series router that can be rack-mounted. All other 800s and 1700s need shelves to sit on.

5. How many serial ports are needed on a ROBO router that uses Frame Relay to connect to three other locations, including the central office?

   Answer: Frame Relay uses only one port to connect to multiple remote locations, each on a unique virtual circuit.

6. How many serial ports are needed on a central-office router that uses Frame Relay to connect to three other locations?

   Answer: Regardless of which site it is, Frame Relay uses only one port to connect to multiple remote locations, each on a unique virtual circuit.

7. The central office has decided to get PPP links between itself and each of the five remote sites. The remote sites are each connected to the central site. How many serial ports are needed at the central site?

    Answer: Because point-to-point circuits have been selected, each circuit needs a serial port to terminate on. Thus, the central site needs five serial ports to talk to the five remote sites.

8. How many ROBO and SOHO locations can a T1 PRI interface on a central router connect to simultaneously?

    Answer: A T1 PRI offers 23 B channels and thus can have 23 simultaneous 64-kbps connections.

9. Which SOHO router can be used to directly terminate a DSL connection?

    Answer: The 827 SOHO router has a built-in ADSL interface.

10. Which WAN connection methods use a serial port to connect to the provider?

    Answer: Both Frame Relay and leased lines (such as PPP and HDLC) use serial ports on Cisco routers.

11. Which condition would cause an Ethernet interface to be up/down?

    Answer: A mispinned cable (bad cable) could lead to the interface being physically up, but logically down.

12. Which conditions would cause a serial interface to be up/down?

    Answer: A variety of issues could cause a serial interface to be up/down. There could be a speed mismatch (speed too fast for the cable); an encapsulation mismatch; a missing clock rate; or a mispinned cable (bad cable).

13. What type of connector and what pins are used for an ISDN BRI connection?

    Answer: ISDN BRI interfaces use the middle two pins (4 and 5) of an RJ-45 connector to connect to the telephone company.

Chapter 4

"Do I Know This Already?" Quiz

1. What pins are used for modem control?

   Answer: c

2. What is the standard for DCE/DTE signaling?

   Answer: a

3. In character mode using reverse Telnet, what is the command to connect to the first async port on a 2509 router that has a loopback interface of 192.168.1.1?

   Answer: b

4. What port range is reserved for accessing an individual port using binary mode?

   Answer: c

5. If a four-port serial (A/S) module is in the second slot (slot 1) on a 3640 router, what are the line numbers for each port?

   Answer: a

6. What is the AUX port line number on a 3620 Series router?

   Answer: b

7. On what interface would you apply the **physical-layer async** command?

   Answer: a

8. In what configuration mode must you be to configure the physical properties of an asynchronous interface?

   Answer: b

9. When should **modem autoconfigure discovery** be used?

   Answer: a

10.   Which of the following commands would you use to add an entry to a modemcap database called newmodem?

Answer: b

11.   Which of the following is *not* a reason to use a chat script?

Answer: d

12.   Which of the following would, by default, trigger a chat script to start?

Answer: d

Q&A

1.   If the user wants to terminate a call, what pin does the DTE device drop to signal the modem?

It drops the DTR signal pin.

2.   What must be done to terminate a reverse Telnet session with an attached modem?

You must press Ctrl-Shift-6, press x, and then execute a disconnect **command.**

3.   Which interface is line 97 on a 3640 Series router?

Line 97 corresponds to slot 3, line 1, which is written as S 2/1.

4.   When flow control is enabled, which pins are used?

The RTS and CTS pins are used.

5.   What is the AT command to return a router to its factory default settings?

The AT&F **command**

6.   Which interface type provides clocking for a line?

DCE provides clocking for a line.

7.   What command lists the transmit and receive speeds for the asynchronous ports on the router?

show line

8.   On which pins does the DTE device send and receive?

It transmits on pin 2 and receives on pin 3.

9. What is the command to manually begin a chat script named remcon?

    The command is start-script remcon.

10. With asynchronous communication, how many pins are used in a DB25 to transfer data and control the modem?

    Eight

11. On what does the DTE device raise the voltage when it has buffer space available to receive from the DCE device?

    The RTS

12. In most cases, when the DTE device is powered on, which pin is raised?

    The DTR pin

13. With what type of bits do most modem consoles operate?

    Most modem consoles operate using eight data bits, zero parity bits, and one stop bit.

14. To configure a modem (the DCE) from a router (the DTE), what parameters must you set up for the connection?

    To configure the modem (the DCE) from the router (the DTE), you must set up the logical and physical parameters for the connection.

Chapter 5

"Do I Know This Already?" Quiz

1. Where is PPP typically deployed?

    Answers: a, c, d

2. What is the difference between interactive and dedicated asynchronous implementations?

    Answer: b

3. Which RFC deals with assigned numbers and protocol types?

    Answer: b

4. Which command assigns a preassigned IP address to an async dialup user?

Answer: b

5. Which two are supported authentication types with PPP on Cisco routers?

Answers: b, c

6. Which PPP option is typically used to provide billing consolidation by entities with dialup users?

Answer: b

7. Which PPP option is typically used on low-speed WAN links in an effort to improve throughput?

Answer: a

8. What encryption algorithm is used in CHAP authentication?

Answer: b

Q&A

1. List the two major components of the PPP architecture.

Answer: LCP and NCP

2. For what reason is it unnecessary to utilize any sort of protocol map commands on a PPP interface?

Answer: PPP is point-to-point. No mappings are necessary because there is no other possible endpoint that could be utilized.

3. List the available PPP LCP options.

Answer: Authentication, Callback, Compression, Multilink

4. If the authentication methodologies on opposite sides of a single link are not configured, what will happen?

Answer: The connection attempt will fail.

5. What command should be issued on a remote access router to keep dialup users from being able to access the user mode prompt?

    Answer: async mode dedicated

6. What encryption algorithm is used in CHAP authentication?

    Answer: MD5

7. What encryption algorithm is used in PAP authentication?

    Answer: None

8. What is one potential security danger in using PAP authentication?

    Answer: Playback attack

9. What happens in the event of a CHAP authentication failure?

    Answer: If the authentication fails, a CHAP failure packet is constructed. It contains a CHAP failure message type and the ID from the response packet. Indication of success or failure is then sent to the calling party.

10. What protocols can traverse a PPP link, and how are they differentiated?

    Answer: Any protocol can traverse a PPP link. There is a 2-byte field in the header that indicates the protocol encapsulated in the payload section of the frame. The most up-to-date values of the Protocol field are specified in the most recent Assigned Numbers RFC. At press time, this was RFC 1700. For more information, see www.isi.edu/in-notes/rfc1700.txt.

Chapter 6

"Do I Know This Already?" Quiz

1. What is the function of LCP (select 2)?

    Answers: b, d

2. Which are PPP LCP negotiable options?

    Answer: e

3. If there is a mismatch in the LCP negotiation, what will happen to the connection?

    Answer: b

4. In PPP Callback implementations, which router is in charge of the authentication challenge and the disconnect of the initial call?

    Answer: a

5. Which LCP option is used to add additional bandwidth to a link capacity as needed and available?

    Answer: d

6. What command shows the status of individual B channels at any given time?

    Answer: b

7. What command enables the real-time viewing of CHAP communications?

    Answer: d

8. What command enables the real-time viewing of dial events?

    Answer: a

Q&A

1. List at least three protocols that can traverse a PPP link.

    Answer: IP, IPX, AppleTalk

2. What is the function of the PPP LCP?

    Answer: The PPP LCP provides a method of establishing, configuring, maintaining, and terminating the point-to-point connection.

3. List the three LCP frame types and their functions.

    Answer: Link-establishment frames are used to establish and configure a link.

    Link-termination frames are used to terminate a link.

    Link-maintenance frames are used to manage and debug a link.

4. List the four PPP LCP options.

    Answer: Authentication, Callback, Compression, and Multilink

5. A PPP Callback router can perform one of two roles. List each and its function.

    Answer: PPP Callback routers can play two roles, that of the callback client and that of the callback server. The client router passes authentication (PAP or CHAP) information to the server router, which in turn analyzes dial string and host name information to determine whether callback is authorized.

6. Where is compression most useful?

    Answer: Compression is most useful on slower-speed links.

7. List the Cisco-supported compression algorithms.

    Answer: STAC, Predictor, MPPC, and TCP header compression

8. If PPP Multilink is not enabled and the **dialer load-threshold** command is entered, will multiple channels be utilized if the threshold is reached? Why/Why not?

    Answer: Yes. The Cisco BOD algorithm will be utilized.

9. If an ISDN call completes successfully and then suddenly disconnects, what is a likely problem?

    Answer: An ISDN call can complete and then suddenly disconnect if there is an LCP option mismatch such as authentication configured improperly or not at all on one side or the other.

10. If IP and AppleTalk are successfully traversing a PPP link while at the same time IPX transmissions fail, what is a possible cause?

    Answer: It is possible that IPX has not been properly configured on the remote end of the link, therefore it doesn't traverse. PPP is obviously configured properly because the connection is up and other protocols traverse successfully.

Chapter 7

"Do I Know This Already?" Quiz

1. Which are the two most common implementations of ISDN?

    Answers: a, d

2. What type of information is carried over the D channel?

    Answer: d

3. Which are the specifications that define Layer 2 and Layer 3 of ISDN?

    Answers: c, d

4. When is it necessary to use **dialer in-band** in an ISDN BRI configuration?

    Answer: d

5. Which two state the difference between a router with a BRI S/T interface and one with a BRI U interface?

    Answers: a, d

6. Which command defines only Telnet as interesting traffic for DDR?

    Answer: b

7. Which is the most common encapsulation in use on BRI interfaces?

    Answer: a

8. An interface that has been configured not to send routing updates is known as what type of interface?

    Answer: d

Q&A

1. How is ISDN different from traditional POTS lines?

   Answer: ISDN replaces traditional analog POTS equipment and wiring schemes with higher-speed digital equipment. The transition from POTS to ISDN changes the way connections at the local loop area are processed.

2. A single bearer channel provides how much bandwidth?

   Answer: 64,000 bps

3. A D channel provides how much bandwidth?

   Answer: 16,000 bps

4. A typical 2B+D implementation utilizes how much total bandwidth overall?

   Answer: 192,000 bps (128,000-bps B channel, 16,000-bps D channel, and 48,000-bps additional overhead).

5. If a router has an interface labeled "BRI U," is an external NT1 necessary to provide the proper connectivity?

   Answer: No. BRI U indicates the presence of an integrated NT1, whereas BRI S/T indicates the need for an external NT1.

6. The **dialer in-band** command is necessary in what circumstance?

   Answer: The dialer in-band **command is necessary in non-native ISDN implementations where the router does not have a BRI interface.**

7. If the **isdn switch-type** command is enter incorrectly, what steps are necessary to correct it?

   Answer: The correct switch type must be entered, the configuration saved, and the router reloaded.

8. What command is used to verify the status of the ISDN layers and what will the output show for Layer 1 and Layer 2 if properly configured and connected to the CO switch?

   Answer: show isdn status **is the command. It will show Layer 1 status activated and Layer 2 will show** MULTIPLE_FRAME_ESTABLISHED. **The Layer 2 output will also show the negotiated TEI(s).**

9. What message is issued by the router to the ISDN switch to initiate a call?

   Answer: The router issues a setup message to the ISDN switch.

10. What message is issued by the router to the ISDN switch to terminate a call?

    Answer: The router issues a RELEASED message to the ISDN switch.

Chapter 8

"Do I Know This Already?" Quiz

1. If the command **ppp multilink** is not entered, what methodology for link aggregation will be utilized?

   Answer: a

2. If you want to use Multilink PPP or Bandwidth on Demand to force the initialization of additional B channels as the utilization of the link(s) already in use reaches approximately 60 percent, which command should you use?

   Answer: c

3. Which of the following is a standard for link aggregation?

   Answer: b

4. Which of the following could be specified under a dialer map-class configuration?

   Answer: a

5. When using the command **rotary-group 32**, what is the dialer interface that will be utilized?

   Answer: d

6. What is the minimum snapshot quiet period?

   Answer: c

7. Which command will designate the use of a two-hour quiet period on a snapshot routing server?

   Answer: b

8. Which command will force the quiet timer to zero and begin the routing update process in snapshot routing?

   Answer: b

Q&A

1. The load of a link is measured on what scale?

   Answer: 1–255

2. Multilink PPP serves what function?

   Answer: Multilink PPP is a specification that enables the bandwidth aggregation of links into one logical pipe. Its mission is comparable to that of Cisco's BoD. More specifically, the Multilink PPP feature provides load-balancing functionality over multiple WAN links, while providing multivendor interoperability, packet fragmentation and proper sequencing, and load calculation on both inbound and outbound traffic.

3. What command can be issued to view the current load of interface Serial 0?

   Answer: show interfaces serial 0

4. What is the principle benefit of dialer profiles?

   Answer: Dialer profiles allow the configuration of logical interfaces separate from the actual physical interfaces that receive or make calls. The separation of the physical and logical interfaces allows multiple physical interfaces to be shared by multiple dialer profile configurations. The logical definition of the differing interfaces can be bound dynamically to one or more physical interfaces on a per-call basis.

5. In the absence of a dialer map statement, what can be used to define the phone number of the remote side of an ISDN link?

   Answer: The dialer string **command**

6. What commands would be entered to bind interfaces Bri 0, Bri 1, and Bri 2 to a common logical interface numbered 24? In the code that is your answer, also assign the IP address of 10.1.1.1/16 to the logical interface.

Answer:

interface BRI0

dialer pool 24

!

interface BRI1

dialer pool-member 24

!

interface BRI2

dialer pool-member 24

!

interface Dialer24

dialer pool 24

7. What is the purpose of a rotary group and how does it differ from a dialer pool configuration?

Answer: ISDN rotary groups are similar to dialer pools. One primary difference, however, is the lack of map class capabilities in rotary groups. The basic concept involves associating multiple physical interfaces with a single logical interface. When a call is placed, the member physical interfaces are scanned and the first available B channel is initialized. According to the needs of the traffic flow, and the capabilities of the remote side, additional B channels can be initialized, provided that there are available channels. The initialization of additional channels also assumes the presence of a Multilink PPP or Cisco BoD configuration.

8. What are the two roles a router can fulfill in snapshot routing?

Answer: **Snapshot server or snapshot client**

9. What are the periods in which a routing table can be placed when utilizing snapshot routing?

Answer: **Quiet and active**

10. What is the minimum active period?

Answer: **5 minutes**

Chapter 9

"Do I Know This Already?" Quiz

1. What information is required of the telco to implement PRI implementations?

Answer: **d**

2. Which are options available for T1 framing and line code configuration?

Answers: **b, c, d**

3. Which command configures the router to forward all incoming voice calls to internal MICA technology modems?

Answer: **b**

4. Which command is useful in viewing the state of Layers 1, 2, and 3 of ISDN simultaneously?

Answer: **b**

5. Which lists the number of bearer channels for BRI, T1 PRI, and E1 PRI?

Answer: **b**

6. Which command details the reason for the call as well as the B channels in use at a given time?

Answer: **c**

7. Which command allows the real-time viewing of the connection phase of a PPP session?

Answer: **d**

8. If a TEI is not properly negotiated, which command can be issued to view the message being exchanged between the router and switch at the appropriate layer?

   Answer: c

9. If a call setup is not properly completing, which command can be issued to view the messages being exchanged between the router and switch at the appropriate layer?

   Answer: d

Q&A

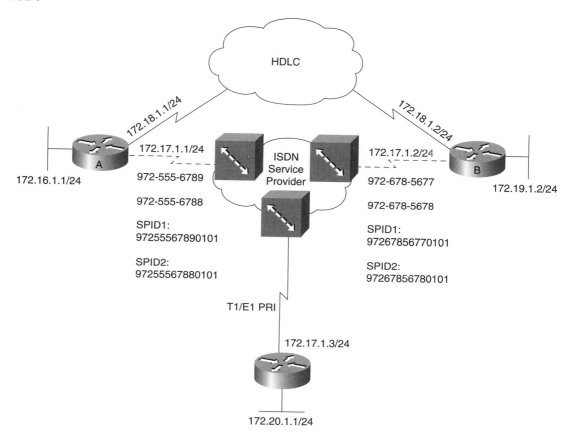

1. List the configuration commands necessary for router C to provide T1 PRI connectivity using B8ZS and ESF. Configure the appropriate IP addressing on interface S 0:23. It is not necessary to get into the PPP/DDR configurations.

    Answer:

    ```
    AS5300C(config)#controller t1 0/0
    AS5300C(config-controller)#pri-group timeslots 1-24
    AS5300C(config-controller)#framing esf
    AS5300C(config-controller)#linecode b8zs
    AS5300C(config-controller)#clock source line primary
    !
    AS5300C(config)#isdn switch-type primary-ni
    AS5300C(config)#interface serial 0/0:23
    AS5300C(config-if)#ip address 172.17.1.3  255.255.255.0
    AS5300C(config-if)#isdn incoming-voice modem
    ```

2. Now assume that router C is being implemented in an E1 environment using the default settings for framing and line code. Because there is only one option for framing (MultiFrame), it is not necessary to enter the command. Make the appropriate configuration changes and list them in your answer.

   Answer:

   ```
   AS5300C(config)#controller e1 0/0
   AS5300C(config-controller)#pri-group timeslots 1-30
   AS5300C(config-controller)#linecode hdb3
   AS5300C(config-controller)#clock source line primary
   !
   AS5300C(config)#isdn switch-type primary-ni
   AS5300C(config)#interface serial 0/0:16
   AS5300C(config-if)#ip address 172.17.1.3  255.255.255.0
   AS5300C(config-if)#isdn incoming-voice modem
   ```

3. Where is signaling information carried in T1 implementations?

   Answer: Signaling information is carried in the SF or ESF frame structure (i.e., in-band).

4. Where is signaling information carried in E1 implementations?

   Answer: Signaling information is carried in a signaling-specific time slot (#16) and is considered out-of-band.

5. What is the difference between SF and ESF?

   Answer: SF consists of 12 T1 frames and utilizes 8000-bps framing overhead. ESF consists of 24 T1 frames and utilizes 2000 bps for framing, 2000 bps for signaling, and 4000 bps for control functions. ESF is considered more desirable due to its management capabilities.

6. To redirect calls to a MICA modem upon arrival at a NAS, what command can be issued on the NAS?

   Answer: isdn incoming-voice modem

7. If an administrator were to feel the need to monitor call setup transactions, what command would be most useful?

   Answer: debug isdn q931

8. To view the number of ISDN connections currently active in a router and the number of B channels in use, what command would be most useful?

   Answer: show dialer

Chapter 10

"Do I Know This Already?" Quiz

1. Where is broadband typically implemented?

   Answer: a

2. Broadband cable technologies are based on which specification?

   Answer: d

3. How is a DOCSIS configuration file loaded onto a cable modem?

   Answer: d

4. Which orbit scheme allows a satellite to remain over the same portion of Earth at all times?

   Answer: a

5. What is the typical round-trip time for a single data packet from ground to satellite back to ground?

   Answer: c

6. Wireless LAN technologies are based on which technical specification?

   Answer: a

7. Which 802.11 specification is most widely deployed?

   Answer: b

8. Which 802.11 specifications are interoperable?

   Answers: b, d

9. Which two are wireless authentication options?

   Answers: a, b

Q&A

1. Data over cable is defined in what specification?

   Answer: DOCSIS

2. What is the name of the organization that governs the cable specification?

   Answer: CableLabs

3. Which DOCSIS component resides in the head end?

   Answer: CMTS

4. Which DOCSIS component is the CPE device?

   Answer: CM

5. What are the bands for downstream and upstream transmissions over cable?

   Answer: 5–42 MHz upstream, 55–750 MHz downstream

6. Satellite transmissions can reach what downstream speed during off-peak hours?

   Answer: 400 kbps

7. What is the altitude necessary to reach geostationary orbit?

   Answer: 35,800 km

8. What is the amount of time necessary to complete one orbit in a medium earth orbit?

   Answer: 6 hours

9. What is the top transmission speed offered in an 802.11a WiFi deployment?

   Answer: 54 Mbps

10. What is the top transmission speed offered in an 802.11b WiFi deployment?

    Answer: 11 Mbps

11. What is the protocol designed to provide security for Wireless Access Point devices?

    Answer: WEP

Chapter 11

"Do I Know This Already?" Quiz

1.   What is the distance limitation of ADSL utilizing 24-AWG cable?

     Answer: c

2.   Into which two general categories can DSL be broken?

     Answers: c, d

3.   If running 1.5 Mbps over 26-AWG cable, what is the maximum allowable distance from the CO?

     Answer: b

4.   Which DSL modulation method is most prevalantly used today?

     Answer: b

5.   Which DSL modulation method utilizes a single channel for all downstream transmissions?

     Answer: a

6.   How many channels does DMT utilize for downstream transmission?

     Answer: b

7.   PPP authentication takes place after which of the following phases?

     Answer: b

8.   In a PPPoE call initiation, the two phases of the setup are what?

     Answers: a, c

9.   Which VCI is the first available for use in ATM end-user configurations?

     Answer: c

10. ATM cells use how large a payload per cell?

     Answer: d

11. The Cisco 827-4V differs from the Cisco 827H in that it:

    Answer: b

12. A large percentage of DSL issues arise from the placement of what device?

    Answer: c

13. Which command will show DSL connection negotiation in real time?

    Answer: b

Q&A

1. What are three things that can adversely affect DSL signals?

   Answer: Loading coils, fiber-optic cables, bridge taps

2. If 26-AWG cable is deployed to support a DSL order for 1.5 Mbps downstream, what is the distance limitation from the CO?

   Answer: 15,000 feet

3. If 24-AWG cable is deployed to support a DSL order for 6 Mbps downstream, what is the distance limitation from the CO?

   Answer: 12,000 feet

4. CAP modulation divides voice from upstream and downstream data transmission. List the ranges of frequency for each of the three traffic types.

   Answer: Voice: 0–4 kHz; upstream data: 25–160 kHz; downstream data: 240 kHz to 1.5 MHz

5. DMT modulation divides the signals into how many separate channels?

   Answer: 256

6. If there is signal degradation or other quality impairments on the line, what will DMT do to correct the situation?

   Answer: DMT will relocate the signal to another channel.

7. What are the two general categories of DSL implemenations and what is the basic difference between them?

    Answer: Asymmetric DSL utilizes mismatched download/upload transfer rates, and symmetric DSL utilizes matching download/upload transfer rates.

8. What is the range of bandwidths available with ADSL offerings?

    Answer: 1.5 to 9 Mbps

9. What is G.lite and what are its advantages?

    Answer: The G.lite standard was specifically developed to meet the "plug-and-play" requirements of the consumer market segment. G.lite is a medium-bandwidth version of ADSL that allows up to 1.5 Mbps downstream and up to 512 kbps upstream. G.lite allows voice and data to coexist on the wire without the use of splitters. G.lite is a globally standardized (ITU G.992.2) interoperable ADSL system. Typical telco implementations currently provide 1.5 Mbps downstream and 160 kbps upstream.

10. In the establishment of a PPPoE session, what options are typically implemented to overcome the security issues brought about in a traditional bridged environment?

    Answer: PPP authentication in the form of PAP or CHAP

11. In the PPP architecture, which portion of the protocol stack deals with link negotiation, packet size, and authentication?

    Answer: PPP LCP

12. What is the purpose of the Discovery phase in PPPoE session initiation?

    Answer: Discovery serves to find the MAC address of the peering device (DSLAM) and obtain a SESSION_ID. It allows the CPE to find all DSLAMs available to it.

13. During the Discovery phase, what is the address in the Destination MAC address field of the PPPoE frame?

    Answer: The destination MAC is the broadcast address ff.ff.ff.ff.ff.ff.

14. PPPoA uses what RFC to define operations for VC encapsulation?

    Answer: RFC 1483 (obsoleted by RFC 2364)

15. List at least three features of a Cisco 827 router.

    Answer:

    ADSL router

    IOS driven

    Recommended for up to 20 users

    Business-class security with integrated Stateful Firewall and support for IPSec 3DES for VPNs

    Differentiated classes of service

    Mission-critical reliability

    PPPoE, PPPoA support

    NAT/PAT

    SNMP, Telnet, and Console configuration access

    Can be shipped to customer premises preconfigured

    Include the Cisco Router Web Setup tool to allow setup by nontechnical personnel

16. What are the two flavors of 827 generally available?

    Answer: 827H and 827-4V

17. A user has had DSL installed in his home. The DSL line trains to the advertised speeds and functions properly. The line is shared for voice and data. When the user lifts the handset, there is a great deal of static on the line. What is likely the cause of the static?

    Answer: The filter was either omitted or placed incorrectly. The filter should be placed between the wall jack and phone or fax.

18. In the event that a **show interface** command is issued and shows the status of the interface as up, line protocol down, what is likely the issue?

   Answer: The interface is properly configured and trying to initialize. However, it is not receiving a proper signal from the carrier. Check the cabling between the router and demarc; if it is sound, contact the carrier for further troubleshooting.

Chapter 12

"Do I Know This Already?" Quiz

1. Which of the following is a characteristic of Frame Relay?

   Answer: a

2. What are the two flavors of Frame Relay virtual circuits?

   Answers: b, c

3. Frame Relay virtual circuits are logically defined by a DLCI. What is the range of valid DLCIs for user traffic?

   Answer: c

4. The Frame Relay star topology is also known as what?

   Answer: b

5. What is an advantage of a partial-mesh network?

   Answer: c

6. Split horizon can cause reachability issues in Frame Relay networks. Which two ways allow you to deal with split horizon problems?

   Answers: b, d

7. With what two different personalities can Frame Relay subinterfaces be created?

   Answers: a, b

8. What mechanism is used to provide dynamic mapping of DLCIs?

   Answer: b

9. What command is issued to disable LMI traffic on an interface?

Answer: c

Q&A

1. What are the two types of virtual circuits and what are the common attributes of each?

Answer: Frame Relay VCs come in two flavors, permanent (PVCs) and switched (SVCs). PVCs are, just as the name implies, permanent, nailed-up circuits. They don't tear down or reestablish dynamically. SVCs are just the opposite. With SVCs, a data connection is made only when there is traffic to send across the link. Frame Relay SVCs are established dynamically and can reroute around network failures.

2. What is meant in the description of DLCIs as being *locally significant*?

Answer: Locally significant means that the DLCI has meaning only on a single leg of a virtual circuit. The switch will assign a new DLCI for the next leg of the virtual circuit.

3. Frame Relay devices fall into one of two possible roles. What are they?

Answer: Data circuit-terminating equipment (DCE) or data terminal equipment (DTE)

4. What are the three supported LMI types for Cisco routers?

Answer: Cisco, ANSI (aka Annex D), and Q.933a (aka Annex A)

5. If the lmi-type is not set on the Frame Relay interface, what will happen, by default?

Answer: LMI will default to Cisco. Should it not be able to establish a conversation, LMI autosense will attempt to contact the switch via the other available lmi types.

6. What are three typical Frame Relay topologies?

Answer: Hub and spoke, partial mesh, full mesh

7. In a fully meshed Frame Relay environment, how many circuits will be necessary to connect 40 routers?

Answer: 780

8. Which Frame Relay topology offers the lowest delay overall for traffic that is traversing between remote sites?

Answer: Full mesh

9. How can issues regarding split horizon be avoided or remedied in a Frame Relay point-to-multipoint connection?

   Answer: Use subinterfaces or disable split horizon

10. When creating a subinterface, what happens if the cast type is not specified?

    Answer: In Cisco IOS Software releases prior to 12.0, it would default to multipoint. As of Cisco IOS Software Release 12.0, the cast type is a required parameter.

11. What is the function of Inverse ARP in a Frame Relay network?

    Answer: Inverse ARP serves to provide dynamic mapping of DLCIs on a router interface.

12. If connecting to a non-Cisco device on the remote end, what command must be entered to make the two routers communicate?

    Answer: encapsulation frame-relay ietf

13. What command would be used to map the next-hop address of 172.16.214.89 to the local DLCI set at 135?

    Answer: frame-relay map ip 172.16.214.89 135

14. What keyword added to the command entered in the answer to question 13 will augment the functionality by allowing routing updates to traverse the link? Restate the command to allow routing updates.

    Answer: The keyword is broadcast. **The command is** frame-relay map ip 172.16.214.89 135 broadcast.

15. Which command will allow the viewing of a PVC with the DLCI 135?

    Answer: show frame-relay pvc 135

16. Which command will allow the viewing of the real-time conversation between the router and the Frame Relay switch?

    Answer: debug frame-relay lmi

17.   In the output of the command **debug frame-relay lmi**, which pieces of output are the most important in ensuring that the link is functional?

   Answer: It is important to see inbound and outbound activity. Status and StEnq messages show *myseq* and *yourseen* values greater than 0, along with *DTE up*. In the event that the link was malfunctioning, *DTE* status will change status repeatedly from up to down and back again. Also, the *myseq* value will increment while the *yourseen* value will remain at 0.

Chapter 13

"Do I Know This Already?" Quiz

1.   In Frame Relay traffic shaping, which of the following is the speed at which you may transmit during noncongestive periods?

   Answer: b

2.   If CIR is 64,000 bps, what should typically be the value of MinCIR?

   Answer: a

3.   In map class configuration mode, what command enables the router to respond to BECN requests?

   Answer: b

4.   In map class configuration mode, what command specifies the CIR if you want CIR set to 512,000 bps?

   Answer: c

5.   In periods of congestion, what is the percentage drop of throughput experienced with each BECN?

   Answer: b

Q&A

1.   List the three possible locations that a Frame Relay traffic shaping definition can be applied.

   Answer: Major interface, subinterface, PVC definition (DLCI)

2. A Frame Relay traffic shaping definition has been applied to a PVC on a subinterface. However, the shaping parameters are inactive. The class definition has been verified. What would keep a properly configured and applied traffic shaping definition from working?

   Answer: The command frame-relay traffic-shaping **has not been entered on the major interface. Therefore, shaping is inactive on all subinterfaces and PVCs residing under that major interface.**

3. The parameter that specifies the minimum guaranteed rate of traffic throughput across the carrier network is known as what?

   Answer: MinCIR

4. If the command **frame-relay adaptive-shaping becn** has not been entered, how will the router respond to BECN requests on that interface or PVC?

   Answer: It will not respond to BECN at all. No change in throughput will occur.

5. If the CIR = 128,000 bps, MinCIR = 64,000 bps, and Bc = 8000 bps, what is the Tc and how long, in seconds, is the amount of time that must elapse once BECN requests have ceased before traffic can begin to step back up.

   Answer: Tc = 125 ms and the interval is 2 seconds (16×125 ms).

Chapter 14

"Do I Know This Already?" Quiz

1. Which command implements dial backup 5 seconds after failure of the primary interface, and keeps the backup interface up for 30 seconds following the return of the primary interface?

   Answer: b

2. Which command specifies BRI1 as a dial backup interface to Serial0?

   Answer: a

3. Which command configures IGRP or EIGRP to use any route that has a metric within the range of one to ten times the value of the metric of the best route in the routing table for a given destination?

   Answer: a

4. Which command will create a backup route to the 192.168.1.0/24 network that will only be utilized in case of the loss of the dynamic route from the routing table?

Answer: d

Q&A

Use Figure 14-2 to answer the following questions.

Figure 14-2 *Network Diagram for Use Questions*

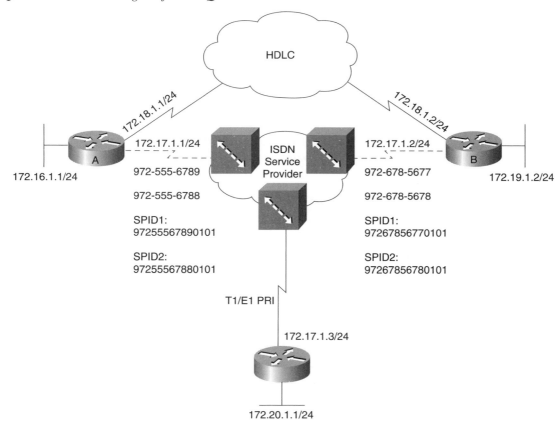

1. Dial backup, in the traditional sense, can be accomplished based on which two criteria points?

Answer: Based on load or failure

2. In the command **backup delay 60 30**, what do 60 and 30 represent?

Answer: 60 is the countdown, in seconds, to initiate backup timer; 30 is the countdown, in seconds, to disconnect backup once the primary has been restored.

3. Configure router A and router B so that the ISDN link is activated only in cases in which the HDLC link is down or has reached 85 percent capacity. The backup timers for failure are at your discretion.

   Answer:

   ```
   !RouterA
   interface serial 0
   ip address 172.18.1.1 255.255.255.0
   backup interface bri 0
   backup delay 5 60
   backup load 85 4
   interface bri0
   encapsulation ppp
   ip address 172.17.1.1 255.255.255.0
   dialer map ip 172.17.1.2 broadcast 9726785677
   dialer map ip 172.17.1.2 broadcast 9726785678
   dialer load-threshold 127
   ppp Multilink
   isdn spid1 97255567890101 9724446789
   isdn spid2 97255567880101 9725556788
   !RouterB
   interface serial 0
   ip address 172.18.1.2 255.255.255.0
   ```

4. To configure an IP routing protocol to support load balancing over multiple equal-cost pathways, what commands must be entered?

   Answer: None. It is a default action to load-balance over multiple equal-cost pathways.

5. Explain the rules behind the use of the **variance** command.

   Answer: The next hop must be closer to the destination (that is, it cannot go back to go forward), and the metric of any suboptimal pathway must be within a multiple of x (where x is the variance configured) of the metric of the best route.

6. Remove the dial backup configuration from routers A and B, and then implement an alternative configuration using the methods described in this chapter to back up the HDLC link.

   Answer:

   ```
   !RouterA
   configure terminal
   ip route 172.19.1.0 255.255.255.0 172.17.1.2 250
   interface serial 0
   ip address 172.18.1.1 255.255.255.0
   interface bri0
   encapsulation ppp
   ip address 172.17.1.1 255.255.255.0
   dialer map ip 172.17.1.2 broadcast 9726785677
   dialer map ip 172.17.1.2 broadcast 9726785678
   ```

```
dialer load-threshold 127
ppp Multilink
isdn spid1 97255567890101 9724446789
isdn spid2 97255567880101 9725556788
!RouterB
configure terminal
ip route 172.16.1.0 255.255.255.0 172.17.1.1 250
interface serial 0
ip address 172.18.1.2 255.255.255.0
```

7. If a router is running multiple routing protocols (RIP, OSPF, EIGRP, and IBGP) and each protocol has a route to a particular destination, which route will be selected to forward a packet to that destination? Why?

    Answer: By default, the EIGRP route will be used. It has the lowest administrative distance of the listed protocols.

Chapter 15

"Do I Know This Already?" Quiz

1. Which network conditions justify the use of queuing?

    Answers: b, c. Queuing should only be used on interfaces that are experiencing congestion or that are not very fast by nature.

2. Which effects does queuing have on a router?

    Answers: c, e. Queuing is normally performed by the main CPU of the router. Thus, the CPU is more stressed and the router itself suffers.

3. Which queuing strategy uses the IP type of service (ToS) bits to help determine egress priority?

    Answer: c. WFQ first attempts to let the smaller packets out before the larger ones. It also examines the IP ToS bits to weight more important packets.

4. How are packets sequenced when using FIFO queuing?

    Answer: c. FIFO queues place packets in the single egress queue when the first bit of any packet arrives on the outbound interface.

5. Which Cisco IOS command is used to create a list of packets that match one or more criteria?

    Answer: a

6. Which Cisco IOS command determines how much bandwidth a particular flow should get during congested conditions?

    Answer: b

7. Which Cisco IOS command determines how much bandwidth a particular flow should get at all times?

    Answer: d

8. What is the difference between CBWFQ and LLQ?

    Answer: c. LLQ is basically CBWFQ with the priority **command used, which guarantees throughput for high-priority, low-delay traffic.**

9. Which of the following compression methods can be used only on point-to-point links?

    Answers: b, c

10. Which of the following compression methods is Cisco-proprietary?

    Answer: c

Q&A

1. Where on a router is queuing implemented?

    Answer: Queuing, or the resequencing of packets, is implemented on an interface of a router. More specifically, packets are reordered as they leave the interface, not as they arrive.

2. When should queuing be considered a viable implementation?

    Answer: Queuing is best used on interfaces that have limited bandwidth (2 Mbps or less). Attempting to queue on faster interfaces tends to use excessive CPU cycles and underutilize the link.

3. Should a queuing strategy be implemented on all WAN interfaces?

    Answer: Queuing might not even be needed on slower WAN interfaces. Queuing is implemented to rearrange egress packets on busy interfaces. If all packets are getting out of the router without any problems, queuing might not be needed. Note that some special handling of high-priority traffic can also justify queuing. And on very high-speed interfaces, queuing is more of a hindrance.

4. When is WFQ enabled by default?

   Answer: WFQ is enabled by default on Cisco serial interfaces that are running at or below 2 Mbps.

5. How does CBWFQ differ from WFQ?

   Answer: CBWFQ allows the administrator to determine how packets are queued, or sorted into flows. The flow assignment is dynamically performed in WFQ.

6. What is the Cisco IOS command to select and sort traffic into various flows in CBWFQ?

   Answer: The Cisco IOS command class-map **is used to divide traffic into various flows.**

7. What is the Cisco IOS command to assign a policy to one or more flows?

   Answer: The Cisco IOS command policy-map **is used to assign a policy to one or more** class-maps**.**

8. What makes LLQ more detailed than CBWFQ?

   Answer: CBWFQ and LLQ use the same configuration commands. The difference is that LLQ uses a priority queue for high-priority traffic (such as voice). The priority queue is always on. CBWFQ only works when the interface is congested.

9. What command is used to create LLQ from a CBWFQ configuration?

   Answer: LLQ uses the priority **command inside of a** policy-map**, compared to the** bandwidth **command that is used for CBWFQ.**

10. What is the actual Cisco IOS command to match all traffic from subnet 10.1.1.0 /24 to network 192.168.1.0 /24?

    Answer: Access lists are used to match IP traffic flows. The following access list matches the traffic shown:

    access-list 101 permit ip 10.1.1.0 0.0.0.255 192.168.1.0 0.0.0.255

11. What are the actual Cisco IOS commands to match the access list in question 10 into a single group or flow?

    Answer: Class-maps **are used to match traffic into flows. The following commands create the appropriate** class-map:

    class-map match-all test-class

    match access-group 101

12. What are the actual Cisco IOS commands to apply a policy that states that "traffic will get 48 kbps during congestion" to the previous flow?

    Answer: Policy maps **are used to apply policy to** class-maps. **The following commands create the appropriate** policy map:

    policy-map test-policy

    class test-class

    bandwidth 48

13. What are the actual Cisco IOS commands used to apply the policy in question 13 to interface serial 0/0?

    Answer: The service-policy **command applies a policy map to an interface. The following commands apply the policy:**

    interface serial 0/0

    service-policy output test-policy

14. List the types of compression supported by most Cisco routers.

    Answer: Cisco routers support Stac and Predictor link compression for point-to-point links. Stac is also used for Frame Relay payload compression. And TCP header compression can be configured for VC-based connections.

15. When should link compression be implemented?

    Answer: Link compression should be used only on point-to-point links, because the entire packet is compressed. The L2 headers cannot be used during transit.

16. Which type of compression should be utilized on VC-based WAN deployments?

Answer: Either TCP header compression or payload compression can be used on VC-based WAN interfaces. Both leave the L2 header alone so that it can be read by the WAN switches in transit.

17. What are the two link-compression algorithms, and which one is considered an open standard?

Answer: Both Stac and Predictor are link-compression algorithms. Stac is considered an open standard. Predictor is a Cisco-proprietary algorithm.

18. When is TCP header compression most effective?

Answer: TCP header compression has its greatest effects on packets that have a small data field. But it can be used for any stream of packets, regardless of size.

19. When can TCP header compression be implemented?

Answer: TCP header compression can be implemented on any WAN interface. Normally, compression is used only on slower links. Any type of compression does cause CPU overhead in the router.

20. What compression options are possible across a Frame Relay link?

Answer: Frame Relay can use payload compression, which actually uses the Stac algorithm, or TCP header compression.

Chapter 16

"Do I Know This Already?" Quiz

1. Which of the following is not a benefit of NAT?

Answer: c

2. Which two of the following are disadvantages of NAT?

Answers: a, c

3. Using simple NAT translation, the NAT software alters what TCP header information?

Answer: b

4. What TCP header information is altered by using NAT overload?

Answer: a

5. What does it mean when a NAT translation is overloaded?

Answer: c

6. What Class B private address space is available from RFC 1918?

Answer: b

7. When should NAT overlapping be deployed?

Answer: b

8. What NAT translation type is generally used for overlapped networks?

Answer: a

9. Which of the following describes the use of NAT TCP load distribution?

Answer: b

10. Which of the following four NAT address descriptions is incorrect?

Answer: c

11. An inside local address is translated to what in a simple NAT translation?

Answer: a

12. What are four types of NAT translations or configurations?

Answer: b

13. What command is used to erase all current NAT-translated sessions?

Answer: c

14. Port address translation is used on what router series only?

Answer: b

15.   What is the maximum number of port handler addresses that can be used on a Cisco 700 Series router?

Answer: c

Q&A

1.   What are the benefits of NAT?

Answer: NAT conserves legal addresses, reduces overlap dysfunction, increases Internet flexibility, and eliminates network renumbering in a changed environment.

2.   The outside global address is converted to which NAT address class?

Answer: The outside global address is converted to an outside local address that is legitimate on the inside of the network.

3.   Why is accountability listed as a disadvantage of NAT?

Answer: With the changes that are made to the addresses, it is harder, although not impossible, for an administrator to know which IP station is sending or receiving packets.

4.   Using overlapped NAT translation, what TCP header information is altered?

Answer: In an overlap implementation, the outgoing IP address and the port assignment are altered, so that the NAT device can use the same translation address, thus saving IP addresses. The port assignment is used by the NAT device to "return" incoming packets to the right end station.

5.   How many Class B private address spaces are available from RFC 1918?

Answer: There are 16 Class B addresses available.

6.   What does it mean when a NAT translation is overloaded?

Answer: It means that a single address known to the outside is being used to translate the internal private addresses. This will conserve Internet-routable address space.

7.   Which two commands would you use to define an overloaded NAT translation using a defined pool of addresses called **transpool** for outbound traffic?

Answer:

```
ip nat pool transpool 123.123.123.1 123.123.123.2 netmask 255.255.255.0
ip nat inside source list 1 pool transpool overload
```

8. When should NAT overlap be deployed?

   Answer: The overlapping of networks typically occurs during a merger of two companies that are using the same private address space. The overlap configuration is put in place as a stopgap while renumbering takes place.

9. What type of NAT translation is generally used for overlapped networks? Why?

   Answer: Simple NAT translation on both sides of the overlap can be used, which would require the administrator to configure and manage NAT on two different routers, presumably at two different physical locations. However using a dual port translation or overlapping configuration on a single router provides a single point for the configuration. This allows for easier manageability, and control of the translation.

10. What command would show which interfaces have been declared as outside or inside?

    Answer: show ip nat statistics

11. Briefly describe the use of NAT TCP load distribution.

    Answer: NAT can be used as a simple tool for TCP load balancing. NAT translates incoming requests for an address location and then, in a round-robin or rotary fashion, processes those requests across a set of mirrored servers, to provide a simple load balance.

12. An inside local address is translated to what in a simple NAT translation?

    Answer: An inside local address is translated to an inside global address.

13. What is the most common type of NAT translation? Why?

    Answer: The most common type is the overloaded translation. Most small businesses do not maintain their own "presence" on the Internet, but rather outsource it to a provider company. In this fashion, the small businesses only require the ability to "surf" the Internet, and therefore do not require more than a single IP address.

14. What is the function of the port handler for the 700 Series router?

    Answer: The port handler, which is unique to the 700 Series router, declares which ports are translated, and conversely which ones will pass untranslated.

15. Can an inside local address be selected from a globally routable address pool?

    Answer: Yes, it can. However, the inside local addresses are generally selected from the private address space.

16. What command is used to erase all currently established NAT translated sessions?

    Answer: clear ip nat translation *

17. Port address translation is used *only* on what router series?

    Answer: The Cisco 700 Series

18. Given the following output, what type of translation is being used on this router?

    ```
    Pro    Inside global    Inside local     Outside local    Outside global
    tcp    103.32.32.1:1098    10.1.0.1:1098    13.43.5.6:23      13.43.5.6:23
    tcp    103.32.32.1:1345    10.1.0.2:1345    13.43.5.6:23      13.43.5.6:23
    tcp    103.32.32.1:1989    10.1.0.3:1989    13.43.5.7:21      13.43.5.7:21
    ```

    Answer: Since the output shows the router maintaining a port assignment and translation, it is either overloaded or overlapped. Since this router output does not distinguish between an outside local or outside global, this router must not be doing the dual translation. Hence, this output shows a router that is doing an overload translation only.

19. Given the following router configuration information, what addresses will be dynamically translated?

    ```
    access-list 1 permit 10.0.0.0 0.0.0.255

    ip nat pool natpool 222.12.12.2 222.12.12.10 netmask 255.255.255.0
    ip nat inside source static 10.0.0.1 222.2.2.1
    ip nat inside source list 1 pool natpool
    ```

    Answer: All addresses belonging to the 10.0.0.0 network, with the exception of the 10.0.0.1 address, since it is being statically described in the third line.

20. What differentiates PAT from NAT?

    Answer: PAT alters the port address, whereas NAT only alters the IP address. You should note, though, that many people refer to NAT and expect that a port assignment is also being tracked. A successful professional candidate should carefully select their words when describing the translation that will be taking place.

Chapter 17

"Do I Know This Already?" Quiz

1. What three options does AAA give you?

    Answers: a, c, d

2. What are some of the combinations of the three services from AAA that you can implement?

Answer: e

3. Authentication identifies what?

Answer: c

4. Authorization can be used by itself. True or False?

Answer: b

5. What are the two primary security protocols for AAA services?

Answers: d, e

6. What standard protocol/port does TACACS use?

Answer: a

7. What part(s) of the packet does TACACS+ encrypt?

Answer: b

8. RADIUS supports what type of communication?

Answer: a

9. RADIUS uses what protocol at the transport layer?

Answer: c

10. What are the two primary access modes?

Answers: a, b

11. An async port can be configured for what type of access mode?

Answer: d

12. Cisco Secure Access Control Server supports which protocols for AAA services?

Answer: e

13. The AAA commands:

Answer: C

14. Authentication can support what option(s) for checking a username database?

Answer: E

15. If you turn on authentication, what other AAA options must also be turned on?

Answer: C

16. What method(s) are available for writing account records?

Answer: D

Q&A

1. What advantages does an AAA server have over a local router database?

Answer: You can configure more specific options for each individual user or assign group variables. CS-ACS also has options for VoIP and enhanced logging.

2. What is authorization used for and how is it assigned?

Answer: It is used to control authorization on a one-time, per-service, per–user list, per-group, or per-protocol basis.

3. Why are accounting records important?

Answer: They enable an administrator to keep track of who used certain resources, including when and for how long they used those resources. This can be beneficial when planning for network growth or troubleshooting problems on the network.

4. Between what devices would TACACS or RADIUS be used?

Answer: Between any device such as a router, switch, VPN concentrator, etc. to an AAA server.

5. List a couple of reasons why TACACS is said to be more secure than RADIUS.

Answer: TACACS uses TCP, which is a connection-oriented transport protocol. TCP has built-in forms of error recovery. TACACS+ encrypts the entire payload of the packet, which RADIUS currently does not support. (The revised RFC for RADIUS is supposed to support encryption.) It has multiprotocol support (example, PPP, SLIP, etc.).

6. What is Character-based mode?

    Answer: It is when a single character is sent not necessarily wrapped inside a frame (such as PPP) and is usually sent on a port that is for direct configuration of a device.

7. Why would you not necessarily want to use a freeware AAA server?

    Answer: You are not guaranteed who has created, manipulated, or built back doors into the code. The encryption algorithm for the username database may not be as strong as what is needed in today's networking environments.

8. What is the name the module of CS-ACS that checks whether the other modules are still functioning and what options does it offer you if one module is down?

    Answer: The module is CSMon and you can tell it to 1) restart the specific service 2) restart all the services or 3) reboot the server.

9. Why must you turn on authentication if you want to have authorization for services on your network?

    Answer: If you don't know who a user is, you don't want to authorize them to do something. Before any user is allowed to perform a task, you must know who they are by way of a username and password combination. Once you have determined that it is a valid user for the network, you can authorize them to do specific things on your network.

10. Why would a network administrator choose to run both RADIUS and TACACS+ on a network?

    Answer: If possible, you should try to stick to one security protocol on a network for ease of configuration and support. The reason a network administrator might choose to run both RADIUS and TACACS+ is that certain Cisco products support only one of the two security protocols. For example, the Cisco VPN 3000 Series Concentrators run RADIUS only with its current releases of code. If a network administrator has already been running TACACS+, but now needs to add VPN support to the network, they may consider running both protocols. When running both security protocols, make sure your AAA server supports both protocols concurrently or you may have to have two different username/password databases, which can lead to problems with end users forgetting which username/password combination is needed for what device.

Chapter 18

"Do I Know This Already?" Quiz

1. What are the three things a VPN network should provide?

   Answers: a, b, d

2. What are the three OSI layers at which encryption is usually performed?

   Answers: a, b, d

3. What is a common application layer encryption standard?

   Answer: a

4. What drawback with regard to routing do you get when you encrypt at the data link layer?

   Answer: b

5. What are three components that you get from a good VPN network?

   Answers: a, d, e

6. The same key is used to encrypt and decrypt in a symmetrical encryption algorithm.

   Answer: a

7. Hashing algorithms give what type of output?

   Answer: a

8. Diffie-Hellman helps with what part of IPSec?

   Answer: a

9. What are the two primary protocols in the IPSec standard?

   Answer: d

10. What protocol number is AH?

    Answer: d

11. What protocol number is ESP?

    Answer: e

12. What is the default mode for Cisco VPN routers to send ESP packets?

    Answer: a

13. IKE is enabled by default on Cisco routers.

    Answer: a

14. Transform sets can have how many AH option sets?

    Answer: a

15. How many crypto maps can be applied to an interface?

    Answer: a

Q&A

1. What options (and how many) would be used in a very strong transform set?

   Answer: It would have one AH option and two ESP options with the strongest algorithm possible with that Cisco IOS version. Example: AH-SHA, ESP-3DES, ESP-SHA.

2. What are three common things provided by a VPN network?

   Answer: Secure, authenticated, access to data, independent of media or connection type

3. Who could use a VPN solution?

   Answer: Anyone who has the need for WAN connectivity could benefit from a VPN.

4. What is a common trade-off in VPN networks?

   Answer: Speed for security or cost versus security

5. What is the primary motivation for the use of IPSec?

   Answer: It solves many of the problems with other encryption methods. For example, it is standards-based, so you are not tied to one manufacturer for equipment. It allows you to encrypt at one side of the network, route through the network, and then decrypt on the other side, whereas an L2 encryption scenario would encrypt the network address, making it impossible to route.

6. Why should you order your isakmp policies from strongest to weakest?

Answer: When two devices try to negotiate an IPSec tunnel, the tunnel originating device will send all isakmp policies that it has configured across to the receiving end. The devices will try to match policies in the order of the first policy from the originator against all policies of the receiver. If there is not a match, it will try the second policy against all policies of the receiver. This process continues until there is a policy match. If there is no policy match, an IPSec tunnel cannot be established.

7. When creating a hub-and-spoke VPN network topology, how do you configure the hub device to distinguish different traffic to be sent to different peers when you can apply only one crypto map per interface?

Answer: You need to create different sequence numbers inside your crypto map and apply the crypto access lists and peer addresses inside each sequence accordingly.

Example:

```
R1(config)#crypto map multi-site 10 ipsec-isakmp
R1(config-crypto-map)#set peer address-for-site1
R1(config-crypto-map)#match address {access-list-number}
R1(config)#crypto map multi-site 20 ipsec-isakmp
R1(config-crypto-map)#set peer address-for-site2
R1(config-crypto-map)#match address {access-list-number}
```

Index

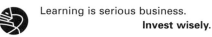